BANKING ON FRAUD

SOCIAL INSTITUTIONS AND SOCIAL CHANGE
An Aldine de Gruyter Series of Texts and Monographs

EDITED BY

Michael Useem • James D. Wright

BANKING ON FRAUD

Drexel, Junk Bonds, and Buyouts

MARY ZEY

ALDINE DE GRUYTER
New York

About the Author

Mary Zey is Professor of Sociology and past Head of the Department of Sociology at Texas A&M University where she teaches and conducts research on Complex Organizations. She has studied such organizations as universities, voluntary organizations, and corporations. Her research is focused on the transformation of corporate control, mergers and acquisitions, and organizational crime. She is the author of *Dimensions of Organizations* and editor of *Decision Making: Alternatives to Rational Choice Models; Complex Organizations: Critical Perspectives,* and *Readings on Dimensions of Organizations.*

ALDINE DE GRUYTER
A division of Walter de Gruyter, Inc.
200 Saw Mill River Road
Hawthorne, New York 10532

This publication is printed on acid-free paper

Library of Congress Cataloging-in-Publication Data
Zey, Mary.
    Banking on fraud : Drexel, junk bonds, and buyouts / Mary Zey.
        p.   cm. — (Social institutions and social change)
    Includes bibliographical references and index.
    ISBN 0-202-30465-5 (cloth). — ISBN 0-202-30466-3 (paper)
    1. Drexel Burnham Lambert Incorporated.   2. Milken, Michael.
3. Securities industry—United States—Corrupt practices.   4. Junk
bonds—United States.   I. Title.   II. Series.
HG4928.5.Z49   1993
364.1'68—dc20   92-42408
                                                                                    CIP

Manufactured in the United States of America

10   9   8   7   6   5   4   3   2   1

For My Son, Jim
and My Mother, Alene

In Memory of my father, Henry Zey

Contents

PART IV
Toward Theory

Preface

Throughout the decade of the 1980s the names of investment banks appeared in the headlines of the *New York Times* and *Wall Street Journal*. These firms and some of their employees were first praised and later vilified as dealings that resulted in massive failures of savings and loans, insurance companies, and businesses large and small came to light. A series of brilliant frauds had increased the concentration of wealth in the country, made the economy more vulnerable to changes in technological, economic, and political processes, and increased social inequality. These frauds had also reduced the perceived legitimacy of industry and government regulatory boards, and the high-yield bond market, reduced business confidence, contributed to the recession, and destroyed individuals' faith in capitalism, representative democracy, and equal justice under the law.

The causes and conditions of these crimes have consistently been interpreted as consequences of excessive greed, obsession with personal power, and other "abnormal" personality characteristics of principal players. The actions of investment banking firms and the economic and legal contexts in which they are embedded have been ignored. Analysis of these deeds as organizational deviance or organizational crime has been nonexistent.[1] Perhaps more important, there have been no organizational studies of the elaborate and sophisticated crime networks created by these actors to support their normal business activities.

In these cases of organizational crime, the responsible parties were positioned in units, departments, and work groups that were critical to their firms. They were able to use their considerable influence and power to control the resources of their own as well as other organizations to commit crimes that were difficult to detect. They worked in organizations that are located at the core of the capitalist system. Thus they breached the trust not only of the organizations with which they did business, but also of the public. This breach of trust renders shaky the implicit agreements on which all economic enterprise rests. The relationship between the public (society at large) and the core of capitalism has been threatened.

When the implicit understanding at the basis of the economic structure of American capitalism, on which the national well-being depends, is breached, it threatens the moral norms of the society. Yet, despite the gravity of these crimes, treatments of them have not analyzed why and how they occur or how they are sustained. We do not seem to want to know how the capitalist system supports such crimes. It is easier to analyze and blame individuals than to analyze the organizations and the systems that they constitute.

We are much more ambitious about analyzing and punishing both street crimes and white-collar crimes against corporations, where the criminal and the crime are more easily recognized and the corporation can be defined as victim rather than central player. This works to the benefit of organizational crimes, which are more subtle and of greater magnitude and pervasiveness than other malefactions. These crimes are subtle, and often invisible, not only because of the nature of their transactions, but because the economic, legal, and organizational contexts in which they take place have been constructed and are being reconstructed by the perpetrators: organizational elites and other professionals who conceal and control illicit behavior. Our social institutions condone and glorify the power these criminals wield through controlling their employing organizations. Newspapers and the business press elevate them to the status of genius. The *Wall Street Journal* heralds them as kings and prophets. Academic institutions and Congress legitimize their behavior by asking them to testify as expert witnesses at hearings and attending their business conferences. Publications reify such conduct as efficient, competitive, and in the interest of shareholders and the economy.

This book examines several major questions: (1) How is securities fraud committed and what are the consequences? (2) What types of organizational and structural contradictions must exist in order to support fraud? (3) What types of economic and legal contexts are developed to support fraud? (4) When and how do corporations control markets and laws? (5) What are the limitations of current theories of organizations and organizational crime and how can better theories be developed?

Two other books have looked at fraud. Susan Shapiro's *Wayward Capitalism* (1984) looks at government control of securities fraud. Diane Vaughan's *Controlling Unlawful Organizational Behavior* (1983) analyzes, from a functional perspective, the government organization developed to control fraud within a drug company. Neither develops or analyzes fraud networks. Although the issue of government control is an interesting one, it is not the focus of this book. Furthermore, the focus is not on the development of control, but on the development of fraud networks. Secondarily, I examine how the economic and legal context is organized to encourage the very phenomenon that it purports to abhor and wishes to restrain. I am interested in exposing how powerful organizations manipulate the legal and economic environments to support their fraud.

PERSPECTIVES AND MODELS OF ORGANIZATIONAL CRIME

The study of deviant economic power and control is in its infancy and involves a number of competing perspectives and theoretical models. Studies of organizational crime have involved a differentiation of focus along two main dimensions: the *unit of analysis* and the *level of analysis*. The unit of analysis has been either organizations or individuals, and the level of analysis has been either the agent or the system. A cross-classification of these two dimensions generates the four cells in Figure P.1. Each cell represents the particular combination of features defining a specific perspective. Cell 1 defines the organizational perspective. Here organizational characteristics (e.g., power, differentiation, formalization) are at the center of the analysis as the causal variables (see, for example, Chandler 1962 and Williamson 1975). In this model, organizational crime is explained as a consequence of the failure of corporate managers who did not organize or structure their firms properly. Corporate crime/opportunism is just another organizational variable, as is efficiency, which the corporation, specifically its managers, is expected to control in order for the organization to achieve acceptable levels of efficiency and effectiveness. Crime is an attribute of the enterprise that can be related to economic performance as measured in the usual ways. Chapter 3 in this book asks the central questions about corporate control and its failures. However, there are other ways to analyze the relationship between organizational characteristics. Specifically, this book analyzes the opposition between organizational structure and actor power resulting in organizational contradictions to expose the dialectical process.

Instead of seeing organizational characteristics as harmoniously integrated for control, I examine the contradictions between the policy and the structure of the organization and the decisions that are made by the management of the organization. I also examine the contradictions be-

Figure P.1. Perspectives on organizational deviance. Adapted from Scott (1985).

Level of Analysis	Unit of Analysis			
	Organization		*Individual*	
Agent	1	Organizational	2	Social background
System	3	Interorganizational	4	Class hegemony

tween the formal goals of the organization and the goals of its departments, and between reward criteria and how employees are rewarded.

Cell 2 defines the social background perspective, in which greed, excessive need for power, level of education, family socialization, insufficient wealth, and club memberships are attributes of deviant corporate leaders (Fligstein 1990a) that result in their becoming corporate criminal elites. In the works of Mills (1956), Merton (1968), and Vaughan (1983), these demographic characteristics plus those of access and opportunity are major predictors of corporate crime. This is the model most often used by journalists who reduce the explanation of human action to negatively valued personal characteristics of greed and obsessive power (for a related work, see Stewart's *Den of Thieves* 1991). Other journalists explain the basis of greed and obsessive power as a result of socialization; some even resort to psychoanalytical explanations (e.g., see Kornbluth's *Highly Confident* 1992). Although I do not dismiss the voluntary actions of organizational elites who commit these crimes, I do not think these individuals possess more self-interest and greed than other elites who are not involved in these crimes. I argue against this model as providing a complete or even adequate explanation of these phenomena. Therefore, there is little consideration of this model in this book.

Cells 1 and 2, the organizational and social background perspectives, which have dominated research studies for some time, share a focus on the role of the agent and tend to isolate this concern from the wider system of relationships within which actions take place. Social relations tend to be reduced to *characteristics of individuals or organizations* and much important information is lost. For this reason, I feel we should look to perspectives at the system level defined in cells 3 and 4, which explain the *relational* features of organizational crime to come to an understanding of its systemic nature.

Cell 3 defines interorganizational causes of organizational crime. Relationships between enterprises are seen as constituted by the environment within which organizations are interacting. Thus interorganizational networks and their larger economic and legal contexts influence the actions of organizations. But organizations also construct the environment in which they exist. Chapter 2 lays out the crime networks of Drexel and its interorganizational nature. Chapters 6 and 7 place Drexel in its legal and economic contexts. This is the first study of organizational crime that lays out both the organizational and interorganizational contexts and bridges the gap between them. Again, the focus is on the contradictions between the organization and the its environment. The discussion highlights the contradictions between the organization's drive for effectiveness and its ability to acquire and use environmental resources.

Cell 4 is the class hegemony perspective, perhaps the least well defined of the four. Although it has never been discussed in the literature as such, it should have emerged from the "structuralist" arguments developed by Poulantzas (1975) and Wright (1978), who are critical of what they term the instrumentalist position (Domhoff 1967, 1983). The class hegemony perspective views the relationships between people as defining the structure of crime. Class exists as a system of positions to which agents are recruited. Class "fractions" are seen as clusters of structurally defined positions [e.g., managers versus shareholders in the managerialist model (Berle and Means 1932)] rather than as groups of individuals possessing particular attributes as in cell 2. This last is the perspective from which I am developing the critiques and constructing the theory expounded in Chapter 8.

This book focuses on the organizational side of Figure P.1: the organizational perspective and the interorganizational perspective. The final theoretical chapter provides implications for the relationship between corporations and financial capital (institutional investors, saving and loans, insurance companies, and funds), which should be the content of cell 4. It argues against social background explanations and opportunity theory, which are based on the individual as the unit of analysis, and against the neoclassical economic, rational-choice explanations that are so popular in today's literature. This book argues for structural embeddedness as an explanation: where organizational crime is a function of structural contradictions in the organization and the organization is embedded in economic and legal relationships that support the crime.

ORGANIZATION OF THE BOOK

In this book I argue against economic organizational theories, and in particular, against agency theory (Jensen 1983, 1986, 1989b). Briefly, agency theory argues that managers, the agents of shareholders (principals), have not managed firms in the shareholders' interest. It further stipulates that in order for capitalist corporations to be profitable and productive, they must be operated in the shareholders' interest. To return control to stockholders (owners), corporations should be highly leveraged. When they are leveraged, managers have to strip out all excess managers, workers, and perquisites in order to pay off the debt. To ensure that the interests of managers are the same as the interests of owners, managers should be paid on the basis of shareholders' returns. Thus salaries, commissions, and bonuses of managers should be tied to the returns to shareholders. The firm should hire financiers to manage and monitor the operations of the firm for shareholders.

Throughout the 1980s, investment bankers and some management and finance scholars agreed that leveraged buyouts could improve the efficiency and effectiveness of firms by disciplining management to return capital to owners. However, by the late 1980s and early 1990s, many of the highly leveraged corporations and later the acquirers had encountered severe performance problems due to the extraordinary level of high-risk debt. The magnitude of the debt was increased by the associated fraud. This book throws into question the value of high levels of debt funded through junk bond issues facilitated by fraud as a method of controlling the opportunism of managers.

The High-Yield Bond Department of Drexel Burnham Lambert, Inc. (Drexel) operated on a hyperrational agency theory model of organization. The bond department retained, as operating capital, approximately one-third of the profits it generated, and another one-third was returned to Michael Milken to distribute as bonuses to the employees who worked on the bond floor. In addition, fees, commissions, and other compensation related to deals were paid by Drexel to the High-Yield Bond Department employees. These employees operated solely to increase profits for the department. Although this is rational from the perspective of agency theory, it created major structural contradictions between the High-Yield Bond Department and the rest of the New York–based corporation. The corporate office created and rewarded the High-Yield Bond Department as it continued to grow and increase its profits through means both legal and illegal. However, the High-Yield Bond Department became more powerful than the central office, which lost the ability to monitor, control, or change the behavior of its own department.

The primary questions guiding this research are: How was Drexel transformed into a major market player and how was it destroyed? What role did Drexel play in the mergers and acquisitions of the 1980s? How did Drexel gain power? What role did fraud play in Drexel's acquisition of status and power?

An important caveat is that the reader should not assume that this is a case study of a single organization at one time period. It is a study of the fraud networks that an investment banking firm formed during the 1980s. The analysis is not limited to the first two chapters, although the development of the networks is presented there. The internal workings of Drexel, the nature of the securities transactions, and the economic and legal contexts that Drexel created and used to facilitate its crime are analyzed in Chapters 4–7. For example, the last half of Chapter 7 lays out the relationships that were formed through the Alliance for Capital Access and the Drexel PAC between Milken at Drexel, Charles Keating at Lincoln Savings and Loan, Dennis DeConcini and the Keating Five, and the Federal Home Loan Bank Board to intervene in the board's ruling on the solvency of Lincoln Savings and Loan and to reform RICO. This is only one way Drexel influenced the legal context in which it did business.

Part I of this book lays out the fraud networks and the consequences of the fraud. The fraud at Drexel became institutionalized through repeated use of three types of fraud networks: (1) external organizations, such as the Boesky organizations, (2) private partnerships composed of Drexel employees, fund managers, bond buyers, and the external legal counsel for the High-Yield Bond Department, and (3) a mix of the networks in (1) and (2). In Chapter 2, I lay out the nature of these networks and the relationships formed by Drexel during these criminal acts. I am careful not to call this deviant behavior for two reasons. First, because these crimes became a normal way of doing business at Drexel and were quite pervasive in other firms in the mid-1980s, to call them deviant would be a misnomer. Second, the term *deviance* generally connotes a functionalist analytical perspective. The functionalist perspective assumes an integrated social system and a consensus of values, neither of which is posited by this analysis. In the functionalist view, crime is abnormal or the act of irrational individuals. In this analysis not only is fraud rational, in many instances it is efficient and extremely useful for the financial elites. It is the normal action of normal people in the capitalist system. The functionalist view cannot help us understand why we cannot eliminate the systemic causes of the fraud.

The details of the Drexel case and investigation tantalize the sociologist to answer questions about the nature of organizational control; organizational and institutional change; organizational power; change in the nature, magnitude, and enactment of organizational crimes; and the relationship between financial organizations and both the state and the economy. Organizational crimes are committed though organizations interacting with other organizations.

Part I of the book consists of three chapters. Chapter 1 describes the chain of events that led to the government's discovery of evidence that was used to persuade the Boesky organization and later the employees of the High-Yield Bond Department of Drexel to cooperate with the government.

Chapter 2 lays out two of the most prominent fraud networks of Drexel and demonstrates how repeated use of these networks institutionalized fraud as a way of doing business. What is important is the power and legitimation of these fraud networks both within and between organizations.

Chapter 3 details the consequences of the fraud, not only for the target and the acquiring firms, but for the victims of these crimes, mostly buyers and institutional investors (savings and loans, insurance companies, and investment funds). In some cases, the fraud made the leveraged buyout (LBO) transactions more efficient; it almost always made the LBO more costly. Of course, ultimately the retirees, annuity holders, and customers of the savings and loans were the real victims. But issuers of the bonds were also victims of fraud, e.g., Kohlberg Kravis Roberts (KKR). Finally, Chapter 3 lays out the consequences of the fraud for U.S. society. The cost to the taxpayer in terms of the national debt is not easily assessed. However, the greater cost, the loss of trust by American citizens in our economic and governmental institutions, is just beginning to be felt.

Part II lays out the core organizational context in which the fraud was developed—the internal structure and policies of Drexel—and the nature of securities transactions, which makes them amenable to fraud. Chapter 4 focuses on the internal structure and distribution of power within Drexel, specifically analyzing how the High-Yield Bond Department maintained its autonomy while gaining control of much of the core of Drexel by dominating strategic contingencies for the firm. At the same time, Drexel established reward structures and other policies that created the major structural contradictions that led to its destruction.

Chapter 5 focuses on the nature of securities transactions—their non-public nature, invisibility, speed, etc. In cases of fraud, there are no actual transactions, only credits against some future favor to be paid back. The innate nature of securities transactions facilitates fraud. Then the question of how these characteristics facilitate corporate control is answered.

Part III focuses on the economic and legal contexts of the development of Drexel's fraud. It was found that the corporations do not passively react to the economic and legal context in which they make transactions. Quite to the contrary, the research found that these investment bankers were powerful initiators of changes in the economic and legal environments in which they were conducting transactions. They were strategically placed (embedded) in the legal and economic networks to facilitate and control the business they conducted.

Chapter 6 places at the center of the analysis the development of LBOs through financing subordinate debt with junk bonds. This junk bond financing was a critical funding mechanism for mergers and acquisitions in the mid-1980s. Through the sale of junk bonds, the third-level, highest-risk debt was issued. Funding was obtained that could not be obtained through other debt instruments. Because junk bonds were the debt instrument of choice for the third-level subordinate debt and since Drexel controlled 40–65 percent of the high-yield bond market between 1984 and 1986, Drexel controlled a strategic contingency for many corporations involved in mergers and acquisitions.

Chapter 7 concentrates on the changes in the legal structure that facilitated mergers, acquisitions, and growth in the junk bond market. Central to this analysis is the role of tax-deductible interest on debt, changes in corporate bankruptcy laws, changes in antitrust laws and their enforcement, the dismantling of the Racketeering Influenced Corrupt Organiza-tion (RICO) Act, under which securities fraud was prosecuted, and control of bank regulatory boards by powerful financial elites. Chapter 7 lays out critical relationships between Drexel, savings and loans (such as Lincoln Savings and Loan), and key congressional actors in controlling regulatory agencies as well as reforming laws under which elite securities firms were being prosecuted.

Part IV, Chapter 8, reveals the contributions of this research to the continued development of theories of organizational crime and economic organizations, and the relationship between the economy, state, and so-ciety. Chapter 8 challenges us to work toward more empirically valid and relevant theories of economic organizations: theories in which power is central to explanation, and theories in which financial organizations are revealed as the driving force of the transformation of corporate control and the economy.

In addition to the findings in each chapter, this research results in several strongly supported observations about the nature of organizational crime. First, the nature of organizational crime can only be understood within the context of the changes and shifts in the internal structure of the organi-zation through which it is executed. This means that we must explore the nature of interdependencies, power, and transaction networks that facil-itate fraud.

Second, organizations involved in fraud are embedded in broader legal and economic contexts that facilitate and support illegal actions. When not naively ignoring or supporting the fraud, the organizations that composed the economic and legal contexts for fraud were often being controlled by actors in the fraud networks.

Third, the fundamental units of analysis for understanding organiza-tional fraud are the relations among corporations—in this case, established and newly generated networks. Relations between individuals are of less importance.

Fourth, the ability of a department to exercise power over other de-partments or organizations is a result of its control over resources that are necessary to those other departments and organizations. In this case, resources consisted of profits and leverage (debt) for takeovers.

Fifth, organizations are subject to economic pressures from buyers and sellers (suppliers) as well as social pressures from competitors and peer groups with which they make transactions.

Sixth, organizational analysis has much to contribute to our under-standing of the most pervasive and significant types of fraud through insight about internal structures of organizations, interorganizational re-lations, and the formation of networks and their subsequent uses in transactions. Merging our knowledge of organizations with our knowledge of organizational crime is fruitful for understanding, monitoring, and controlling such conduct.

Seventh, rational-choice and economic organizational theories are not useful for understanding complex fraud. They may be good at explaining certain types of market transactions, but not others. They are no better at explaining economic organizations than noneconomic organizations. In fact, the aspects of the organizational and institutional environment that they treat as assumptions are the ones that perpetuate the fraud.

Much of this book is based on field research that reveals the little-understood nature of investment securities transactions, the intricacies of interorganizational relations, and the secretive and invisible transactions between those involved in misconduct. The data were collected in a series of case studies of various networks. This investigation presents empirical data not available in published sources and gathered by a variety of social science methods. Data were gathered from the Securities and Exchange Commission (SEC); from depositions and presentencing hearing documents (Fatico Hearings) of the United States District Court of the Southern District of New York; from interviews with former employees of Drexel; from trading and official documents related to the cases; and from numerous articles from the *Wall Street Journal* as well as other journalistic accounts. In all cases, events that are discussed here have been verified through two or more informants or data sources.

NOTES

1. The term *organizational deviance* is not used in this book because it is most often applied to individual personal behavior within the organization rather than organizational actions. The term *organizational crime* is used because the unit of analysis is the organization. In some cases the crimes were not pursued or proven by the prosecuting attorneys.

Acknowledgments

I wish to thank two people who worked with me on different stages of this manuscript: Laurie Silver and Kim Sweeny. Kim spent many hours searching the University of Wisconsin libraries (main, business, and law) for the sources that I required in writing this book. Without exception, she brought more to her work and mine than I requested. But more than that, her enthusiasm as she began the sociology doctoral program at the University of Wisconsin—Madison was my inspiration in the early stages when the book was more amorphous than I could tolerate. Laurie Silver has similarly sustained me, working many nights from six until midnight after putting in an eight-hour day in two other jobs. Laurie is an excellent editor and a wonderful friend, who worked with me throughout the summer and early fall of 1992 to edit and put the finishing touches on the final manuscript. I owe a great deal to the support of these two fine women.

I would like to express my gratitude to Dick Scott and the Stanford Center for Organizational Research (SCOR) for providing a supportive environment for my work during the fall of 1991. Much of the first draft of the book was written at Wisconsin and Stanford in 1991. There are a number of people who listened patiently as I told them of the latest interview I had conducted or the latest testimony I had analyzed. I would like to thank these friends for their thoughtfulness. Both my friends at Wisconsin: Laurie Edelman, Marilyn Whalen (now at Oregon), Andy Michener, John DeLamater, Nadine Marks, Cora Marrett, Richard Schoenherr, Wolfgang Streeck, Franklin Wilson; and my friends at Stanford: Jim March, Cecilia Ridgeway, Bob Sutton, Lex Donaldson, Jeffrey Pfeffer, and Bill Barnett. A special thanks to Michael Useem for his kind words on an early draft of the manuscript.

Finally I would like to thank three of my closest friends who have always supported my work: Steve Murdock who read parts of the final draft. Alex McIntosh, who came up the title, *Banking on Fraud*, over a plate of *pad thai*, and Letitia Alston, who assisted me in editing the rough draft of the book.

Part I

Doing Fraud and Its Consequences

Chapter 1

An Error and Its Chain Reaction

MARCH 21, 1986—BOESKY AND MOORADIAN'S ERRORS

Michael Milken had agreed to raise $660 million for Ivan F. Boesky from the sale of bonds through Drexel. Boesky needed one billion dollars by March 21, 1986, for arbitrage purposes. He prepared to dissolve Ivan F. Boesky Corporation and create a new privately owned entity, Ivan Boesky Limited Partnership. The Boesky $660 million bond fund was known as the Hudson Fund and was scheduled to close on March 21, 1986, giving Boesky access to one billion dollars in capital. (A list of central actors appears at the end of the book.)

At the Hudson Fund closing, Drexel would earn $24 million in financing fees (3.6 percent). Milken would receive a $5 million equity interest in Ivan Boesky Limited Partnership (a conflict of interest, given that Milken, as an investment banker, would have an interest in an arbitrage organization). But Boesky still owed Milken $5.3 million from various Milken and Boesky collaborative trading. Boesky and Milken generally made trades at below the market value or did trading "favors" for each other (these favors are elaborated on in Chapter 2). When he learned that Milken would not let the closing for the $660 million proceed until he received his $5.3 million, Boesky knew he had to do something.

That very day, accountants at the accounting firm OAD, Inc., were reviewing Boesky's books for the purpose of issuing a "comfort letter." This was not a full audit, but was designed to reassure investors of the financial health of Boesky's new partnership. Ivan F. Boesky Corporation was dissolved at 4:00 P.M. However, Peter Testaverde, the OAD auditor, had found an unexplained ten-thousand-dollar account payable some time after 4:00 that afternoon. Setrag Mooradian, Boesky's accountant and bookkeeper, thought it was minor and told Testaverde that he did not know what the entry on the ledger was. Mooradian had a much more pressing matter to worry about—Milken's $5.3 million (*U.S. v. Michael Milken* 1990e, p. 65).

3

But Testaverde insisted that he had to have some documentation on the ledger entry. Mooradian testified that he thought Testaverde could over-look such a small amount, given that there was a billion dollars hanging in the balance. After several protracted attempts to change Testaverde's mind, the pressure of coming up with and transferring Milken's money caused Mooradian to blurt out, "Why the fuck do you care about ten thousand dollars when I've got $5.3 million sitting over here?" Mooradian immediately knew he had made a mistake because the Milken debt was not part of the corporate record. It was in the secret set of books where Mooradian and Charles Thurnher, one of Milken's bookkeepers, kept separate tallies. Mooradian was planning to make the payment to Milken later that day or the next, after the audit.

Testaverde immediately asked, "What $5.3 million?" Mooradian told Testaverde, "Forget I ever mentioned this. We can't talk about it now." Testaverde retaliated by preparing to leave without giving Mooradian the requisite comfort letter. Mooradian persuaded Testaverde to stay, but he had to admit to Testaverde that he had a $5.3 million account payable with no documentation, no bills, no invoices, nothing but Boeksy's usual when dealing with Milken: undocumented instructions. Testaverde had to confer with OAD senior partner Steven Oppenheim to confirm that the accounting firm would accept what ever documentation Mooradian could produce.

The accounting firm called Boesky. Boesky called Mooradian, according to the accountant's testimony, and cursed him, hung up on him, and then called him back to continue, "You stupid fucking bastard." Now Boesky had to document his clandestine dealings with Milken. If he did not pay Milken the $5.3 million, Milken would not sell bonds to raise the $660 million for the Ivan Boesky Limited Partnership. If he paid Milken the money, he had to document the ledger entry because of Mooradian's inadvertent outburst in front of Testaverde. If he could not acquire doc-umentation from Milken, OAD would not issue the comfort letter, which was essential. Mooradian reported Boesky called him four or five times, with new epithets on each occasion. Mooradian reported that he feared he would lose his job (*U.S. v. Michael Milken* 1990e, p. 66).

Because the market was closed, cutting him off from other sources of revenue, Boesky, under pressure to complete the transaction, did some-thing he had never done before as far as the records demonstrate. First he called Milken and asked him to provide a bill for the $5.3 million, thus creating the paper trail that could damn them both. Second, he told Mooradian to issue a check for $5.3 million to Milken.

MILKEN'S ERROR

Milken tried to cover the gaffe by billing Boesky for "consulting," without elaborating in the typical invoice fashion, which included a statement of the services performed, the hours worked, the dates of each service, and the associated fees. The memo arrived in Boesky's office on March 24 and read, "For consulting services as agreed upon on March 21, 1986, $5,300,000.00." The cover letter from Thurnher was equally cryptic and read, "Mr. Boesky, Please send your remittance check for the attached invoice directly to me at the address listed below." It was the High-Yield Bond Department address at Drexel, Milken's turf, not the firm's New York corporate headquarters. The Ivan Boesky Limited Partnership was born with nearly one billion dollars in assets.

The government would use this transaction as evidence that Boesky's and others' testimonies specifying trading relationships between Milken and Boesky were true.

THE ANNUAL PREDATORS' BALLS

The 1986 Predators' Ball, as the Drexel High-Yield Bond Department Annual Conference was called by bond issuers and buyers, featured Larry Hagman of "Dallas" flashing his Drexel Express titanium card with a ten-billion-dollar credit line while admonishing, "Don't go hunting [for takeover target firms] without it." This was a direct reference to Drexel's prowess in corporate takeovers. This preceded a Madonna look-alike dancing and lip-synching to her "Material Girl,": "I'm a double-B girl living in a material world," an obvious play on junk bond ratings and bra sizes. Then Dolly Parton sang in person. This was a dazzling spectacle demonstrating the personality endorsements money could buy. Even more important, however, it was a presentation of Drexel's power and corporate flash, a corporate culture unusual in the investment banking world.

In addition to Drexel's stated aim of advertising the success of the High-Yield Bond Department, the annual conference had other purposes. A second outcome of these meetings was that they supplied a direct link between the corporate buyers and sellers of bonds. Here they met and came to know the particular nature of each other's financial status. As a consequence of this information, raiders could more easily select their next targets. Here, where power was defined as the ability of one firm to take over another, was the arena in which acquirers defined their relationship to their next acquisition.

The balls had a third purpose. They were a massive legitimizing process in which the use of junk bonds to finance mergers and acquisitions was validated to buyers and sellers by the congressmen who had the greatest power over financial legislation. Representative Timothy Wirth of Colorado, and Senators Bill Bradley of New Jersey, Alan Cranston of California, Edward Kennedy of Massachusetts, and Howard Metzenbaum of Ohio all attended.

Academicians legitimized the junk bond process for both the legislators and the corporate executives. Edward Altman, a prominent New York University professor of finance, speaking at the 1985 conference, demonstrated that market data from 1978 through 1984 (a period that did not include a major recession) confirmed Milken's thesis that a diversified portfolio of junk bonds yielded substantially higher returns with no greater risk than U.S. Treasury Bonds. These were the data used by Keating and his sales staff at Lincoln Savings and Loan (LSL) to sell bonds issued by American Continental Corporation (ACC), the parent company of LSL, through Drexel, to unsuspecting LSL bond customers. However, the pitch used by the sales staff reportedly was that these bonds were not only as safe as government bonds, but were guaranteed by the Federal Deposit Insurance Corporation (FDIC). These actions later led to the indictment and trial in both California and the federal courts of Keating, who was also the chief executive officer (CEO) of ACC. Keating was found guilty on seventeen of eighteen counts of securities fraud in California and was ordered by the federal courts to pay plaintiffs $3.3 billion (Salwen 1991b).

The fourth purpose of the Predators Ball was to serve as a mechanism for political contacts and payoffs. Congressmen were paid large sums of money to make fifteen- to twenty-minute addresses that advocated the expansion of the junk bond market. Drexel would subsequently hold fund-raising dinners for many of these same congressmen. For example, Timothy Wirth, a Colorado Democrat, who chaired the Subcommittee on Telecommunications, Consumer Protection, and Finance of the House Committee on Energy and Commerce in 1984 and 1985, had introduced several antimerger bills, one outlawing greenmail. In 1985 Wirth was a speaker at the annual conference. Drexel employees donated $23,900 to his successful Senate campaign. The antimerger legislation was dropped.

David Aylward, who worked as Wirth's assistant, left his job researching antimerger legislation to help organize the Alliance for Capital Access, which became the official Drexel lobby opposing federal limits on junk bond financing. Prior to 1985, when this lobby was established, Drexel did not have a strongly visible lobby.

Drexel executives also contributed $56,750 to the campaign of Senator Alfonse D'Amato of New York, who was at the time chairman of the Securities Subcommittee of the Senate Banking Committee. In 1985 alone, D'Amato received over $17,000 from Drexel. Although he had been drafting legislation to limit corporate takeovers, by the time his bills were brought to the Senate floor in December 1985 they had been purged of all antitakeover statutes.

Senator Alan Cranston, one of the Keating Five, received $41,740 from Drexel in 1986. Another of the Keating Five, Senator Dennis DeConcini, received an equivalent sum from Drexel. In the end, of the more than thirty bills drafted in 1984–1985 to regulate corporate takeovers, not one passed.

SEPTEMBER 17, 1986—BOESKY'S SURRENDER

On September 17, 1986, Boesky surrendered to federal authorities, gave evidence against Drexel, Milken, and others, and became an undercover operative for the Department of Justice. Boesky had approximately six months from the time the Ivan Boesky Limited Partnership was founded until he surrendered to federal authorities in which to realize benefits from his newly formed partnership.

Drexel was implicated. Although the company had reported to the *Wall Street Journal* that it had over one billion dollars in capital plus over half a billion dollars in a litigation budget, legal counsel for Drexel knew that the firm could survive the financial hardships of a government RICO (Racketeering Influenced and Corrupt Organizations Act) indictment for only a short time. Estimates of survival were no more than a year, and indictment was an imminent threat.

THE PARADOX

Drexel's relationship to the social order is a paradox. Employees of Drexel saw the firm as the great American success story. Throughout the mid-1980s, Drexel was the fastest-growing securities firm in the United States and the most profitable Wall Street firm, with a net income of $545.5 million in 1986. Revenues exceeded $4 billion and the firm's capital grew to more than $1.8 billion (Smith 1988). Michael Milken was dubbed the "junk bond king" by the prestigious *Wall Street Journal*. He had achieved legendary status and was credited with creating the market in junk bonds almost single-handedly. These achievements alone must have made the employees of Drexel feel they were "doing the right thing". Society was rewarding the firm and its employees. There is no doubt they felt invincible.

Drexel controlled the largest portion of the high-yield bond market in 1986 and 1987 (Smith 1988). The annual salaries of the traders and salespeople in the High-Yield Bond Department were in the millions. Michael Milken made over $550 million in 1986 in bonuses alone. However, within months Dennis Levine, a Drexel investment banker, pleaded guilty to securities fraud. He was the first. Ivan Boesky followed suit in 1987.

Not only did Wall Street and academicians sing Drexel's praises but Milken himself contributed to the legitimation process. On Thursday, September 8, 1988, the day after Drexel was indicted by the Securities and Exchange Commission (SEC) in one of the largest indictments in the history of Wall Street, Milken said:

> During the almost 20 years that I have worked in the financial services industry, I have always tried to create value for society, investors, and the

many companies that we have had the privilege to finance and the millions of employes [sic] they employ. Drexel Burnham and I have a record of ethical dealings with thousands of community leaders, customers and clients of which I am proud." (Stewart and Hertzberg 1988b, p. 1A)

It is probable that Milken believed this statement when he made it, as it is consistent with the press's portrait of him, his employees' support of him, and the public's idolization of him.

However, by April 1988, he must have begun to doubt the image he had helped create. Although he had testified several times before, when a congressional committee subpoenaed Milken to testify on April 28, 1988, he appeared but refused to answer questions, invoking his Fifth Amendment right against self-incrimination. Drexel supported Milken's taking the Fifth Amendment, reminding the public that Milken had "made an enormous contribution to financing the country." Milken also refused to testify because he had been under grand jury investigation by the Southern District of New York for nearly eighteen months. However, despite his legal problems, the press continued to refer to him as "the most powerful figure in U.S. finance" (Ricks 1988).

In 1987 Drexel's net income fell 79 percent to $117 million (Drexel 1987), the largest percentage drop among investment banking firms. It was a dramatic contrast with Drexel's previous year's performance, which topped the industry at $545.5 million (Drexel 1986a). When the stock market crashed in October 1987, Drexel took heavier than average losses because of the decline in the junk bond market, which did not bottom out until 1989. Drexel's 1987 annual report did not attribute any of the decline to the government's ongoing investigation of the firm.

DECEMBER 1988—DREXEL PLEADS GUILTY

In December 1988, Drexel pleaded guilty to six felony counts. In the midst of Drexel's financing of the largest takeover in the history of capitalism, Kohlberg Kravis Roberts's (KKR) acquisition of RJR Nabisco, the Justice Department approved the filing of RICO charges against Drexel and brothers Michael and Lowell Milken. Indictment under the RICO statute meant bond would have to be posted for the amount of any assets identified in the government's fraud charges. The Justice Department's tactic of threatening indictment under RICO was a critical blow to Drexel because its ability to conduct business depended on its assets. Drexel's assets would be effectively frozen at the same time it was participating in its largest deal ever with its most profitable client, KKR.

Ultimately survival of the firm was the major objective. Drexel's CEO Frederick Joseph and Drexel's lawyers negotiated with Rudolph Giuliani, U.S. attorney general for the Southern District of New York, Bruce Baird, assistant U.S. attorney, and the U.S. Attorney's Office.[2] Drexel pleaded guilty in exchange for two concessions from the government: that Drexel's pleas would not speak to Michael Milken's guilt or innocence (Joseph did not want it to appear as though he was selling Michael Milken out to the government) and, more importantly, that the fines assessed on Drexel would not bankrupt the firm. The agreement consisted of the following major points:

1. Drexel was allowed to say that it could not disprove the government's claims against it and Milken.
2. Drexel would not have to admit Milken's guilt, but would have to cooperate in the government investigation of Milken.
3. Drexel would agree to plead guilty to six of the nearly one hundred charges the government had brought against it.
4. Drexel would have to pay $650 million in fines and restitution.
5. Drexel could not pay Michael and Lowell Milken their 1989 bonuses. (Michael Milken's bonus was reported to be $200 million.)
6. Michael and Lowell Milken would have to leave Drexel or be fired.

The settlement was announced by the Justice Department shortly before Christmas 1988. Drexel survived the fines and guilty pleas and successfully completed its part in KKR's takeover of RJR Nabisco for a record $25.07 billion (later reported by KKR to be over $26 billion). Drexel's fees for the acquisition were approximately $600 million, nearly the same amount it was fined for all its fraudulent dealings up to that time.

A COLLAPSING HOUSE OF CARDS

The evidence used to reconstruct events discussed below was obtained from testimony of a long list of Boesky and Drexel employees who became state witnesses after they watched previous government targets plea-bargain and cooperate with federal investigators. Of course, Boesky not only cooperated with the government, but wore a hidden transmitter to assist the government in obtaining evidence against his network of colleagues. Boesky's bookkeeper, Setrag Mooradian, who had been suspended by the SEC on a prior charge, supplied information concerning the $5.3 million that Boesky owed Milken as a result of their collaboration. Mooradian had destroyed the secret records of that transaction, but was able to reconstruct them with the assistance of Maria Termine, his assistant.

Mooradian proved valuable in explaining the Boesky-Milken securities transactions to the SEC. In addition to other types of fraud, Boesky and Milken had been able to avoid securities registration and taxes through their manipulations.

Both of Milken's bookkeepers, Charles Thurnher and Donald Balser, were granted immunity from prosecution so the court might obtain the other side of the record keeping and securities transactions between Boesky and Milken. Thurnher testified that Milken, who kept no invoices or billing records, decided how much of the $5.3 million was owed to the High-Yield Bond Department and how much to the New York office (*U.S. v. Michael Milken* 1990e, p. 101). Thurnher testified that he could not say from his own knowledge that Milken's allocations were correct.

Boesky gave evidence against Martin Siegel and Kidder, Peabody, the firm for which Siegel worked as an investment banker before he came to Drexel. The U.S. Attorney's Office dropped two of the three felony, counts against Siegel in exchange for his cooperation in confirming Boesky's testimony, which exposed Robert Freeman (code name, Goldie), head of arbitrage for Goldman, Sachs. Freeman played a role in transactions that involved warrant skimming and insider trading. In August 1989, he appeared in federal court and agreed to plead guilty to a felony count and resign from Goldman, Sachs, where he had worked for nineteen years. In exchange for a reduced sentence, he testified to gaining inside information on KKR's takeover of Beatrice Foods and causing others to trade on this information.[3] See the Appendix for others who traded evidence or were prosecuted.

MARCH 1990—THE GOVERNMENT'S OFFER TO MILKEN

In March 1990, Michael Milken was made an offer he should not have refused. The government offered Milken a guilty plea on only two counts, or three if the deal provided immunity for his brother, Lowell. But Milken would neither admit wrongdoing nor cooperate with the government in uncovering wrongdoing in Drexel.

The deadline to accept the government's offer was March 29. Milken did not accept and was indicted under the RICO statutes on ninety-eight counts. A $1.2 billion bond was set.

APPENDIX

Cary Maultasch, a trader for Drexel in Beverly Hills, was indicted on two felony counts in connection with insider trading with Princeton/Newport, the first investment banking firm to be indicted under the RICO statutes. Maultasch resigned from Drexel. In August 1988, he gave evidence against Milken and Drexel in exchange for reduced charges.

James Dahl, who handled the Boesky trades for the High-Yield Bond Department, was implicated by Boesky and Maultasch and received a target letter in September 1988 from the government telling him he was about to be indicted. As a consequence, he testified that his name had been signed to trades that had been executed by Michael Milken (*U.S. v Michael Milken* 1990a, pp. 1173–213). Dahl's evidence exposed not only Boesky and Milken but Dahl's client Thomas Spiegel, head of Columbia Savings and Loan. In exchange for his revelations, Dahl was granted immunity. He provided accounts of the Diamond Shamrock/Occidental Petroleum insider trading on the part of Milken and associates. Dahl was the first member of Milken's High-Yield Bond Department to testify against him. Milken's employee network was beginning to crumble.

Terren Peizer, another High-Yield Bond Department salesman, provided information on David Solomon, CEO of Solomon Assets. Peizer kept the record (the so called blue binder) of Milken's use of Solomon assets and his trading on inside information on behalf of the Finsbury Fund of Solomon Assets. According to Peizer, the Solomon arrangement, which focused on the Finsbury Fund, a high-yield bond fund, was overseen by Drexel lawyer Lowell Milken. Peizer testified that Lowell Milken told him how to keep records on the Solomon transactions. Further according to Peizer, Michael Milken had instructed him not to comply with the government requests for information. Peizer testified that Milken told him, "If you don't have any documents, you can't comply" (*U.S. v Michael Milken* 1990a, p. 770). This was an attempt to cause Peizer to destroy evidence. Judge Kimba Wood, who sentenced Michael Milken, cited Milken's willingness to destroy evidence as one of several grounds for the severity of his penalty.

Many of Michael Milken's former associates at Drexel and its client firms testified at his presentencing hearing, including Michael Davidoff, Boesky's head trader; Cary Maultasch, trader in the High-Yield Bond Department; Peter Gardiner, member of the convertible-bond side of the High-Yield Bond Department, the salesman who replaced Maultasch when he went to the New York office; Patsy Van Utter, trader for the High-Yield Department; Terren Peizer, bond salesman for the High-Yield Bond Department; James Dahl, the High-Yield Bond Department's top trader; Kevin Madigan, legal counsel for the High-Yield Bond Department; Craig Cogut, external legal counsel for the High-Yield Bond Department with responsibility for employee private partnerships and organizer of the Alliance for Capital Access, Drexel's lobby; Fred Joseph, CEO of Drexel; and Joseph Harch, first vice-president of corporate finance under Fred

Joseph (1985–1986) when Joseph was CFO. Fund managers and lawyers for clients testified for the government. These included Benalder Bayse, Manager of First Investment Management Corporation's high-yield funds from 1985 to 1989; Aubrey Hayes, Manager of General Electric's bond fund; and R. Theodore Ammon, legal counsel for KKR from 1984 until the time of his testimony.

NOTES

2. Both Rudolph Giuliani in Manhattan and the SEC in Washington through the Department of Justice were involved in the indictment of Drexel and the Milkens.

3. Beatrice Foods changed its name to Beatrice Company Incorporated in the mid-1980s.

Chapter 2

Fraud Networks of Drexel

Fraud at Drexel was carried out through ordinary relationships established with other investment bankers, buyers, and sellers. But Drexel also established extraordinary relationships such as private partnerships and the Boesky collaborations, which were sophisticated networks for fraud activities.

One purpose of this chapter is to present both the ordinary and the extraordinary networks. Only a limited number of examples are presented for the sake of clarity. Figure 2.1 presents a fuller picture of how issuers and buyers were connected in both the ordinary and extraordinary networks. Only cases in which fraud is involved are presented.

A second purpose of this chapter is to make clear that the unambiguous position of the government was that these acts were unlawful. However, these acts often developed over long periods of time through a gradual accumulation during stages of a process. Various parts of the process were not illegal until they were linked together and used in ways that were different from those originally intended. Illegal innovations were often employed when the market was not functioning to favor the High-Yield Bond Department's position. Some acts, viewed from the perspective of those "bearing the risk" and "doing the deals," were not illegal. But most of the time actors knew they were breaking the law and went to extensive measures to conceal these fraudulent transactions.

This analysis was conducted to determine not only the structure of the networks, but the content of the interaction in the networks. Specifically, the purpose was to determine who initiated the links between organizations and who controlled the interaction. The central question was, Who had the power in the network: the issuers, the buyers, or the investment bankers? The intent was to discover whether corporations control banks or banks control corporations.

In addition to exploring the direction of power, the analysis was conducted to expose how the fraud was used in the issuing and selling of high-yield bonds to facilitate mergers and acquisitions and in some cases as a necessary component of the financial transactions. In fact, the mergers and transactions could not have been executed without the fraud.

The High-Yield Bond Department and Drexel linked three type of actors

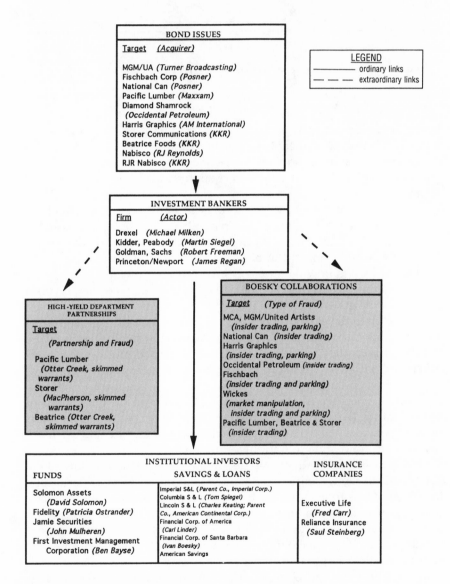

Figure 2.1 Fraud networks between Drexel and external organizations.

into a network that is characteristic of investment banking firms: issuers of bonds (corporations whose bonds were sold to raise capital); buyers of bonds, in many cases institutional investors (corporations, investment funds, savings and loans, and insurance companies); and traders and sellers of bonds in investment banking firms (both Drexel and other investment banking firms). Some fraud was committed through these standard networks created to conduct normal business.

However, employees of Drexel also created special or extraordinary networks through two types of organizational entities: Boesky collaborations and privately held partnerships, whose principals were Drexel employees and other members of the ordinary networks. These extraordinary networks were the essential mechanism used to defraud issuers and buyers of bonds. Although some of the transactions conducted in these extraordinary networks were legal, they were also the sites of most illegal transactions. Because they were entities independent of Drexel, they were difficult for the firm to oversee and thus were easily manipulated by the High-Yield Bond Department. Milken also, on occasion, created intricate relationships between the Boesky organizations and one or more of the limited partnerships in order to conduct fraudulent transactions.

ORDINARY NETWORKS

Issuers of Bonds

Corporations issue bonds when they wish to raise capital. In a leveraged buyout, the acquirer funds the takeover by issuing debt, in the form of bonds, on the target firm. As early clients of the High-Yield Bond Department of Drexel, such raiders as Carl Linder, T. Boone Pickens, and Saul Steinberg used these mechanisms. They realized that the largest pool of money was to be made in mergers and acquisitions, specifically in leveraged buyouts, which increasingly meant that a public company—one traded on a stock exchange—was taken private. KKR executives Henry Kravis and George Roberts became Drexel clients later. Issuers of junk bonds were double-bound to the Milken network. Drexel sold their junk for them. In the process, Milken generally raised more capital than they needed, creating surplus capital. In exchange for underwriting their bond sales, Milken expected them to use some of this capital to buy the junk bonds of other corporations from Drexel.

Although Drexel issued bonds for many firms, only a limited number of these were entangled in fraudulent transactions. The targets and the acquiring firms are listed in the uppermost box in Figure 2.1. Normally the transaction was executed by the investment bankers selling these issued bonds to institutional investors, some of which are listed in the large box at the bottom of Figure 2.1.

Buyers of Bonds

Buyers of bonds include not only individuals, but corporations and institutional investors. Institutional investors include such organizations as investment funds, savings and loans, and insurance companies (see Figure 2.1). The High-Yield Bond Department at Drexel assembled a network of junk bond customers that included such executives as Thomas Spiegel, the head of Columbia Savings and Loan; Charles Keating, the head of LSL and most importantly, Fred Carr, the head of Executive Life Insurance Company.

Many of the issuers of bonds were also buyers. For example, when Drexel was selling Wickes[4] stock in December 1986, some of the firms doing the buying were also sellers, among them Allied, Amcor, Atlantic Capital, Bass Investment Limited Partnership, CSL Realty Advisers, Columbia Savings and Loan, Executive Life Insurance Company of New York, First Stratford, Golden Nugget, NBC Holding, Presidential Life, Reliance, Princeton/Newport (*U.S. v. Michael Milken* 1990a, pp. 480–84).

The High-Yield Bond Department also sold bonds to fund managers in other securities firms: Patricia Ostrander, who managed a high-yield bond fund for Fidelity; John Mulheren, who managed Jamie Securities; and David Solomon who managed Solomon Assets, which due to heavy investing in Drexel's junk bond offerings grew to over $2 billion in employee pension and annuity funds in 1986. The Solomon-managed junk bond fund, the Finsbury Fund, invested solely in offerings from Drexel's High-Yield Bond Department.

Milken's relationship with Solomon Assets is an example of fraud through the normal investment banking network. Among Milken's original six guilty pleas, counts four and five were to wrongdoings in connection with Solomon's Finsbury Fund (*U.S. v. Michael Milken,* 1990c, pp. 45–51). The Solomon fund reimbursed Milken for the commissions to pay Drexel salesmen. In order to capture these commissions, Solomon simply inflated the price paid by the Finsbury Fund for the junk bonds. Milken kept a cut for himself. In return for these lucrative commissions, Milken generated phony tax losses for David Solomon's personal trading account.

Solomon, with Milken's assistance, defrauded the American taxpayer of over eight hundred thousand dollars in 1985 alone. In addition, the Finsbury shareholders were defrauded by an undetermined amount of money (*U.S. v. Michael Milken* 1990a, pp. 717–57, testimony of Terren Peizer,). Alan

Rosenthal and Terren Peizer, two Drexel traders, kept a notebook that was the balance sheet between Milken and Solomon Assets.

Investment Bankers

Normally investment bankers work with other investment bankers to underwrite takeovers. In some cases, one investment banker may put the deal together and other bankers may do the financing. This was the case with Kidder, Peabody and Drexel. Martin Siegel at Kidder, Peabody had contacts to put the deal together, but often had to rely on the High-Yield Bond Department at Drexel to issue the third-level subordinate debt. Before Siegel moved to Drexel, he and Milken often worked on the same takeover. Sometimes they worked for the same firms. Sometimes one worked for the acquirer and the other for the target.

In January 1983, Diamond Shamrock Corporation retained Kidder, Peabody to represent it in a takeover of Natomas Co., a small oil company. Siegel testified that he had informed Boesky of the impending takeover. If Boesky bought Natomas stock, it might threaten Natomas into feeling that they could be taken over by a hostile raider—Boesky—and thus soften them to a friendly takeover from Diamond Shamrock. Siegel recalled that his review of the data from the merger revealed that Boesky had acquired eight hundred thousand shares, which netted him a profit of $4.8 million (*SEC v. Martin Siegel,* 1987, pp. 7–8).

Boesky testified that Milken had called him in early January 1985 to tell him to buy Diamond Shamrock and simultaneously sell short Occidental Petroleum. Michael Davidoff, Boesky's chief trader, bought 3.5 million shares of Diamond Shamrock and tried to sell Occidental, but could only sell nineteen thousand shares (*U.S. v. Michael Milken* 1990c, pp. 65–70, redacted). Occidental was a Milken client. Occidental hired Drexel to examine the transaction and issue a "fairness opinion" assuring Occidental's board that a merger between Occidental and Diamond Shamrock that would result in one share of Occidental being swapped for one share of Diamond Shamrock (a one-for-one swap) was fair.

The reason that Milken told Boesky to buy Diamond Shamrock and sell Occidental was that Occidental was trading at approximately nine dollars more per share than Diamond Shamrock. Thus Diamond Shamrock would increase in value and Occidental would drop. This meant that Boesky would make money. It also meant that Milken would make money. Milken could not trade directly on this merger because he was representing Occidental. However, Boesky testified that the Shamrock/Occidental deal was one in which Boesky and Milken were sharing in the profits. Again, it was understood that they jointly held what Boesky was buying.

In the presentencing hearings, James Dahl, a Drexel trader, testified that he heard Milken and Boesky make the deal to share in the profits and that he also overheard Milken call Boesky the following week and tell Boesky to sell Diamond Shamrock when Diamond Shamrock decided to back out of the deal. But Boesky had bought such a large position he could not unload it in a market that knew the deal was off. Dahl testified that he heard Milken complain that the department had lost money on the Diamond Shamrock/ Occidental transaction (*U.S. v. Michael Milken* 1990a, pp. 65–70). Dahl's testimony led me to conclude that when Milken and Boesky's collaborative trades made money Milken paid Boesky for his share of the profits with Drexel favors and professional consulting. When their collaborative trades lost money that Boesky had put up for Milken, Drexel's High-Yield Bond Department was held accountable. Milken is reported to have explained to Dahl that Drexel's High-Yield Bond Department held a position "off line" with Boesky (*U.S. v. Michael Milken* 1990d 65–70). Milken testified that he committed no crimes other than the six counts to which he pleaded. Diamond Shamrock/Occidental trading was not part of the Milken plea. Although this charge was dropped by the government as part of the plea agreement, it is yet another case of insider trading. Milken's attorneys did not address the Diamond Shamrock/Occidental trading in their reply to the sentencing memo (*U.S. v. Michael Milken* 1990d, p.65).

Milken did other *favors* for those who purchased bonds. For example, he revalued securities for Charles Keating of LSL, one of the buyers in the High-Yield Bond Department ordinary network. At the time that the Home Loan Bank Board had defined LSL as insolvent, Drexel was helping Charles Keating retain the appearance of solvency by revaluing securities. One such security was Playtex bonds. Keating purchased these securities from Drexel at a fraction of their price as a sweetener for other securities that LSL was buying. Keating then sold them among three of the corporations that he headed, finally selling them back to LSL. Each time the securities were sold, Milken, who was the authority on the value of such bonds, would revalue them at a higher price. After one and one-half years, they were resold to LSL and appeared to be worth thousands of times Keating's original purchase price. Through many similar manipulations, with Milken's assistance Keating attempted to make LSL's bottom line appear much larger than it was. The ploy worked temporarily, until the bank regulators had Lincoln's assets reassessed by other valuators and discovered the gross overvaluations of a number of bonds that Milken had revalued. The bank was placed in receivership.

EXTRAORDINARY NETWORKS

In addition to using the established investment banking network of sellers, bankers, and buyers to commit fraud, Drexel established relationships with the Boesky organizations, created some private partnerships, and used other existing partnerships expressly to defraud the sellers and buyers of bonds.

The Boesky Connection

According to Maultasch's testimony, Milken illegally passed information through Maultasch to Boesky regarding MGM and Pacific Lumber. Maultasch also passed inside information to Boesky about Harris Graphics. In each instance the information concerned a merger or acquisition transaction (*U.S. v. Michael Milken* 1990a, p. 187). Boesky invested in these companies' stocks in a fifty-fifty collaboration with Milken. Milken pleaded guilty to several counts of using Boesky and his organization both to manipulate stock and to accumulate stock positions, specifically, to using the Boesky organization to manipulate MCA stock and to accumulate stock positions in Fischbach, Harris Graphics, and Diamond Shamrock/Occidental Petroleum mergers. The government presented testimony that Boesky also traded on Milken's behalf on two KKR acquisitions: Storer Communications and Beatrice Foods.

The fraud process that Milken and Boesky set up entailed Milken's subordinates informing the various Boesky organizations that impending mergers or takeovers not yet made public were about to be announced or that target firms were about to settle. Access to this type of nonpublic information allowed Boesky an unfair advantage in trading stock. According to their agreement Milken would make good any losses that the Boesky organization incurred on behalf of the Boesky-Milken collaboration. Likewise profits, minus a Boesky commission, were due Milken on the investments that were made on his behalf.

The Partnership Connections

The second type of external entity that the Drexel High-Yield Bond Department accessed to facilitate its fraudulent activity was the privately held partnerships consisting of employees and associates of the bond department.

The department hired its own legal counsel, who worked with official external legal counsel hired by Lowell Milken. The external legal counsel for the bond department was autonomous from Drexel and therefore was not monitored by the home office. It was this external legal counsel and Lowell Milken who established the private partnerships that Michael Milken used for both legal and illegal transactions. These partnerships were established instantly and then combined to create larger pools of resources for the purpose of temporarily supplying capital to facilitate takeovers. It was these partnerships that Michael Milken used for the purpose of skimming warrants and equities in several of the Drexel underwritings.

Two such partnerships were involved in the skimming of equities from two KKR takeovers. MacPherson Partners was established to skim equity from Storer Communications before its bonds were sold to the various funds some of whose managers, such as Patricia Ostrander, were part of the partnership. The MacPherson partnership was a corporation in which funds from other partnerships and trusts were pooled to generate enough capital to underwrite the takeover of Storer Communications, a deal Drexel felt was too risky. Otter Creek Partners served the same function for a somewhat different set of actors to skim equity from Beatrice Foods before its bonds were sold (see Figure 2.1).

THE ROLES OF THE BOESKY ORGANIZATIONS

The cases presented below were chosen from a large range of cases to represent the various uses of the Boesky organizations by the High-Yield Bond Department.

Insider Trading, Parking, and Market Manipulations with the Boesky Organization in the Wickes Conversion

The Wickes transaction demonstrates Milken's use of Boesky's organizations for purposes of market manipulation, parking, and accumulation of stock through insider trading. The government held that, in January 1985, Wickes—under the leadership of CEO Sandy Sigoloff—was undertaking an aggressive corporate acquisition campaign, which necessitated raising a substantial sum of money. By March 1985, Drexel had won out over Salomon Brothers as Wickes's investment banker. Over the next few years Wickes paid Drexel $118 million in fees in connection with various acquisition attempts, both successful and unsuccessful (*U.S. v. Michael Milken* 1990a, p. 5–6).

The assets of Wickes were structured though common stock, which did not pay dividends, and three other classes of securities. Two of these were debentures and the third was approximately $200 million in preferred stock. A portion of the preferred stock was categorized as 2.50. It was this 2.50 preferred stock that was manipulated by the Boesky organization on behalf of Drexel.

The preferred stock was attractive to investors because it was scheduled to pay a 10 percent dividend for each of the three years from 1985 to 1988. Two features of the 2.50 preferred increased its particular desirability: First, at the holder's option, each share of 2.50 preferred was convertible into 6.16 shares of common stock. Thus if the common stock began selling at a high price, 2.50 preferred holders could take advantage of the higher value at a favorable rate of exchange, by converting each share of their preferred to 6.16 shares of common stock and selling the common stock at the increased price. Second, the 2.50 preferred was not callable by Wickes until May 1, 1988. However, it could be called and converted if and only if Wickes common stock traded at or above a price of 6–1/8 ($6.125 per share) for twenty of thirty consecutive trading days—a highly unlikely event. Thus, it was probable that Wickes would be locked into paying the 10 percent annual dividends to its 2.50 preferred stock investors unless the investors themselves decided to exchange the stock for common stock. However, by including in the contract the clause about common stock trading at or above a set price for a certain number of days, Wickes had designed a way in which it could make the stock callable and potentially avoid paying out $15 million in dividends.

From the point of view of Wickes, these dividends inhibited its acquisition campaign because the $15 million, which it was obligated to pay out to its shareholders, would diminish the equity it had to invest in future buyouts. Wickes could not generate the acquisition capital through sale of common stock because there was little market for additional common shares. Issuing more stock would have driven down the price of each share. Thus Wickes and Drexel knew that they would have to "flush out" the convertible preferred. On September 4, 1985, Drexel wrote a letter to Mr. Mallory, a Wickes executive and the link to Drexel (*U.S. v. Michael Milken* 1990a, p. 9, government exhibit 2), suggesting that Wickes offer holders of 2.50 preferred seven shares of common stock for each share of preferred. This move was calculated as an incentive to the holders to convert voluntarily because each share of preferred stock was estimated to be worth only 6.16 shares of common stock and shareholders would acquire an additional 0.84 shares of common stock for each share of preferred stock. In exchange Wickes would be getting out from under the dividend burden and thus be able to take part in the merger and acquisition game, which was considered to be the most lucrative activity of the mid-1980s.

On December 20, 1985, Wickes offered to exchange both the preferred Series A and the 2.50. The terms of the 2.50 were exactly as Drexel had suggested. The terms for the Series A preferred were six shares of common stock for each share of preferred. Under previous agreement, holders of Series A preferred stock had been entitled to 5.5 shares of common stock. Thus they were receiving an incentive of 0.5 shares of common stock for each share of preferred series A they held. However, few investors were willing to convert their preferred shares because the price of common stock was too low.

A few months later, Wickes and Drexel saw an opportunity to force the issue. Presumably due to market forces, between March 23 and April 22, 1986, Wickes common stock closed at or above 6–1/8 on 19 out of 28 days. For Wickes to be relieved of future dividend payments by forcing pre-

ferred investors to convert their shares to common stock, the stock had to
close at or above 6–1/8 on one of the next two days.

On April 4, 1986, Wickes CEO Sandy Sigoloff had a meeting with Drexel
and Milken at the Predators' Ball. Wickes was launching an offer for
National Gypsum. Sigoloff was depending on Drexel to engineer the
conversion of Wickes preferred stock to supply the necessary capital for
the National Gypsum acquisition as well as other acquisitions. The offer
for National Gypsum was announced on April 8, but was not successful.

On April 23, 1986, Wickes closed at 6–1/8, thus triggering the conversion. By this mechanism, all preferred stock was automatically converted
into common stock, for which Wickes paid no future dividends. The
government produced a record of the telephone call from Sigoloff to
Milken, congratulating him on the success of *Project 400*, the code name
for triggering the conversion (*U.S. v. Michael Milken* 1990a, p. 21, government document 15). Congratulations were in order because Drexel had
underwritten the conversion of the 2.50 preferred by Wickes (pp. 20, 21).
If the common stock had not closed at or above 6–1/8 on twenty out of
thirty consecutive days, Drexel stood to lose handsomely. Congratulations were in order from Milken's colleagues because the Underwriter
Assistance Committee, an internal peer review committee established to
review the risks of potential underwriting activities (discussed at length
in Chapter 4) had labeled the underwriting of the conversion of $153.7
million of the 2.50 preferred as exposing Drexel to some reasonable risk,
however, the committee concluded that the High-Yield Bond Department
could go forward (p. 22).

As a result of four calls on April 23, 1986, from Cary Maultasch in the
New York office of Drexel, to Michael Davidoff, Boesky's head trader,
Seemala Corporation, a Boesky organization, purchased 1.9 million shares
of Wickes common stock. Davidoff placed the first three orders, one for
one million shares at 3:14 P.M., a second for five hundred thousand shares
at 3:45 P.M., a third for one hundred thousand shares at 3:49 P.M., to drive
the price of Wickes common stock to 6–1/8 or above. The final order for
three hundred thousand shares occurred at 4:00 P.M. The last purchase was
necessary because in order for the stock to close at 6–1/8, to effect the
trigger, at least three hundred thousand shares had to be purchased at
6–1/8 or above . Because the Boesky organization could not know how
many shares had already traded at 6–1/8, they purchased the full amount
required to ensure the proper closing price to trigger the conversion.

The Boesky organization bought half of the shares that traded on April
23. All were purchased in the last hour of the market. During that hour,
the stock was always selling at or near its highest price. Since these
purchases were made long after the National Gypsum takeover had failed,
it was reasonable for the government to conclude that Boesky was not

purchasing Wickes because he had inside information on a Wickes takeover of National Gypsum. Thus it was not possible to claim Boesky's behavior was due to his anticipation of an impending rise in Wickes common stock valuation. The Boesky organization obviously did not buy the common stock for arbitrage purposes. Boesky's white sheets showed that he began selling Wickes the very next day, on April 24, 1986. Between April 24 and May 15 he sold his entire holding at a net loss of four hundred thousand dollars (*U.S. v. Michael Milken* 1990a, pp. 24–25). Now anyone who had held one share of 2.50 preferred was holding seven shares of common stock, which was falling in price because the market was flooded with Wickes common. Boesky was not acting in his best interest as an arbitrager. He was not acting as an arbitrager at all, but as a conduit for Milken.

Michael Davidoff's testimony sheds light on the chain of events that brought about the Wickes preferred-to-common conversion. Davidoff stated that, to keep Boesky informed, he called him from the floor of the exchange, where Davidoff was buying Wickes common stock at the direction of Drexel. Boesky affirmed the buys. Davidoff further testified that the stock was being purchased not for Seemala Corporation but for Drexel (p. 46).

Davidoff exchanged his full cooperation for government immunity. He testified that Michael Milken's bond trader Cary Maultasch requested the purchase of the 1.9 million shares of Wickes common between 3:00 and 4:00 P.M. on April 23 through Seemala Corporation. Maultasch, who had worked in the High-Yield Bond Department as a convertible securities trader from June 1983 until August 1985, when he went to the New York office where he handled the Boesky organization's trading, corroborated Davidoff's depiction of the purchase of Wickes common stock to trigger a conversion of the preferred. Maultasch added another link to the chain: He reported that he called Davidoff to make purchases at the request of Peter Gardiner, a Milken trader on the bond floor, and reported back to Gardiner as Davidoff made the series of purchases. Maultasch stated that Gardiner had instructed him to have Boesky buy the stock (p. 90). Gardiner later testified that he had not instructed Maultasch, but that Michael Milken had instructed him several times that day to sell Wickes (as unsolicited) in order to cause it to close at or above 6–1/8. (It was against the law for Drexel to solicit buyers for these securities. The nature of the transaction, solicited or unsolicited, is recorded and is therefore traceable by the SEC.) Milken's defense tried to make it appear as though Maultasch had been taking action on his own to ensure the closing of Wickes common at the required price.

After the transaction was complete, Davidoff transmitted the information concerning the total purchase of Wickes and the price to Maultasch. Maultasch gave the information to Charles Thurnher, who was the accountant for Drexel's High-Yield Bond Department. He kept Milken's books of the Boesky-Milken collaboration third-party trades for each other.

Insider Trading, Parking, and the Use of a Client to Induce "Play"
with the Boesky Organization in the Takeover of Fischbach

Drexel used Executive Life Insurance Co. (a bond customer) and Boesky to manipulate a target on Victor Posner's behalf. As a raider, Posner's strategy was to use Sharon, his company, to purchase large stakes in firms, thus "putting them into play" and buying them up only to sell off their parts at a profit to Sharon. To do this he needed vast amounts of capital. This is where Drexel entered into his scheme.

In 1980, Posner made an initial sweep to acquire Fischbach Corporation, a construction company, by purchasing 5 percent of its stock and filing the required Schedule 13-D statement disclosing Sharon's position to the SEC. As a result Fischbach's management threatened to sue Posner for antitrust violation. In turn, Posner agreed not to purchase more Fischbach stock unless someone else obtained more than 10 percent of Fischbach in a takeover attempt and filed a 13-D with the SEC.

This did not stop Posner, however. He had Milken underwrite a debt issue for Pennsylvania Engineering, a Posner-held company, to finance his takeover of Fischbach and he enlisted Milken to assist him in organizing a raid on Fischbach. In December 1983, Drexel junk bond customer, First Executive Life Insurance Co. operated by Fred Carr, filed a schedule 13-D with the SEC disclosing that it had acquired 13 percent of Fischbach. This action created the appearance of a takeover bid. There is no evidence that Carr conspired with Milken, only that he bought the Fischbach stock that Milken requested him to buy. Carr generally took Milken's advice in these matters. Since Carr's purchase broke the 10 percent ceiling for the established standstill, Posner went into action to take over Fischbach.

Little did Milken and Posner know that insurance companies do not file Schedule 13-D, but rather 13-G. Carr had inadvertently filed the wrong form. In any event, the terms of the agreement required that a 13-D schedule be filed to break the standstill. Thus, Posner could not proceed with the takeover. If the takeover went forward, Fischbach could sue Posner for breach of the agreement. They would be in court, and this would buy Fischbach time and probably lead to a decline in the price of the stock. The use of Executive Life as a decoy had failed. A new decoy was needed.

Milken called on Boesky to purchase a large stake in Fischbach. Boesky bought both stock and convertible debentures. Boesky was buying in his own company's name and Milken was guaranteeing him against loss. According to Boesky's stock purchase records, he bought just under 10 percent, but on July 9, 1984, he purchased a 145,000-share block of Fischbach held by Drexel's High-Yield Bond Department, triggering the ceiling on the standstill agreement between Posner and Fischbach.

Not knowing about Milken's connection to Posner and Boesky, Fischbach assumed that a hostile raider, Ivan Boesky, was mounting a takeover. The standstill broken, Posner, with Milken's backing, was free to take over Fischbach. However, the New York office of Drexel stepped in to tell Milken that the deal was too high risk. Stephen Weinroth, from Drexel's Corporate Finance Department in New York, flew to the West Coast to convince Milken that Posner's Pennsylvania Engineering was not financially secure and to inform him that it was under investigation for securities fraud. In defiance of the New York office, Milken had the High-Yield Bond Department underwrite the deal in February 1985, with $56 million in high-yield bonds on Pennsylvania Engineering.

Drexel had a difficult time selling the Fischbach bonds. Milken is reported to have had Dort Cameron III, a former Milken employee who worked for the Bass Family Investment Partnership, buy large quantities of the bonds. Drexel absorbed the rest of the bonds and sold them at later times. What was in it for Drexel? Three million dollars for the deal and the placement of the debt.

Milken had guaranteed Boesky's position. The Boesky-Milken position in Fischbach was reported to the SEC as Boesky's alone to conceal Milken's purchase of shares in a company that his client was taking over. Milken conspired with Boesky in Posner's takeover of Fischbach. These facts are set forth in *U.S. v. Michael Milken* (1990c, pp. 30–37, redacted). Michael Milken pleaded guilty to the Fischbach dealings and conspiracy as one of his six counts of securities fraud. However, Milken's defense insisted that he did not instruct Boesky to buy Fischbach stock or guarantee him against losses at the time of Boesky's original purchase (pp. 81–82). Since Milken later paid Boesky to compensate him for losses, it is difficult to suppose that there was no former agreement and that Boesky just happened to be buying the stock because of his great insight into the market.

This was the deal that revealed the Boesky-Milken link to the SEC, not because the SEC could detect it from the transaction (it was difficult to detect[5]), but because, after Boesky sold the Fischbach stock he held on Milken's behalf, he calculated a loss of $5 million, which Milken had assured him Milken would incur. Naturally, Boesky wanted it reconciled as soon as possible. The transaction could be detected only by matching the quantity and price of the stock that Pennsylvania Engineering bought and Boesky sold. Pennsylvania Engineering bought precisely the same amount of Fischbach stock and debentures that Boesky sold, and at the same price (*U.S. v. Michael Milken* 1990e). Fischbach went the way of many Posner-acquired corporations. Its assets were drained, workers were fired, and the company declined.

Initiating a Takeover for Purposes of Self-Dealing with Boesky
in the Takeover of Harris Graphics

Perhaps the best example of Milken's use of the Boesky organization was one in which Boesky's execution of trades for Milken was restricted entirely to self-dealing—that of Harris Graphics (see *U.S. v. Michael Milken* 1990c, pp. 79–82). The circumstances of this takeover were even more advantageous for Boesky and Milken than the others described here, because they both held stock in Harris Graphics and would benefit if the stock's price were driven up in a takeover bid. The employee partnerships had purchased 1.2 million shares of Harris Graphics for $1 per share when it was formed. Other major investors were Fred Carr of Executive Life, and Saul Steinberg of Reliance Group.

Harris Graphics's management needed to raise capital and in early May they decided to make a simple stock offering through Drexel. But Drexel knew that such an offering would dilute its holdings as well as many of its customers' holdings in Harris Graphics (by making each share worth less). Harris Graphics hired Milken to make its offering, which was to take place on May 22, 1985. In early May 1985, "Milken told Boesky that he wanted the Boesky organizations to buy more than 5 percent of Harris Graphics' common stock, . . . that he would guarantee Boesky against loss on the portion, and that he would share any profits with Boesky 50%-50%." At this same time the High-Yield Bond Department at Drexel was acting as consultant to AM International, which was considering making an offer to buy Harris. By September of that year, "Milken directed Boesky to increase their Harris Graphics position to more than 5 percent and to file a Schedule 13-D" with the SEC (*US. v. Michael Milken* 1990c, pp. 79–82). This served notice to the market that Harris Graphics was in play.

Harris Graphics withdrew its plans for an offering and began to defend itself. Boesky continued to buy Harris Graphics, and Saul Steinberg increased his holdings to over 5 percent and filed with the SEC. Harris Graphics undoubtedly thought that two raiders were competing for the takeover. When Drexel presented AM International to Harris, with a friendly bid of $22 per share, saving Harris from the two hostile opponents, AM International was defined by Harris Graphics as a "white knight." By May 1986 the two companies had decided to merge.

The government concluded that

> Milken used the Boesky Organization to effect the corporate destiny of
> Harris Graphics' management. Drexel could not take overly hostile steps to
> force the sale of Harris Graphics. Through his illegal arrangement with
> Boesky, however, Milken was able to "put Harris Graphics into play" and
> create an opportunity for undisclosed trading profits. (*U.S. v. Michael Milken*
> 1990c, pp. 78–82)

What appeared to be Boesky's profits were actually Milken's profits. Prior to his sentencing, Milken admitted that he had acted unlawfully with regard to Harris Graphics.

The government charged that "The Boesky Organization presented Milken with the opportunity unlawfully to influence and manipulate the equity securities markets particularly in mergers and acquisitions, and thereby enhance Drexel's ability to consummate and profit from such a transaction" (pp. 29–30).

Through Boesky's purchases, Milken and Boesky owned about 8.4 percent of the company. The Drexel and Milken partnerships' holdings in Harris Graphics were sold for approximately $30 million. Drexel earned its customary fees, in this case $6.3 million, and the Boesky-Milken collaboration made $5.6 million on its sale of Harris Graphics.

Several types of misconduct are apparent in these transactions. Boesky was trading on inside information supplied by Milken. There is disagreement between the government prosecution and the defense as to whether the announcements of the takeovers were public before Milken instructed Boesky to buy. Since Boesky was buying for himself and Milken and filing SEC documents in his name only, there was a false filing of SEC documents. Assuming that Boesky paid the taxes, there was tax fraud by Milken.

The network formed by Milken and Boesky had major consequences for the target firms, which might not have been taken over had Milken not been linked with the Boesky organizations and other buyers. The major benefits went to the raiders and acquirers who were building empires through Milken's control of these financial markets. Of course, Drexel as well as the investment bankers who represented the targets, benefited handsomely.

Insider Trading with the Boesky Corporation in the Takeover of MGM

After KKR's takeover of Storer Communication the word spread concerning the power of Milken to finance the largest of takeovers. Ted Turner, head of Atlanta's Turner Broadcasting as well as the owner of the Atlanta Braves and WTBS, had founded the increasingly successful Cable News Network (CNN). Turner employed Milken on the West Coast to buy MGM/United Artists, a much larger and more established firm. Turner wished to reduce his expenses by gaining direct control over MGM/UA's classical film library for use by Turner Broadcasting.

In what seemed to most a conflict of interest, Drexel represented both MGM/UA and Turner. Milken on the West Coast was assuring Turner that Drexel could raise the funds for the takeover of the larger film giant. The *U.S. v. Michael Milken* Sentencing Memo (1990c, p. 4–89) notes that the *Wall Street Journal* reported on August 16 that "Despite the Drexel [highly confident] letter, it remained unclear," even if Drexel were successful in raising the money, how Ted Turner would support the hugh amount of debt that it would have to take on in order to take over MGM/UA.

Michael Davidoff testified that, from early 1985 through mid-1986, he traded stock for Michael Milken and Cary Maultasch as a result of Ivan Boesky giving him "permission to execute the order on their behalf" (*U.S. v. Michael Milken* 1990a, p. 48). Davidoff testified that he had received orders from Milken to buy stock and warrants in MGM/UA and carry them as a Seemala position in 1985 and 1986. Subsequently, Maultasch testified that he had been told by Milken to have the Boesky organization trade securities for him in connection with MCA, Harris Graphics, MGM/UA, and Pacific Lumber (pp. 84–89). It is also important to note that when the government disclosed the charges in the sentencing memo (pp. 84–89) Milken denied the insider trading charge (*U.S. v. Michael Milken* 1990d, p. 96, note 44).

The government established that Turner's takeover of MGM/UA was a matter of public record on August 7. Milken's defense attorney then attempted to document that there was an agreement in principle on the deal on August 5. The date is important because, "Boesky first purchased MGM/UA shares [for the Boesky/Milken collaboration] at 23 7/8 on August 5th" (*U.S. v. Michael Milken* 1990a, p. 65). According to Davidoff, these transactions were made at Milken's request and for him. Milken's defense attorney was not able to establish that there was an agreement in principle on August 5, leaving the reader of the court records with the impression that the trades were made for Milken on information he had because he was financing Ted Turner's takeover of MGM/UA.

Boesky bought MGM/UA stock and Boesky and Milken shared the profits fifty-fifty. There was no public knowledge of Milken's ownership. Boesky's purchases of MGM/UA stock worked to Drexel's advantage because they lent credibility to the idea that Drexel could execute the takeover. Otherwise, why would such a wealthy arbitrager become involved in purchasing such large quantities of MGM/UA? The market did not know that half of these shares belonged to Milken. The collaborative buying executed by Boesky served a second purpose, that of convincing Drexel's bond buyers that the MGM/UA bonds were a good purchase despite their high price.

The Milken/Boesky collaboration made $3 million in the trading of MGM/UA stock. In addition, Drexel made $66.8 million in financing fees for raising the $1.4 billion for Turner's takeover of MGM/UA. Drexel could rationalize these large fees, not because they had much work to do on the takeover (it was not a hostile takeover), but because they had to restructure the deal due to the questionable economic capacity of Turner Broadcasting to cover the debt.

THE ROLES OF PRIVATE PARTNERSHIPS

The private partnerships were originally formed by Milken as an avenue for him to invest on behalf of employees of the High-Yield Bond Department, to free them from investing so they might spend their time trading and selling for Drexel. In order to accomplish this, he assured them that the privately held partnerships would net them greater returns than they could make by investing individually in the market. The following discussion will focus on the two major partnerships, Otter Creek and MacPherson.

Insider Trading with Otter Creek in the National Can Takeover

This transaction is an example of the use of a private partnership rather than the Boesky organization for purposes of insider trading. Otter Creek was founded in 1979 and consisted of assets of Michael and Lowell Milken, and a large number of the employees, at one point numbering thirty-seven, of the High-Yield Bond Department. Otter Creek's management committee was headed by Lowell Milken. During Posner's attempted takeover of National Can in 1984–1985, Otter Creek acquired large holdings in National Can. The government produced documents verifying that on January 3, 1984, just days after the decision was made and before the public announcement, National Can had agreed to a Drexel-financed leveraged buyout, Otter Creek bought 10,000 shares of National Can. On January 5, National Can's board met and agreed to pursue the buyout. That same day Otter Creek bought another 31,300 shares followed by 2,000 shares two days later. On January 12, National Can publicly announced the Drexel-led takeover.

The obvious heavy trading of Otter Creek just days before a takeover triggered an investigation of insider trading by the New York Stock Exchange (NYSE). Drexel called Otter Creek's trading "unsolicited transactions" in a "nondiscretionary account." Drexel reluctantly, after much time admitted that the investors in Otter Creek were Drexel employees, but then stated that Otter Creek and Drexel had no connection to National Can (U.S. House of Representatives, 1988a). The High-Yield Bond Department was financing the takeover, and investors in Otter Creek were members of the bond department. They were directly linked to National Can. Milken denied any involvement and argued that he did not know that National Can was contemplating a buyout prior to the public announcement (see Stewart 1988).

Lowell Milken was not only the Otter Creek partner investing for the partnership, he was also head of compliance for the High-Yield Bond Department. Because of this he could trade in the stocks of clients who were soon to be announced as takeover targets financed by Drexel, and he could supply misleading information to the NYSE investigating committee. The committee's report concluded that Otter Creek had "no known connection to National Can." The committee either did not make the link between Otter Creek and the National Can takeover or did not pursue the apparent connection.

Insider Trading through the Boesky Organization and Skimming Warrants through MacPherson in the Pacific Lumber Takeover

The Pacific Lumber takeover is perhaps one of the best example of how Drexel combined the two extraordinary networks of the Boesky organization and the private partnerships to effectively execute a takeover and maximize their return.

In September 1985, Maxxam Group Inc., a real estate developer that was a junk bond buyer in Drexel's network, targeted for takeover Pacific Lumber Company, one of the nation's largest owners of redwood forests. Unlike MGM/UA in Ted Turner's takeover, Pacific Lumber fought to retain its autonomy. Maxxam Group retained Drexel, and Milken directed Boesky to begin purchasing Pacific Lumber stock in order to pressure it into the Maxxam deal. Within weeks Boesky, with Milken's collaboration, had purchased over 5 percent of Pacific Lumber stock, requiring Maxxam to offer a much higher price for the company than it had originally. Boesky's filing of Schedule 13-D with the SEC made no mention of Milken's shared interest in the stock being accumulated, again leaving the perception with Pacific Lumber and the public that Boesky alone was threatening the takeover. It took only one month for Drexel to convince Pacific Lumber to capitulate. On October 22, 1985, Pacific Lumber agreed to the takeover at $40 per share (*U.S. v. Michael Milken* 1990c, pp. 82–84).

Milken benefited on both sides of the acquisition: from his share of the collaborative investment and also from the increased fees that resulted because the Boesky-Milken collaborative investment drove up the stock price.[6] Because higher stock prices increased the debt load required for the deal, the risk associated with the bonds issued on Pacific Lumber also increased. Drexel convinced Maxxam that buyers of these securities required warrants as incentives to invest. Maxxam issued 250,000 warrants, which were to be offered to bond buyers but were instead retained by one of the Milken employee partnerships whenever the bonds were sold to institutional investors. Drexel earned a fee of $20.5 million and received equity warrants. As a result of the warrant skimming, the equity stake to the partnership was even greater than the fees to Drexel.

Pacific Lumber, now controlled by Maxxam and under immense pressure to meet the debt from the leveraged buyout, harvested large tracts of virgin redwood forests in the northwest United States to meet its debt obligations and regain solvency.

Insider Trading with the Boesky Organization and Skimming Warrants through the MacPherson Partnership in the Storer Takeover

In 1985 Henry Kravis, a partner in KKR, was involved in making a bid for Storer Communications, a Florida-based cable TV network. For this takeover, Martin Siegel of Kidder, Peabody was acting as KKR's investment banker and strategy adviser, while Milken was arranging the financing for the bid through Drexel's High-Yield Bond Department (see Figure 2.2).

The takeover of Storer Communications was set at a price of $2.4 billion. One might think that KKR had to come up with this money. Nothing is further from the truth. They invested only a fraction of the price, $2.5 million of their own money. They leveraged the takeover on Storer's equity. To add insult to injury, because KKR was a "boutique" takeover firm, it charged Storer, the target, $23 million in fees, for taking it over. It might seem somewhat ironic to charge the company you are taking over a fee for acquiring it, but the irony is multiplied when one realizes that the Storer investors were actually paying the fee of KKR, the acquiring firm. Storer was essentially helpless to argue with its acquirer over the magnitude of the fee. KKR's explanation was that it was a little less than 1 percent, which was the standard Wall Street fee. But of course this was not the entire cost to Storer.

Milken could not trade in the Storer stock because he was doing the financing. He again had Boesky acquire a position for their collaborative venture. Boesky is reported to have purchased $1 million of Storer stock on Drexel's advice, which increased the stock price. He later sold it on instructions from the High-Yield Bond Department.

The money that Drexel's High-Yield Bond Department made trading through Boesky was substantial, but represented only a small portion of the total gain. From the Storer financing, the High-Yield Bond Department made nearly $50 million in fees, a small amount in comparison to the large amounts made by the employee partnership from skimming Storer warrants. The MacPherson partnership retained the valuable equity, which was offered by KKR as an incentive to institutional investors to buy the Storer high-risk bonds.

Thus Milken was deceiving KKR, if, indeed, KKR did not know that the buyers of the Storer junk bonds were not receiving the warrants with their junk bond purchases. Milken represented the bonds to KKR as too difficult to sell without the equity sweetener (*U.S. v. Michael Milken* 1990a). In turn, some fund managers were deceiving the shareholders of the funds they managed by keeping the warrants (equity), thereby shorting the customer instead of allowing the warrants to accompany the bonds into the investment funds they managed.

But if KKR was a boutique takeover firm, why did it need Drexel? In the Storer takeover as with the later Beatrice Foods takeover, Drexel generally came up with buyers for the part of the loan that KKR could not sell on its own, the third-level, subordinate, or junior debt. KKR could come up with the largest part of its financing: the first- and-second level debt, which was easy to sell to public pension funds that it controlled. The senior debt was neither high risk nor difficult for KKR to sell. This debt was secured by the assets of the acquired company. KKR often acquired its senior loans

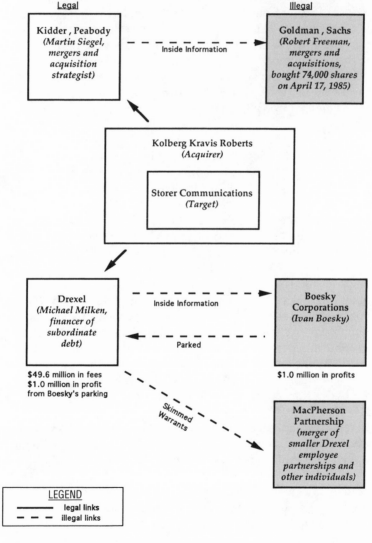

Figure 2.2 Fraud networks of Drexel: KKR's acquisition of Storer Communications.

from banks that were investing in KKR funds. The third part of the loan was the junior debt, which was high risk and, if the target failed, was paid back only after all other loans were secured. In exchange for taking this greater risk, KKR (but actually Storer) would pay a much high rate of interest on these bonds than any other: 14–18 percent. Only since October 1990, has it come to light that KKR paid much more than it initially agreed to pay for the privilege of doing business with Drexel. It also relinquished large sums in the form of warrants.

How and why could Drexel charge such large fees to another investment banker, especially KKR, which controlled extensive wealth and had its own networks? Of course, the first answer was that Drexel was doing the largest deals in the high-risk bond market—it could sell these less attractive bonds more quickly because it had the capital to underwrite bridge loans and it had a ready market (its network of buyers). But more importantly, it could render favors far beyond investment banking services normally rendered on a nonmanipulative basis. It coerced the target to sell by threatening takeovers by Boesky or other raiders. It could ensure before the takeover that, if it could not place the bonds with institutional investors, one of the Milken privately held partnerships would take them until they could be placed. Drexel not only drew from its own assets, but also from the partnership assets. No other investment banking firm had Michael Milken and his partnerships standing behind it and in some cases, for a limited period, standing instead of it.

Thus Drexel was often the linchpin in the deal because it sold the portion of the debt that was the most difficult to sell. It took the high-risk bonds, which previously were sold to insurance companies and pension plans. Now Drexel bought them outright or underwrote them so that KKR could acquire its funding instantly and act quickly. Efficient transaction time was often the key to a successful takeover. The junk bond market was not only an acceptable market in which insurance companies and pensions funds invested, but the public had become convinced that it was an acceptable place to trade on a diversified basis. The public was generally investing in high-yield bond funds such as the one Patricia Ostrander managed for Fidelity.

With regard to KKR's takeover of Storer Communications, KKR made an offer for Storer Communications in May 1985 for $75 per share. At approximately $2 billion, it was the largest leveraged buyout ever proposed, and KKR requested its main investment banker, Michael Milken, help organize the financing. Knowing that KKR was attempting to purchase Storer, Milken caused an Ivan Boesky organization, Seemala Corporation, to buy approximately 124,000 shares of Storer common stock between July 8 and July 16. To avoid disclosure of the real owner—Milken and Boesky had made an agreement that any profits or losses were Drexel's—Boesky filed the usual disclosure document with the SEC stating that Seemala had purchased more than 5 percent of Storer's common stock. On July 16, a few days before Boesky disclosed his ownership, Comcast offered to buy Storer for $82 a share plus securities. By the end of July, Comcast had raised its bid to $83.50 per share plus securities. KKR immediately countered at $90 per share, plus securities, and then immediately raised its own offer to $91 per share, plus securities. Comcast conceded defeat, presumably because KKR had overbid the value of Storer.

Even KKR thought the $2.4 billion that it paid for Storer was excessive. When Theodore Ammon of KKR was asked whether he was concerned that KKR was paying too much for the company, he replied, "I was concerned. I think it's fair to say a number of people in the firm were concerned. . . . But not so concerned that we weren't willing to give it a try" (*U.S. v. Michael Milken* 1990a, pp. 816–17).

Because the subordinate debt was often the most difficult to sell, Milken made a case to Ammon that Drexel would have to offer some form of additional inducement if they wanted to create a market for the high-yield bonds. Milken asked for an "equity kicker" in the form of warrants. The warrants were supposed to be worth $2.05 a share and Drexel would sell them, in some proportional ratio, for 7.4 cents a share to those who purchased the subordinate debt. The warrants were actually worth a great deal more than $2.05 each. As the stock rose in value so would the warrants.

Milken persuaded Ammon to offer 32 percent of Storer's equity in the value of the warrants. This meant that KKR was offering one-third of its equity to have the deal done by Drexel and it was losing that same portion of Storer. Although Milken agreed to pay $10 million for the warrants, he later renegotiated to a mere $5 million for this one-third interest, which was represented as inducement to buyers of the subordinate debt.

The Storer warrants were sold three years later, reaping the equity investors a return of 50 percent per annum. KKR and its investors paid $218 million for 51 percent of the Storer equity, while the Milken partnership paid only $5 million for 32 percent of the equity in the form of warrants. The warrant holders made many times more than the regular equity holders. But Drexel had KKR in a bind, because if KKR refused to supply warrants as part of the deal, Drexel could have refused to sell the subordinate debt.

In fact, Milken and his partnerships, not Drexel, bought the debt. Milken ran the subordinate debt, plus the associate warrants through the MacPherson partnership and then sold the debt to insurance companies and investment funds. The warrants remained with the MacPherson Partnership. Thus Milken not only made money from the investment banking fees and underwriting the subordinate debt, he and his partnerships also benefited directly from the ownership of the equity in the form of warrants.

MacPherson was made up of trusts of Michael's and Lowell's children, and contributions from the external legal counsel for the High-Yield Bond Department, some account managers for the mutual funds, and savings and loans officers that were regular buyers of Michael Milken's high-yield bonds. The warrants did not go into the accounts of the funds that invested in the Storer bonds, but into the personal accounts of the managers. Hearing testimony clarified that these warrants were used to reward past business and to serve as incentive for future business that Milken expected and required of his network participants. Further, these account managers testified that they did not disclose the acquisition of these warrants to their employers, nor did they share the warrants with the ultimate purchasers of the bonds—the fund clients.

Aubrey Hayes, the senior vice-president and manager of taxable fixed-income portfolios for General Electric, testified voluntarily that during a meeting at GE's headquarters in which Drexel and KKR were attempting to sell Storer securities, he specifically asked if there would be equity participation (warrants) for the bondholders. Aubrey Hayes reported that in the presence of the KKR representative, "I was told that the deal was going along very nicely and there would not be any equity available." Hayes reported that he did not hear of the availability of equity "until several days before the deal was finally priced and offered for sale. . . . Mr. Berger [of the high-yield department of Drexel] called me and indicated to me that there would be equity available and that I would be able to receive equity in the deal" (*U.S. v. Michael Milken* 1990a, p. 664.) Presumably the salespeople from KKR, which had invested 32 percent of Storer's equity in this inducement, and the salesperson from Drexel knew that equity was available, but they were not offering it to the buyers of bonds. The equity was later offered directly to the fund manager by Berger.

Hayes went on to negotiate with Drexel. As part of this negotiation it was stipulated that General Electric would increase its purchase of Storer high-yield bonds and in exchange would receive warrants. Berger testified, "I had an understanding that if equity was in the deal, we would be willing to increase the size" (p. 666). General Electric committed to 7 percent of the senior subordinate debt for $35 million, and in turn Drexel allowed General Electric to participate in the equity offering.

General Electric Pension Fund's public trading ticket showed that on December 12, 1985, Drexel sold 1,970 warrants of SCI (Storer) Equity Association to General Electric for $50 each for a total of $98,500. Hayes testified to the purchase and that Drexel simply informed him of the number of warrants he could purchase. Hayes presumed it was directly related to the magnitude of the bond purchase. Some two months later, February 3, 1986, after General Electric had sold its bonds, Drexel made a market for Storer warrants held by General Electric. The trade ticket was approximately $1.1 million. Thus General Electric made approximately $1 million in profit from the warrant transaction.

KKR is reported to have been very upset about the fact that Drexel negotiated these valuable warrants, which were to be used to induce the sale of the subordinate debt and that this equity ultimately ended up in the personal accounts of fund managers and Drexel executives and consultants. It seemed that not even Milken's most valuable customer, KKR, was above being defrauded by Drexel. Ammon, the KKR executive who managed the Storer deal, reported that he did not know that a Drexel partnership had managed to acquire the warrants, which were the equity kicker in the sale of the preferred stock. He reported that a year and a half later, in mid-1987, during the Beatrice deal he began to suspect wrongdoing.

Ammon said that he discussed the issue of the Storer warrants with Peter Ackerman, Drexel's agent to KKR, and that Ackerman told him Drexel executives deserved the warrants because they had risked some of their money in making the deal happen by buying a large portion of the preferred stock and holding it for several days. Ammon reported that he and Ackerman then "had a fairly vitriolic exchange, and at the end of the day we agreed to disagree. He saw it one way and I saw it slightly differently" (*U.S. v. Michael Milken* 1990a, p. 806). Ammon did not report his dissatisfaction to Michael Milken. He did not press charges against Drexel for misrepresenting how the equity kicker would be used. As a matter of fact, when it came time to finance subsequent deals in which KKR acquired Beatrice and later RJR Nabisco, Drexel did the high-risk, difficult to sell part of each deal. KKR did not stop doing business with Drexel over the equity skimming.

The bottom line seemed to be that no other company had the capital concentration and the ability to close such large, high-risk deals in such a short time. Drexel controlled a strategic contingency and eliminated normal market risks. The network link was so important to both of the companies that at the highest levels of each firm there seemed to be almost an implicit agreement that the other could do no wrong. Frederick Joseph, Drexel's CEO, in testifying about a conversation with Henry Kravis, CEO of KKR, said that KKR did not seem to be concerned about the loss of $225 million in Storer warrants that went to MacPherson, the Milken partnership. However, the content of his testimony demonstrates that Kravis wanted to inform Joseph that he knew that Drexel had profited excessively and that reciprocity was due. Joseph testified that Kravis said some people thought

> he should be troubled, or he should do something about Drexel's affiliates' purchases of as much equity as they ended up with of Storer and Beatrice, but in substance that he thought that was baloney and sort of waved it off. (*US. v. Michael Milken* 1990a, p. 1043).

These warrants, valued at $225 million, could have been retained in Storer or could have gone to the purchasers of the bonds. Thus both KKR and the bond purchasers lost to the benefit of MacPherson Partnership.

Skimming Warrants through the Otter Creek Partnership
in the Beatrice Takeover

At this same time in 1985, KKR made a bid for Beatrice Companies, a Fortune 500 conglomerate. This was KKR's first really hostile takeover, and the press was heavily involved in publicizing the bids and counter-offers. KKR seemed to have billions of dollars at its disposal, and billions were required to take over Beatrice. Thus the numbers of bidders were few and very select. When KKR acquired Beatrice for $5.6 billion and assumed $2.6 billion in debt, it charged Beatrice a $45 million investment banking fee. The fee was charged before KKR did anything for the acquired firm.

KKR had allied itself with Donald Kelly, a former Beatrice chairman of the board. This was an attempt to threaten Beatrice's management into accepting KKR's terms for the takeover. If Beatrice did not capitulate, KKR would take it over and replace management with Kelly and his associates. This hostile takeover was the turning point for Jerome Kohlberg, who soon after resigned his position as senior partner of KKR, leaving his cousins Henry Kravis and George Roberts to run the firm (Bartlett 1991).

Martin Siegel of Kidder, Peabody was representing KKR. He was organizing the takeover and was reporting its progress to Robert Freeman, head of arbitrage at Goldman, Sachs, who was buying large quantities of Beatrice not only for himself, but also for Goldman, Sachs. The information was vague enough that it escaped strict definitions of insider information.

Beatrice agreed to KKR's takeover at a price of $50 per share in November 1985. But on January 7, 1986, KKR learned from Drexel, which was doing the financing, that it could not finance the deal at $50. The price would have to be lowered or the financing would have the be altered. Either choice would send a message to the market about the value of Beatrice. The next morning, January 8, Freeman unloaded his option position. When Freeman called Siegel to confirm the trouble, Siegel did not yet know of KKR's financing problems. Freeman knew this confidential information (although he was not working on the deal) before Siegel, who was KKR's investment banker. The network was so fast in communicating accurate information that people outside the deal knew about deal problems before the deal strategist. Siegel confirmed the problem with KKR and then called Freeman to verify that his information was correct. That afternoon Freeman sold one hundred thousand shares of Beatrice and the right to buy another three hundred thousand shares. Of course, since he was selling before the information was public, Freeman made extremely profitable transactions. Beatrice was finally sold to KKR at $40 per share.

Siegel's information saved Freeman 20 percent of his investment. Of course, neither Siegel nor the arbitrage unit that he advised at Kidder, Peabody could trade on the Beatrice takeover because Siegel was KKR's investment banker. Kidder, Peabody got the lucrative investment banking fees for doing the deal. However, Milken and Drexel got the much more lucrative financial fees. While Kidder, Peabody made $7 million, Drexel made approximately $50 million. Siegel was watching Michael Milken wield enormous power in putting together the takeover of Beatrice Foods and wanted to be a part of those deals. Siegel would later take a position with Drexel's High-Yield Bond Department for just that purpose.

Milken again induced KKR to provide warrants, in this case Beatrice warrants, as a sweetener in order to assist him in selling the high-yield bonds. His argument was that he needed to offer equity to his buyers in order to get them to purchase high-risk bonds. Again Milken ran the deal through a privately held partnership, Otter Creek, which retained the warrants. The high-risk bonds were then sold by the fund managers who were part of Milken's network and were themselves sharing in the Milken profits. The warrants, which represented a 24 percent interest in Beatrice, were provided by Beatrice at 25 cents a share and sold for $26 a share or a total of $650 million. In this instance, KKR agreed to sell 24 percent of Beatrice in warrants for the nominal sum of $7.9 million, as an incentive to bond buyers. The profit for these warrants when the partnership sold them was over $275 million. Most of these warrants ended up in the closely held partnership of Michael Milken—Otter Creek.

BOND BUYERS AND THE EXTRAORDINARY NETWORK

Buyer: Fund Managers Payoffs through MacPherson

The case of Patricia Ostrander is an example of fraud through one of the employee partnerships of the High-Yield Bond Department. A member of the ordinary network of Drexel buyers, she was linked to the extraordinary network through MacPherson, an employee partnership. Patricia Ostrander was a Fidelity High-Yield Bond Fund manager in the mid-1980s.[7] She became, at Milken's discretion, a member of MacPherson Limited Partnership, and was identified in the Milken presentencing hearing as a recipient of money from one of Drexel's takeovers. However, she was not indicted until mid-October 1991 (Lambert and Schmitt, 1991). Ostrander violated securities laws by accepting unlawful compensation in connection with investments she made on behalf of pension plans she managed.[8] MacPherson Limited Partnership, which was used to skim warrants from KKR's takeover of Storer Communications, paid her $750,000. Storer intended the warrants to be sold as a sweetener (equity of high value) to funds that purchased its high-yield bonds as a reward to fund shareholders for taking a risk. Instead Fidelity shareholders took the risks, and Ostrander, along with her partners in MacPherson, received the equity.

Buyer: Illegal Compensation of a Buyer through MacPherson

The buyer network of fund managers, savings and loan officers, and insurance firms was organized through the High-Yield Bond Department and stood ready even before a trade was conceived. The department's control of its environment was so far-reaching that in some cases it could define who became a manager for the major funds that were its clients. For example, Benalder Bayse was an investment adviser in high-yield bonds for Mitchell Hutchins Asset Management, a Drexel client. Mitchell Hutchins Asset relied on Drexel, which controlled the lions share of the market. Roy Johnson managed the Mitchell Hutchins Asset account at Drexel.

In 1985, Benalder Bayse was attracted from Mitchell Hutchins to First Investors Management Company where he managed the First Investors Fund for Income, the First Investors Special Bond Fund, Executive Investors High-Yield Fund, and Life Services High Income Fund. Among those represented were the Minneapolis Teachers Retirement Fund and ICH, an insurance company fund (*U.S. v. Michael Milken* 1990a, pp. 599–601). Between 1985 and 1989, Bayse was promoted to vice president at First Investors.

But what was most interesting was how he was recruited to First Investors. He testified that Roy Johnson at Drexel in Los Angeles called him one day and told him, "there was going to be job opening, a very lucrative job opening in New York for a high-yield manager, and that in fact there had been a request for candidates for that job, and he wanted to submit my name" (pp. 605–06). Bayse further testified that Roy Johnson told him that First Investors wanted to fill the position quickly and that he should immediately send his qualifications to Johnson, who would get them to First Investors.

When the government asked if Johnson was acting solely on his own initiative, Bayse responded that Johnson "told me that Michael Milken had, in fact, found this job opening and that he had asked the salesmen if they had any candidates that might be available for it" (p. 607). Bayse further testified that after he had faxed Roy Johnson his handwritten qualifications, a few days later he received a call from David Crayson, president of First Investors saying that he would like to meet with Bayse to discuss the possibility of Bayse working for First Investors.

After the interview was over, Johnson called New York and told Bayse that "he thought the interview went well," and that it was important for Bayse to meet Johnson and talk about this opportunity. Bayse learned from Johnson that this was an important account and that Johnson would be covering the First Investors account for Drexel. In mid-1985, before being offered the job, Bayse met Johnson at the Stanhope Hotel in Manhattan.

Bayse testified that after Johnson told him how profitable the First Investors account was for Drexel, "He, in fact, told me that he wanted total control over the account before they could endorse me for the job." Bayse reported that he told Johnson that was impossible. Bayse further testified that in response Johnson, "basically told me that they would think about it. He knew I was a good manager and he would want to consider this and he would get back to me."

Bayse reported that after he had been given the position at First Investors, Johnson told him that "Mr. Milken had *made* various investors like Fred Carr and Tom Spiegel and David Solomon" (*U.S. v. Michael Milken* 1990a, p. 615, emphasis added). From talking to the investors in his new department, Bayse discovered that his predecessor had been so heavily influenced by Drexel that he did not make his buy decisions based on credit reports, but on Drexel's recommendations. As a consequence, Bayse found his newly acquired high-yield department in disarray. He reported turning the department around in two quarters. At the same time he helped Drexel begin the reciprocity process that would hook him into its network. Just three week after he took the position at First Investors Bayse asked Drexel's Roy Johnson if he could invest in Town and Country. Roy Johnson sold Bayse, in a personal account, twenty thousand dollars in Town and Country warrants, which Bayse understood were the equity in conjunction with Drexel's recent offering of Town and Country bonds. Bayse reported that in two or three weeks he sold the warrants back to Drexel for a nine-thousand-dollar profit. Thus Drexel had provided Bayse a nine-thousand-dollar bonus through the sale and repurchase of Town and Country warrants.

Bayse now owed Roy Johnson a personal favor. When Johnson called to sell Bayse third-tier, subordinate debt in Storer, Bayse bought, on behalf of First Investors, $50 million worth of the less-risky, 15 percent interest bonds. Johnson wanted Bayse to take the higher risk, high-yield preferred, but Bayse felt they were too low on the capital structure. During the negotiation, when Johnson became convinced that Bayse was not going to buy the preferred, he put Michael Milken on the phone to persuade him. Bayse made a $10 to $11 million investment in the higher risk, higher yield Storer preferred as a result of his conversation with Michael Milken. Bayse testified that there was no equity kicker offer made to him at the time of his purchase of Storer preferred on behalf of First Investors (*U.S. v. Michael Milken*, 1990a, p. 624). After Milken and his partnerships had underwritten KKR's takeover of Storer, in January 1986, Bayse raised the issue of equity in the Storer takeover on the basis that he had been a good customer (having purchased large quantities of the bonds and the higher risk preferred stock). He was told that he could buy into a private partnership, MacPherson Limited Partnership. Bayse invested $8,800 in one hundred thousand warrants; he paid 8.8 cents per warrant. The government asked

Bayse what Johnson told him concerning the other investors in MacPherson and Bayse replied:

> The only other name he mentioned was David Solomon. However, he did tell me that I had reached the major leagues. I was accompanied in this by a lot of well heeled individuals, and that I should be very proud of being in this league. (*U.S. v. Michael Milken*, 1990a, p. 627)

Bayse testified that the warrants were offered to him personally and were never connected to the nature of his purchase of Storer preferred stock for First Investors (p. 628).

Bayse testified that he bought Republic Air, Documentation, and John Lair at the suggestions of Roy Johnson. Drexel was making a market in each of these securities (pp. 633–36). He testified that he did in hindsight feel that others might think there was some impropriety in his dealing on information he received from the securities firm with which his employer was doing business.

Ironically, in 1986 Bayse published an article in *Bottomline* entitled "How to Tell High-Yield Bonds from Real Junk," explaining that credit analysis is crucial in managing these securities (1986). Yet he testified to a method of decision-making that rested more on the advice of Drexel salesmen than on the methods he advocated in his article. Somehow the disparity between his method of operation and the rational calculus he presented leads one to asks how these rationality myths were created and perpetuated. From 1985 to 1989, the funds under Bayse's management rose from $400 million to roughly $3 billion (*U.S. v. Michael Milken*, 1990a, p. 601).

Buyers: Savings and Loans

Before the Reagan administration, savings and loans had been restricted to investing in home and other real estate loans. People who were not risk prone knew that their deposits in these institutions were insured for up to one hundred thousand dollars by the government. Those who invested large sums of money relied on the fact that they were dealing with conservatively managed organizations.

Under the Reagan administration banks were deregulated, which meant they were allowed to buy riskier securities. Risky securities paid higher interest rates than real estate loans. Receiving higher rates for investments allowed savings and loans to compete with commercial banks in offering higher deposit interest rates. In order to offer higher rates, these bankers had to invest in riskier securities. Bankers bought high-yield bonds from Drexel for this purpose. Among the bond purchasers were American Savings, Centrust, Financial Corporation of America, Lincoln Savings and Loan, Columbia Savings and Loan, and Financial Corporation of Santa Barbara. Risky investments by savings and loans made the failure of these institutions more likely, especially in a depressed economy.

DISCLOSURE OF THE MILKEN/BOESKY CONNECTION

Both Boesky and Milken employees reported having observed transactions between their bosses. Michael Davidoff, Boesky's head trader,
testified that he helped Setrag Mooradian, head bookkeeper for Ivan
Boesky and Seemala Corporation, keep a list of securities that were traded
for Drexel and securities that Drexel held for Seemala Corporation under
Drexel's name (*U.S. v. Michael Milken*, 1990a, pp. 50–51). Cary Maultasch
testified that he obtained information on the purchase of Harris Graphics,
Pacific Lumber, Wickes, and MGM/UA by Boesky for Milken and gave
this information to Charles Thurnher, a High-Yield Bond Department
accountant, who was keeping the records of transactions Boesky's organization made as favors for Milken (p. 96). Similarly Maultasch testified
that Michael Davidoff asked him to purchase Helmerich & Payne through
Drexel as a favor. When Maultasch told Michael Milken of the requested
purchase, Milken asked him, "Can you get him to do less?" Presumably
Milken did not want such a large quantity to appear on the Drexel books.
Later Milken is alleged by Maultasch to have asked him to "get it off the
page," which means to trade it out of the Drexel account. This same event
was also reported to Charles Thurnher, who was keeping the books on the
Boesky-Milken collaboration for Milken.

EVENTS LEADING TO BANKRUPTCY

The junk bond market, which had been deteriorating steadily throughout the year, crashed by the fall of 1989. The mergers and acquisitions
business slowed. Drexel's revenue stream from trading and underwriting
high-yield bonds declined substantially. Because the high-yield bond market was illiquid, Drexel and its unregulated affiliates[9] became dependent
on the short-term credit markets, borrowing as much as $1 billion, on an
unsecured basis, through the issuance of commercial paper (Breeden 1990,
p. 3). Critical events followed.

September 1988. The SEC filed an injunction against Drexel Burnham
Lambert (DBL) and Group for fraud. Subsequently, DBL and Group
agreed to enter pleas of guilty to six counts of felony violations of the
federal securities laws and mail fraud statutes.

March 1989. Drexel settled with the United States on felony insider
trading charges by agreeing to pay $650 million to the government and
defrauded investors. Without admitting or denying the allegations in the
SEC's complaint, DBL and Group consented, among other things, (1) to
pay $350 million into a fund, required by the United States Attorney

General's Office, for the benefit of persons injured by DBL and Group's violations of the federal securities laws; (2) to pay $15 million as a civil penalty under the Insider Trading Sanctions Act of 1984, as part of $300 million in civil and criminal penalties agreed to with the United States attorney general; (3) to cooperate in the SEC's continuing investigations; (4) to retain an independent special appraiser to review investment company related operations; (5) and to effect changes in DBL's personnel and establish advisory procedures (Breeden 1990, p. 19).

Fall 1989.   By fall 1989, Drexel's fortune was tied inextricably to the junk bond market it had created, a market that was crashing. Drexel was a highly leveraged company, with substantial unsecured short-term borrowing at the top echelons or holding company level. Drexel did not have and could not obtain committed bank lines of credit to support its unsecured borrowing.

December 1989.   Standard and Poors lowered the rating of Drexel-issued commercial paper because Drexel's primary assets, which were privately placed debt and equity investments and non–investment grade corporate debt, became increasingly illiquid. This illiquidity, coupled with the declining revenue flows from the junk bond market, precipitated the lower rating. The lowering of the rating made it even more difficult for Drexel to refinance its short-term debt as it came due. This led to increased insolvency.

January 1990.   To counter the growing insolvency, Drexel withdrew approximately $400 million from DBL (the broker-dealer) and the government bond dealer (GSI) thereby substantially reducing the capital of both firms. This created further risk. Now DBL customers and broker-dealers could be subjected to liquidation by the Securities Investor Protection Corporation (SIPC) (Breeden 1990).

February 7, 1990.   The SEC and the NYSE took action to ensure that DBL's capital could not be further depleted without the consent of the SEC and the NYSE. According to Breeden (1990), this was necessary, in part, because regulators were unable to value accurately DBL's portfolio of securities to determine if the firm had sufficient capital. The SEC took action under its net capital and customer protection rules. The NYSE had authority to set net capital requirements for its member organizations and impose restrictions on withdrawal of funds from member firms. Neither the SEC nor the NYSE had regulatory oversight of the activities of the parent holding company, Drexel. They did have oversight for DBL and GSI.

February 1990.   The majority of the assets on the books of DBL and GSI had been liquidated. The total assets of the two firms were reduced from $20 billion on February 1, 1990, to $8 billion a month later. Seventy-five percent of DBL's customer accounts had been transferred to other firms through actions of financial regulators.

February 13, 1990.   Frederick Joseph called the SEC to advise it that Drexel was inclined to seek relief under Chapter 11 of the Federal Bankruptcy Code. Ironically the holding company was unable to meet the interest payments on its maturing debt. At approximately 11:00 A.M., Drexel issued a statement announcing its default on almost $100 million in loans (Breeden 1990).

CONCLUSIONS

The legal positions defined by the government are unambiguous, and do not make allowance for the process by which activities may become illegal, either through slow accretion or by subsequent redefinition of the law. For example, private partnerships were organized from the bond floor for the purpose of investing pools of funds for employees. Later these funds were merged to provide a legal structure to underwrite takeovers. An example of this was the MacPherson Limited Partnership Fund, which was used in the takeover of Storer Communications. In the process of closing the deal, Milken persuaded KKR to put up one-third of the equity in Storer in the form of warrants to be sold at a discounted rate to the buyers of the high-risk Storer bonds. Otherwise, Milken claimed, he would not be able to convince the institutional investors to buy such high-risk bonds. However, instead of issuing the warrants to the purchasers of the bonds as he had represented to KKR, he distributed them to the members of the MacPherson partnership. These securities represented approximately one-third of the total equity of Storer. The MacPherson partnership was thus guilty of warrant skimming.

Drexel held that this was not illegal. Milken's attorneys stated that MacPherson investors were entitled to this equity because they incurred risks in underwriting the takeover. The attorneys held to the capitalist assumption that suppliers of capital, such as MacPherson partners were entitled to compensation for financial hazard. At question here is the level of compensation and the extent to which KKR and the bond buyers were defrauded. The government argued that they lost substantially. The government also alleged that the purchasers of the bonds were defrauded because they did not receive the equity that KKR had intended to accompany the debt. Kravitz of KKR testified that MacPherson investors, by retaining the warrants, had violated an oral agreement.

Evidently, the jury in the Patricia Ostrander case agreed with the government that investors in Fidelity funds that purchased the Storer bonds had been defrauded. The government charged Ostrander with two counts of fraud because she, as a principal in MacPherson, received warrants (a bribe to buy the bonds) valued at thirteen thousand dollars for purchasing the high-risk bonds for the Fidelity fund she managed. In conjunction with this transaction, she did not report ownership of these warrants and thus was in violation of federal reporting laws. She was later found guilty of these charges.

Certainly, those who feel the market and not the state should control transactions and eliminate those who act fraudulently would hold that it was appropriate for Ostrander to net the $750,000 that she received from her investment of thirteen thousand dollars. After all, this is a cost of doing business in the capitalist system. Much of the ambiguity exists over assumptions that lie at the base of our economic system and the question of who should control the market, the state or financial firms.

The High-Yield Bond Department at Drexel executed millions of transactions. Only a small portion of these were illegal. Because the illegal transactions were embedded in the legal transactions, they were difficult, if not impossible, to detect. They were exposed initially by errors made by Boesky's bookkeeper and the responses Milken made to those errors. These mistakes led the investigators from Boesky and his bookkeepers to all those who gave evidence to the government in the wake of the ensuing investigations.

The High-Yield Bond Department was innovative in it's use of Boesky's organization and the private partnerships only when its normal and legal means of doing the deals were blocked. For example, the department had Boesky manipulate the market only when Wickes did not close at the requisite 6–1/8 on the nineteenth day. Thus when the normal means of reaching the ends or doing the deal were not accessible, it used innovative means. In this case the innovative means were illegal; in other cases they were not. When the illegal acts were not detected they became part of the pattern of doing business and were repeated. As the number of transactions increased, they became in many cases the most effective method of doing business and their legality and legitimacy were not questioned. They were no longer kept secret from employees of the High-Yield Bond Department or from the Boesky organization.

The fraud networks were called into action when normal market mechanisms were not functioning in favor of Drexel. Thus, the Boesky organization manipulated the market and bought positions on Drexel's behalf when the market was not moving in the desired direction. Likewise, when

Drexel could not finance a deal or defined it as too risky, Milken's employee partnerships were used to perform such functions in lieu of and on the premises of Drexel. Warrants were skimmed as incentives for the partners. The partnerships became a functional alternative to Drexel's financial capacity.

This analysis supports the financial capital and bank control models, which are squarely lodged in conflict traditions, with assumptions well suited to the interorganizational perspective. The focus here is not on the form or structure of the network, but on the content and direction of the power relationships. This is an effort to expose the sources of power.

As holding companies and conglomerates expanded early in the century, investment banking firms increased in power. The earliest studies of such networks were conducted by Jeidels (1905). These studies were influential in the classic statements of Hilferding ([1910] 1981), who argued that the concentration of banking and industry leads to their fusion into the monopoly form of money capital. In the financial capital model, financial capital forms itself into units of capital with varying mixes of banking and industrial interests. The units are not integrated enterprises, but are loosely coupled allies linked through intercorporate shareholders, indebtedness, and various kinds of interlocks. Certainly Drexel had all of these characteristics of the financial model; however, in the financial capital model the corporation, not the financial firm, is dominant. These models describe distinct empires or spheres of influence (Rochester 1936; Perlo 1957; Aaronovich 1961), groups of companies pursuing a corporate strategy through the control and use of financial capital.

In my findings, the majority of the links within the network, as expected, run between financial and nonfinancial companies rather than being confined within each sector. But the initial relationship is from the investment bank to the corporation; instead of from the corporation to the bank as posited in earlier theories. Whereas Hilferding held that the tendency of organized capitalism was toward cartelization of the whole economy, we are not examining the pervasiveness of these links, but their nature.

The bank control model is often mistakenly equated with the financial capital model, but in fact differs. The bank control model holds that banks are the power centers within the networks. Banks are seen as possessing an independent base of power because of their ability to grant or to withhold long-and short-term loans. Investment banks, and in particular Drexel, could simply refuse to do the deal, thus limiting the expansion of the acquirer. In an effort to protect their investments, banks seek a wide range of interaction with the corporations they lend money. Banks subordinate the interests of the various corporations in a common strategy aimed at maximizing bank interests. The strongest statement of bank control is made by Fitch and Oppenheimer (1970), who define this relationship as "bank terrorism." Weaker arguments are made by Kotz (1978) and Mintz and Schwartz (1984). The networks form clusters around banks, but it is assumed that the director interlocks are created by bankers sitting on industrial boards rather than industrialists sitting on bank boards. Thus the links are directional indicators of the flow of power.

Drexel controlled not only the acquiring firms but also the buyers of the bonds by requiring that they make purchases, by influencing who would become fund managers, by illegally compensating fund managers, by revaluing securities to inflate the bottom line of savings and loans, and by revaluing securities to deflate their value for tax purposes. To extend this model, when Drexel employees loyal to the High-Yield Bond Department were placed on the boards of target firms, the purpose was to protect the bank's investment by obtaining information concerning the continued solvency of the target and the possible need for restructuring given the large debts carried as a result of the leveraging. A second function was served: The issuers of bonds were also buyers, and members of the board were in a position to know the types and quantity of investments the firm was making. The investment bankers/board members also performed the function of supplying information about future takeovers, which were the core of Drexel's business.

In their ten-country analysis of interlocking directorates, Stokman, Ziegler, and Scott (1985) conclude that although the U.S. networks showed a low level of centralization, there were links connecting the larger corporations to a very large number of banks represented in the networks. When this study was conducted on data from 1976, commercial banks and insurance companies were the centers of the networks. In his conclusion, Ziegler (1985) points out that as a result of the strict separation of commercial and investment banking, the absolute concentration of banking in Great Britain and the United States was less than might have been expected. In fact, until this study, investment banks had not been included in such analyses. There were more commercial than investment banks among the most frequently interlocked corporations. Among the top twenty companies there were eight banks. But Ziegler concludes that "this high degree of 'bank-centrality' in the Anglo-American countries, far from creating centralized networks, was actually preventing the formation of large centers" (p. 267). Commercial banks had no directors in common. In addition in 1976, bankers in the United States less often sat on the boards of industrial firms than industrialists sat on the boards of banks (Stockman and Wasseur 1985).

Given what was occurring at Drexel, it would be interesting to discover if these trends changed by the mid-1980s. It stands to reason that as the mergers and acquisitions period of the 1980s accelerated, more investment bankers found their way to corporate boards. Also, the analysis of data from other countries leads us to believe that this trend should have increased over that decade. First, the separation of commercial and investment bank functions was decreasing due to deregulation and changing practices whereby existing regulations were not being enforced. Second, the tendency toward clustering in interlocking directorships seemed to be especially pronounced when holding companies acted as financial intermediaries, allocating and monitoring capital among corporations from various industries. Whether ownership ultimately belonged to families, government, or stockholders made little difference. Thus interlocking through banks was a clumsy technique for holding companies to coordinate the activities of independent and unrelated firms (Stigler 1968, p. 261). Certainly Chandler (1977) would find this an inferior managerial technique for organizing marketing and production, but it seems to be a satisfactory device for monitoring capital allocations among financial interest groups. It is the creation of these holding companies that is explored by writers from the financial capital and bank control perspectives, and it is the transformation from multidivisional firms to holding companies that results from the financial conception of control (Fligstein 1990a). It was the continuation of this transformation that Drexel was financing.

NOTES

4. Wickes was a lumber and building materials retailer. Wickes's CEO was Sanford (Sandy) Sigoloff.
5. Milken's name was neither on the transaction nor directly linked to the purchase.
6. The process of skimming warrants is more fully elaborated in the Storer takeover in the following example.
7. She left Fidelity in 1987 to become, by 1991, president of her own firm, Ostrander Capital Management.
8. "Ms Ostrander was found guilty of two counts of accepting an illegal gratuity and one count of violating federal reporting requirements stemming form a $13,000 investment she made in a deal set by Drexel's junk bond department" (Moses 1992).
9. Drexel Burnham Lambert Group Inc.(Drexel) is the holding company parent of Drexel Burnham Lambert Inc. (DBL), a registered broker-dealer, and Drexel Burnham Lambert Government Securities Inc. (GSI), a registered government securities dealer, DBL Trading Corp. (DBL Trading), an entity that engaged in extensive foreign exchange and commodities trading, and DBL Internal Bank, Nv, a Curacao corporation through which Drexel conducted many of its foreign operations (Breeden 1990). The junk bond market as well as mergers and acquisitions were carried on by the holding company, Drexel.

Chapter 3

Consequences of Fraud-Facilitated Leveraged Buyouts

The ultimate issues for study are, Has the national interest, in the form of better economic performance, been advanced? and Has the national interest in the form of citizens' well-being been advanced? We may never be able to answer these questions fully because of the interrelatedness of the objectives. However, to begin, we must examine ramifications of junk bond fraud-facilitated LBOs for the various actors in Drexel's networks as well as for society as a whole. Just who suffered and in what ways? This examination leads us to conclude that Drexel's securities fraud of the 1980s had pervasive consequences, not only for Drexel and the companies targeted for the takeovers, through which fraud was perpetrated, but also for the issuers of the bonds who supplied equity to sweeten the sale of the junk bonds to insurance companies, savings and loans, and investment funds' management firms.

CONSEQUENCES

In the early 1960s, the established business community was aware of, but relatively unaffected by hostile takeovers. They did not touch the business elite. By 1968 the threat posed by hostile takeovers had been recognized and was formally acknowledged by the passage of the Williams Act, which imposed regulations on the utilization of these transactions (Jarrell and Bradley 1980; Schipper and Thompson 1983).

Although its early practitioners had brought the hostile takeover to the attention of the business world as an innovation, the process was generally defined as an illegitimate, if not an illegal aberration. Takeovers were likely to be initiated by acquirers who were outside the established business elite, such as Ronald Perelman, T. Boone Pickens, and Carl Icahn, and the deals were likely to be made by investment banking firms that were not among the ten top-ranking firms. However, by the mid-1980s even the largest firms were either involved in hostile takeovers or targets of such takeovers. The largest investment banking firms either represented the raiders or defended the targets.

Initially, these buyouts had been financed by high-quality, investment grade bonds. Michael Milken helped bring about the flowering of the hostile takeover by introducing the use of junk bonds, or high-risk debt, to fund mergers and acquisitions. Because any corporation can issue non–investment quality debt, if an investment banking firm can sell it, these instruments create capital, or liquidity, very rapidly. The more liquidity is available, the greater the opportunity for fraud. The opportunity for fraud increases as the number of transactions increases, and because of the characteristics of the transactions discussed in Chapter 5, the fraud was easy to conceal. Milken's use of junk bonds to fund buyouts compounded the investment risk structure because it created a financing mechanism with high-risk securities instruments for a base and because it increased the opportunity for fraudulent transactions.

Innovative financial activities increase the opportunity for fraud precisely because they are new. No one except the innovator knows exactly how the new instruments work. Participants who have not seen the new processes in operation before are unaware of the details of the normative structures associated with them. When some of the players do not know the standard, it is easier to incorporate fraud in the transaction. Furthermore, when some aspects of the process are invisible, the opportunities for fraud are compounded.

Fraud increased the efficiency of merger transactions by improving the capital position of the acquirer. Fraud helped make it possible and easy for companies to buy other companies. The innovation of junk bonds and the attendant fraud catalyzed perniciously the transformation of the purpose of mergers and acquisitions: Companies became acquirers of other companies to make a profit rather than to reduce competition or increase productivity. Junk bonds and fraud helped create a market for corporations. Whatever problems might have been anticipated from the concentration of wealth and power associated with corporate mergers and acquisitions were exacerbated by the change in their purpose and the increase in their occurrence. Additionally, the consequence of fraud itself was to concentrate power and resources in the hands of those privy to the crime.

Thus many large U.S. corporations significantly augmented their leverage during the 1980s. Debt was considered necessary for efficiency and effectiveness (e.g., Jensen 1989a, 1989b). However, the first year of the 1990s saw an increase in the number of bankruptcies and a restructuring of target firms, and acquirers. In addition, there was a rise in the number of failures of savings and loans, insurance firms and investment firms that purchased junk bonds. These corporate and bank failures have been attributed to excessive leverage and the associated costs of high debt and reduced managerial flexibility. Although it is understood that fraud expedited these LBOs, the failures have never been linked together through the fraud that occurred in each of the deals.

Michael Jensen (1986, 1988, 1989b), extending a thesis first suggested in 1932 by Berle and Means that the interests of corporate owners and managers are separate, exposed the dysfunctional effects of such a separation. In his seminal works, Jensen argued from the standpoint of agency theory that debt provided a number of governance benefits that are often lacking in firms with low debt and high–equity capital structures. Jensen makes three major contentions. First, he assumes that debt can motivate or act as a disciplinary force for executives to achieve organizational efficiency and thereby augment the value of the firm. He presumes high levels of debt and increased threat of bankruptcy force managers, who would otherwise use free cash flow to invest in low-return projects (such as expanding markets or research and development), to focus on organizational efficiency. Here organizational efficiency means efficiently returning capital to owners and efficiently paying off debt. Managers are forced to increase efficiency in order to ensure that they have satisfactorily high cash flow to repay debt and associated interest payments. Improvement in efficiency is thus expected to maximize the profits of the firm for shareholders (Jensen 1986).

Second, Jensen (1989b) assumes that the debt of highly leveraged firms tends to be held by a relatively concentrated group of banks and financial institutions. This is empirically the case (Eccles and Crane 1988). Presumably these debt holders, in contrast to equity owners, have a greater incentive to monitor and control managerial behavior. In fact, Jensen suggests that Wall Street (i.e., investment bankers) can more effectively monitor and discipline a firm's management than its CEO or board of directors. The assumptions are that investment bankers will monitor in the interest of organizational owners and that what is in the interest of organizational owners is in the interest of the organization. That is, owners are the organization.

Third, Jensen (1989b) argues that shifting funds from wasteful practices of firms to banks' and bondholders' control ensures, at the very least, that these resources are moved form low-return-producing firms to more productive ones.

Jensen's suppositions are curious against the backdrop of Nobel laureates Modigliani and Miller's 1958 classic article "The Costs of Capital, Corporation Finance, and the Theory of Investment," which put forward and empirically supported the idea that the value of a firm is independent of both the degree of its financial leveraging and the level of its dividends paid in a tax-free environment. This research implies that strategic activities to enhance value are independent of a firm's capital structure. In contrast to Jensen, these two economists present, as a rationale for increasing the use of debt financing, the idea that such manipulation is consequence free.

Merton Miller supports this position again in his 1992 research. He reiterates that the value of the firm is independent of its capital structure. However, he does note, as do others (Hall 1990; John 1991; Kaplan 1989; Smith 1989), that a firm's value may be enhanced by leverage because corporate income tax laws allow substantial gains from writing off interest costs and allowing accelerated depreciation of assets financed through debt.

Jensen theorized that managers are motivated by debt to change their strategies and this change in behavior causes firms to be more efficient (Jensen and Meckling, 1976). Modigliani and Miller suggest, on the basis of empirical research, that the debt to equity ratio of firms has no consequences for efficiency and is therefore irrelevant. The theories of Jensen and his students have been credited with fueling the massive use of debt financing for mergers in the 1980s (see Jensen 1989a, 1989b, for his strongest advocacy of this position). Empirical evidence indicates these theories are erroneous.

Although, the fraud-facilitated, debt-financed buyouts may not have had negative consequences for the value of firms to owners, they did affect the employees of targets and acquirers, the debt purchasers, and society. Further, management decisions to invest in debt as opposed to research and development and market expansion had long-range consequences for the firm. These effects were greater in some economic environments than others. Thus, the capital structure of the economy had much to do with the success or failure of target firms. Firms that took on heavy debts in the 1980s could not survive under their debt payments in the recession of the 1990s. In economic periods in which debt-financed mergers increased, investment bankers did have control, not over managerial decisions, but over merger and acquisition success through the control of debt capital.

I agree with Jensen that investment bankers were and are powerful, but not for the reasons he proposes. Furthermore, I find, contrary to Jensen's theory, that junk bond–financed LBOs caused many organizations to fail rather than to become more efficient or to create more value. Junk bond–financed LBOs have negative consequences: They constrain managers to use scarce capital to cover interest payments on debt, which becomes more costly as interest rates decline in economic recessions. Organizations must repay debt rather than focus on growth and effective business practices. Long-term development is forgone.

I argue that the level of debt that many targets took on was increased by fraud because fraud raised the costs of bonds, commissions, and other fees associated with the takeovers. According to Jensen, investment bankers were monitoring and controlling the opportunism of managers. Ironically, however, no one was monitoring and controlling the opportunism of investment bankers. A wide range of firms was affected by the fraud-infested LBOs of the 1980s (targets, acquirers, and institutional investors). Not all firms suffered the same outcomes or suffered to the same extent. Due to space limitations, only one or two examples of each type of consequence are presented below. Many others exist. Some have been discovered; others are yet to be.

CONSEQUENCES FOR TARGETS

Most empirical research during the 1980s found the target's shareholders to be winners in a takeover, if they sold their stock at the right time. Generally the price of stock is bid up. Subsequently, the price paid is as much as 80 to 100 percent above the original price of the stock. Organizational economists often argue that the stocks were originally underpriced and that the sale price represents the real value. There is no more evidence to support this assumption than to support the assumption that the stocks are overpriced after they have been bid up and the acquirer pays an inflated price for the corporation.

As we shall see, even though the target firm's shareholders may do well in a takeover, this does not mean that the corporation itself does well. The corporation may be split up and sold off. It may be drained of its assets, which may be used to pay off the transaction costs as well as other costs of the acquirer. In addition to employee firings, one of the first consequences for the target is the elimination of its research and development.

The conglomerate corporations or holding companies, created by these mergers and acquisitions, brought about two innovations: First, they accelerated a model of diversification wherein a small core staff of executives managed large "portfolios" of various size firms, each of whose products or services was unrelated to those of the others (unrelated industries). Second, it promoted the acquisition of existing companies through the purchase of available shares in the public market and the purchase of remaining shares at above-market prices. Through this process, a market in the buying and selling of corporations came into existence.

In the decade and a half since the publication of Williamson's *Markets*

and Hierarchies (1975), economic theories of firms have evolved from regarding corporations as more efficient than markets for exchanges where
information is unequal, relationships are enduring, actors are boundedly
rational and guilefully self-interested (opportunistic), to regarding corporations as commodities to be bought and sold on the market. The
acquisition of a corporation now creates a temporary relationship. On the
assumption that components may be more valuable than the integrated
firm, companies and their parts are purchased, reorganized, and then sold
again to make a profit.

This leaves us with the question, For whom is this market in corporations valuable? In order to justify the creation of a market in corporations,
economists have made several assumptions. They suggest that most U.S.
firms carry too little debt, that debt is good, and that the firms that are taken
over have built up too much equity and are not being managed well
(meaning that they are not making adequate use of productive assets).
Thus, economists recommend, these firms should be bought, their managers should be replaced by more effective managers, and capital should
be allocated to more effective firms.

This line of reasoning answers the question of who benefits with "the
stockholder." Profits are created for the stockholder at the expense of the
corporation and future productivity. This point of view ignores what
Williamson (1975) and generations of scholars before him found: that
efficiency in corporations rests on relatively stable social relationships. The
constant radical recalculation of self-interest undermines the effectiveness
of the networks that link issuers or sellers to intermediaries and buyers.

Granovetter (1985, p. 496) argues that personal ties are often of utmost
importance in managing market relationships, especially between sellers
and buyers. Enduring personal relationships are more likely to lead to
delivery of the commodity promised, because of the binding effects of
expected future exchanges. Continued interaction is more likely to lead to
trust, which in turn further binds the actors. When the actors in the
organization are highly mobile, due to the fluidity imposed by repeated
reorganizations, there is less pressure to deal honestly and in good faith.
The supplier or the issuer does not have to deal with the purchaser again,
because of movement to a new job, or movement of the firm to a new
owner. Employees who are being laid off have no incentive to act fairly.
There is no reason for a self-interested actor who is operating opportunistically in an environment of fluctuating relationships to deal honestly.
Fraud is much more likely. Fraud becomes the rational, self-interested
method of doing business.

There is reason to believe that the market in American corporations had
a high cost for American society, the economy, and the corporations that
were bought and sold. If efficiency was the goal, it may not have been

obtained. However, efficiency may not have been the highest value for these corporations. Research indicates that firms subjected to protracted takeover battles do very little work, and experience little growth during and immediately after the takeover period. At best, managers are working to preserve the corporate entity rather than making it more effective or efficient. At worst, they are thinking about preserving their own jobs and power, and how to bail out with the greatest number of organizational resources. And rightfully so, because, in the posttakeover period, most managers are replaced, workers are fired, corporations are divided, and parts are sold. The remainder is restructured, socially and financially, sometimes repeatedly. It is difficult to imagine that this process does not cause inefficiencies in the functioning of the organization.

Takeovers have negative consequences, not only for the management of the firm, but also for employees. Restructuring generally means that a large portion of the employees of the organization are fired or persuaded to take early retirement. These people generally do not find employment at the same salary level. Approximately one-third of displaced workers in the 1980s did not find employment at all. This undoubtedly contributed to the high unemployment of the early 1990s.

The research and development activities of the target corporation are generally greatly curtailed or abolished. For example, when RJR Nabisco was taken over by KKR, a plant that was being built near Raleigh, North Carolina, for RJ Reynolds was left uncompleted. The production expansion of these corporations and therefore the economic expansion of American industry are greatly altered by such actions.

All of this is justified in the name of efficiency. However, if efficiency rests on at least some stability of social relationships within and between organizations and these relationships are radically disrupted by the constant threat of takeovers, and if the goal of the merger and acquisition movement of the 1980s was to make inefficient firms more efficient, then the strategy of turning American corporations into commodities and operating them as predominantly financial entities was the wrong strategy. Findings demonstrate that junk bond–leveraged takeovers merely transfer wealth from bidder shareholders to target shareholders with a reduction of research and development and productivity of the target.

CONSEQUENCES FOR THE ACQUIRING FIRM

Dennis Mueller at, the University of Maryland has found that, "Whatever the stated or unstated goals of managers, the mergers they have consummated have on average . . . not resulted in economic efficiency." But more importantly he finds it "impossible to prove from the available empirical evidence that the performance of either the individual merging firms or the economy at large are significantly better as a result of all the mergers that have occurred in this country." He concludes that: "When one looks at the real effects of mergers on operating forfeitability, growth in sales or market shares, one finds no evidence in the United States that mergers have improved internal efficiency." Indeed, in his view, the empirical evidence suggests "there is at least as good a chance that slowing down merger activity would increase efficiency in the corporate sector on average" (1977, p. 344).

In a more recent analysis, Ellen Magenheim and Dennis Mueller (1988) reported on their study of long-term stock prices of seventy-eight acquiring firms that had announced mergers or tender offers between 1976 and 1981. They found that, although acquiring firms had experienced abnormal positive returns in the years prior to the acquisition, their postacquisition performance declined significantly, by as much as 42 percent. The authors infer that the bidder's loss may equal or exceed the target shareholder's gain (Magenheim and Mueller 1988).

But what about performance in the mid-1980s, during the time of the fraud discussed in Chapter 2? Using 1975–1983 data, which included fifty-six cases of hostile tender offers, Edward Herman and Louis Lowenstein (1988) compared the profitability of successful bidders before the tender offer with the profitability of the target (surviving firm) after the acquisition. They found that, in the 1970s buyouts, bidders were more successful than targets. Even though they paid high prices, their performance continued to improve in the years after the acquisition. In the early 1980s buyouts, the targets generally enjoyed outstanding results prior to takeovers. Before the buyout, the bidder continued to pay its shareholders enough to yield price-earning ratios that were almost two times the market average; however, after the bid, it suffered sharp declines in profitability. This may have been due to the inflated prices that were being paid for the target stock. If it was difficult for the acquiring firm to maintain its profit level in the early 1980s, it was even more difficult in the mid- and late 1980s. Not only did the prices paid for targets become more inflated, but the fraud committed by those who executed the transactions increased, increasing transaction costs.

Other researchers have supported this picture of takeovers as producing wealth transfers from bidder shareholders to target shareholders, rather than real social gains. In order to understand factors leading to disappointing performance, David Ravenscraft and F. M. Scherer (1987, 1988) undertook three separate studies using (1) Federal Trade Commission "line-of-business" data on twenty-seven years of mergers, over five thousand acquisitions, (2) sell-offs of businesses using line-of-business data; and (3) intensive reviews of fifteen specific mergers that resulted in sell-offs. They too found the target was significantly negatively affected by takeovers. The acquirer did not improve the operations of the target firm.

Franko (1989) showed that research and development investments are positively related to long-term corporate performance. Examining global competition through changes in market shares held by leading firms in fifteen major industries from 1960 to 1986, he found the amount of resources allocated to research and development to be the primary predictor of subsequent sales growth performance relative to competition. Thus, firms following aggressive takeover strategies may be trading research and development for expansion through acquisition, which may have pernicious long-range consequences both for firms and for American industry, particularly in sectors depending on high rates of innovation.

There is growing evidence that the significant investments necessary for acquisitions inhibit research and development by draining resources normally directed to these functions. Hitt, Hoskisson, Ireland, and Harrison (1991) found strong support for the negative effects of acquisitions on research and development investments and of diversifying acquisitions on the filing of new patents. Further, these researchers found that acquisitions have a stronger effect on research and development investment than diversification. In fact, managers may use acquisitions as a substitute for innovation. They may acquire technology and products that are new to their firm but not innovations in the marketplace. Thus over the long run, without research and development investments, corporate innovativeness may decline. A long-range consequence of junk bond–leveraged buyouts may be a significant reduction in the organizational performance of the acquirer.

Leveraged buyouts can force an acquiring firm to sell stock in its acquisitions. This reality contradicts Jensen's prediction that leveraging activities would lead to the privatization of firms as acquirers bought up the stock of targets. KKR provides an example. By mid-1988, KKR had taken over Safeway Stores Inc., Duracell Inc., Motel 6 Inc., and Beatrice Companies (which owned Avis, Playtex, and a number of other companies). In early 1990, KKR had completed its largest takeover, RJR Nabisco, for $26.4 billion. However, shortly after RJR Nabisco was acquired, Moody's downgraded RJR Nabisco debt because the company was overleveraged. Subsequently, the value of RJR Nabisco bonds dropped to fifty-six cents on the dollar, necessitating financial restructuring. As part of the RJR Nabisco takeover, Peter Ackerman of Drexel had sold something dubbed "reset bonds," a new form of junk bonds, which had an adjustable interest rate between 25 and 30 percent. This was an historically high debt service.

In 1991, KKR restructured RJR Nabisco's debt to a service rate between 17 and 17–3/8 percent. However, Nabisco was still in danger of insolvency. If Nabisco was bankrupted, its debt payment would become the responsibility of KKR. Therefore, KKR made a transformation from the largest issuer of debt to the largest seller of stock by taking public its best performing companies: Duracell, AutoZone Inc., Stop & Shop Companies, Owens-Illinois, and RJR Nabisco (Anders 1992: B1). KKR made this move to raise capital to pay off Nabisco's recently restructured debt. Nabisco's resources were depleted by the costs of the takeover and KKR was paying off the debt with shareholder-generated monies, a direct reversal of the leveraging process in which it had been a leader in the later 1980s.

Similar forces came to bear on other conglomerate acquirers.[10] Holding companies had relied on the constantly increasing returns on investment of the 1980s to make a profit and pay the record debt services their targets had to support to issue junk bonds. However, by 1989, after the collapse of the junk bond market, interest rates began to decline. Acquired companies were forced to try to pay high interest rates on their own debt with the ever-dwindling interest rates they could get from new investments. Thus, to avoid bankruptcy, many acquirers were forced to sell stock in their new acquisitions. It appears that Jensen's 1989 prophecy of the end of the public corporation was proven false by 1991. Leveraged buyouts had led to the brink of insolvency and beyond, not to privatization of all American corporations.

CONSEQUENCES FOR INVESTMENT BANKERS

The goal of the leveraged buyout activities of the 1980s was not to build a better industrial base or strengthen the economy. The goal was to create even greater numbers of financial transactions in order to generate ever higher profits and larger fees, enlarge commissions, increase interest rates, and enhance bonuses. The related fraud was an intended consequence for some but not for others. Efficiency of production was not the central activity of this economy. Rather, the central activity was financing the purchasing of firms. Such actions were very profitable for the investment bankers, attorneys, and boutique takeover firms. But what value was created?

These financial firms and their employees made a great deal of money in a short time. It would have taken industrial corporations decades to make this amount of money through expanding production. However, these resources did not go back into production. They went into the accounts of financiers, investment bankers, and lawyers.

Takeovers are fiercely advocated by those who are opposed to "managerialism," those who are against the separation of ownership (stockholders) and control (for an analysis of this separation, see Berle and Mean

1932). Those who advocated hostile takeovers (see Jensen 1988) recommended management be stripped of the power it had not wielded in the interest of owners. The opponents of managerialism constructed the myth of vested interests, alleging that managers had controlled corporations for their own vested interests, to the detriment of the interests of owners/stockholders. Those who analyze power and control in American corporations find the interests of managers and owners to be much more unified (Useem 1984, Chapter 2, presents a different analysis of this issue).

The hostile takeover was said to concentrate control in the hands of owners—shareholders. But takeovers did not have this effect. Stockholders are seldom organized appropriately to control a corporation either before or after it is acquired. The hostile takeover effects a transfer of ownership to the acquiring firm. Control of the acquired corporation is also beyond the means of the target firm's managers, who must defer to the acquirer.

These takeovers are initiated by holding companies managed by financiers, accountants, and lawyers who have no knowledge of, or interest in, the particular production process, markets, and strategic decisions necessary to direct the acquired industrial corporation productively. The ability of the acquirer to control the day-to-day functioning of the target firm is also quite limited. This transfer of target firm control to a small group of holding company executives who are unfamiliar with its business is a direct challenge to the traditional practice of multidivisional firms.

CONSEQUENCES FOR THE JUNK BOND DEPARTMENT EMPLOYEES

Most theories of fraud make the acts sound deviant or irrational. When fraud is a normal way of doing business and employees are committed to the department or firm for which they work, fraud is rational not only in terms of creating and increasing productivity for the firm, but also in terms of actions for the employee. It would be irrational or deviant for the actor not to be involved in fraud. Commitment includes compliance with demands for conformity, even involvement in acts that are not legal, and total loyalty to the organization. At Drexel, members of the junk bond department felt a sense of allegiance that transcended Drexel's plea of guilty to six counts of fraud (perpetrated for the most part by members of that department), Drexel's bankruptcy, and the indictment of Michael Milken and his colleagues from the bond floor.

What originated as self-interested acts of opportunism as traders acquired their first million was no longer rational after the Justice Department began its prosecutions. It is not rational to continue to act opportunistically when the risk of being caught is high and sanctions are severe.

However, social cohesion within the department was high: The extent of feelings of obligation to the collective good and to the friends worked with for many years was striking. Few employees left the High-Yield Bond Department. Their allegiance was apparent in their testimony throughout the trials and the presentencing hearings. Within the organization there was a moral code that supported this loyalty and protected the actions of others in the group.

Cooperation occurred as a result of impending crisis. Bond floor employees cooperated with the Justice Department, not only because they recognized the beneficial consequences of doing so, but also because they recognized the untoward consequences of refusing to do so. Noncooperation would have surely resulted in their prosecution. Most cooperated as part of plea-bargaining agreements.

There were many odd juxtapositions in the situation of bond floor employees. On the one hand, they had the opportunity to acquire unprecedented wealth; on the other, they faced job and income loss. On the one hand, they had the opportunity to gain high status and prestige among an elite group of financiers; on the other, they faced the negative status of an impending prison term. The tightly knit group of securities professionals to whom they were so committed offered little support in times of crisis. However, in the end, most important was a paradox: Many of the bond floor employees had great power and control, even control over the market, yet they could not control the legal structures by which they were being indicted and prosecuted.

Members of the external legal counsel for the High-Yield Bond Department received large fees and became involved in privately held partnerships. These partnerships, MacPherson and Otter Creek, shared in warrants that should have been retained by the acquired corporation or sold with high-risk bonds as equity incentives.

Fund managers who became involved in these privately held partnership acquired equity for themselves that should have gone into the funds they managed. They did not disclose these acquisitions to their employing organizations. Some of them traded on inside information from Drexel's salespeople and traders who were themselves putting target companies into play. Fund managers' benefits were small compared to those of Drexel's salespeople and traders, especially Michael Milken. As was demonstrated in Chapter 2, the bonuses and partnership returns that the employees of the High-Yield Bond Department received were beyond imagination.

CONSEQUENCES FOR SAVINGS AND LOANS

In this game of mergers and acquisitions, the holding companies, such as KKR, were the largest winners. They leveraged targets in order to acquire them, often leaving a company in such an unstable state that it had to be restructured shortly after being taken over, thereby taking on additional debt (for example, RJR Nabisco's second restructuring). In contrast, companies like KKR grew in wealth through the exorbitant acquisition, management, and other fees charged before, during, and after takeovers. While the acquired corporations clearly incurred tremendous losses, the investors who bought their junk bonds were even greater losers.

Savings and loans were experiencing a period of deregulation and, as a consequence, extensive diversification. As they purchased high-risk securities, that risk was shifted to the Federal Savings and Loan Insurance Corporation (FSLIC). By law, federally chartered savings and loans are allowed to hold 1 percent of their assets in unrated bonds. An additional 10 percent of their commercial lending authority may be used to purchase non–investment quality bonds. Thus 11 percent of total holding can be junk bonds. State-chartered savings and loans in some states can devote larger fractions of their assets to junk bonds. Approximately fifty savings and loans failed due to purchases of such bonds.

Columbia Savings and Loans

In 1985, ten savings and loans (out of 3,180 FSLIC-insured institutions) held $4.64 billion in junk bonds. This was 77 percent of all junk bonds held by savings and loans. According to Taggart (1988) five of these institutions were in California and three in Texas. Both of these states have the most liberal regulations for state-chartered savings and loans. Taggart goes on to point out that "a single institution, Columbia Saving and Loan Association of Beverly Hill, California, held approximately $1 billion in junk bonds"(p. 18) in 1985. By June 1986 this figure had increased to $2.3 billion, or 28 percent of its assets (Hilder 1986). Little did these two authors know in the mid-1980s that by the end of the decade, junk bonds would have led to the demise of Columbia Savings and Loan.

Stein (1989) reported in Barron's that when Columbia Savings and Loan purchased junk bonds, Drexel would sometimes combine the debt offering with an equity kicker. The equity was the real value in these deals. The depositor's money went to purchase the bonds while the equities went to insiders and the former CEO of Columbia Savings and Loan, Thomas Spiegel. This was accomplished by retaining the equity in privately held partnerships organized from the high-yield bond floor. The bondholders and depositors whose holdings were reduced to near nothing by the junk bond crash of 1989 were the victims not only of the violation of Columbia Savings and Loan of the federally established limit on investment in these bonds, but also of the loss of the equity that was the real value in many of these deals. As discussed in the previous chapter, the equities were worth anywhere from sixty to a hundred times the value at which they were purchased by these partnerships.

In August 1989, Columbia Savings and Loan had about 35 percent of its asset mix—nearly $5 billion—devoted to junk bonds. This was far more than any other savings and loan at that time. When the stock market crashed in 1987, Columbia's earning declined some 40 percent. Rising interest rates in 1988 further decreased its earnings (Heins 1988, pp. 153–56).

In *Business Week*, Kerwin (1990a) reported that Columbia Savings and Loan Association of Beverly Hills had been on the verge of seizure by the Office of Thrift Supervision. Most of Columbia's $591 million dollar loss in 1989 came when, in keeping with regulations, the bank was forced to write down the value of its high-yield bond portfolio to market levels. It tried to retain its solvency by selling off $2.9 billion in junk bonds acquired from Michael Milken. Columbia Savings and Loan had little hope of raising the $700 million still needed to bring it into line with federal standards of solvency.

The Office of Trust Supervision filed a civil lawsuit against Thomas Spiegel, seeking $5 million in penalties and the repayment of $19 million in corporate funds that Spiegel allegedly spent for personal benefit. On September 16, 1991, the Resolution Trust Corporation (RTC) sold part of Columbia Savings and Loan to investors and liquidated the remainder for $1.2 billion (Thomas 1991).

Lincoln Savings and Loan

Charles Keating, Jr., chairman of American Continental Corporation (ACC) based in Phoenix, Arizona, parent company of Lincoln Savings and Loan based in Los Angeles, was indicted on fraud charges by the SEC in early March 1991. Keating was head of the largest bank failure in the history of banking—the $2.6 billion failure of LSL. The government seized LSL in April 1989, shortly after ACC filed for protection from creditors under Chapter 11 of the U.S. Bankruptcy Code.

As will be explained more fully in Chapter 7, Charles Keating purchased large quantities of high-yield bonds from Drexel's High-Yield Bond Department. The government allegations against Keating included the allegation that he defrauded twenty-three thousand investors in LSL branches by selling them $250 million in unsecured bonds, which were represented as secure. Many of the investors were retired. Some of them claimed that LSL had falsely told them that the bonds were federally guaranteed and as safe as certificates of deposit. These bonds are reported, by Salwen (1991b, p. A5), to have been used to fund operations of ACC, the parent company of LSL. Thus LSL may have been operating as a broker-dealer for bonds of its parent and may have been in conflict of interest.

The SEC investigated the marketing efforts associated with LSL's sales of ACC bonds, and whether LSL or ACC personnel engaged in selling practices that violated federal securities laws. The SEC sought to determine whether there were misrepresentations of material facts concerning the risks associated with the debentures, whether sales personnel improperly pressured depositors to purchase ACC bonds, and whether ACC satisfied prospectus delivery requirements. Further, the SEC examined whether the self-underwritten selling of ACC bonds by LSL met the legal requirements for exemption from the broker-dealer registration requirement (Breeden 1989).

Lincoln chairman, Robin Symes, testified that examiners had concluded by 1987 that ACC was at financial risk, but Charles Keating never told the bond purchasers. Instead salespersons were briefed, often immediately after bad press, about the solvency of the corporations.

On December 5, 1991, in a Los Angeles Court, Charles Keating, Jr., was found guilty of seventeen of eighteen counts of fraud in connection with ACC's bond sales by branches of his Phoenix company, LSL. California law allows a top executive to be held criminally accountable only for those wrongful acts that he knew about, intended, and aided. He was found to be guilty of making false statements and omitting material information about the safety of $250 million of subordinated debentures purchased by some seventeen thousand investors. The sixty-eight-year-old Keating was sentenced in April 1992 to ten years in prison for these seventeen counts alone (Stevens 1991).

Keating was federally indicted on RICO charges and in July 1992 was found guilty of defrauding thousands of investors of LSL. Plaintiffs charged that they had lost $288.7 million as a result of the purchase of fraudulent securities, including junk bonds, which were represented as being federally insured bank certificates. The jury awarded these investors $3.3 billion in damages from Keating alone. Another $5 billion in awards were levied against three codefendants. Keating's lawyers have declared him bankrupt and therefore the claimants will recover nothing from him. However, the jury made other awards to be paid by Keating associates, who do have assets: $900 million in triple damages against Saudi Arabian Investment Corporation; $2.3 million in compensation and punitive damages against Continental Southern, Inc.; and $1.96 billion against Conley Wolfswinkel, a real estate developer. It is possible that the investors will recover some of their losses from these codefendants. The failure of LSL is reported to have cost the American taxpayers $2.6 billion (Freudenheim 1992).

CONSEQUENCES FOR PENSION FUNDS

In establishing a contribution plan, an employer agrees to set aside a fixed amount of money for each employee's retirement, based on salary. How much the employee receives varies among employing organizations based on how well the funds are invested. Neither annuities nor defined contribution plans carry a government guarantee, but some plans do carry Public Benefits Guarantee Corporation Insurance.

Barlett and Steele (1992) found that during the 1980s, nearly two thousand businesses used their pension funds (an estimated $21 billion) for purposes other than the benefit of employees and their spouses. This does not include the billions that businesses diverted to other uses after substituting inferior plans or unguaranteed securities (see below).

How did Drexel gain access to pension funds? In order to justify their actions, the investment banking firms and the raiders had to convince the securities industries as well as political leaders of two things. First, as Drexel testified before a congressional committee in 1985:

> Drexel believes that corporations that have undergone restructuring as a result of acquisition activity or strategic change have evolved into stronger companies better equipped to compete in today's domestic and international markets. An unsolicited acquisition can also result in the replacement of management with a new team better able to realize the full potential of a target company. . . . Merger and acquisition activity result in a shifting of assets to more productive uses.

The assets that were shifted included pension funds. The phrase *more productive uses* was not defined by Drexel. Their second assertion was that American corporations' pension plans were overfunded. This means that the securities that the pension funds held exceeded the amount that the pension plan would have to pay out in the future. These corporate owners further argued that the extra money belonged to the company, not the employees, regardless of whether potential raises were held in pensions in lieu of being paid out. The third assertion was that American corporations were underleveraged relative to competing Japanese and German firms, which put them at a decided disadvantage. The second assertion is explored in this section.

Simplicity Patterns Pension Funds

Victor Posner found Simplicity Patterns had $100 million in investments and pension funds in 1979. Within months, Posner acquired 7 percent of the its stock for $7.1 million. By the end of 1980 he owned 1.2 million shares, or approximately 9 percent of Simplicity. Drexel, Posner's investment banker, having a vested interest in the price of Simplicity stock, reported to its investors that Simplicity was vulnerable to a change in management and that such a change was a valid reason for speculating in shares for those who were interested in short-range profits. Simplicity was in play.

In 1981, NCC Energy, a London oil and gas company, bought 15 percent of Simplicity's stock. Their investment adviser was Drexel, and their account was handled by Peter Ackerman from the High-Yield Bond Department. NCC Energy bought out Posner for $22 million (approximately $10 million in profits to Posner). Later that year, Carl Icahn, another of Drexel's clients, appeared and purchased 1.6 million shares of Simplicity, or 11.2 percent of the outstanding stock, then 13 percent, and made a tender offer to buy another 18 percent, effectively blocking NCC Energy's takeover bid. One month later, Waltons Bond, Ltd., made Icahn's holding company a $26.5 million dollar offer for its 1.8 million shares (a profit of $15 million in one month for Icahn). Posner's and Icahn's combined profits of $25 million reduced Simplicity's assets. In January 1982, NCC Energy took over Simplicity and began to drain its assets further.

By April 30, 1982, the smaller shareholders filed a lawsuit against NCC Energy and Waltons Bond alleging self-dealing, on the basis that NCC Energy, and Waltons Bond and Cook International had "failed to disclose that they intended to use the cash assets of Simplicity to finance their acquisitions of Simplicity stock" and further that they "intended to use the cash assets of Simplicity to prevent Birmingham [NCC's Parent Company] from being forced into receivership." When NCC Energy could no longer meet its debt and Birmingham went into receivership in England, Waltons Bond returned $10 million to Simplicity. In May 1982, NCC Energy sold its 20 percent interest and Waltons Bond sold its 13 percent interest in Simplicity to Charles Hurwitz, a Houston financier and Milken client. Hurwitz immediately began investing Simplicity assets in takeovers of sugar refineries (Domino brand) and real estate (Twin Fair Holdings, Inc). Hurwitz changed the name of Simplicity to Maxxam Group Corporation.

Due to the drain of Simplicity assets, in 1984 the union of Simplicity's workers was required to make wage and benefit concessions. Simplicity management put pressure on the workers by announcing that, if they did not agree to reduce wages and benefits to 1982–1983 levels, it would move the plant from Niles, Indiana, to the southern part of the United States to garner tax, utility, and labor cost savings, not to mention the possibility that the union might be broken. The workers took the cuts and the city of Niles gave the corporation a 50 percent property tax break on plant improvements. The corporation had extracted the revenue it was using for mergers and acquisitions from the workers and city of Niles ($1.9 million in savings to Maxxam through Simplicity). Within a month after the employees and city of Niles made concessions, Hurwitz announced that Simplicity would be sold to Triton Group, Ltd. [as reported by Barlett and Steele (1992, pp. 146–61) from the South Bend Tribune and Niles Star 1984]. He was making no commitment to Nile or the workers in exchange for their sacrifices.

The reason that Simplicity was a good acquisition for Triton Group was because Simplicity had a good cash flow, about $12 million, which resulted in a 14 percent pretax profit in 1983. Triton had a tax loss carryforward of about $400 million to shelter future earnings. Triton was the new name for the former Chase Manhattan Mortgage and Realty Trust of Massachusetts, a real estate company that had gone into bankruptcy in 1979 and was acquired by Fuqua Inc. in 1983. Due to favorable tax laws, Triton was able to cancel out Simplicity's profits with its own past losses. Thus Triton Group did not pay federal income taxes on combined three-year profits of $100 million ($13 million for 1985, $11 million for 1986, and $76 million for 1987) because it owned Simplicity. The was legal under the tax codes.

In December 1986, Triton removed $7.8 million of the $8.5 million in Simplicity's employee pension fund, leaving less than one-eighth of its assets. This was less than 8 percent of the pension fund's original assets because it had been raided previously in 1983 for $2.9 million by Charles Hurwitz. Triton used the pension funds to purchase Simplicity Series B preferred stock until all the outstanding shares of Simplicity were re-deemed (SEC 1986). These outstanding shares of Series B stock were owned by Hurwitz's Maxxam Group, Inc., which had received the stock as part of a $65 million package of cash and notes when Triton bought Simplicity. Triton had used Simplicity employees' pension funds to pay for Triton's purchase of Simplicity.

By 1989, not only had Simplicity's $100 million in 1979 assets been depleted, but this highly profitable firm was $120 million in debt. By June 1989, the latest company to buy Simplicity, Borrows, defaulted on the loan, with Simplicity bearing the debt.

Iowa State Pension Funds

The Iowa State Pension Fund has invested over $375 million, approx-imately 10 percent of its total $4 billion fund, with KKR. Some of that money has been used for LBOs and ultimately ended up in the high-yield market. Other than the policies that a fund establishes to regulate its investors, unlike banks, there is no limit to the amount that pension funds can invest in high-risk securities. It is possible that because half of Iowa's commitment to KKR has been invested in RJR Nabisco and is not highly diversified, it is at greater risk. Its fate truly depends on that of RJR Nabisco.

Certainly, these pension funds would have profited more if privately held partnerships of Drexel employees had not taken the half-million in equity kickers from the warrants of KKR targets in the sale of their bonds. If these warrants had been sold with the high-yield and preferred secu-rities as was intended, they would be in the pension funds that ultimately purchased these securities. Likewise, had Drexel salespersons, traders, and executives taken less of the profits and instead passed them on, there would be less loss to pension funds. Finally, if the warrants that were sold with bonds had been purchased back by Drexel at a higher rate, the funds would be in better condition. Many of the state pension funds (Oregon, Washington, New York, Michigan, and Wisconsin) that bought into the high-yield bond market created by Drexel were suffering from fiscal short-falls by the end of the decade.

LINKING PENSION FUNDS TO INSURANCE COMPANIES

In still other cases, during takeovers, pension funds were drained from the employees' plans and inferior plans of less value were substituted. Cannon Mills Corporation was a company that until its 1982 takeover by David H. Murdock provided a pension fund insured by the Pension Benefits Guaranty Corporation. Before selling Cannon in 1986, Murdock terminated the pension plan with assets of nearly $103 million covering its twenty-three thousand employees. He removed $36.6 million from the fund to invest in two corporations and used the remaining $66.4 million to purchase annuities from an insurance company, Executive Life Insurance Company.

The annuities, unlike the pensions, were not insured by the Pension Benefits Guaranty Corporation. Not only were the annuities not guaranteed, the insurance company that purchased the former pension funds was not regulated as to the amount of its assets that could be held in high-yield securities. As noted below, Executive Life, the purchaser, was heavily invested in high-yield bonds from Drexel. It was seized by the California Insurance Commission in April 1991 and is at present the largest insurance company to have failed in the United States. It is currently returning somewhat better than seventy cents on the dollar to its investors.

In 1991, James B. Lockhart III, the Pension Benefits Guaranty Corporation's executive director, testifying before a House Budget Committee, warned that there was "at least $40 billion of unfunded liabilities in the defined benefit pension system." This is the amount that it can be required to pay out to employees of already failed corporations. This government agency is already operating at a deficit, and if it has to be bailed out, it most likely will be bailed out at the expense of the American taxpayer in much the same way the savings and loans were bailed out after the 1980s savings and loan fraud.

CONSEQUENCES FOR INSURANCE COMPANIES

The crash of the high-yield bond market in the late 1980s and the demise of Drexel and subsequent imprisonment of its junk bond king, Michael Milken, did not greatly affect insurance companies. In looking at the assets used by insurance companies to back pension annuities and guaranteed investment contracts, Marcia Parker and Hillary Durgin (1990) concluded that junk bonds are a small portion of all insurance companies' assets (less than 3 percent industrywide). The collapse of the junk bond market, which might trigger pension insurance or annuity defaults, would not significantly impair the overall health of the insurance industry. However, some select insurance companies held substantially larger portions of their assets in junk bonds.

Jonathan Laing reported later that year (1990, pp. 10–11) that a special committee at IDS Financial Services projected that twenty to thirty-four of the hundred largest U.S. life insurance companies could become insolvent should the United States suffer a severe economic decline. Based on the fact that investment income and annuity premiums account for nearly 60 percent of the total income of U.S. life insurance companies and that insurers own some $60 billion of the estimated $200 billion in junk bonds outstanding, the industry overseer had cause for concern.

Executive Life Insurance

First Executive Corporation based in Los Angeles had two subsidiaries: Executive Life Insurance Company of New York and Executive Life Insurance Company of California, which in turn underwrite not only insurance policies but also pension plans.

Joseph Harch was employed at Drexel from 1984 until February 1990. In 1985 he was first vice-president and in 1986 he was managing director in the corporate finance department in the New York Office. He testified that corporate finance was the department within the firm that called on potential corporate issuers, proposed capital-raising transactions to companies, and provided merger and acquisition advisory services and other corporate functions (*U.S. v. Michael Milken* 1990a, p. 396). His connection with the High-Yield Bond Department was that his department originated the transactions, the purpose of which were to raise capital, "perform all the necessary due diligence, to get the transaction into a position to be marketed" (p. 396). The role of the High-Yield Bond Department was that "once the transaction reached a certain point in time where there was a selling document in the form of either a private placement or a publicly registered prospectus, and the High-Yield Bond Department would be mainly in charge of marketing the securities that had been packaged" (p. 396). Joe Harch was the senior corporate finance person in charge of the Wickes corporate account (p. 397). He testified that one Executive Life company bought a nine-hundred-thousand-share block and later the other affiliate bought a four-hundred-thousand-share block of Wickes.

Drexel, Pacific Lumber Pension Fund, and Executive Life

In the name of Maxxam, corporate raider Charles Hurwitz acquired Pacific Lumber through a leveraged buyout. The buyout was underwritten by a Michael Milken $900 million junk bond transaction on Pacific Lumber. First Executive, one of Drexel's biggest junk bond customers, bought more than one-third of that debt. Hurwitz used Pacific Lumber's $97 million pension fund to pay for a $37.3 million Executive Life annuity to cover all employees and retirees as of March 1986. This allowed him to recapture more than $55 million, which was used to pay down some of the debt that was taken on in the takeover (Yoshihashi 1991, p. A4). The Pacific Lumber employees and retirees who were dependent on the company pension fund were now dependent on Executive Life.

In 1989, a group of active and retired Pacific Lumber employees sued Hurwitz and Maxxam, the corporation he had established in the takeover, over the use of the pension funds for the purpose of paying down the debt. The suit accused Maxxam of buying the annuity in exchange for Executive Life's purchase of the junk bonds. Maxxam denied any improprieties, maintaining that Executive Life was the lowest bidder on the annuity. They further maintained that the use of pension funds for other company purposes was common practice at the time of the buyouts (Yoshihashi 1991).

Executive Life's Failure

Executive Life's total assets increased from $6.3 billion to $14.4 billion in 1986 (Gilbert 1987, pp. 22–25). Ironically, that same year, New York State insurance regulators imposed a fine of $250,000 on Executive Life Insurance of New York, whose CEO was Fred Carr. Central to the fine was First Executive Life's reliance on high-yield junk bonds to generate future flow of income. As late as 1989, Kerwin (1989) reported that Milken, who then faced a ninety-eight-count federal indictment for securities crimes, raised capital for First Executive and held stock in two companies in which First Executive was a major shareholder. In other words, Carr continued to rely heavily on junk, which made up 51 percent of his $17-billion portfolio. By February 1990, Kerwin was reporting the same $8-billion portfolio in junk bonds held by Executive Life, but was also reporting that these junk holdings had led to an accelerated run on First Executives's annuities by policyholders (Kerwin 1990c, p. 41).

In April 1991, the California State Commissioner of Insurance, John Garamendi, announced that his agents had seized control of Executive Life. "Of Executive Life's $10.1 billion in assets, $6.4 billion is junk," reported *Time* magazine (Castro 1991). These junk bonds were acquired from Michael Milken's High-Yield Bond Department in the 1980s. Henri Bersoux, a spokesman for the American Council of Life Insurance, reported: "No other company of that size or larger has invested so much of its assets in high-yield bonds." First Executive reported a $465.9 million fourth-quarter loss and, during the week it was reported, two-hundred sixty clients a day cashed out their policies. The psychological and economic cost to those who cashed out their policies is unknown, as well as the losses of those who retained their policies.

Executive Life of California and Executive Life of New York had $3.1 billion in more than three hundred guaranteed investment contracts outstanding at the end of 1990, much of that retirement related. There were another 178,000 annuity holders for whom the company had established reserves of more than $2.5 billion. The pension holders were Revlon and state of Alaska employees (Yoshihashi 1991, p. A4). As a consequence of Executive Life's heavy investment in high-yield bonds and subsequent failure, these holders received only a portion of their health and retirement benefits.

Executive Life Insurance Company of California was placed in conservatorship on April 11, 1991, while Executive Life Insurance Company of New York was placed in rehabilitation during the week of April 15, 1991. Both California and New York regulators stated that they seized the insurers to prevent their collapse and to halt the outflow of cash. The insurers had $15 billion in state pension fund assets, making this the largest collapse in the history of the insurance industry (Loomis 1991, p. 61–62). As the companies failed with $12.2 billion in obligations, regulators were trying to decide how to protect customers. At present it seems that since no buyer can be found, the assets will have to be sold and the policyholders paid a fraction, perhaps less than 50 percent of the cash value of their policies.

On July 9, the *Wall Street Journal* (Karr 1991) reported that the collapse of Executive Life had far-reaching consequences. The employers of the pensioners were not covering these losses for their employees and retirees. As of mid-1992, most of those covered by these two companies have lost their benefits.

Sale of Executive Life

By November 1991 the only bidder left for Executive Life Insurance of California was the nation's insurance guaranty fund, the National Organization of Life and Health Insurance Guaranty Associations, but it did not pass all the financial and legal hurdles set by the state insurance department. The state commissioner of insurance, John Garamendi, said that the bid did not offer sufficient new capital to back Executive Life's extensive junk bond portfolio. There is still an outside hope that either the French bank, Credit Lyonnais, or a group led by the San Francisco investment banking firm of Hellman and Friedman can put together a deal to take over the company.

Under the bid by Credit Lyonnais, a French investment group, Altus would buy most of Executive Life's junk bonds for about $3 billion (about one-half of their reported value), thus providing liquidity for one of Executive Life's major assets. A second French allied investors group would acquire the rest of Executive Life and infuse it with an additional $300 billion. Under the Hellman and Friedman offer, Executive Life's junk bonds would be retained and $300 million in cash would be contributed as an initial capital base backed by an additional $700 million in guarantees (Rose 1991, p. 3A–5A).

Altus and Credit Lyonnais have an inside track because Leon Black, former head of mergers and acquisitions (M&A) for Drexel, is acting as an advisor for Altus, the prospective acquirer of Executive Life's vast $3 billion junk bond holdings, which were issued to Executive Life by Drexel. Thus Black not only profited from the issuance of this junk, but is now profiting from its greatly devalued resale.

CONSEQUENCES FOR MILKEN

For Drexel the consequences of mergers and acquisitions and the expansion of the junk bond market were positive until the market failure of 1987. Their involvement in fraud did not have such a benign outcome. As a consequence of the collaboration between Boesky and Milken, Boesky was able to give the government detailed descriptions of Milken and associates' insider trading and securities fraud. The High-Yield Bond Department and Michael Milken had underwritten $660 million for Boesky's new Ivan F. Boesky Limited Partnership, and as Boesky was closing out his old Ivan F. Boesky Corporation, he still owed Milken $5.3 million from multiple deals in which they had collaborated.

As already detailed in Chapter 1, Mooradian, Boesky's bookkeeper, testified that on the morning of March 21, 1986, the day of the closing, Boesky did something he had never done before: He told Mooradian to "issue a check for $5.3 million" and to record the check as a "trading commission." This was the beginning of the end of the fraud, the junk bond market, and the merger and acquisition craze of the 1980s.

After Drexel pleaded guilty to six counts of securities fraud and paid $650 million in fines in 1990, Milken pleaded guilty to six related counts of securities fraud in 1990 and paid $600 million, $500 million of which was for restitution to those injured by the fraud of Drexel. In February 1992, Milken agreed to pay an additional $300 million in penalties to those who had filed civil law suits. Thus Milken paid $900 million. Former officers of Drexel (Peter Ackerman, Milken's top associate, who received large bonuses; Leon Black, head of M&A; Lowell Milken, Michael's brother, who Milken protected from prosecution; Joshua Friedman; Marc Rappaport; and Warren Trepp, Milken's head trader) paid another $300 million, and insurers are expected to add another $100 million to bring the total to $1.3

billion. Financial presses, including the *Wall Street Journal* (Moses 1992) estimated that Milken would be left with $500 million in personal wealth. This is an exceedingly low estimate, perhaps one-third of what it should be, because the estimates of his worth before the fines were low.

Milken has been given three years to manage the disposal of his investment partnerships assets, which will contribute to the settlement. He will manage this process from his prison cell at the Pleasanton Federal Prison Camp in California.

Milken admitted no role in the savings and loan frauds and failures, which were largely the result of the frauds and the failure of the junk bond market. The payment will be made to individuals who suffered losses as a result of Milken's control of the fraud networks outlined in Chapter 2. It also settles litigation with the FDIC, which charged Milken with coercing savings and loan officers into buying overvalued and high-risk securities, which resulted in the failure of these banks. There is a direct link to the savings and loan failure in that settlement money will go into a restitution fund for investors who can prove they were defrauded by the defendant and into the U.S. Treasury to cover the savings and loan bailout costs. Another $1.3 million will go to Drexel's fixed creditors (Moses 1992).

The settlement was expected to aid in the bankruptcy reorganization of Drexel, which was scheduled for a confirmation hearing for March 5, 1992. Under the settlement, the Milken brothers were required to drop the more than $300 million in claims against Drexel.

CONSEQUENCES FOR NATIONAL EMPLOYMENT

What is the difference between the financial conception and the manufacturing and sales conceptions of control of a firm for employment? One of the major differences is in the way they calculate growth through acquisition. For example, in the infamous Deloitte analysis of KKR (conducted by Deloitte of Deloitte and Touche, a prestigious accounting firm), a discussion of the number of jobs that KKR was generating was included. A spokesperson for the Deloitte analysis reasoned that it makes no difference when counting Motel-6 employment, whether Motel-6 buys motels that hire sixty people as a result of a takeover or builds motels and hires sixty more people. In each case sixty people are employed.

Long and Ravenscraft (1984) examined this financial position and disagreed. They argued anyone who takes a larger look at the entire economy would see that a takeover results in the hiring of sixty fewer people than would be hired if a new motel were built. There is a difference between buying an existing company and building a new one through expansion into new markets and building from scratch. When you acquire an existing business, the people who were originally employed in the business may be retained or they may be laid off. If they are retained under the new ownership it is obvious that there is no creation of new jobs or growth in the economy. However, if they are fired and the new ownership employs others, it may appear that jobs were created, when all that has occurred is a substitution. Some new people have obtained work, but the employees of the former company are out of work. On the other hand, under the manufacturing definition of growth, if a new company is built, new jobs are created and employment that did not formally exist in the economy is created. Thus not only are the people who were working in the firm that is not taken over still working, but jobs have been created for the people in the new firm.

Acquisition does not necessarily mean economic growth even though many acquisition studies confuse the two. The fundamental difference is demonstrated in an example: Consider that in a leveraged buyout the acquirer lays off one thousand employees of the acquired firm and then buys a company with twelve hundred employees. The financial concept would be that the leveraged buyout had created two hundred new jobs. But prior to the buyout both firms together had employed twenty-two hundred employees, while after the buyout one thousand fewer people had jobs. The effect on the economy is the loss of one thousand jobs.

As I attempt to demonstrate throughout this book, the money that was to be paid to the employees who were left jobless often ended up in the pockets of investment bankers, fund managers, lawyers, and congressmen. In 1992 the American public's confidence in its social institutions including banks, insurance companies and government was at an all-time low. The scandals were in the venue of the daily news and the outcomes of the trials and pleas of Milken, Boesky, Levine, and Keating, were thoroughly reported by the press as though there were some way to improve the faltering economy and as though their punishment in some way repaired a greater moral order.

CONSEQUENCES FOR THE NATIONAL ECONOMY

We have been looking at mergers, leveraged buyouts, and securities fraud from the perspective of organizations involved in these activities. A series of larger questions focuses on the country and its economy: Do these activities contribute to productivity? Do they promote new products, new methods of production, and technological advance? Do they contribute to the reindustrialization of the United States? Are they laying a foundation for a better corporate America?

What if mergers and acquisitions as well as securities fraud undermine efficiency defined as productivity, and obstruct or divert money that would otherwise be used for research and development? If this is the case, they would also subvert United States competitiveness internationally. We have just begun to ask and, more recently, to answer these questions, but we have some evidence that the picture is not bright. The results regarding the value of acquisitions for the shareholders of acquiring firms have been decidedly mixed (Amihud, Dodd, and Weinstein 1986; Fowler and Schmidt 1988; Lubatkin 1987; Lubatkin and O'Neil 1987). Ravenscraft and Scherer (1987) conservatively estimated that acquirers had divested one-third of all acquisitions made in the 1960s and 1970s by the early 1980s. Porter (1987) also reported that acquisitions often did not yield anticipated outcomes and eventually led to divestitures. Both Porter and Ravenscraft and Scherer have suggested that the divestitures are largely the result of inadequate performance. Even Jensen (1988) found that the returns to acquiring firms from acquisitions vary closely around zero.

CONCLUSIONS

There is substantial and growing evidence that junk bond–funded leveraged buyouts have no real value for the acquirer, the target, research and development of the firms involved, long-term American competition, managers of targets, or employees. In fact, the actors who benefit most are the shareholders of the target and the numerous transaction professionals (deal makers): investment bankers, lawyers, financial consultants. Thus the result has been a transfer of wealth from employees and managers, pension funds, and widely dispersed shareholders to private owners and their transaction operatives.

It is clear that unregulated markets based on self-interest are inefficient for production. At the same time it is not at all clear that regulation and monitoring are inefficient. Indeed, it is often argued by Block (1990, pp. 69–72) that regulation enhances efficiency because formal controls equalize information, and guard against fraud. Certainly the inefficiency of fraud in the cases of LSL and First Executive have increased costs not only for those who lost their jobs because of takeovers or insolvency, but for those directly involved in the purchase of securities, and for those indirectly involved, who suffer the loss of their pensions or of their savings.

NOTES

10.   An acquirer buys stock in a target firm sufficient either to control it or, in some instances, to take it private (by buying all the stock). To pay for this purchase, the acquirer issues bonds on the target. Any junk bonds that are issued carry extraordinarily high rates of interest. The acquired firm now has to pay back the cost of its own acquisition plus tremendous amounts of interest on the debt. The acquired firm often buys junk bonds from other targets to amass the money necessary to pay its own debt principal and interest. If the cost of the debt is rising, an acquired firm can buy bonds that are paying more interest than it must pay on its debt and, in this way can remain solvent. If the cost of debt is falling, an acquired firm cannot earn enough on investments to repay its own debt and risks insolvency if its cash flow is too low.

Part II

Toward Understanding Fraud

Chapter 4

Structural Contradictions and the Failure
of Corporate Control

The changes which took place in Drexel in the 1970s and 1980s accelerated the transformation from sales and marketing control to financial control of American corporations. While it was facilitating the transformation of corporate forms from multidivisional firms to holding companies, however, Drexel itself was making a transition from a departmental to a multidivisional form. The High-Yield Bond Department was the first department to evolve into a divisional form: The High-Yield Bond Department in Los Angeles was a product line as was the Investment Grade Bond Department in New York. This particular High-Yield Bond Department was a major actor in the transformation of corporations from multidivisional firms to holding companies, but was itself a division of a privately held corporation that had only recently gone public.

According to Chandler, the most efficient response to increased complexity and expanded administration is the multidivisional form of firms, where decision-making authority is allocated to the various functional operating units [1962, pp. 37, 383; 1977, pp. 286, 339; Williamson (1975, 1983) makes a similar argument.] Chandler suggests holding companies are inefficient because they are legal entities with small centralized administrative offices that act as portfolio managers in independent operating subunits, where lines of authority and communication are often unclear and confused (1962, p. 40).

In multidivisional firms, middle management coordinates product flow, while top management defines and allocates resources for future activities (Chandler 1977, p. 143; 1990b, p. 594). The modern managerial firm is efficient because it has internalized market functions and decentralized decision-making (pp. 175–80, 411–14; Williamson 1975). Recently, Chandler (1990a, 1990b) has articulated a more specific logic of development. The logic of the "managerial enterprise" is the dynamic logic of growth and competition that drives modern industrial capitalism (1990a, p. 435). According to Chandler, strategies that pursue economies of scale and scope create oligopolistic industries, which remain efficient because the competition for market and profits sharpens the skills of middle management and tests and enlarges top management's skills and authority over middle management (1990b, p. 36).

This argument assumes that middle managers are operating in the interest not only of their division, but of the organization. It assumes that the managers of divisions implement rational and efficient solutions to maximize the profits of the division and at the same time those of the organization. The model also assumes a rational, consistent relationship between policy made at the corporate level and practices implemented at the divisional level, and between the formalization of rules at the top level and control decisions made at lower levels. It assumes that managers at lower levels not only have less authority than upper-level managers, but have less resource-based power and therefore are bound by the decisions made at the corporate level. Further, it assumes that upper-level managers understand the direction of the organization and correctly perceive and control both the goals and policy decisions being made as well as the organization's external environment and are capable of acting to pursue a rational course of action (Prechel 1991). Finally, it assumes that rewards are allocated consistently, based on management's ability to perform its functions.

Assuming such a rational model is a point of departure for understanding what was occurring in Drexel. Organizational misconduct can be understood as a consequence of rational social action that emerges as a result of organizational contradictions, both within the organization and between the organization and its environment. How the structures of the organization, the market, and government limit actions within the organization and affect the transformation of the organization is central to our understanding of how organizational misconduct takes place.

Organizations change as a consequence of the outcomes of contradictions and crisis (Benson 1977b, p. 4; Heydebrand 1977). *Contradictions* entail an opposition or incompatibility between two components of the organization that are necessary for its existence (Lyng and Kurtz 1985). *Crises* do not occur unless these contradictory structural imbalances disallow the organizational adaptation required to attain goals (Heydebrand 1977, p. 89). Contradictions always exist, but crises occur only at critical points, when an organization must undergo reorientation and restructuring in order to survive. Faced with a crisis of internal or organizational/ environmental contradiction, if the organization does not make a significant transformation, it may not survive (Zammuto and Cameron 1985).

Drexel's internal operation revolved around sophisticated, complex, and often secret compensation packages, and the retention of authority, while decisions were decentralized to the departmental level. In the case of the High-Yield Bond Department, Drexel returned 33 percent of the profits it generated for the firm as an operating budget for the department. Another 35 percent of the profit it generated was returned to the head of the department, Milken, in the form of a bonus pool to be distributed to the personnel of the department.

Drexel employee compensation operated in consonance with the premises of agency theory (Jensen 1989b), which suggests that subunits and employees be rewarded based on their contribution to the profits of the organization. However, upper-level management was unaware that the rational assumption that subunit profit maximization would lead to organizational efficiency was contradictory. Drexel evaluated all subunits on their profits in much the same way a holding company evaluates its separate firms. Thus it was to the High-Yield Bond Department's advantage to do as many deals with as high a return as possible (generally also meaning a high risk) not only because of the fees, but because it meant the bonus pool that Drexel returned to the department would be larger. Yet many of the larger deals were higher risk, which put the corporation at risk for the benefit of some of its departments.

In order to execute these high-risk deals, the subunit had to gain autonomy, separate itself from the control of the corporate decision-makers and monitoring system, establish its own functions, and increase its profits in whatever manner was most efficient, including those which disregarded legal boundaries.

Drexel was fueling the mergers and acquisitions of some of the largest American corporations throughout the mid-1980s, which resulted in their being disassembled and sold as commodities. At the same time, control within Drexel was shifting from the traditional bankers to the trading and M&A departments. This shift not only expanded Drexel's growth but increased the contradictions between the East Coast office of Drexel and its High-Yield Bond Department. Milken, through the innovative use of junk bonds to finance LBOs, created his own department, separated that department from the corporation, then used that department to create an extensive network of buyers and sellers, and ultimately used that network as a power base to control the corporation. The same networks that were used to defraud were Milken's major sources of power against internal constraints.

It may appear that the transition of power within Drexel was moving from finance to sales, but this was not the case. Through his networks, Milken not only traded, but underwrote and financed the largest takeovers in the history of American capitalism. For a number of years the High-Yield Bond Department controlled the strategic contingency of profits for

Drexel. This allowed Milken to restructure the department to provide it and his work with maximum autonomy. This newly developed structure then provided a context in which he expanded the functions he performed for his division, which enabled him to expand and control both his issuers and buyers. Control over these networks enabled him in turn to control Drexel's management.

A second set of contradictions existed between the hierarchy of authority and the decentralization of decision-making to the middle-management level of department heads. This contradiction became increasingly apparent as the power of the High-Yield Bond Department increased due to the proportion of the corporate profits it generated and its disarticulation from the home office in New York. This process, which will be discussed below, consisted of departmentalization, spatial separation, and the duplication of corporate functions in its new location on the West Coast.

The New York office attempted to regain control of the West Coast High-Yield Bond Department by instituting an internal monitoring system called the Underwriters Advisory Committee. This committee was to use a process similar to those Hage (1974) describes for hospitals that monitor doctors who perform too many unnecessary operations: A peer review panel passed judgment on each operation (in the case of Drexel, on each deal). However, Drexel's committee was made up of bankers in the home office who were separated from direct oversight of the bond floor. Thus control through direct communication and feedback from a peer committee was not a successful method of control. The development of Drexel and its struggle to maintain control of the High-Yield Bond Department is the subject of this chapter.

HISTORY OF DREXEL BURNHAM LAMBERT, INC.

Drexel was founded under the name F. M. Drexel, Exchange Broker, in 1837 in Philadelphia, by an established portrait painter named Francis Martin Drexel (Hopkinson 1952, p. 13). In 1871 the firm of Drexel, Morgan and Company was opened in New York to engage in both commercial banking and investment banking. For the first few years the Drexels dominated both the New York City and the Philadelphia firms, but in 1876, after the retirement of Joseph W. Drexel, his son Anthony J. Drexel headed the parent firm, while Morgan assumed leadership in New York (Carosso 1970, p. 21). From that time on, although they were a partnership, they operated under two different names and in two different cities: J. P. Morgan and Company in New York and Drexel and Company in Philadelphia. While the partnership was the wealthiest and most prestigious in the nation, Drexel enjoyed less prestige than the company associated with the financial acumen of the legendary J. P. Morgan.

But both banks had a great deal of power. Both were associated with powerful individuals, and at the turn of the century, a small number of powerful individuals (mostly financiers) controlled the U.S. economy. Financial institutions were more powerful than nonfinancial institutions, since nonfinancial institutions were dependent on them for large sums of capital. For example, John D. Rockefeller was dependent on James Stillman, and Edward H. Harriman was dependent on Jacob Schiff for capital.

From the turn of the century, corporations were linked through their boards of directors. Perhaps the most interesting of the studies of interlocking directorates, for our purposes, is Mizruchi's 1982 study, which, unlike other studies (Useem 1984; Burt 1975), included financial institutions. Mizruchi found that the nature of power in the business world in the early 1900s was reflected in interlocks. Among 166 firms in 1904, 154 were completely connected. Among the 25 most central firms in the network, 14 (56 percent) were financial institutions, even though only 25 percent of all the firms in the network were financial institutions. This varied from 68 percent in 1912, to 32 percent in 1919, and to 48 percent in 1935.

Mizruchi found that later in the century the importance of individuals declined while the importance of the corporations that they had founded remained stable. The importance of financial institutions also declined. Had his analysis extended into the 1980s he probably would have found the importance of financial institutions expanded, as investment banks and raiders took center stage, transforming mergers and acquisitions into takeovers and LBOs.

The role of investment bankers was also transformed. Instead of supplying the capital on which corporations had become dependent, the investment bankers of the 1980s were the originators of the takeover, defining the target, finding the appropriate acquirer, underwriting and counseling the raider, using knowledge obtained in previous transactions in which the target was involved. Thus investment bankers not only regained their power in the 1980s, they surpassed their earlier status, as many of them (such as KKR) became merchant bankers with large portfolios of corporations.

In the 1930s, efforts were made to curtail the power of bankers. With the passing of the Glass-Steagall Act in 1934, the separation of investment banking activities from commercial banking was mandated, and J. P. Morgan and Company and Drexel and Company were required to dissolve their partnership. The Morgan firm opted for commercial banking and is now known as Morgan Guaranty Trust. Drexel took on the investment banking function. In 1966, Drexel merged with Harriman Ripley and

Company, a New York–based firm with blue-chip investment banking clients. In 1970, Drexel Harriman Ripley obtained a badly needed infusion of capital—$6 million from Firestone Tire and Rubber Company—and became Drexel Firestone.

In the early seventies, Wall Street was not healthy. Many firms were dying, the recession of those years crippled the securities market, and spiraling inflation prohibited many small firms from taking risks that would surely have led to their demise. Like other investment banking firms, Drexel Firestone was not in an economically viable position in the early 1970s. It had close to $1 billion under management, some investment banking clients, and about $10 million in Firestone money. It was in need of capital. Its major assets were a small number of prestigious clients. In 1973 Drexel merged with Burnham and Company, a submajor investment banking firm founded by I. W. "Tubby" Burnham in 1935. In the early 1970s, Burnham and Company was worth only about $40 million. It had a good research department, and its international equity arbitrage and retail businesses were profitable. The firm had always been profitable, largely because Burnham was not a risk taker and watched his capital carefully, but Burnham's clientele was not blue chip.

Burnham desperately wanted to move into the majors. Above the majors were the "special bracket" firms. At that time this elite category of firms consisted of Dillion, Rad and Company; the First Boston Corporation; Kuhn, Loeb and Company; Merrill, Lynch, Pierce, Fenner and Smith; Morgan Stanley and Company; and Salomon Brothers. After that came the "major bracket" firms, which included Drexel. Burnham and Company was in neither of these two brackets, and wanted to move up.

The firms merged in 1971, but employees of the two firms avoided each other. The firms were incompatible not only in their market orientation, but also in the backgrounds of their employees. Burnham and Company consisted mostly of Jewish traders, who survived on their marketing skills. Drexel employees were WASP, old guard, hard sell. In 1974, when Fred Joseph was hired as head of finance on the Drexel Firestone side of the company, he was one of three Jewish employees, along with Tubby Burnham and Michael Milken, the head of trading and sales for the newly formed convertible and non–investment grade bonds.

Milken worked in the more prestigious Drexel side of Drexel Burnham, in one corner of the investment grade bond department. High-yield bonds had not yet reached departmental status. It is ironic that the department that would propel Drexel to its highest status was not its Blue-Chip Equities or its Investment Grade Bond Departments, but the low-grade, High-Yield Bond Department, which according to Podolny (1991) had no prestige in the investment banking community.

SOCIALIZATION OF THE JUNK BOND KING

Michael Milken, similar to Henry Kravis and George Roberts of KKR came from a home in which business was the center of family life. Bernard Milken, Michael's father, was an accountant; from the time he was ten years of age, Michael watched his father prepare tax returns. The bottom line was the method used to measure success from the very beginning of Milken's socialization. It was quite natural for him to major in business administration at the University of California at Berkeley, graduating in 1968. While many of his peers at Berkeley were involved in broader social issues of the 1960s, which led them to invest their time in protests and critical analysis of the system, Milken was investing in markets for his fraternity brothers.

While at Berkeley, Michael Milken discovered the work of W. Braddock Hickman (1958). Hickman, through studying data on corporate bond performance from 1900 to 1943, found that a low-grade (non–investment quality) bond portfolio, if very large, well diversified, and held over a long period of time, was higher yielding than a high-grade portfolio. Hickman's findings were updated by T. R. Atkinson (1967) in a study covering 1944–1965. This work was later to become Milken's bible. After obtaining his B.A. in business administration, Milken moved to the Wharton School of Finance, where he obtained his M.B.A. in 1970. During the summer of 1969, Milken began working at what was then Drexel Harriman Ripley in Philadelphia. He worked for Drexel part-time throughout his two years at Wharton and after graduation was hired full time at Drexel to work in the Wall Street office as head of research for fixed-income securities. Shortly after, he moved to sales and trading.

Milken's background was not on a par with the upper-class, ivy league–educated elite investment bankers of the special-bracket and major-league firms. His chances of employment in one of the premier firms on Wall Street were therefore not high. Drexel was not a major player among investment bankers at that time and the match between Drexel and Milken was thus a good one.

During the 1970s recession, Milken used Hickman's (1958) advice that corporate bonds were typically undervalued in the market at or near the date of default. As a result, investors selling at that time suffered large losses, while those purchasing obtained correspondingly large gains. Milken bought the bonds of failing firms across a wide range of industries. As defaults became imminent and bondholders panicked, Milken was able to purchase securities at a fraction of their original price. The key question was which defaulting firms would survive and which ones would not. Milken had an exceptional ability to determine the survivors. He made money for himself, his traders, the firm, and his investors by being able to answer this question correctly. This ability would catapult him to the center of financial markets in the mid-1980s.

In 1973, Burnham was told that Milken wanted to leave Drexel Burnham because Milken felt he had low operating capital. Milken's value to the firm was already evident. Burnham gave Milken a position of $2 million, which at that time was a large amount of trading capital. That year Milken made $2 million in profits (a 100 percent return) for Drexel Burnham. The next year Burnham doubled Milken's capital. Milken was supposed to report to Fred Joseph, then Head of Finance. However, Burnham, who was above Joseph in the hierarchy, determined Milken's operating capital and compensation. This was an irregularity in the corporate hierarchy.

From 1977, when Drexel offered the first non–investment grade issue, until 1989 when the government required that Drexel fire him, Milken headed the High-Yield Bond Department. Drexel was the undisputed leader in this market. It had ties to a range of issuers and investors in the junk market that was simply unmatched by other major participants. These networks allowed Drexel to place high-yield securities in volumes that were beyond the capabilities of its competitors. Podolny writes:

> So dominant was Drexel's position in the high-yield market throughout much of the 1980s that one banker commented that it was "probably the closest thing that the financial markets had ever seen to a pure monopoly." As the end of the decade neared, the higher status banks began to chip away at Drexel's privileged position. (1991, pp. 56–57)

Those individuals who bridge the boundaries between the investment banking firm and its issuers, buyers, and competitors gain information, access to networks, and resources that give them power. Those who control external dependencies can use the power garnered to gain control over internal strategic contingencies (Perrow 1970; Hickson, Hinings, Lee, Schneck, and Pennings 1971; Salancik and Pfeffer 1974).

Milken controlled the strategic contingencies of access to and knowledge of a financial mechanism through which takeovers of the largest American corporations could be achieved. From his earliest days in the investment quality bond department in New York, he had studied small and sometimes failing firms. He knew their assets and their potential. By 1983 he had revolutionized Drexel and to some extent the investment banking industry by redirecting his department to finance assaults on some of the nation's largest and most well established firms, including Gulf Oil, Phillips Petroleum, Revlon, Disney, and Union Carbide. Milken created the junk bond market by putting together deals that needed capital, which he supplied in the form of high risk bonds.

As a consequence, by 1983 Drexel had made a transition from relative obscurity to a place among the top ten U.S. investment banking firms (based on assets). By 1984 it was the nation's second largest financial underwriter of corporate stocks and bonds. In 1987 and 1988 Drexel was sixth among the top ten M&A departments of investment banking firms, behind Goldman, Sachs; First Boston; Shearson and Lehman; Morgan Stanley; and Merrill Lynch. Drexel completed 126 deals in 1987, which totaled $22.7 billion, and 158 deals in 1988, which totaled $39.0 billion (*Wall Street Journal* 1989).

The industry—and sometimes the New York Office of Drexel—were stunned by the rise of the High-Yield Bond Department and by its aggressive tactics. The High-Yield Bond Department was not part of the more sedate East Coast establishment. It provided a wide range of M&A services for its clients, duplicating and surpassing the M&A functions of the East Coast office. It advised the acquiring firm, devised tactics designed to stampede a sale (such as "two-tiered tender offers") or to deter mergers and takeovers (such as the "poison pill" or "scorched earth"). It provided data on firms that were potential targets and potential takers, and helped its clients plan for all possible alternatives.

Other investment banking firms began to restructure their M&A departments to emulate and compete with Drexel and indeed to share in the growing number of M&A and the high-yield bond market. [For an extensive discussion of how a corporation becomes a role model, see DiMaggio and Powell (1983) and Meyer and Rowan (1977).] Some were unable to make the transition (see Lewis 1989). While the investment banking industry tried to define how to become involved in such a market, Milken's traders became multi-millionaires, he made billions, and the High-Yield Bond Department underwrote takeovers of some of the largest corporations in the United States, including Beatrice Foods and RJR Nabisco.

STRUCTURAL CONTRADICTIONS AND THE FAILURE OF CORPORATE CONTROL

At the beginning of the 1980s Drexel was faced with capital accumulation problems. Industrial growth in the United States was slowing and the economy's industrial growth was plagued with recession. Financial markets were weak as industries tried to compete with Japan and Germany. Organizational research was dominated by two seemingly contradictory responses to these problems. The first consisted of decentralization of decision-making, cooperative information sharing, and communication within organizations. The second, inspired by Williamson's and Jensen's variation on neoclassical economic theories, focused on hierarchical control. The decentralized response concentrated on cooperative teamwork; high levels of communication; decentralization of decision-making to departments where decisions are put into operation; diminished boundaries between department level managers and the managed; and departmental, middle-level manager, and employee autonomy (e.g., Huber and McDaniel 1986; Kanter 1989a, 1989b; Powell 1990b). The second approach concentrated on control through hierarchy and reward structures. Managers are distanced from the decision-making of departments through computerized accounting systems and a conception of departments as independent profit centers. Control is maintained by an elaborate system of extrasalary compensation. Here middle-level management work (especially decision-making discretion) is degraded or eliminated, but the objective realities of middle managers are obscured by the ideology of decentralization (e.g., Carter 1985; Smith 1990).

At Drexel, Milken—who was a department head, a middle-level manager—gained control of the reward system for his High-Yield Bond Department. Upper-level management could not use it to control him or the members of his department. He allocated the bonuses for his department from the 35 percent of profits returned to him, and he had total control over these funds. Drexel could not bring Milken to heel because Milken controlled a sizable portion of corporate profits and brought business to other departments (such as M&A). If Drexel had tried to direct him, Milken could have taken his knowledge of the market and techniques to another firm. His networks of buyers and issuers would have followed him.

Both contradictory mechanisms were occurring at Drexel. In order to understand this, it is necessary to differentiate between the location of decision-making related to the work of the organization and authority as predictors of organizational outcomes. Rational legal authority to control the organization may rest at the top of the organization, while discretionary decision-making may be relegated to middle- and lower-level managers in the organization. At Drexel, decision-making related to making a profit became more rational/calculative, which placed control in the centralized accounting and corporate finance departments that Fred Joseph controlled as CEO, but this same profit motive caused a shift of accountability and discretionary decision-making related to capital accumulation to the departmental levels, where the same rational/calculative mechanism pits one department against another and all of them against the organization.

The pressure for capital accumulation is not specific to investment banking firms, nor is it a recent occurrence (see Marx [1867] 1976). Capital accumulation is the mobilization, transformation, and exploitation of inputs to increase the capital of the firm. It is a broad process that encompasses not only what the junk bond department did but also what investment banking firms do for themselves. Some researchers have demonstrated how accumulation constraints have historically resulted in a change in formal control in corporations [e.g., economic constraints (Edwards, 1979; Gordon, Edwards and Reich 1982), legal constraints (Fligstein 1990a)]. Others argue that rational calculation affects organizational forms (e.g., Carter 1985; Markus and Pfeffer 1983). In the case of Drexel, both constraints for capital accumulation and rational calculation led to a restructuring of Drexel, which focused on the High-Yield Bond Department.

We know little about how formal control affects organizational hierarchies or the distribution of decision-making and authority. Advocates of decentralizing decision-making to the departmental level have not explained how the decentralization of decision-making is possible when several thousand professionals work in the organization. Thus the questions to be answered in this chapter are, Does the firm simultaneously maintain control over the highly interdependent process while decentralizing decision-making? If so how is this accomplished? If not why not? The question is not whether decentralization and centralization are occurring, but rather what is being decentralized and what is being centralized.

CONTRADICTIONS OF CORPORATE CONTROL AND DEPARTMENTAL AUTONOMY

In order for Drexel to control the functioning of its High-Yield Bond Department it had to be able to monitor and administer the work of its employees and the transactions taking place within the department. From the time Milken established his own semiautonomous unit in the corner of the High Quality Bond Department in New York until Drexel closed its doors in 1990, this monitoring became increasingly more difficult.

Hierarchy of Authority

The internal networks of investment banks are flat, broad, and flexible, in contrast to product-producing organizations, which have more hierarchical structures. The links are likely to be made horizontally between departments rather than up and down the hierarchy. According to Eccles and Crane (1988), the structure is flat because the speed with which the deals have to be transacted makes the function of coordination more important than control. Information is the major input and communication the most important process of the organization. Managers are more likely to be facilitators than evaluators. Departmental lines are not sacred, as managers move back and forth across departmental lines to obtain deals, make deals, and close deals.[11] Any attempt to restrict information would inhibit the rapid cooperation necessary to the making of deals. A major question answered in this section is, What happens if control is completely lost to efficiency of communications and transactions?

Even though Eccles and Crane (1988) minimize the role of the hierarchy of authority in investment banking firms, the hierarchy at Drexel was very much in existence. But while the hierarchy of authority was well established in the New York office, it did not control the High-Yield Bond Department. Power and influence overwhelmed the formal authority structure; status, prestige, and rewards did not follow the line chart of the organization. Informally and often formally throughout the mid-1980s, the corporate office in New York functioned to carry out the explicit and sometimes implicit wishes of the High-Yield Bond Department. For example, during testimony on the Wickes acquisition, it became clear that buying on the high-yield and convertible bond floor was done at the bequest of Milken, who directed the actions of those in the New York office. As detailed in Chapter 2, on April 23, 1986, the very day of the conversion of Wickes preferred, Michael Davidoff, head trader for Boesky, purchased 1,900,000 shares of Wickes for Boesky's Seemala Corporation, at the verbal request of Cary Maultasch, block equities trader in the New York office of Drexel. Maultasch testified that he had purchased the stock at the request of Peter Richard Gardiner, who sat on the convertible equities side of the high-yield bond floor. According to Gardiner's testimony, as late as April 23, Michael Milken could tell Gardiner to have Wickes close at a certain price and knew that he would communicate this to Maultasch, who would communicate it to Davidoff, who would purchase it in one of Boesky's accounts (*U.S. v. Michael Milken* 1990a, p. 250).

None of these actors were in the High-Yield Bond Department. Gardiner's department head was technically Gary Winnick, head of the convertible bond department, and later Alan Rosenthal, who held the same position. Even after Maultasch moved back to the New York office in 1985, Rosenthal set his salary. But Maultasch considered Michael Milken his boss, even though he was not in the direct chain of command. The government asked, "If you had to say who was your boss at that time [the time he was working in the New York Office], would you say Mr. Milken or Mr. Rosenthal?" Maultasch answered, "Overall boss was Mr. Milken" (p. 179). Thus the contradiction between the hierarchy of authority and the locus of power destroyed the control mechanisms of the organization, replacing them with Milken's control of strategic contingencies.

DEPARTMENTAL AUTONOMY
THROUGH DIFFERENTIATION

Milken took little interest in the prestigious client list of blue-chip investors at Drexel because the interest rate on the investment grade bonds favored by those clients was not much higher than that of risk-free U.S. treasury bonds. Milken was interested in the below–investment grade bonds (those rated Ba1 or lower by Moody's, BBB+ and below by Standard and Poor, or unrated bonds). These bonds were known by several different euphemisms based on their riskiness: "fallen angels," "chinese paper," etc. The higher interest rates offset the exceptional risk. If the company did well, the bonds could be upgraded in the future, making them more valuable and less risky. (Milken himself offset the risk to investors by guaranteeing that he would make a bid on the bonds if the investor needed liquidity; however, Drexel did not guarantee that investors would recoup their full investment.) In return, Drexel received high commissions (4 to 5 percent as opposed to less than 1 percent for high-grade bonds).

Product Specialization

At the beginning of his career, Milken was under considerable pressure to prove himself and the profitability of the high-yield bonds he advocated. In the summer of 1970, Milken, through Drexel, published extensive information on and began trading almost exclusively in these bonds, which created liquidity where previously none had existed. By 1973 Milken wanted to differentiate the high-yield bond sales from the high-grade bond sales at Drexel Burnham. This was the only way he could demonstrate to the partners that he was making the profits of the department. Milken was the first person at Drexel and possibly the first in any investment banking firm to specialize in the selling of high-yield bonds [although Taggart (1988) credits Lehman Brothers with having underwritten the first bonds that were below investment grade from the start with the issue of Institutional Investor bonds in 1985]. He felt it was more like selling stock than investment grade bonds because the salesperson had to know about the company, its earning trend, and its cash flow. It was exceptionally difficult because buyers had to be convinced that the rating agency was wrong and the true value of the bond was actually higher than its rating. Finally buyers had to be convinced that if the company went bankrupt, its asset pool was sufficient that the high-yield bonds they were buying would not be vulnerable.

Departmentalization

Indeed this was specialized work, and Milken wanted autonomy to do it, in the form of a department differentiated from the investment grade bond department. The Drexel Burnham partnership was still in its creation stage; therefore, Milken's requests were more easily accommodated than they might have been in an older, more established firm. As head of the

High-Yield Bond Department, Milken could demonstrate its profitability, which gave him power. The separation of the High-Yield Bond Department from the Investment Grade Bond Department gave Milken autonomy. And the combination of power and autonomy gave him the ability not only to control the functioning of the department, but to screen its functioning from executives at Drexel's East Coast office.

Spatial Differentiation

In 1974, only one year after the merger of Burnham and Company and Drexel Firestone, Frederick Joseph arrived at Drexel Burnham as the head of the newly constituted firm's corporate finance department. The two companies were still operating separately. They retained their different cultures and clients. Burnham and Company was aggressive and willing to change with investment banking's role in mergers and acquisitions, while Drexel Firestone was the more conservative firm, which appealed to blue-chip investors.

In an attempt to increase autonomy and greater control over his department, in early 1978 Michael Milken announced that he was moving his entire department to Los Angeles, ostensibly for the benefit of his family. But within the firm it was understood that he wanted greater distance to obtain more autonomy from Burnham, who was breathing down his neck about the volume of his positions and the high risks associated with his deals. Joseph, on the other hand, became more important as Milken's first line of defense in the home office in New York, supporting and defending him in the move to the West Coast.

Bruck's work gives us some insight into why Milken had the power to move the most profitable department of Drexel to the West Coast, where no other firm had such a department of any consequence. She writes that, at the time of the announcement, "Milken's profits were so astronomical that when the profits and losses of all the departments in the firm were calculated, the others canceled one another out and Milken's profit figure was that of the firm, overall" (1989, p. 51). Burnham and Company was economically strong enough to take over Drexel Firestone at a time when it had little or no prestige, but it was not strong enough to keep its most profitable department (including about twenty traders and sales research people) in New York or even on the East Coast.

This was the most significant, though not the last step that Milken took to separate and differentiate his unit *within* Drexel. It afforded him greater autonomy from the home office and at the same time greater control over his unit. The separation of the High-Yield Bond Department from other departments and from the management of Drexel cut down on the daily conflict between the other managers of Drexel and his traders. His traders were quickly becoming millionaires and many other Drexel employees wanted to join the High-Yield Bond Department in its wealth.

To further differentiate it from the New York investment banking establishment, Milken did not just move the Bond Department to Los Angeles but to the intersection of Wilshire Boulevard and Rodeo Drive in Beverly Hills, a high-rent retail rather than financial district address. They moved into a building which was owned by Michael and Lowell Milken. Thus the Milken brothers benefited not only from rent and from tax breaks, but also from an increase in the value of the property.

Corporate managers argue that autonomy confers success. The reasoning is that because they are in touch with the external environment, acting as the interface between the customer and the internal operations of the corporation, they can make better decisions than upper-level management, if they are given the autonomy to make decisions. Thus they claim that autonomy makes them more successful. I posit that the relationship between autonomy and success may be just the reverse. Those units in an organization that are most successful may have the power to differentiate themselves from the executive control of the organization. Those which are not successful do not. Success confers autonomy. Thus success in the case of the High-Yield Bond Department led to greater and greater autonomy. This success was symbolized by the financial world's labeling this five-story building the "West Coast Headquarters of Drexel Burnham Lambert."

CONTROL OF THE BOND DEPARTMENT: RATIONALITY AND OPPORTUNISM

The bond floor is the social context in which traders learn from mentors the rules of trading, including rationality and opportunistic self-interest. This is not an attempt to deny the existence of self-interest and rationality in human behavior, or to deny that there is a self- or organizational selection of those who are more self-interested into this type of work. But in the context of the trading floor such drives are clearly defined, given meaning, and cherished, and command respect and status.

The trading floor of an investment banking firm is constructed to generate cooperation and trust among traders, but only to a limited extent. Opportunism and self-interest are more highly cherished. Most of the time the opportunistic self-interest is overriding. Whereas in larger firms selection of a new employee occurs by the recruit roaming the bond floor until someone takes him or her in at a desk. In the High-Yield Bond

Department, the traders were often hand-chosen by Milken. He chose only those who were at the top of the game, those who had been mentored or had learned from exchange partners and peers that rational, self-interested opportunism was the only valued strategy for action on the trading floor. The interplay between the rules and the actions of the traders was nowhere more apparent than on the bond floor. Meyer, Boli, and Thomas (1987) suggest that institutional rules render the relations between actors and action more tautological than causal: "Actors enact as much as they act: What they do is inherent in the social definition of the actor itself. Consequently, rules constituting actors legitimate types of action, and legitimated action constitutes and shapes the social actor" (1987, p. 22). Self-interested, opportunistic, and illegal behavior was considered legitimate and became the norm. The more legitimate it became; the more it shaped the traders.

Self-interest and opportunism are reinforced by the reward structure. The basic definition of bond traders' work is that they perform the dual roles of broker and dealer. As brokers, they match buyers with sellers, thereby earning a commission from the firm. As dealers, they trade bonds for their own accounts, either buying or selling to create profits for the firm. As we have seen, at Drexel this was not such an objectively rational process. Opportunism was profitable because traders were paid a bonus and commissions that far exceeded their salary—at any one time, nearly everyone on the bond floor was a millionaire. Thus doing the deal was more important than the firm's welfare. The firm was of little relevance because the trader could not move up the corporate hierarchy. Status, prestige, and wealth depended on a continuous stream of transactions. More important than the number or the size was the profit made from each trade, and deregulation of commissions made profits variable and competitive.

Without a doubt the bond floor and bond traders are the closest parallel to the neoclassical market and economic man that exists in contemporary American society. The goal of bond traders is personal wealth, through entrepreneurship in a competitive market. The department, if not the firm, supports this goal of personal wealth because the department's capital accumulates with the individual's compensation. Although traders as well as bankers rationalize, when asked, that they are doing this work for the "rush," or "high" that they obtain, aside from this and the admitted goal of wealth, there is a third explanation: "the mastery of the deal." This might be interpreted as a seeking of power and control over the firms involved, but this would be a superficial interpretation. Most of the traders talked of the craft of "doing the deal," of the strategy of putting the deal together in a short time, under pressure from competitors and market volatility (risk). Status comes from the commissions and bonuses, but esteem, respect, and prestige come from doing the biggest deals. And in this more than any other profession, mastery of the craft resulted in the goal of personal wealth. The trading floor attracts those who desire wealth and rewards them for achieving their goal. The means of doing the most profitable deals are through opportunism. Therefore it is rational that rational actors do not stop at the bounds of the law, but cross it to commit unlawful acts.

Williamson defines opportunism as "self interest seeking with guile" (1975, p. 26). Among the types of opportunism that he elaborates is selective or distorted disclosure of information in a transaction. Two of the most common types of opportunistic disclosure are "laying off" bonds, which involves offering incomplete information in order to make a profit at the expense of one's transaction partner and "showing a bid," which involves offering false and deceptive information on the street to support a position. The street bid is withdrawn after the deceptive information is communicated. Both of these types of opportunism can be engaged in alone without the support of others in or outside one's firm. Because they are nonpublic, they are not easily verified and therefore difficult to detect. Traders often define incomplete and deceptive actions, such as these, as "in the gray area"—not really illegal. When asked if there is not a law against these acts, the respondent will often reply that they are "the way business is done," meaning that they are common practice. The market regulation is ignored as a matter of general practice. No particular strategy is necessary.

On the other hand, trading on inside information from another firm, market manipulation, and parking, as described as Chapter 2, are defined as illegal. The traders all know that these activities are illegal, but they rationalize that "everyone is doing it." These illegal transactions necessitate specific strategies and arrangements between firms and actors in firms. The traders have to confront their partners in crime; someone else knows. This is particularly difficult because of the self-reliance and individualism that the traders have internalized as the basis of trading, and the competition and lack of trust between traders both on the floor and between firms. Although they have learned the gray areas and the technical manipulations as part of their socialization, they generally do not ask for assistance or support in their work. How could they ask for support in the clandestine, illegal acts used to exploit others in the market? The answer to this question is found in the nature of the organizations in which they worked, and also in the particularly supportive economic and legal contexts for opportunism described in Chapters 5 and 6.

Competitors entered the junk bond market. The market grew rapidly, contributing to the difficulty of socializing the novice trader. The institutional rules of investment banking were changing as was the firm's control over its employees. To confound matters further, the Reagan administration was not enforcing the regulations that existed and the traders knew this.

Structure of the Bond Floor

Who was in control of the Drexel bond floor: the self-interested traders, the firm, or the head of the High-Yield Bond Department? The arrangement of the bond floor begins to expose Milken's need to control those in his department while maintaining his autonomy from the firm. According to Patsy Van Utt's testimony, the trading floor of the High-Yield Bond Department was arranged in an X configuration. The high-yield bond traders formed the upper part, the arms of the X, the convertible-bond traders formed the legs of the X, and Milken sat in the center. That is, the high-yield bond traders formed a V in front of Milken's desk, while the convertible-bond salespersons formed a V behind Milken's desk. The support staff sat in a line behind the traders/salespersons. "On either side you had, I believe at that time, private placement or capital markets group to either side and an equity department" (*U.S. v. Michael Milken* 1990a, pp. 376–81). The compliance officer had a desk in one corner of the trading floor.

Milken sat in the center of the X facing the high-yield bond traders. His assistants sat in desks behind him, facing each other. Maultasch testified that Milken sat in one center portion of the X, while Gary Winnick, the head of the convertible-bond traders, sat in the other center portion of the X. The High-Yield Bond Department fanned out from Milken and the convertible-bond traders fanned out from Winnick (p. 165). The traders' desks were arranged to form the X and they sat outside and inside the arms of the X. Peter Gardiner (pp. 286–87) testified that two persons sat on the outside and two on the inside of each of the four arms of the X. There were two people on the leg and he was the person at the end on the inside of one leg of the convertible-bond side on the X. Thus there were eight traders/salespersons on each V, four on each arm and four on each leg when all the desks were filled. Gardiner testified that his desk at the end of one leg was no more than twenty to forty feet from Milken's desk. Behind the X formation was a set of conference rooms for meetings with clients and private conferences among employees. Milken sat with his back to the conference rooms and facing the high-yield bond traders.

Van Utt described the atmosphere on the bond floor in the following way:

> A lot of noise. Most of us were always on the phone. Michael was always on the phone. Most of us were always on the phone. It was quite loud. There was a lot of usually calling back and forth. If you were on the phone

with an account, and you needed to get a trading market from one of the traders or you had an order for something, it was kind of a constant calling out. There was a lot of energy generated and a lot of noise on the trading floor usually. (p. 379)

From this one can conclude that not only could Milken communicate directly with all of the traders on the floor, but also that the traders could communicate directly with each other. This not only facilitated communication and feedback, but also direct control, especially the monitoring of trades. Van Utt testified that Milken would call out directions to the traders while he was on the phone. He was in constant dialogue with the traders (p. 385). Gardiner testified that "it was not infrequent that Mike would shout directives to the troops in the course of the day" (p. 295).

Cary Maultasch testified that Michael Milken, as frequently as once a week, would ask him to execute trades for him. Maultasch would execute trades on equities, either with common stock, with straight bonds, or with warrants attached to bonds. Maultasch further testified that Michael Milken asked nearly everybody, including clerks who handled the orders and the convertible-securities traders, to execute trades for him.

This picture of the relatively small High-Yield Bond Department trading floor is very different from the normal trading floor in which individuals are trading fast and furiously on their own account and in their own self-interest. Here the traders were controlled to trade in the interest of the department. Milken's trades took precedence over any trade that might be on their personal agenda. The work of the department was loud, fast, and furious, but the arrangement, control over, and downward direction of communication left no doubt that the department head had discretionary decision-making power over the operation of the floor.

Status of Drexel and Control of the Bond Department

Investment banking firms are arranged hierarchically into what is called brackets—the higher the bracket the more prestigious the firm (as mentioned above with regard to Burnham's early aspirations for Drexel mobility). The highest bracket is the special bracket. Although the composition of the special bracket changed in the 1980s, the special-bracket firms were typically Morgan Stanley; First Boston Corporation; Goldman, Sachs; Salomon Brothers; and Merrill Lynch. Drexel generally appeared in the "majors," the category under the special bracket.

This ranking of firms can be seen in the *tombstone*, the ad placed in the financial press to announce an offering. The tombstone generally lists in the first and second positions the firms that are the principal and comanager. All other investment banking firms involved in the offering are listed below. The size of the type denotes the importance of the firm in the offering. Drexel was often listed as comanager until the mid-1980s. When managing LBOs, Drexel was more often the principal.

In analyzing the status of investment banking firms, Podolny wrote that "the most significant actors in one market are usually among the most significant actors in another, and a corporation's selection of a bank for services in one market may lay the groundwork for the choice of the same bank in another" (1991, p. 57). Drexel entered the decade of the 1980s with low status and reputation—it was not a major player in any of the equity or bond markets. This changed as the junk bond market grew. As Drexel came to dominate the junk bond market, it was able to increase its underwriting presence in other markets. However, the other departments at Drexel never developed the same presence or status in their market that the High-Yield Bond Department did.

By the mid-1980s Drexel's status had increased substantially. From 1984 to 1987, the volume of underwriting that Drexel did was greater than either of the more prestigious firms of Goldman, Sachs or Morgan Stanley, but they did not recognize Drexel as having shifted from the majors to the special bracket, because LBOs represented only one type of market and Drexel's status had not changed substantially in other markets. Among LBO underwriters, Drexel was the largest and the most prestigious. For example, in 1988 when KKR initiated the takeover of RJR Nabisco for $25.07 billion, there were two competitors for the underwriting: Shearson, Lehman and Drexel. Shearson ranked somewhat above Drexel in status in the debt market because of its activity in the investment grade market. Shearson was working with RJR Nabisco to bring the company private and had allied itself with Salomon Brothers, which ranked fifth as an underwriter of junk bonds, which would in large part provide the financing for the takeover. Shearson was doing the deal and Salomon would do the financing. But KKR with the backing of Milken and Drexel had amassed $5.6 billion to pursue acquisitions. Podolony reported that this was more than twice the size of the next largest fund devoted to this purpose, and that KKR's capital represented more than one-quarter of the asset pool in the world targeted for use in LBOs (1991, p. 61). With Drexel's financial backing KKR was therefore a more formidable force than Shearson with Salomon's financial backing.

George Roberts, general partner of KKR, insisted that the most knowledgeable investment banker in the junk bond industry should be used—he wanted Drexel and Michael Milken. Peter Cohen, chairman and CEO of Shearson, wanted to be at least coadvisor on all auctions and have the fees go to Shearson. Roberts insisted on Drexel as lead manager, but Salomon Brothers refused to comanage on a deal that would be led by Drexel.

Although by this time, Drexel had been indicted for securities fraud, this was not the real reason for Salomon Brothers balking. They were willing to be comanager on a bond underwritten by Shearson because if Shearson were the lead underwriter, the financial world would know that Salomon was doing the financing. Throughout the industry, Salomon was generally perceived to be superior to Shearson in the underwriting of junk bonds. However, the industry also knew that Drexel had been the leading financier of LBOs since 1984. If Drexel were the lead underwriter and Shearson were comanager, everyone would know that Drexel was doing the financing. Because of Salomon's status in the high-grade bond market, it would be an insult to be asked to take second place to Drexel when it wanted to be the greatest power in financing LBOs (Burrough and Helyar 1990).

In the mid-1980s, the higher status firms were attempting to remain as aloof as possible from the disreputable tactics of Drexel. However, they also saw that Drexel had not only moved into the ranks of the top ten revenue-generating investment banking firms, but was involved in junk bond LBOs, which many of them had not yet mastered. Gradually they became involved. For example, Morgan Stanley joined with Drexel to finance Ronald Perelman's takeover of Revlon; Goldman, Sachs leveraged Macy's in a $4 billion takeover; Merrill Lynch, Shearson, Lehman, and First Boston's Bruce Wassenstein were all involved in the takeover markets in the mid-1980s. They may have held Drexel in disdain, but imitation was the sincerest form of flattery.

Status of Traders and Control of the Junk Bond Department

Before the 1980s, traders and investment bankers, although they worked in the same firms, occupied very different social ranks. Investment bankers came from established financial families, attended ivy league schools, obtained prestigious MBAs, held memberships in the right fraternities and the right social clubs. Traders had none of these characteristics. They were held in disdain by bankers as not only lower class, but uncouth, brutish, and uncultured. Even more important, bankers felt that traders were retained by investment banking firms to perform the function of trading the stocks and bonds that resulted from deals that only bankers could do.

The 1970s saw a shift in corporate power from sales and marketing to finance and accounting, which served to reinforce the greater power and status of the bankers and financiers in most investment banking firms. However, within investment banking firms there was a shift in power from finance and banking to trading and sales. This switch was due to the change from a fixed-commission structure to variable commission rates, the expansion of mergers and acquisitions as the method of growth, and the LBO as the debt instrument of favor. Because commission rates had been de-regulated, firms began to compete with each other on the basis of commissions. Clients whose corporations had done business with one prestigious firm for generations became involved in transactional banking—that is, seeking out the firm that offered the lowest commission for each new deal. Buyers of the bonds were interested in obtaining the highest interest rate. Both issuers and buyers were interested in having the deal close quickly. The trader's ability to do the deal depended on the capitalization of the firm, the trader's knowledge of issuers and financial instruments, and the extent of the trader's networks to sell the entire bond offering.

By their function, bankers were often too far removed from the execution of the deal, whereas traders were at its very heart. Bankers thought of themselves as agents who facilitated the transaction for their clients. Bankers were intermediaries. Traders thought of themselves as the principals, not their clients. As principals, traders would use the firm's capital to take a position (to buy bonds or stocks). In this way investment houses became merchant bankers. Milken invested not only Drexel's capital but the traders' profits (held in private partnerships) in bankrupt or nearly bankrupt companies, as well as companies that were on the rise, but were underrated. Trading became the major profit center in most investment banking firms in the 1980s, which caused the bankers to hold the traders in even greater disdain, although they respected their power.

Typically investment bankers collect information about issuers' and buyers' needs and attempt to meet these needs through structuring deals. Competition between investment banking houses has increasingly important because corporations issuing equity or debt instruments now use multiple firms to complete transactions. The number of banking organizations involved depends on the number and kinds of services needed. In the mid-1980s the number of banking firms used in an acquisition depended on the amount of capital needed. For example, both Drexel and Merrill Lynch were required to underwrite KKR's takeover of RJR Nabisco. Eccles and Crane reported that "between 1984 and 1986, for example, 124 companies used 5 or more investment banks to lead transactions" (1988, p. 53).

The links to buyers or investors are as complex as those to issuers, with equity salespersons, analysts, and portfolio managers all needed to support traders. Eccles and Crane (p. 37) found that between large investors and large investment banks, over one hundred people can be linked in complex networks.

Investment bankers are linked to their competitors through syndicates for underwriting and distributing securities. The more frequently two firms serve as comanagers for each other's deals, the more robust and numerous become the links between the initially competing organizations. Comanagers are generally of nearly equal status. Multiple links are formed between firms representing acquirers and targets in takeovers and mergers. The larger the number of links, the greater is the potential for innovative interorganizational programs, both legal and illegal.

CONTRADICTIONS OF AUTHORITY AND CONTROL

Both Cary Maultasch and Peter Gardiner testified that they could make small transactions, defined as less than $5 to $10 million, without supervision. However, Alan Rosenthal or Michael Milken had to approve a single transaction in the neighborhood of $10 million or more (*U.S. v. Michael Milken* 1990a, p. 232). Alan Rosenthal reviewed Gardiner's transactions on a daily basis, and Gardiner testified that Milken "often spoke to me during the day about transactions that I had made or would make or that he would like me to make and asked me to account for them in instances when I had made them" (p. 232). Rosenthal, the department head, had direct supervision, but Milken had overall supervisory rights.

In response to the government's question regarding how he would describe Michael Milken's role in supervising his trading, Perter Gardiner replied,

> He too reviewed transactions sheets and from time to time in the morning would ask me about trades that had occurred in the convertible department. Also from time to time during the day, if he heard of a specific transaction occurring or he had a specific interest in a transaction of a security that I traded, he would ask and supervise in that sense. (p. 232)

There seemed to be a direct line of supervision on the high-yield bond floor but there was far looser coupling between the High-Yield Bond Department and the chain of command in the New York office.

The Underwriters' Advisory Committee

In the early 1980s, as the New York office realized that it was losing control of the West Coast operation, it instituted what Drexel called the Underwriters' Advisory Committee. This oversight committee was established because the partners and some of the hierarchy in New York felt that many of Milken's deals were too high risk. The committee was made up entirely of five New York office employees; no one from the High-Yield Bond Department served on it. The committee's major responsibility was to review each deal and decide if it should be closed and then advise the High-Yield Bond Department and the New York office.

Milken's staff was to wire the specifics on each deal to New York, exclusive of information on the profits. However, Milken had information on the profits wired along with other specifics. Many times, the information was wired to New York, but before the committee could meet and communicate its decision back to the West Coast, Milken would have closed the deal and registered the profits with the New York office. The committee believed that Milken often did not communicate his information until he was nearly ready to close the deal. The West Coast office felt the New York office was too slow in responding to deals in which timing could make or break the transaction.

The New York office had records of deals in which the committee withheld approval. On many occasions the committee admonished Milken for making high-risk deals and deals that were unapproved or disapproved. Before the Storer deal closed, a banker flew to the West Coast to advise Milken not to do the deal. Milken closed the deal. Nevertheless the New York office did not withhold Milken's commissions, fees, and portions of his bonus related to these deals nor did it fire him for his insubordination. In fact, it rewarded him, which was de facto approval.

The Chinese Wall and Compliance

Securities traders and investors are duty bound to avoid conflicts of interest. It is against the ethical norms of securities firms and in many instances against the law to abuse privileged positions or privileged information for purposes of personal or corporate gain. Access to such information can lead to self-dealing, which is the exploitation of insider positions for personal benefits. When brokers, traders, or dealers act as agents of others in giving investment advice, in trading or doing deals, or in managing funds, numerous conflicts of interests are possible. These range from the fraudulent appropriation of clients' funds to advising the client in favor of securities in which the adviser has an interest. This is even more likely when an investment firm combines banking, underwriting, investment management, and market making functions. In these cases it is not only the nature of the transaction—that the commodity is symbolic rather than physical—that facilitates the fraud, but also the fact that these functions overlap at their boundaries.

The most serious attempt by investment banking firms to ensure ethical behavior is the construction of what is called a "Chinese wall." A Chinese wall of silence, through which no information should flow in any form between parts of the firm performing different and potentially conflicting functions, is the investment banking firm's assurance to the public that the firm is on an even playing field when investing in the market. In an investment banking firm there are information barriers, intended to prevent a firm's traders from acting on confidential information entrusted to it by clients. These barriers are particularly strong between investment bankers and traders, including arbitragers. This means that the firm should not invest in or create markets in securities managed in its corporate finance department. Thus the operation of the trading floor should be separated from the operations of the corporate finance and the M&A departments to prevent traders from making deals based on information gained in the securities network. On the other hand, it should also prevent traders from making a market for the benefit of corporate clients such as Drexel did for Wickes. Additionally, it should prevent traders from acting on the temptation to invest funds in securities that their firm is trading.

The effectiveness of the Chinese wall depends on both the structure and the culture of the organization. In some cases the culture may work against the structure to prevent the Chinese wall from functioning. Structurally the most effective Chinese walls, those with physical separation and compliance officers, are located in relatively large firms. The reasons can be found in elementary organizational theory. Only the largest firms can afford the separate locations and the additional compliance personnel. In Weber's (1947, [1903–1906] 1985) and Blau's (1970) terms, increases in size lead to increased spatial differentiation and horizontal division of labor.

One might expect that when Michael Milken moved the High-Yield Department to the West Coast this would provide a spatial separation that would maximize the effectiveness of the Chinese wall; however, this was not the case. Milken duplicated corporate functions by creating a separate underwriting function, separate corporate finance, and separate deal making, along with the normal functioning of the High-Yield Bond Department. Milken advocated that the High-Yield Bond Department could more efficiently perform all of these functions than deal with the New York office. All of this was sheltered by the department's own compliance officers and legal counsel.

However, these same measures, which, according to the firm, are for the purpose of ensuring the separation of functions to impede the flow of information and enforce restraints, may be instituted to legitimize the corporation in the eyes of the government. The proliferation of compliance rules, regulations, and structures that accompany the hiring of personnel may not occur solely for the purpose of regulating the investment bank, but may also be for the purpose of reporting to the regulatory agency what it wants to hear and to keep the firm informed of regulatory changes. Since investment banking firms are routinely sued, the establishment of spatially separated departments and the hiring of compliance officers may be the best way to demonstrate to the regulators that the firm is working to ensure that it is in compliance, when, in fact, it has little intention of complying. In other words the elaboration of these structures may exist to conceal the very actions they purport to prevent.

The Chinese wall is developed as a signal that the firm is sensitive to the reconciliation of conflicts of interest. Wolfson (1980) has described how these pressures have contributed to the construction of elaborate forms of Chinese walls in investment banking. Herzel and Colling (1983) have shown that for the past twenty years the Chinese wall has spread through financial institutions because courts and regulators have been ready to accept the existence of an effectively policed wall as an important evidentiary aid in lawsuits, making more credible a defense against charges of insider trading and related securities fraud.

THE CONTRADICTION OF AUTHORITY
AND ECONOMIC INCENTIVE SYSTEMS

Drexel implemented the agency model of incentive systems to its fullest. Jensen (1989b), the leading advocate of agency theory, characterizes public corporations as the main engine of twentieth century economic progress in the United States. But he feels the public corporation has "outlived its usefulness in many sectors of the economy and is being eclipsed" (p. 61). According to Jensen, organizations that are taking the place of the public corporation use public and private debt, rather than public equity, as their source of capital. Their primary owners are not individual shareholders, but large institutional investors, pension funds, insurance companies, and entrepreneurs. Jensen characterizes takeovers, corporate breakups, divisional spinoffs, and leveraged buyouts as manifestations of the massive organizational changes taking place. He feels that these changes are not only positive but should be encouraged because the separation of ownership and management is "the central weakness of the public corporation" (p. 61). Furthermore he feels these leveraged forms of organizations have made "remarkable gains in operating efficiency, employee productivity, and shareholder value. Over the long term, they will enhance U.S. economic performance relative to our most formidable international competitor, Japan, whose companies are moving in the opposite direction" (pp. 61–62). Jensen feels LBOs, at premiums, demonstrate that market prices are undervalued:

> Indeed the fact that takeover and LBO premiums average 50 percent above market price illustrates how much value public-company managers can

destroy before they face a serious threat of disturbance. Takeovers and
buyouts both create new value and unlock value destroyed by management
through misguided policies. (pp. 64–65)

Jensen seems to be oblivious to the inflated value of the junk bond market
that underwrote these buyouts. He does not seem to realize the centrality
of the high-yield market in creating the new surplus of capital (debit
capital) that was being used in these LBOs. Rather he writes: "The widespread waste and inefficiency of the public corporation and its inability to
adapt to changing economic circumstances have generated a wave of
organizational innovation over the last 15 years—innovation driven by the
rebirth of 'active investors'" (p. 65).

Jensen sees the finance conception of the firm as paramount. He states
that, consistent with modern finance theory, these organizations are not
managed to maximize earnings per share but rather to maximize value,
with a strong emphasis on cash flow. The model Jensen builds is around
highly leveraged financial structures, and pay-for-performance compensation systems.

Jensen feels that publicly held corporations have a tendency to reward
management through promotion rather than annual performance bonuses, creating a cultural bias toward growth (p. 66). Organizations must
grow in order to generate new positions to feed their promotion-based
reward systems. In turn he sees this growth as an enhancement of the social
prominence, public prestige, and political power of senior executives.
Jensen advocates that compensation be tied to performance and be returned to the employees in the form of commissions, bonuses, fees, and
ownership. He uses LBO associations as exemplars of his finance model
of incentive structures. He points out that "LBO Associations usually have
higher upper bounds than do public companies, tie bonuses much more
closely to cash flow and debt retirement than to accounting earnings, and
otherwise closely link management pay to divisional performance" (p. 68).
Jensen does not seem to be aware of the potential for fraud and exploitation
connected with LBOs, which greatly influence the outcomes of the samples
on which he bases his conclusions.

More importantly, Jensen, like other economic organizational theorists,
does not understand the contradictions that arise between the goals of the
organization and those of the organizations' subunits. In Drexel, a mul-
tifunctional firm, the goals of increasing the bonuses, commissions, and
salaries of the High-Yield Bond Department became inconsistent with
long-term growth and, in the end, survival of the corporation. The drive
to increase these rewards for the department was a major personal motivation for fraud. After Drexel's indictment, the corporation did not
withdraw these incentives. Joseph proposed reducing them in order to

save Drexel from bankruptcy, but the members of the High-Yield Bond Department protested and Joseph withdrew his proposal. To have altered the lucrative bonus system would have destroyed the morale of the employees of the High-Yield Bond Department. These compensation plans— especially in the High-Yield Bond Department—drained much-needed capital from the corporation after it pleaded guilty and Milken was fired. Inefficiency and ineffectiveness set in as Drexel tried to keep key personnel from taking offers from other firms by increasing their already exorbitant compensation packages. Due to corporate commitments, the compensation packages of those involved in the fraud were not terminated. Milken was paid his annual bonus even after he was severed from Drexel.

Rewards and the Corporate Culture of Drexel

Frederick Joseph came to Drexel in 1974 as head of the corporate finance department, and immediately set about defining a new corporate culture that was consistent with economic models of the firm. He wanted to build a firm more powerful and successful than Goldman, Sachs, the top investment banking firm in the United States. To do this, he wanted to appeal to medium-sized growth companies, a realistic goal. It meant that Drexel and Company would have to adjust its sights downward from Ford and the Fortune 500 companies it wanted, but was unable to attract, while Burnham and Company would have to adjust its sights upward. But the differential between what each of the partners wanted and the new standard was much greater for Drexel than for Burnham. This meant that if a partner brought in a deal with a medium-sized firm, he would have to be rewarded in the same way as someone who brought in a large and prestigious firm.

In keeping with his newly established goals, Joseph fired about one-third of his bankers in the corporate finance department and began to assemble more aggressive bankers and traders, not out of the major firms, but from the unranked firms on the level Burnham and Company had occupied. For these bankers to work for Drexel was a vertical move. Joseph's other major recruiting ground was Shearson, where he had previously worked. He assured the new bankers and traders that their continued aggressiveness would be rewarded through the establishment of new compensation structures.

Milken and Burnham had already negotiated a major change in the corporate culture by bringing the compensation package into line with the financial conception of the firm, which was based on the assumption that employees work harder if they share in the profits of the firm. The corporation allocated some portion of corporate profits to each department as a bonus to be divided among the employees by the department head, thus conceding decision-making and monitoring power to the departments, as is the case in most multidivisional firms (Chandler 1962, 1977). Joseph instituted a formula for corporate finance's bonus pool that would increase the pool and at the same time change the nature of the allocation system. Then head of corporate finance, he negotiated with management that a fixed percentage of the operating profits of the department would go into the pool, with increments for certain kinds of deals. Money from this pool was later called bonuses, and the employees who were the most productive were compensated more handsomely by their bonuses than through their relatively smaller salaries. Joseph set up criteria for the distribution of the pool to the departments within Drexel. Through the allocation of rewards based on these criteria, he began to establish a new, more competitive corporate culture among departments and employees of the corporate finance area.

In 1973, just one year before Joseph came to work for Drexel, Milken started with $2 million in capital, and generated a 100 percent rate of return, earning bonus pools for himself and the members of the High-Yield Bond Department that approached $1 million in a system negotiated with Burnham. Milken had negotiated a corporate compensation package for his department that was somewhat better than average. Because Milken was working in areas with which Joseph was unfamiliar—unrated bonds—Milken was able to renegotiate with Burnham the High-Yield Bond Department's compensation arrangement to provide an even stronger performance incentive than existed for the rest of the corporation. Milken and his semiautonomous high-yield bond traders would receive 35 percent of the profits attributed to their activities. Milken was given the discretion to allocate this bonus money in any way he saw fit. Burnham also gave Milken additional finder's fees of 15 to 30 percent of the profits attributable to any business the bond department brought into the firm. With regard to the work of the High-Yield Bond Department, the firm kept as little as 33 percent. The bonus structure for the High-Yield Bond Department was a closely held corporate secret. Burnham was afraid it would cause envy and poor working relations if other departments learned of it.

The two cultures of bankers and traders existed at Drexel, but less separately than in most investment banking firms that had multiple strong departments vying for power. Stratification between the East Coast bankers and the West Coast traders was much less than might have been expected because the status of the bankers at Drexel was not as elevated as in the more prestigious firms, and therefore, there was less social distance between the bankers and traders. At the same time the greater compensation of the West Coast traders reduced the status gap. The great spatial distance between the two and the overwhelming power of the

high-yield operation on the West Coast also eliminated conflict that might
have been fueled by greater proximity in space between the authority-
based power of the East Coast bankers and the economic power of the West
Coast traders. When conflicts did occur they most often focused on the
compensation packages and the lucrative private partnerships of the High-
Yield Bond Department employees.

The New York headquarters was designed to be both a control center
and perform corporate functions for departments on the East Coast as well
as the West Coast. Many of these functions were duplicated by the West
Coast office. This laid bare the nature of the power structure within Drexel.
New York could not replace Milken and the High-Yield Bond Department,
but they could replace it by replacing many of the functions it performed.

Corporate Compensation

Drexel was the first investment banking firm, since the time of its early
partner J. P. Morgan, to engage in merchant banking, the practice of a firm
using its own capital to finance its deals (in this case as a debt participant).
By the mid-1980s Drexel had equity stakes in about 150 firms. In some cases
Drexel invested directly in the bonds, which were later converted to
equity. In other cases it took warrants from a company and latter turned
the warrants into stock. Unlike other investment banking firms, Drexel
took warrants from some companies as promotional accompaniment to
sell to buyers when bonds were high risk. It sometimes retained the more
valuable warrants as was described in Chapter 2. At other times they took
warrants as payment for services rendered, a practice shunned by most
reputable investment banking houses.

When Drexel took an equity stake in a firm, it became an owner. Drexel
did not concentrate on the control that ownership gave it over these firms,
but argued instead that this deterred it from doing deals that were too high
risk. If Drexel owned a portion of the company it had a stake in seeing that
the firm remained solvent. This made Drexel a partner with both the issuers
and buyers of the bonds—no one wanted the company to get into trouble.
But the rationale was faulty because Drexel, knowing the market, could
sell its stake if it saw the company falter, whereas buyers generally did not
have such a comprehensive knowledge of the market. Milken supported
the idea that a manager will work harder for a company if he has invested
his capital in the company, than if he does not. Likewise he believed that
an investment banking firm with a stake in a company will make sure the
deal is good. Thus, Milken and Drexel held substantial stakes in many of
the companies for which they were transacting deals, often owning both

their debt and their equity, sitting on their boards, and informally influencing management decisions for which capital was required.

Employee Compensation Packages as Control Mechanisms

The Financial Accounting Standards Board (FASB), which oversees accounting rules in the United States and which is overseen in turn by the SEC, works in part to improve the accuracy of managers' reported salaries and earnings. But accountants are currently instructed by management to treat various components of compensation such as stock options and commissions differently from salaries and bonuses. As a consequence, its stock options are neither added to the corporation's compensation expenses nor deducted from the corporation's pretax earnings. Cowan (1992) reports Graef Crystal, a Berkeley economist, found that, in 1990, 274 of 292 major American public corporations awarded stock options to their CEOs with an average value of $13 million per company. These figures are deleted from the firms' combined compensation expenses, as reported by their boards or reported as pretax earnings for tax purposes. Crystal estimates that if these figures had been noted, it would have lowered corporate earnings by as much as 10 percent (Cowan 1992).

Crystal found that if the thirty largest companies in each major industrial country in 1990 were examined, the estimated annual salary, bonus, and present value of long-term incentives such as stock options offered to CEOs would compare as follows: $3.2 million for the United States, $1.1 million for Great Britain, and $0.5 million for Japan. The lowest-paid bond trader in the High-Yield Bond Department at Drexel in 1986 rivaled this Japanese figure. Michael Milken's salary that year far outstripped that of the U.S. CEOs in 1990. In fact, Milken's compensation for three days' work was equivalent to that of the CEOs' yearly compensation.

Peter Gardiner, a trader in the High-Yield Bond Department, testified that when he was hired in 1985, his salary was $10,000 per month or $120,000 per year. By December of that year he was making double that salary or $240,000 a year. In mid-1986 this increased to $450,000 per year, retroactive to the beginning of 1986, exclusive of bonuses and commissions. Peter Gardiner was the lowest-paid trader in the convertible securities department as of April 1986. Bruce Newberg, who was leaving the High-Yield Bond Department in 1986 and whom Peter Gardiner was replacing, made $1.5 million in salary. After Bruce Newberg left, Peter Gardiner took over his accounts: Elliot and Associates, Princeton-Newport, Kaufman Alsberg, Trust Company of the West (*U.S. v. Michael Milken* 1990a, pp. 230–33).

In 1984 Dennis Levine was hired by Drexel. His letter of appointment at Drexel, dated January 18, 1985, revealed that he would receive a base salary of $140,000, about twice his base at Shearson Lehman, one thousand shares of Drexel, and a minimum first-year bonus of $750,000 or one-half again his bonus at Shearson Lehman. In 1986, Martin Siegel moved to Drexel from Kidder, Peabody for $3.5 million per year, a $2 million signing bonus, and a block of Drexel stock for which the value was not stipulated. The package was worth approximately $6 million. He was hired to work with Michael Milken to establish a firm bond between mergers and acquisitions and Milken's High-Yield Bond Department. This meant that he could expect an even higher bonus the next year as a result of finders fees and other compensation.

Michael Milken's compensation package was directly tied to the high-yield bond issues, which grew from $15 billion in 1976 to $125 billion in 1986. According to Joseph's calculations, in 1987 the High-Yield Bond Department was entitled to $700 million in bonuses. Milken had authority to distribute this in any way he saw fit. Michael Milken kept $550 million in bonuses from Drexel, dividing the remaining $150 million among the employees of his department. He earned approximately $1.5 million a day and this was only a fraction of his compensation, but it was more than Drexel's profits for the year—approximately $525 million. He was earning additional revenue from his private partnerships: MacPherson, which held the Storer warrants, and Otter Creek, which held the Beatrice warrants, Pacific Lumber warrants, and National Can stocks, to name just a few. The Otter Creek distribution alone was $437.4 million. Milken's net worth was estimated to be approximately $3 billion in 1986. Of course, he held large quantities of high-yield bonds in which he traded; and although his net worth undoubtedly increased in 1987 to nearly $5 billion, it most certainly declined between late 1987, when the market crashed, and 1989, when the bottom fell out of the high-yield bond market. Milken was doing better than Drexel, but Drexel was not doing poorly.

In 1986 alone, Drexel reported $4 trillion in transactions, $5 billion in net revenue, and pretax net income of $2 billion. It owned 49.9 percent interest in a complex of offices in Manhattan's World Trade Center, into which it planned to move in 1987.

Corporate Strategies for Tying Bonuses to Profits
and Commission to Employee Control

Profits from investment banking transactions are generally retained by the corporation. But as described above, Milken negotiated a large portion, 35 percent of the profits be returned to him, as a departmental bonus pool. In addition, he negotiated one-third of the profits from his department be returned to his department as a capital base for its operation. This is an unusually large amount, but Milken had the power to negotiate such returns not only because he was successful, but because the firm knew that no other Drexel department could generate a higher return on its capital.

Milken made it mandatory that his traders reinvest a certain portion of their bonuses and commissions in trading accounts and partnerships that he controlled. This increased his trading base and had the additional advantage of controlling the employees. The traders could not complain about the rate of return on their investments because returns were exceptionally high through the mid-1980s. In fact, many of the traders were quite pleased with the investment program. As long as they remained in Drexel's employ, they prospered. However, if they wanted to leave, it was difficult to withdraw their money. Liquidity was not easily achieved because Milken had the partnership assets invested. Through these incentives (one positive and the other negative), Milken not only controlled the turnover rate of his department, which remained low throughout its existence, he also controlled the spread of knowledge technology by insuring that no one left with his database or trading secrets.

On October 23, 1990 Fred Joseph testified about the elements of the compensation package that employees at Drexel received (*U.S. v. Michael Milken* 1990a, pp. 1031–35). He explained that a profit-sharing formula had been negotiated in 1973 between Drexel and Milken by Burnham when he bought Drexel. "It effectively created a profit participation pool equal to an ascending scale percentage of the operating profits and it ascended up to 35 percent, and that formula I believe was unchanged from 1973 on" (pp. 1031–32). Joseph reported that in addition to the profits, finders fees were paid into that pool based on origination of investment banking business by High-Yield Bond Department members and a commission pool came off the gross revenue, which was used to compensate people in the High-Yield Bond Department (p. 1032). This commission pool was allocated among departmental employees by and at the discretion of the department head, Michael Milken.

Both the profit-sharing pool and the commission pool were allocated to the High-Yield Bond Department employees by and at the discretion of Michael Milken. Joseph reported,

> After the department head made the allocations they were reviewed by senior members of the firm to be sure that the head of the department was being fair to the people in the department, and we never had a problem in the high-yield department of it not being fair. (p. 1032)

Joseph reported that Milken's profit sharing and commissions also came from this pool and that Milken "essentially kept the residual of what was left in the pool after he had fairly compensated his personnel" (p. 1032).

Partnerships as Control of Employees and Fund Mangers

Joseph further testified (*U.S. v. Michael Milken* 1990a) that the LBO partnerships that Milken had formed for his employees were highly coveted by employees of the New York office in the mid-1980s. The partnerships shared in the equity from takeovers. The corporate finance professionals were especially envious of the profitability of these partnerships and wanted to participate. In 1986, Drexel constructed a policy that allowed corporate finance employees to participate in the partnerships as the High-Yield Bond Department employees had done in the past. The firm used the equity partnerships to reward and retain the most talented employees, who were responsible for generating the high volume of LBO business and the very substantial fees that came as a result of that business. The second function of these partnerships was to keep the traders working on the High-Yield Bond Department deals as opposed to spending their time trading on their own portfolios. And a third function was to increase the loyalty of these highly knowledgeable actors to the bond department.

Joseph testified under cross-examination that the policy to have corporate finance, the High-Yield Bond Department, and the firm share in those equity securities was established in April 1986 out of

Concern by some members of the corporate finance department that the high-yield department might be buying strip equity, as they call it, from leveraged buyouts in the aftermarket for their own accounts as opposed to for joint accounts, as it was called. (*U.S. v. Michael Milken* 1990a, p. 1086)

Two employee units were cut into the partnerships at a reduced rate. According to Joseph's testimony (p. 1086), the High-Yield Bond Department received 50 to 60 percent, corporate finance received 25 percent, and the firm received 20 to 25 percent.

These partnerships extended to the managers of funds and other clients who were in charge of making fund and institutional buys. One partnership in the MacPherson Investments was made up of Dayton Investments, a trust for Michael's, and Lowell's children, Crystal Partners, a group of lawyers (including Craig Cogut and Richard Sandler of the Victor, Cogut, and Sandler law firm—legal counsel who actually operated on the bond floor) who advised the High-Yield Bond Department, and a number of fund and institutional investment managers. MacPherson Investments was established to reward the institutional investment managers and the fund managers. They received an equity kicker, which was associated with the bonds that KKR sold in connection with the financing that Drexel did for KKR's takeover of Storer Communications.

The limited partnerships were so rich that they were able to underwrite takeovers in Drexel's stead, that is, when Drexel had taken on too much debt. Joseph testified that before Drexel actually signed an underwriting agreement in connection with the financing of the acquisition of Storer Communications, Milken asked for a $250 million commitment from Drexel to KKR. When Joseph told him that Drexel was not prepared to make such a large commitment, Milken asked Joseph, "Would it be okay if we did it" I took the "we" to mean the high-yield department, principals of Milken, maybe their families, maybe the partnerships." Joseph testified that Milken then said, "You know that equity goes with the preferred or will go with the preferred" (pp. 1039–41). Joseph understood that Milken was taking the equity through the partnerships. Whether or not he knew that it stayed there instead of going to the buyers is unknown.

The result was that Milken did not use the $1.5 billion equity kicker as he had promised to reward the ultimate buyers of the Storer preferred stock that KKR was selling to finance its takeover. Instead Milken ran the preferred stock and the equity kicker through MacPherson Investments and then the preferred convertible was sold off to other buyers or to Drexel. The equity was retained by MacPherson.

Thus both the ultimate buyers of the preferred issues as well as KKR were defrauded in order to reward and retain the loyalty of this select group of fund and institutional investment managers, who had purchased the preferred. MacPherson Investments purchased the warrants at 8.8 cents per warrant in January 1986 as part of the financing of the Storer LBO; it purchased additional shares in early 1986 from General Electric for 80 cents per share. It later sold them for $2.50 per warrant, an increase of 41 percent.

The fund managers and fiduciaries had not informed their employing organizations of their purchases and therefore there was no approval of the purchase, which is necessary under disclosure law. Drexel employees did not file the appropriate forms to report their purchases of these securities. Furthermore "there were restrictions on the investing in securities by members of the trading department that made a market in those securities without the express consent of the department head or, in the case of a department head of the senior officer of the firm" (p. 1050).

Atlantic Capital purchased some of the Storer preferred and thus ended up with SCI warrants. This equity was later sold to MacPherson Investments, Joseph testified (p. 1053). Drexel also bought some of the SCI preferred and thus had a right to purchase warrants, but that right was not known to anyone outside of certain employees in the High-Yield Bond Department. There was no indication in the firm's books and records that it had that right other than a "letter of agreement," which was sent to Atlantic Capital when it originally bought the preferred and the associated warrants. But when Drexel, under government subpoena, conducted a search of its records, it could not find the agreement. A copy was not filed in the High-Yield Bond Department, nor with Drexel in general (p. 1055). Thus Milken had subverted equity that Drexel should have owned.

Joseph testified that he did not know about MacPherson Investments until Craig Cogut, the external legal counsel for the High-Yield Bond Department, informed him in October or November 1988. The fraud had taken place in the last half of 1985, some three years earlier. Drexel had a policy that its employees could not give favored treatment to managers and fiduciaries of institutional investor accounts. But these rules were ignored and there was evidence that when the corporation knew of non-compliance it did not enforce these rules.

Drexel's Fees

Drexel's fees were substantial. In the Storer transactions they were in the magnitude of between $40 and $50 million. But the fees were often multiplied by two when Drexel worked for both the buyer and the seller in a merger. Drexel is known to have been Ronald O. Perelman's investment banker. In 1985, Milken helped Perelman take over Revlon. When Perelman needed a buyer for Revlon's troubled Technicon unit, Milken introduced him to Parker G. Montgomery, also a client of Milken's. Montgomery bought the Technicon unit from Revlon for his company, Cooper Development. In February 1987, *Business Week* reported the fees that Drexel received as described in the prospectus (Hamilton and Dobrzynski 1987). From the 1986 sale, Drexel advised Cooper Development for a fee of $1.5 million in its bid to buy Technicon. Drexel pocketed $9 million to place the $300 million junk bond issue that paid for Technicon. Drexel served as underwriter for CooperVision common stock and other bond issues. Through Drexel Investors, it held an "indirect" interest in Cooper Technicon. Finally, a Drexel employee sits on the board of Cooper Technicon, now the main subsidiary of Cooper Development, with the standard salary for board members.

In October 1986, Montgomery tried to merge Cooper Development and LaserSonics. A Drexel representative sat across the table from him acting as financial adviser for LaserSonics. LaserSonics paid Drexel $200,000 to provide a fairness opinion on Montgomery's offer. The question was, In which corporation's interest did Drexel operate? Certainly, if not a real conflict of interest, such a network of advising relationships gives the appearance of conflict of interest.

CONCLUSIONS

By late 1978, the demand for high-yield bonds had far outpaced the supply. Eleven high-yield bond mutual funds had been created. Less than two years after Drexel sold its first junk bond offering, Texas International Company, there was a $2 billion market. Drexel was at the center of the transactions that produced the market.

Milken, but not Drexel, had maximum control over his operation. He had created a financial instrument, junk bonds to be used in LBOs. He could execute the sale of the bonds efficiently through the use of "highly confident" letters. He controlled an extensive network of issuers and buyers. He controlled the trading capital of Drexel and privately held partnerships. He had a knowledge of the market and knew the price of each bond and the prices at which it had traded. He knew and had created many of the financial trading instruments that were being adopted for LBOs across the investment banking industry. He had developed not only a most lucrative incentive system for his traders, but one that bound employees to the department. He had control over the decision-making for his department and had broken the authority by which Drexel tried to constrain his actions. Through this power base he gained autonomy from the bureaucracy and supervision of the home office in New York. This autonomy from Drexel and the use of fraud networks allowed Milken to function efficiently and effectively on behalf of his department and the employee partnerships.

The internal transactions of Drexel were taking place within a hierarchy of authority where the profit center managers were struggling for rewards and status. This struggle was intense because of the implementation of a reward system in the form of salary increases, bonuses, commissions, and participation in private partnerships that was based on not only profit center performance but individual performance. The departments were placed in a primarily competitive relationship with each other. This relationship is consistent with exchange autonomy (Eccles and White 1988) and agency theory (Williamson 1975). Both are based on the premise that the greater corporate good comes from each profit center manager's pursuing his or her own self-interest, a management philosophy in keeping with the political economy of Adam Smith. This philosophy remains appropriate where profit center interdependencies are small and the pursuit of self-interest does not lead to locally optimal decisions that are suboptimal for the firm as a whole. Both of these conditions were absent at Drexel.

Contrary to the organizational theory notion that autonomy leads to success, in the case of the High-Yield Bond Department success (i.e., profitability) led to autonomy and autonomy led to greater control over the subunit and to subunit efficiency (through both legal and illegal means). Instead of structure leading to strategy as Chandler would have us believe, strategy led to structure and control.

Fligstein (1990a) found that manufacturing firms moved toward integrated structures and conceptions of control. However, Drexel's strategy for control was financial, a method consistent with the holding company form, but inconsistent with the departmental form of Drexel's structure. Drexel was divided into departmental units each controlled by profit as the ultimate goal. Upper-level management delegated decisions to the department heads and attempted to maintain control through the allocation of rewards and control of integrated functions. When it lost control of these functions to the department, it tried to regain it through peer supervision in the form of the Underwriters Advisory Committee. Through control of the strategic contingency of corporate profits, the High-Yield Bond Department successfully functionally differentiated and then spatially differentiated itself from the New York headquarters. It then duplicated the various functions of the corporation (accounting, legal, etc.) but more importantly it constructed control mechanisms that reversed the direction of normal control from the corporation to its subunit, resulting in subunit control over the corporation with extensive contradictions of structure and decision-making. As a consequence the goals of the subunit (profit) were sustained at the expense of corporate goals (growth and later survival). The formal structures such as the Underwriter's Advisory Committee, the Chinese wall, and compliance were subverted to the benefit of profit. As corporate control diminished, the High-Yield Bond Department was able to create alternative structures (the Boesky collaboration and the private partnerships) to facilitate deals and thus meet employee goals of larger compensation packages. Incentive structures that were designed to create loyalty to the corporation functioned to create loyalty to the subunit, because Milken controlled their allocation. They were of such a magnitude that individual compensation and subunit profits were more important than the survival of Drexel. These rewards caused employees to place the corporation at risk in two ways: (1) the risk associated with the deals and (2) fraudulent acts through the networks discussed in Chapter 2.

Rational models of organizations might lead us to assume that a growth in bureaucratic structures to multidivisional/multinational globalized firms would mean greater control and therefore a reduction in fraud; that bureaucratization of ownership means that the markets are dominated by rule-bound institutions permeated by professional ideologies. In this kind of system it would be assumed that the scale also acts as a check on fraud; that gross fraud would rarely occur in large corporations because fraud is characteristically a solitary vice, committed by a few in secrecy. The routinization of policies and procedures, and formalization of rules and modes of decision-making in bureaucracies are obstacles to fraud, as they are to other types of innovative behavior. The dominance of sophisticated and highly educated personnel should provide strong incentive to ethical practices and high standards.

However, the enactment of bureaucracy and crime are both political processes in which some actors come to control the organization through control over strategic resources, positions, the organizational structure, and information. In Drexel's case the fraud was not the result of one person's behavior, but became embedded in the standard operating procedures of the organization. Bureaucratization may either raise standards of conduct or, in the case of Drexel where structure and decision-making were in contradiction, routinize corrupt conduct in a way that makes it difficult to recognize and reform. These procedures and ways of making decisions become established ways of doing business, a part of the corporate culture of the organization. In some cases this corrupt culture extends to one department only, in other cases it extends through the entire organization. Chapters 1 and 2 of this book demonstrate that in the case of Drexel, it extended to the organization and outside the organization to a network of organizations. In the case of Braithwaite's (1984) analysis of pharmaceutical companies, it extended to the entire industry.

It is important to keep in mind that the disarticulation of the High-Yield Bond Department from the corporate structures of Drexel served the function of decentralizing the power of Drexel over the department. The High-Yield Bond Department became disarticulated from the corporate structure in which it had developed, and in turn, began to coopt the corporate structure to function on its behalf. The horizontal and vertical differentiation, the spatial separation, and the high levels of vertical and horizontal communication are all characteristics that facilitate innovation (Hage and Aiken 1967; Zaltman, Duncan, and Holbeck 1973). Innovation may take positive forms, such as inventing new junk bond markets and program change, or it may take negative forms, such as new methods of fraud. Structural facilitation knows no differences between legal and illegal acts, between actions that lead to positive or negative outcomes.

NOTES

11. The deal is a process. Parts of the deal are often executed by different departments. Often M&A obtains the deal, Trading and Sales sell the bonds, and bankers close the deal. The departmental lines are important because later the reader will find that Milken takes over all of these functions!

Chapter 5

The Nature of Securities Transactions
and Market Control

Weber saw capitalism and bureaucracies developing together, emerging side by side as parts of the same rational processes. However, Williamson (1975) understood hierarchies as alternatives to markets, markets being the more rational (self-interested) process. Although these two scholars do not define rationality in the same way, they both contribute to our understanding of the relationship between markets and firms. As a third perspective on the relationship between markets and firms, I wish to examine how corporations though both fraudulent and nonfraudulent actions can be understood as mechanisms for controlling market transactions. Corporations use their resources to control the competitiveness of the market in which they do business in multiple ways. We will examine eight of these mechanisms: (1) unequal access to information, (2) elimination of competition through diversification, (3) vertical integration and vertical disintegration, (4) predatory pricing, (5) political influences, (6) control over uncertainty of the client's environment, (7) control over techniques that manipulate the market, and (8) purchase of employee loyalty. After we have examined the characteristics of securities transactions that can encourage fraud, we will examine the ways that corporations control competitiveness and afford opportunities for fraud.

CHARACTERISTICS OF TRANSACTIONS AT DREXEL

Although interorganizational relations receive intense scrutiny and analysis (Aldrich 1979; Pfeffer and Salancik 1978), misconduct and unlawful transactions between organization are seldom analyzed from an interorganizational perspective (for exceptions, see Zey 1989; Vaughan

1983). Focusing on securities fraud reveals some neglected but critical elements of interorganizational relations: The nature of transactions, methods of communicating transactions, and methods of monitoring transactions afford opportunity for, facilitate, and in some cases generate unlawful interorganizational relationships. The nature of securities transactions themselves contribute greatly to the ability of investment bankers and other corporations to control markets. Securities transactions are characterized by twelve major attributes that facilitate fraud. Some of these characteristics may apply to other types of transactions, but the following generalizations were drawn from the transactions in the networks that I studied and are therefore more specifically applicable to securities transactions, including those in other financial capital firms such as savings and loans. One would not expect them to apply to industrial capital corporations.

1. Control of Strategic Contingencies

A firm is vulnerable to the misconduct of another firm when it has no alternative firm with which a transaction can be made. A deal must be made with a specific partner regardless of whether it is performed legally or illegally. Thus, one organization controls strategic contingencies that are necessary for its transaction partners to do business.

A single department, some believe a single person, controlled the strategic contingency that gave Drexel its power. The High-Yield Bond Department supplied the financing for the third-level subordinate debt for the M&A deals that Drexel underwrote. Even KKR, the most powerful M&A company of the 1980s, depended on Drexel to finance this debt for its largest takeovers. Perhaps Kravis said it best after he found that Milken and associates' partnerships had skimmed Storer warrants, which KKR had agreed to make part of the deal to reduce the risk to the ultimate buyers of the highly risky debt. The government attorney thought that, since Milken had convinced KKR to sweeten the offer with these warrants, Kravis would be angry that Milken had skimmed them before the debt was sold. Kravis could not afford to get angry. He knew no other investment banker had a network large enough to sell the high-yield Storer debt. He said, "We just wanted to get the deal done" (U.S. v. Michael Milken 1990a, p. 1098). Drexel controlled the strategic contingency of financing the third and last portion of the deal. Kravis had no competitive alternative.

2. Control of Functional Alternatives

Milken's privately held partnerships controlled a critical functional alternative. When Joseph decided that Drexel could not make good on his promise to underwrite a deal because of the risk involved, Milken turned to his privately held partnerships, which had ample resources to underwrite even the largest deals for his best customers. When Joseph decided not to underwrite KKR's takeover of Storer, Milken turned to his functional alternative and with Joseph's consent financed the takeover (*U.S. v. Michael Milken* 1990a).

3. Numerous and Complex Transactions

Numerous and complex transactions often inhibit the organization's ability to discriminate between legal and illegal actions. When the transactions are numerous and complex, there may be no normative standard for the conduct. Information about the transaction may be incomplete, or information may exist, but the organization may not be able to process it or may not be able to apply it to the circumstances of the particular transaction taking place. The organization may have to make decisions about transactions when it is not at all certain that these transactions should be made.

The numerous and complex transactions are a perfect morass in which to embed illegal transactions. A small number of Drexel's transactions may have been illegal, but they were difficult to detect because they were so few among so many. If a firm operates legally most of the time, it is hard to determine when or even if it operates illegally because there are so many complex transactions to examine.

4. Specialized Methods of Trading

The methods of trading securities are specialized transaction processes. The securities move from the seller to the investment banking firm to the buyer in a progression so that the buyer cannot know the nature of the securities or what the seller intended. Because the fund managers and savings and loan officers who purchased Storer high-yield bonds did not know that Storer had designated millions of dollars in warrants to be sold as a sweetener with the bonds, some of them were unaware that the warrants had been skimmed off by the MacPherson and other partnerships on the way to the customer. They were at the mercy of Drexel and the High-Yield Bond Department for ethical treatment.

5. Transaction Processes Are Invisible

These intricate and specialized transaction processes do not leave a paper trail. They are computerized transactions in which the recording method is arbitrary and unique for each firm. No two firms have the same methods of recording the buying and selling of securities. Because the recording process is invisible and nonpublic, fraud is often undetectable. Practices are elusive. Indeed, the fact that these transactions are elusive gives the trader a sense of security about communicating insider information because of the known difficulty of detection.

6. Systematic Monitoring Is Impossible

These invisible transactions are almost impossible for the SEC and district attorneys to monitor. What they can monitor is the accounting records kept by the firm. As we know (Hirsch 1986; Carruthers and Espeland 1991) accounting records not only serve to rationalize organizational decisions, they are also symbolic myths used to legitimize the organization's interpretation of its transactions to the external environment (Meyer and Rowan 1977). Boesky's bookkeeper and chief accountant, Setrag Mooradian, presented the formal accounting records to the auditor. What the auditor did not know at the beginning was that there was another set of records in which the many transactions between Boesky and Milken were recorded: for example, Boesky's parking for Milken and Boesky's trading on Milken's behalf. Because no actual paper exchanges took place, the transactions were impossible to monitor.

7. Monitoring is General

The volume and diversity of daily transactions between securities firms and their clients and customers make rules and procedures necessary for the routinization of exchanges. In the same manner that formalization develops to coordinate and control intraorganizational activities, formalization emerges as a mechanism by which organizations attempt to cope with the variety and multiplicity of interactions with other organizations in their networks.

In order to standardize and make these complex transactions more efficient, technology was developed for recording and processing these complex transactions—both accounting procedures and computing systems. Transactions are encoded in special language created for processing, storing, and retrieving masses of information. Because of the specialization of buyers, sellers, and investment bankers, organizations vary in both the rules and procedures governing exchanges, and accounting procedures and computing systems created to keep track of transactions. Not only does this make it difficult for regulatory agencies such as the SEC to monitor these transactions, it is even difficult for the parties to the exchange to monitor them. Finally, it is nearly impossible for an organization such as Drexel to monitor the numerous transactions that take place in all of its departments and, at the same time, maintain efficiency. Monitoring would require additional documentation and personnel and a requisite slowing of transaction time.

The SEC monitors these transactions only at known points of trouble. The monitoring process does not observe each transaction or even a systematic sample of firms or transactions within a firm. It monitors some problem organizations and some trouble spots in markets, but the process is in no way systematic or complete. For most securities organizations, most of the time, monitoring of their transactions and accounting is nonexistent. This leaves the organization free to engage in innovative transactions that are sometimes unlawful.

8. Transactions Based on Trust

In spite of all the complexities of modern securities transactions and their invisible nature, these transactions are based upon a considerable amount of trust. No matter what the degree of supervisory restriction imposed on employees, elements of trust remain. If strict controls were imposed on all corporate personnel, then embezzlement, management fraud, and other illegal conduct would be greatly reduced, but very little business would be done. Because of organizational constraints to monitoring, trust becomes a concomitant to interorganizational exchange almost by default. Monitoring by firms themselves becomes a matter of observation based on sampling and spot checks, tapping indicators that will lead to discovery of fraud.

KKR must trust Drexel. When a firm that is dealing in good faith is actually unknowingly dealing with a firm that secretly acts fraudulently, it may not discover the fraud for months, years, or ever. On the other hand, in the securities industry, when a firm acts fraudulently, it must collude with other firms that act fraudulently. It must network with other firms that are willing to make unlawful transactions. These unlawful transactions must also be based on trust. Drexel and Milken had to trust Boesky in order to commit fraud. These relationships of trust are developed over long periods of time, through multiple and complex transactions. They are based on being able to count on the other person and the other organization in critical times when there are billions of dollars hanging in the balance. These relationships become formalized as does the method of communication used.

9. When Doing Fraud, Exchanges Often Do Not Exist

When a transaction is known to be fraudulent, the parties do not actually make an exchange. They credit the score card of the other party, to be drawn down at a later time. Since Milken did not actually give Boesky money, but rather gave him information and services and commitment to reimburse funds lost, there was no actual transaction. On the other side, Boesky was charging Milken fees for trading, the use of his money, and manipulating the market. Hundreds of transactions were made by Boesky on Milken's behalf, but no financial exchange was made between them. If these transactions had been legal, the actual exchanges between Milken and Boesky would have taken place as the transactions took place. Only in the final analysis of settling the balance sheet did money have to change hands. When Boesky wrote Milken the check for the difference in the accounts, the process was visible for the first, and possibly only time.

Capital transactions can exist by agreement alone. If no paper or computer trail is left and nothing changes hands between the parties of the transaction, then it is impossible to detect the transaction. Thus when Boesky paid Milken the $5.3 million in order to balance their books, numerous transactions had taken place, but money had not changed hands and there were no records of these transactions. There was only the accounting of Boesky's bookkeeper, Mooradian, and Milken's bookkeeper, Thurnher. The two were very careful to pay each other with trades or favors. Thus it was stupid for Boesky to write Milken a check for $5.3 million in March 1986, because for the first time there was evidence of their secret arrangement. It gave the government a clue about where to begin to trace the transactions. Milken had to cover the mistake by billing Boesky for consulting—another formal document that was detectable by the government.

10. Methods of Communication Are Cryptic

The method of communication becomes formalized and cryptic. Traders may communicate with each other several times a day or even several times an hour in a specialized professional language that the common person, as well as the courts, have a difficult time decoding. The meanings of words and phrases become established, based on large numbers of past interactions. Little needs to be said. When Peter Gardiner called Davidoff, Boesky's head trader, and asked for a "favor," Davidoff knew that this was an off-the-record transaction, that it would be recorded in the *unofficial* records, and that Milken would make good on any losses Boesky incurred as a consequence. These transactions were coded in specialized language created for processing, storage, and retrieval in a separate system from the legal transactions that were carried on by these two organizations.

11. Transactor Is Invisible and Impersonal

Computers are a direct link to organizational resources. The skillful thief does not have to be present, execute the theft at the time of the transaction, or personally take possession of the diverted funds. Thus the actor can be separated from the act in distance, in time, and by interstitial transactions through dummy corporations, which are difficult to trace. The impersonal nature of computerized theft, the efficiency of transactions, and the ability to recode the system to disguise illegal transfers all facilitate illegal conduct.

12. Technology Is Sophisticated

Complex methods for recording and processing transactions present opportunities for violation. Highly diversified companies with numerous businesses have complex accounting procedures that allow creative accounting—and thus fraud. The tendency of accounting procedures to facilitate unlawful behavior has been exacerbated by the advent and proliferation of computers and other electronic equipment, which dominate securities firms. While these new technologies complete and record transactions with increased speed and efficiency, they simultaneously offer faster and more efficient ways to misappropriate funds and alter records.

SYSTEM INTERFACE PROBLEMS

These characteristics do not by themselves explain why securities fraud occurs. While all investment banking firms have the same transaction characteristics with which to deal, they do not all become involved in fraud. Likewise, these transaction characteristics do not explain why the High-Yield Bond Department chose legal means of conducting business on some occasions and illegal means on other occasions.

The answer lies at least partially with the organization's interface with the market. Many times the rules of the market and the need of the organization to complete the deal meshed and there was no reason to resort to actions outside the law. However, if Drexel could not complete the transaction, it was left with the transaction costs and no return on capital. In some cases the transaction costs were not high because Drexel had already collected large portions of the fees, but an incomplete transaction could be disastrous in initiating the next deal, because news of failure travels fast and reputation among issuers is important.

For example, when Wickes wanted to force an exchange of common stock for the more desirable preferred stock of its shareholders, Drexel was left in a situation in which it was at the mercy of the market. In order to save Wickes $15 million in dividends, Wickes common stock had to close above 6–1/8 for twenty of thirty consecutive days. On the twenty-eighth day of the thirty-day period, the market on Wickes had closed at 6–1/8 or above for only nineteen days. It had to close above 6–1/8 in one of the next two days.

Milken and the convertible bond department had tried to sell Wickes common stock all day in order to increase the closing price of Wickes. They had contacted all of their buyers and still the market in Wickes was below the magical price of 6–1/8. The market was not working for them. Drexel required an immediate completion of the transaction in order to close the deal for Wickes, and Milken went outside the regular market mechanisms to make it happen.

After working through normal market channels for nearly a month, the High-Yield Bond Department was down to the last hour on the next to the last day to complete the deal. Gardiner testified that Milken asked him as well as others to look for "unsolicited" buyers of Wickes common. (It was against the law for Drexel to solicit buyers of stock in which they were dealing.) In the last hour before the market closed on March 23, 1986, when Milken knew that it could not close above 6–1/8, he called Maultasch in New York and asked him to call Boesky (*U.S. v. Michael Milken* 1990a, pp. 239–66). Before the market closed, they had completed a series of four calls to ask Boesky to buy additional shares of Wickes common stock. Boesky bought a total of 1.9 million shares of Wickes common stock in the last hour before the market closed, resulting in the market closing up, at 6–1/8. This triggered the conversion of Wickes preferred for Wickes common. Drexel made the market work for Wickes.

Drexel was unable to devote direct resources to a legitimate resolution of the problem. Legally it could not buy the stock itself. Nor was it legal for Drexel to solicit the sale of Wickes common stock. Yet it had to effect the purchase of the stock within a two-day period in order for the conversion to transpire. The market was inflexible and unresponsive to Wickes's and Drexel's needs and could not be legally negotiated. Thus Drexel resorted to manipulating the market unlawfully in order to complete the transaction its customer required.

Drexel's reputation was in danger, and the stakes were high. If the market had not closed at 6–1/8 or above, the preferred stock, which carried a high dividend, would not have been converted and Wickes would have had to pay out $15 million in dividends. If Wickes's resources were diminished, it would not only be costly for Wickes, but it would ultimately mean that Wickes would have diminished resources to continue its acquisition process, which would in turn hurt or at least not help Drexel. Drexel had a great deal to gain from causing Boesky to manipulate the market in Wickes stock.

Boesky purchased the stock in his organization's name to conceal the real identity of the owner. Milken unlawfully used the resources of Boesky's organization. Boesky misrepresented the stock as his in reporting its purchase to the SEC. Since Boesky was not linked to Milken in any way that was detectable by those outside their organizations, it would be difficult to prove that Milken had caused Boesky to purchase Wickes common stock on his behalf. There was a low probability of detection—any evidence could be considered circumstantial. The communication with Boesky's organization was through Michael Davidoff, Boesky's head trader, and then it was so cryptic and vague as to be difficult to prove its meaning. The nature of some transactions was known only to Boesky and Milken and was shrouded in such secrecy in the organization that even Davidoff and Peter Gardiner disagreed about which organization should incur the losses as the stock adjusted to its real market value after the conversion was triggered.

The Storer transaction is another example of system interface problems that cause transaction irregularities. In this case, the interface problem was between the High Yield Bond Department and Drexel. Milken had worked up the deal with Storer. All that was left was the underwriting of the third-level subordinate debt by Drexel. When Milken laid the deal out to the New York office, Joseph informed Milken that Drexel would not be able to underwrite the debt. Milken had already issued a "highly confident" letter and made a commitment to KKR that Drexel would underwrite the takeover of Storer. Milken had made a commitment, but Drexel did not want to risk its resources on this deal. Milken could either let the deal fall through or find another way to finance the third-level debt.

Milken then put together the MacPherson Partnership, which underwrote the high-yield debt as KKR took over Storer. As detailed earlier, the deal was complete, but the bonds were run through MacPherson and the warrants were skimmed off. KKR was defrauded, because it was led to believe that the warrants were necessary in order to sell the junk bonds. The funds that bought the bonds were defrauded, because they should have been the recipients of the warrants. Kravis of KKR, when told much later that the warrants had not gone to the buyers of the bonds, rationalized that he had to have the capital and that getting the deal closed was more important than who got the warrants. Drexel explained the irregularity by saying that the private partnerships had taken considerable risk by underwriting this transaction and that they were entitled to the equity.

If Drexel had been able to underwrite the transaction, there would have been much less opportunity for fraud because the bonds and warrants would have traveled through Drexel, where they would have been visible to both the New York and Beverly Hills offices. When the system interface problem between the High-Yield Bond Department and Drexel occurred, Milken took care of the problem by creating a functional alternative to Drexel that would do the deal he had pending. This alternative did not have the same internal control structures as an investment banking firm, nor was it subject to regulation by the SEC as was Drexel. The partnership not only allowed Milken to resolve the interface problem but also facilitated the skimming of the warrants. When transactions are complex and monitoring is general and nonsystematic, organizations can resolve problems, such as blocked transactions, through fraudulent actions.

Summary of Transaction Characteristics and Fraud

When transactions between organizations are strategic to their functioning, functional alternatives to external resources, complex and numerous, specialized, invisible, difficult to monitor, based on trust, cryptic, computerized, or insubstantial, they provide opportunity for illegal conduct. However, it is reasonable to assume that the potential for violations of the law increases when these characteristics combine. When a large number of these factors interact to provide opportunities for unlawful behavior then the *transaction system* of the organization facilitates the illegal behavior. The organization is thus supporting illegal behavior.

When the crime is of such magnitude and complexity that it requires a network of organizations for its execution, the public can only see small parts of the crime at a single viewing. Thus the offense often appears to be reduced to the act of an individual actor or a few actors. In many cases the characteristics of the organization both allow opportunities for and facilitate the fraud. But characteristics of the transactions and the networks are equally as important. The crime is lodged in the relationship between organizations. In these interorganizational fraud networks, both victims and perpetrators are organizations.

CORPORATIONS AS MECHANISMS OF MARKET CONTROL

Many of the assumptions of the neoclassical economic model (the pure market economy model) are not valid for the market transactions carried on by economic organizations. An understanding of where these assumptions break down will help us understand how fraud occurs.

Unequal Access to Information

The neoclassical model, which Williamson takes as a point of departure, assumes that market mechanisms rest on equal access to information. Anyone should be able to trade on any information he or she has because of the assumption of equal access. But many times the buyer has information deficits; and the costs of making up the deficits are prohibitive. For example, equal information would mean that when buying Drexel-issued high-yield bonds from the sale of Storer and Beatrice, a fund manager would know that the fund was to receive the equity kicker that KKR provided to entice buyers. This is a part of the value of the bond purchase. But the fund manager had no way of acquiring this information. Neither organizational controls within Drexel nor SEC regulations reduced the inequality of information. Thus some of the mechanism that should have been built in to overcome the inefficiencies of the market transaction were not. For example, SEC filings could have been required to carry information about what is offered with a trade, including sweeteners. Mechanisms that are built into market transactions to "increase efficiency" can be used to defraud the market.

Interference with Competition

Competition and cooperation are concepts that assist us in differentiating between ideal markets and corporations. In neoclassical economic theory, perfect competition requires that actors act in their own self-interest and that there are many economic units so that no single unit can affect the prices of goods. In addition the ideal model assumes that transactions are isolated, ephemeral, impersonal, unaffected by context, and based on complete information. Competition eliminates inefficiencies in the market. As each buyer and seller seeks to maximize profits and minimize costs, both overpriced and underpriced goods are eliminated.

But it will become obvious in the next two chapters that the economy does not function according to the neoclassical model. In contemporary society, vertical integration, horizontal integration, diversification, and conglomerations are organizational mechanisms that transform and redefine markets.

Some markets are more important to the economy of a country at some times than are other markets. For example, during periods in which industrial expansion is defined in terms of LBOs, the junk bond market becomes critical because it provides access to the key debt instrument. When a holding company builds a portfolio of unrelated firms, the competitor is no longer someone in the same industry sector who is buying the same materials and courting the same buyers but anyone who has access to capital to fund takeovers. A holding company gains control over the capital market, not the product market. Thus, if KKR had access to the investment bank that controlled 40–65 percent of the high-yield bond market, it controlled the essential capital market.

Drexel not only controlled the junk bond market, it could intervene in the competitive process of the takeover. The High-Yield Bond Department at Drexel had the advantage of being able to manipulate the perception of competitors and the target. Through Milken/Boesky collaborations, Milken could present the appearance that a fierce arbitrager (a competitor of the highest order) was attempting to take over a target, thus forcing the target into the arms of Drexel's client. The client would pay a higher price as a result of a bidding war with the (putative) competitors. Fees to Drexel were based on the price paid by the client. Thus the Milken/Boesky collaboration inflated the fees paid Drexel through the High-Yield Bond Department. In addition, Boesky would sell the stock of the target just before the deal was closed by Drexel, which netted the Milken/Boesky collaboration substantial profits.

Drexel had eliminated competition by diversifying to incorporate firms that gave the pretense of being competitors and thereby controlling the price.

Vertical Integration/Vertical Disintegration

If we concede to Coase's ([1937] 1988), Williamson's (1975), and North's (1990) arguments that firms arose as a way of controlling the anarchy of market competition, we can understand how firms took on characteristics that were not in accordance with the classical and neoclassical principles of competition. The extent to which a firm can control competition is controversial among organizational theorists. Although I do not think that firms arose as a result of a need to control competition, I do think that firms as well as markets are socially constructed. Firms deal with the anarchy of competition in the market by absorbing transaction costs.

These three institutional economists and Neil Fligstein (1990a) demonstrate that many transactions that were previously carried out in the market are now lodged in the firm. According to Coase, "firms will emerge to organize what would otherwise be market transactions whenever the costs of organizing a transaction become less than the costs of carrying it through the market" (1937, p. 7). This view is consistent with the vertical integration of the post–World War II period of U.S. capitalism, in which firms bought their suppliers, their distributors, their retailers, and their franchisers. When the product is capital as it has been in the last fifteen years, a similar process occurs. New firms emerged in the 1980s, which were called *venture investment bankers*. They not only provided capital for ventures, but actively participated in the decision-making and recruiting of the firms they financed. They provided consulting and helped to target firms for their client's takeover. They were fully integrated firms that dealt in what had been market transactions. They were integrated above the product level at the financial level.

A securities firm can limit its market transactions and reduce its uncertainty or access to its suppliers and customers through vertical integration. It substitutes vertical integration for external procurement of resources and services. If a firm integrates vertically, it has control over the inputs it needs from the external environment as well as a built-in market for its output. Thus the firm has reduced its price competition by eliminating transactions with the external environment, which can be not only expensive but uncertain. This gives the firm greater control over price, because it is setting the price for thousands of transactions it would have to perform with the marketplace.

Milken vertically integrated the High-Yield Bond Department by hiring its own legal counsel, accountants, bookkeepers, underwriters, and compliance officers. Although the New York office performed each of these functions for Drexel as a whole, the bond department by operating as a separate division not only gained control of the environment external to Drexel but limited the control of the home office. At the same time, the High-Yield Bond Department was vertically disintegrated from the rest of Drexel in order to limit Drexel's control over the high-yield bond operation. The bond department routinely charged the New York office high prices—some thought higher prices than the New York office would have paid in the marketplace, for comparable services.

The High-Yield Bond Department vertically integrated its issuers and buyers, and when it could not control the price by legal means, Milken constructed alternative controls over these transactions—the fraud networks. As Williamson (1975) points out, economic actors can be more efficient if they absorb many of the costs of exchanges and manage rather than engage in transactions. Instead of relying on the pricing mechanisms in the external market, managers direct their resources to controlling the market, sometimes lawfully and sometimes unlawfully.

Diversification

The boundaries between the junk bond market and Drexel's High-Yield Bond Department were virtually nonexistent, since the market was created and fueled by Drexel and in turn sustained Drexel and a few other powerful investment banking firms. Drexel did not have to make the transition from product-producing to money-producing as did many firms. That is, it did not have to make the transition from making decisions and policies about production, to making decisions and policies about distribution and marketing, to resolving uncertainties about capital.

Paradoxically the antitrust regulation that Fligstein (1990a) defines as the determinant of the transformation from the marketing conception to the financial conception of control of firms reduced horizontal and vertical integration. By law, a firm could not acquire another firm or portion of a firm that produced a product that it needed or that could enhance its production line. Growth began to bring on expansion through the acquisition of unrelated firms—diversification. The commodities produced had no value to the holding company. They were of value only because they could be turned into capital for the corporation to acquire what was of value—more capital. The newly acquired corporation had to show a profit in a short time or it would be sold. Each diverse entity was evaluated on its short-term performance and ability to generate surplus capital (p. 193).

A corporation had to be certain that its price-to-earnings ratio was not too high or it would become a target. It had to maintain a considerable amount of debt to keep from becoming too attractive.

Acquiring firms became capital markets. They themselves internalized capital markets by becoming commodities for national and internal trade. Each newly acquired corporation was a capital producer or loser. The corporations that were held by the acquiring firm had nothing in common with each other. Fligstein called these "the central banks" for their subsidiaries. "Growth in the firm is produced by investing in products that provide a relatively high rate of return. When product lines do not perform, they are sold" (p. 193).

These firms could not regulate themselves, as we learned in Chapter 4, and they were socially inefficient, as we learned in Chapter 3. In the case of American firms, this resulted in the closing of plants and the loss of American jobs, extremely high corporate debt, a failure to invest in the expansion of production facilities, and the abolishing of research and development. All of these lead ultimately to the deterioration of long-range profits and to national recession, if not depression.

Predatory Pricing

Conventional wisdom is that, as organizations expand in size and gain large market shares, they are able to limit access to the market through predatory pricing. That is, because they control a large market share and have the advantage of large amounts of capital, they can lower the price of the commodity they sell and drive competitors, who are operating on a smaller scale and require larger profit margins, out of business.

Drexel was similarly able to limit its competition through predatory pricing, not by reducing its price but by raising so much capital that no other investment banking firm could compete with it. Drexel limited its competition through its control over access to capital and information. Thus no matter to what level the price was driven, the issuer had to pay Drexel's commission because no other investment banker could underwrite the third-level debt and create a market for the bonds.

To insure the elimination of competitors, Drexel often used Boesky to drive the price of the stock, and therefore the acquisition, above the ceiling at which other investment bankers could compete. Thus by using Boesky and the covert transactions of the Milken/Boesky collaboration, Drexel was able to further reduce the effects of the market through predatory pricing. When competitors entered the market, Milken could cause Boesky to buy on his undisclosed behalf and drive the price of the stock so high that competitors could not raise the capital to do the deal because they did not have access to buyers and could not sell the debt.

Political Power to Limit Competition

In Chapter 7, we will discover that through indirect networks with Keating and others, Drexel had access to select congressmen who not only made the laws under which securities fraud was prosecuted but also influenced the regulation of some of their bond buyers.

Through Keating, Milken was indirectly linked to the regulators of the savings and loans. Both Keating and Drexel made large campaign contributions to key congressmen, who allegedly intervened on behalf of LSL in attempts to persuade regulators of the solvency of the insolvent bank, and to pressure the regulatory board to increase the legal limits on the portion of the bank's assets that could be held in high-risk, high-yield securities.

At the same time Congress was involved in influencing the regulation of Drexel's savings and loan clients, it was attempting to reform RICO, the most stringent law under which securities fraud is prosecuted. Both Keating and Milken were indicted under RICO and were making large campaign contributions to Senator Dennis DeConcini, who wrote the reform of the RICO bill, and his colleague Alan Cranston (Zey 1990). Some, though not all, of these contributions were made through legal political action committee (PAC) contributions. Others were made through illegal contributions, some of which were returned to Keating and Milken when discovered by the media (see Chapter 7).

Control over Efficiency of Transaction and Issuer's Uncertainty

"Highly Confident" Letters. Drexel was able to limit its competition and establish loyalty among clients by issuing "highly confident" letters. Drexel devised "highly confident" letters as a method of quickly tapping a segment of the placement market for high-yield bonds when doing a deal. An undercapitalized acquirer such as Carl Icahn or T. Boone Pickens could enhance the credibility of his bid by obtaining a letter stating that Drexel was highly confident that it could raise a specified amount of capital to help finance a tender offer. Drexel would then obtain commitments from its network of investors to purchase these unregistered, unrated bonds immediately prior to the takeover.

Immediately after the takeover, the securities would be registered with the SEC and become tradeable, affording the network of buyers a market for the securities. These securities would typically consist of various levels of subordinated debt with high rates of interest. In some cases the debt carried high rates of interest, which issuers paid by selling off the assets of the target (Kuhn 1990).

Until the very end, Milken never defaulted on a "highly confident" letter. Typically, when such letters were issued, Drexel had not yet sold the bonds, but the bond issuer was certain that its bonds had a market— that Drexel could raise the capital to support the takeover. The client had higher assurances of acquiring the capital than if it had to compete in the market. Thus clients were often biased toward Milken and later became loyal repeat clients because Milken made good on his promises to raise their capital. This in turn contributed to the growth of Drexel and the Milken partnerships and allowed them to be even more confident about the size of the deals that could be underwritten and the fees and interest rates that could be charged.

Competitors were limited because they could not assure the sale of the bonds as efficiently as Drexel. They did not have the established network of buyers. Milken did not have to actually contact his customers—he knew he had a market for the bonds. Thus Drexel controlled efficiency and a sizable market for its clients.

Bridge Loans and Merchant Banking. Another tactic used by Drexel was that of the *bridge loan*. A bridge loan is intended to be interim financing. It is high priced and limited term, typically no longer than six months, and induces the issuer to find more permanent financing immediately after the deal is closed. If the loan is extended, it is at an increasing rate of interest.

The bridge loan is typically the most subordinate debt that is held on the issuer and therefore is the highest risk. Because of this, the holder can charge a fee of 1 to 3 percent for assuring the loan. On large deals, Drexel often made bridge loans. Drexel was itself highly leveraged and therefore its capacity to provide bridge funding was limited. If Drexel could not make the loan, Milken would call on the capital from his privately held limited partnerships in order to close the deal. This was the case with regard to KKR's takeover of Storer (*U.S. v. Michael Milken* 1990a; see Chapter 2).

Both "highly confident" letters and bridge loans backed by Milken's private partnerships gave Drexel the extra advantage of speed—minimizing the time that competing purchasers or a reluctant target would have to mount a competing offer. A target company's shares might be purchased pursuant to a cash tender offering, and effective control obtained in as little as twenty days. On the other hand, the registering of securities (through the SEC) to be used in the exchange offer could take four to six weeks or more. Then the offer had to be open for an additional ten days. Thus through these two techniques the investment banking firm could shorten the execution time considerably.

Buying Loyalty of Employees to Control Knowledge.   Trust is an essential component of the neoclassical market model. It is often a side effect of the mechanisms that corporations and society implement (professionalization, regulations, SEC registrations) to compensate for information inequality. However, when individuals act opportunistically by continuously recalculating their self-interest and the social structures that were established to mitigate this self-interest are suspended, the basis for loyalty and trust in the system is destroyed. The result is the spread of misconduct and unlawful activities, which increase efficiencies of the controlling firms.

Drexel was very careful to reward its employees well. But Milken rewarded the bond traders and salesmen even better. This not only created loyalty to Milken rather than the New York office, but it also ensured that they would be less likely to leave Drexel to take positions with Drexel's competitors. Neither Milken nor Joseph wanted them to leave Drexel and take their knowledge of the functioning of the high-yield bond market (including both its legal and illegal tactics) and Drexel's innovative methods of doing business to their competitors. Drexel bought this commitment with excessive salaries, commissions, and bonuses. This was an important method of keeping these traders and salesmen at Drexel. Their exit was undesirable because they had greater (unequal) information, which would have been an asset to competitors. Thus buying the loyalty of his employees kept them from taking positions with competing firms and thereby was a method of reducing competition.

Milken wanted to ensure that they did not use their unequal information to trade for themselves, so he restricted trading during work hours, offering his employees participation in privately held partnerships as an alternative to participating directly in the market. Market competition was reduced because the employees were so embedded in Drexel that they did not perform personal transactions in the marketplace, nor did they move into the labor pool and thus equalize the spread of information, which would have spurred competition. The stronger Drexel became, the more embedded the employees and Milken became in the culture they had created, and consequently the more the employees were controlled.

Summary of Methods of Market Control

The point has been made that the high-yield bond market did not operate at the high level of efficiency it would have under some natural equilibrium process with open access to information and free-market mechanisms based on competition. In fact, there was relatively little control by the market and substantial control by the corporation. Indeed, we are hard put to differentiate between the operation of Drexel's High-Yield Bond Department and the high-yield bond market. Market efficiency was sacrificed for the transaction and short-term corporate efficiency of Drexel.

CONCLUSIONS

Those who model decision-making under uncertainty, specifically situations in which there are things the decision-maker cannot know, maintain that decision-makers make inferences on the basis of what they do know (Arrow 1992). Thus if we do not know if someone is telling the truth, we ask ourselves whether it looks like he or she is telling the truth. We try to protect ourselves from the unknown: How will it affect me if he or she is not telling the truth? Thus if we think someone may be competing unfairly by trading on inside information, we ask: How can I protect myself? On a more macro level, if we know that securities transactions are elusive, complex, secretive, and invisible, and can be executed cleanly through high technology, then we know the answer to the first question. Yes, it looks like fraud could be easily committed, and thus this is a high-risk proposition.

One answer to the next question is to construct legal restraints against fraud and insider trading. Another is for securities firms and the industry to create controls against insider trading, and securities fraud. But the incentives for honesty would have to be greater than the rewards for committing the fraud. Thus the defrauder must be fired, serve a severe prison sentence, and be fined an amount greater than that stolen plus profits from the theft. This seldom occurs.

Because of the nature of these transactions, the probability of being caught is low and the probability of being seriously sanctioned once caught is even lower. Many times the securities firm benefits at the same time as the employee as a result of the firm's commission on a sale. What is in the interest of the employee is in the interest of the organization; thus the organization has nothing to gain and in fact loses if the employee is caught and sanctioned.

The employing organization may indirectly encourage misconduct to attain organizational goals. Not only does each of these transaction characteristics present opportunities for unlawful behavior, but when transactions exhibit several of these characteristics, the ways in which they combine in the transaction may compound the opportunities for illegal activities. Indeed, the transactions of some organizations may create opportunities for violation. Management may direct employees to objectives that cannot be achieved legally, for example, to make certain that a stock closes at a certain level in order to trigger the exchange of preferred for common stock. The organization itself and systems outside the organization such as markets or regulatory agencies may block completion of the transactions as legal processes, thus creating the impetus to search for alternatives. Unlawful behavior or misconduct may be the only effective alternative and is likely to be chosen if the stakes are high and the chances of detection low.

The organization is always assessing the costs of such illegal behavior against the costs of not obtaining organizational goals. Many times illegal behavior is less costly to the organization than failure to achieve goals. Failure to achieve organizational goals may result in the failure of the organization. Thus, not only do employees have to be sanctioned, but firms must be sanctioned in order to inhibit such misconduct.

The incentives would have to be imposed from the external environment, through the legal system. The problem is that the sanctions are so weak that the securities industry employees are rewarded for committing the crime, paying the fine, and doing the time. In other words if there is to be deterrence, the cost of securities fraud must be greater than the benefits to the firm and employees.

Part III

Toward Understanding Fraud
as Structurally Embedded

Chapter 6

Economic Context

The purpose of this chapter is to place the fraud-facilitated junk bond transactions squarely in the context of the LBOs that were the major method of funding mergers and acquisitions during the 1980s. In so doing I will demonstrate the role of Drexel in the merger and acquisition movement of the 1980s. The analysis in this chapter demonstrates that mergers and acquisitions, the major methods of expansion during the 1980s, increased at a faster rate than in previous decades; that LBOs were the major method of financing these mergers and acquisitions; that the critical segment of the LBO was the difficult to finance third-level subordinate debt; and that most of this third-level subordinate debt was financed through the sale of junk bonds. Drexel controlled 40–65 percent of the junk bond market during the mid-1980s and thus was at the heart of the merger and acquisition movement. Many of the transactions that were antecedent to or directly involved in these takeovers had significant fraud associated with them.

It was relatively easy to commit fraud in the junk bond–financed LBOs because this method of leveraging was a Drexel/Milken creation. As with all innovations, there was no standard legal method of executing such LBOs. The lawfulness or unlawfulness of various aspects of the LBO were determined post hoc as they became known to Drexel's transaction partners and the government. Some aspects of these transactions that were unlawful are without a doubt still unknown. Because they are invisible in the ways defined in Chapter 5 they may never be known. The definitions of what is legal or illegal remain ambiguous, creating constant incongruity for the organization. The line between a good business transaction and illegality often became blurred. Merton notes, "On the top economic levels, the pressure toward innovation not infrequently erases the distinction between business-like striving this side of the mores and sharp practices beyond the mores" (1968, p. 195). Achievement of organizational goals through illegal behavior reinforces the occurrences of that behavior in the organization. Perpetuated over time, this conduct, which society defines as illegal, comes to be defined as standard business practice within the organization, although employees do know that it is against the law. The choice to do business illegally becomes an efficient strategy for conducting normal business as well as for doing business that could not be done within legal realms. These illegal strategies, which are successful for one firm, are then adopted by competing firms. Competition escalates the illegal conduct as the firm becomes even more efficient than competitors driving illegal innovations into new areas of the organization.

By demonstrating the power Drexel had in the transformation of corporate structures from multidivisional firms to holding companies and the transfer of capital supply from equity to debt, I hope to show the reader how the High-Yield Bond Department used its power to gain control over the internal workings of Drexel (discussed in Chapter 4) and how it was able to wield power in the legal arena (to be discussed in Chapter 7).

For the past one and one-half decades, firms (hierarchies) have been defined as an alternative method of governance and control to that of markets (Williamson 1975, 1981, 1985). This perspective led Eccles and White (1988) to conclude that the concerns of economists and sociologists cannot be easily isolated from one another. Actors in more recent economic organization models are boundedly rational and act opportunistically some of the time. Organizations are intended to be rational but are not. This is in contrast to the ideal-typical neoclassical economic model, which was developed around distinctions between economic and social organizations, in which actors are assumed to be hyperrational and never to act opportunistically. Also in contract to neoclassical models, newer models describe prices as constructed by organizational actors (Corey 1930), rather than something offered up by a reified market. Fligstein and Dauber argue that "the determination of the value of resources to be exchanged is tied to the explication of the social relationships between the actors through the form, content, and language of the negotiation itself" (1989, p. 2).

More recently, we have come to the realization that markets like organizations are socially constructed. Baker (1984, p. 775) found that trading among actors exhibited distinct social structural patterns that dramatically affected the direction and magnitude of option price volatility. My observations of the development of internal and external controls that function in investment banking firms also indicate that neoclassical models do not apply, neither transaction cost models (Williamson 1975, 1985) nor agency theory models (Jensen 1986, 1989b). The development of controls is not the result of hyperrational, profit-maximizing actors in efficient, external markets and of efficient firms working to become even more efficient. Managers are neither optimizing nor satisficing. Instead they are attempting to survive and, in so doing, are gaining power by constructing new strategies and structures based on their analyses of ways to control organizations and their environments.

At the same time, the economic context in which these new courses of action are developing are not conducive to rational, profit-maximizing courses of action. They are developing in an economic environment in which the major corporate structure is making the transition from a multidivisional structure to a holding company, based on the financial conception of firm as defined by Fligstein, and accounting methods as defined by Prechel (1991). These views define the purpose of the firm singularly: to increase short-run profits. Mergers and acquisitions became the major method of growth for the largest companies during the period described earlier. Fligstein (1990a, p. 2) documents this trend when he finds that between 1947 and 1985 the asset concentration of the five hundred largest manufacturing companies increased from 42 to 76 percent. Most of this increase occurred through mergers.

According to Fligstein, the holding companies of unrelated corporations came about because of antitrust laws' restrictions of horizontal and vertical differentiation, the instability of relations with competitors, and managers' search for survival mechanisms in the face of economic crisis. Mergers and acquisitions were the methods of expansion through which this new organizational form of unrelated industry companies was created. Mergers and acquisitions of the 1980s were largely a phenomenon underwritten with debt by investment banking firms and the leverage instrument of choice, high-risk, high-yield (junk) bonds. As we saw in Chapter 2, various types of fraud facilitated the execution of many of LBOs of the mid-1980s.

These mergers and acquisitions may have been beneficial for short-run growth and profitability of these firms, though even this assumption is now in question. They may have had a less positive effect on the expansion of firms through research, development, and innovation in various product sectors. For the economy as a whole, the effects were even less positive.

The questions that we want to explore in this chapter are: What were the characteristics of the economic environment in which fraud-facilitated LBOs were such a prominent occurrence? How did the new finance-oriented managers change the structure of the firms? What was the role of investment bankers in this redefinition and restructuring? And why were junk bonds the debt instrument of choice in executing LBOs?

These questions focus the analysis squarely on the relationship between the acquiring firms and their investment bankers. What is the relationship between managers' ideas about the nature of their firm and its goals and the nature of the financial institutions with which it does business? The production and service firms that offer stocks and bonds, institutional investors who are clients, and competing investment banking firms provide constant information and feedback on the performance of the investment banking firm. At the same time, the regulatory agents and laws of the government affect the actions of these banking firms as they influence the agencies and members of Congress who make the laws.

The crucial question of how the strategy and structure were developed was answered in Chapter 4, while the characteristics of the transactions that facilitated the fraud were discussed in Chapter 5. The economic context in which they developed and Drexel's articulation with its external economic environment are addressed here. This chapter analyzes the relationship between Drexel's fraud and the economic context of mergers, LBOs, and the development of the junk bond market and capital markets, which Drexel both helped create and functioned within. Drexel's security fraud developed, at least in part, out of these relationships. I argue here that the fraud developed as a result of the relationship between Drexel's goal of short-term productivity, specifically the High-Yield Bond Department's need for short-term profits, and the functioning of the economic environment in the 1980s.

1980s TRANSFORMATION OF CORPORATE CONTROL

The 1980s were an incredible period of reorganization of financial assets among the largest corporations in the United States, the greatest period of acquisitions and mergers in the history of American capitalism. Corporations were motivated by the spectre of increased competition with Japan and second with Germany. The number of mergers and acquisitions exploded from 1,565 in 1980, having a combined value of $33 billion, to 3,487 in 1988, having a combined value of $227 billion (Adams and Brock 1988). Between 1980 and 1988, some 26,000 mergers and acquisitions, having a value of over $1 trillion took place among American corporations (Adams and Brock 1989, p. 12).

Many companies were involved in multiple takeovers. Prominent among these was the merger of Nabisco and Standard Brands in 1981, a $2 billion deal, which combined the 152nd and 128th largest manufacturing firms. (Both were food manufacturers: Nabisco made Oreo and Fig Newton cookies, Ritz crackers, Shredded Wheat, and Cream of Wheat, while Standard Brands made Planter's nuts, Royal gelatin, and Baby Ruth and Butterfinger candy.) The resulting conglomerate jumped to fifty-fourth on the Fortune 500. In 1985, R.J. Reynolds (twenty-third largest industrial firm) acquired Nabisco Brands for a price of $4.9 billion. By December 1989, RJR Nabisco had been purchased through a LBO by the largest merger and buyout firm, KKR, for $25.07 billion. This last buyout took place over a two-year period ending in 1988, during which RJR

Nabisco became the target first of F. Ross Johnson (the president who had guided it through its mergers), when he attempted to dissolve the food and tobacco conglomerate. Then, KKR, in an effort to expand its status as the nation's largest LBO, intervened with a $25.07 billion bid and ultimately closed the deal at a little over $26 billion, much of which was underwritten by Drexel.

Although the acquisitions of the late 1970s and the early 1980s were not hostile takeovers involving junk bonds, the decade progressively moved in that direction. DuPont's purchase of Conoco, the ninth largest U.S. oil company, for $7.68 billion marked the beginning of the merger and acquisition period. Conoco's stock nearly doubled, from $50 to $98 a share, largely due to Boesky's purchasing of large blocks of stock. Hostile takeovers can be traced to the Drexel-financed, T. Boone Pickens's attempted takeover of Gulf Oil (Lipton, Fogelson, Brownstein, and Wasserman 1987).

This wave of reorganization through mergers and acquisitions has led organizational theorists to focus on the dominance of financial considerations. Their agreement on the importance of financial considerations is obvious. What they do not agree upon is the origins of the view of the organization as a financial entity. Financial economists assume that managers and particularly owners push the corporation in this direction in order to maximize efficiency and returns to the shareholder. Thus, the *end* of maximizing efficiency is used to justify the *means* of mergers and acquisitions. Organizational sociologists, on the other hand, are more interested in the *processes* by which mergers and acquisitions become a driving force. They suggest that the social construction of managers' worlds is important in promoting a worldview that rationalizes mergers and acquisitions as appropriate actions based on efficiency. They recognize that the consequences were not efficiency. Nevertheless, takeovers did have consequences.

Takeovers of the 1980s were advocated in theory by some economists early in the decade (Altman 1990a, 1990b). Transactions cost analysts (Williamson 1975, 1981, 1985) and agency theorists (Fama and Jensen 1983a, 1983b; Fama 1980) advocated efficiency through the reduction of transaction costs and agency costs, respectively. Williamson advocated the elaboration of hierarchical, organizational control over the market through converting market transactions to organizational transactions. But Jensen, to a greater extent than Williamson, contributed to the merger frenzy by advocating the reduction of costs through the reduction of management costs (agency costs) and increased monitoring of management (agency). By the end of the decade, he announced the death of the American public corporation. He believed that in the 1990s American corporations would be privately held and shares would no longer be traded. After over forty years of economic prosperity without significant depression, he felt that bankruptcy was no longer a serious threat to most managers. He maintained that stockholders' assets were being squandered by managers and that this trend should be reversed by bringing corporations to the verge of bankruptcy through increased indebtedness. In this circumstance, managers who had been all too powerful, could be brought under the control of shareholders to manage firms in the interest of shareholders.

Jensen, from his academic position at the University of Rochester, in 1976 argued that the interests of managers (agents) and shareholders (principals) were opposed and that the problem could be solved through takeovers, during which managers would be required by owners to purchase equity in the firm. If managers were also owners, their interests would be brought into line with the interests of the acquirers, and if the takeover were financed with debt, the owners would hold even greater control over managers because in order to pay off the enormous debt and its interest, managers would have to become more efficient. Jensen and Meckling rhetorically argue, "Why don't we observe large corporations individually owned, with a tiny fraction of the capital supplied by the entrepreneur in return for 100 percent of the equity, and the rest simply borrowed?" (1976, p. 330). Corporations moved in this direction in the last half of the 1980s, but the trend was short-lived.

Jensen's culture of leveraged American corporations was reinforced by Arthur Laffer's (1985) culture of leveraged American government. Laffer described a model under which the government *should* cut taxes and willingly accept big deficits for a year or two, assuming that a stronger economy would expand the tax base so much that the government would soon recoup the loss. Leveraging the U.S. economy should therefore not be feared. Laffer had no way of knowing that the Reagan and Bush administrations would leverage the American economy, not for a year or two, but for more than a decade.

That which Jensen and Laffer only theorized about, Drexel did. With the willing participation of T. Boone Pickens, Carl Icahn, Ted Turner, and more effectively Jerry Kohlberg, Henry Kravis, and George Roberts, Drexel facilitated the takeover and privatization of many large corporations. Sociologists have suggested at least two alternative approaches to explain the merger and acquisition movement. The first is the extension of control over firms by banks and financial institutions: financial control theory. Underlying this theory is the assumption that corporations have become more vulnerable to financial manipulation (Mintz and Schwartz 1985; Kotz 1978; Brancato and Gaughan 1989). The second sociological explanation rests on the assumption that managers with a new definition of the firm have come to power, and this financial conception of the firm has spread to lesser firms (through isomorphism, the imitation of successful forms, as described by Powell and DiMaggio 1990). This, coupled with lax antitrust policies and tax cuts for corporations supported by the Reagan and Bush administrations, led to increased mergers (Fligstein 1987, 1990a).

Fligstein maintains that the reorganization of financial assets of the largest corporations can be understood as a result of the social embeddedness of managers' actions. He finds that, in corporations with a financial conception of the firm, "managers are more likely to engage in stock repurchases, mergers, divestitures, and the purchase of stock of other firms" (Fligstein 1990b, p. 3). Merger targets tend not to engage in forms of financial reorganization. As a consequence they are easy prey for raiders. Fligstein interprets the role of bankers on boards of directors not as bankers controlling corporations, as does Mintz and Schwartz (1985), but as lenders who are trying to protect their loans during times of possible merger. Fligstein concludes that there is no evidence that the financial "facts" of the firm promote reorganization, and thus the strictly economic explanation is not substantiated.

Fligstein's (1990a) interpretation of the merger and acquisition movement implies that the acquiring firm must have managers who can analyze and interpret financial information, make decisions about it, and act upon it in order for financial reorganization to occur. These finance-oriented managers can better interact, not only with bankers on their boards, but with investment bankers who underwrite their debt. There is ample evidence from our analysis of Drexel that the finance capital perspective in which corporations control banks is not as strong as the bank control model in which the investment banking firm initiates, manages, and controls the takeover of corporations. But this leaves unanswered the question of whether banks control because their managers hold the financial conception worldview or because of their greater power.

MERGERS AND ACQUISITIONS AS THE AVENUE TO GROWTH AND PRODUCTIVITY

William Baxter, President Reagan's first chief of the Justice Department's Antitrust Division said, "Merger activity in general is a very important feature of our capital market by which assets are continuously moved into the hands of managers who can employ them efficiently" (1983, p. 315). Attorney General William French Smith (1991) agreed that interfering with mergers would be an error of substantial magnitude, and Edwin Meese III linked mergers to U.S. competitiveness. These government officials believe that antitrust law should be adjusted to facilitate the expansion of mergers and LBOs. In the words of Malcolm Baldridge, secretary of commerce,

[T]rade patterns have changed, but the antitrust laws have not. It is not that some parts of those laws are irrelevant today; it is the fact that they place additional and unnecessary burdens on the ability of U.S. firms to compete. (1986, p. 22)

These officials as well as many academicians believe that merger-induced restructuring is necessary if American industry is to achieve productive efficiency, technological innovation, and global competitiveness. They further advocate changes in antitrust regulation to eliminate the practice of nonenforcement, and thereby recognizing what corporations have already realized in practice—their greater power over the state in enforcement of regulations.

Did these mergers indeed promote efficiency, technical progress, and international competitiveness, or were they destructive to the economy? Is it productive to buy out and merge today in order to divest tomorrow? What of the investment bankers who obtain large fees for both the union and dissolution of these conglomerates? Is it more productive to spend for the formation and dissolution of these conglomerates rather than for expansion through research and development of new products and growth of the production infrastructure? Would these monies be better spent on the plant and human resources to increase productivity than on banking fees? I believe that it may be necessary to diversify through mergers, but I question whether it makes sense to do this through LBOs, expansion of the junk bond market, and the securities fraud that accompanied these innovations, which in some cases were the innovations themselves. Peter Drucker points out that it is one thing to be efficient doing things right. It is quite another to be efficient doing the right things (1984).

Perhaps mergers and LBOs funded by junk bonds are not the right things for us to be doing. Perhaps we are involved in these mergers and junk bond–financed LBOs because they benefit those who are the most powerful in our society—wealthy shareholders, or because investment bankers have the ability to do the deals efficiently, and to "do them well," not because they are economically sound for the United States.

The 1980s period of mergers and acquisitions was different from previous periods. Altered circumstances and values of the late 1970s led the CEOs of major corporations to search out means to improve the performance of their existing enterprises in the face of Japanese competition and rising oil prices. The normal process of research and development was defined as too slow. The problem of competitiveness in the United States, unlike Japan and other nations where the government sustains corporations, was reduced to survival—compete or fail to exist. Thus in financial terms, the problem of competitiveness was reduced to short-term profitability. In order to increase short-term profitability, managers not only had to decrease costs, but they also had to increase profits while maintaining their own stock prices at a high level to fend off possible takeovers from other firms. One way they could increase profits was to purchase existing firms, selling off the less profitable parts, and restructuring the remaining parts to increase the profitability of the acquired divisions or merging the acquired divisions with the acquiring firm to restructure in a more efficient manner. They could not afford to increase productivity through research and development because the uncertainty and length of time that are essential elements in research and development are not geared to short-term profits.

LEVERAGED BUYOUTS AND LEVERAGED TAKEOVERS

To credit Drexel or Milken with the innovation of the LBO would be a mistake. Any business historian will be quick to note that both LBOs and high-risk (junk) bonds have been with us since the time of J. P. Morgan, who (in 1901) merged eight steel companies at a cost of $1.4 billion—$570 million of which U.S. Steel took on in debt (Anders 1988).

What is a leveraged buyout? *Leveraging* simply means using debt to finance an acquisition, and pledging the acquired company's assets as collateral for the loans. Thus the suitor company will borrow money short term (a bridge loan) for the purchase and then, when the transaction is completed, sell off pieces of the property to obtain funds to repay part or all of the short-term debt. The acquirer might sell off all the less-profitable parts to pay the debt and keep the centerpiece to add to its conglomerate. The resulting acquisition of that centerpiece is sheer profit. Just as investors pool their funds to create LBOs, companies use the equity in their own organizations to leverage themselves in order to engage in a buyout. In his testimony before the hearings of the Senate Finance Committee, Secretary of the Treasury Nicholas F. Brady (1989, p. 28) testified that the typical LBO involved the acquisition of a public corporation by a small investor group, frequently including the target corporation's management and one of the LBO funds that pool capital for this purpose. These funds are generally accumulated by investment bankers. The investors either merge with the target or make a tender offer for its stock. The target corporation's share-holders surrender their equity, common stock, for cash and/or debt of the acquisition corporation.

The investing group generally supplies only 15 percent of the LBO's total capitalization:

Around one-third of the LBO's total capital would be subordinated debt, initially in the form of bridge loans which would later be replaced with so-called junk bonds. The bridge financing (roughly 30 percent) often comes from an investment bank, with the junk bonds purchased by pension funds, specialized limited partnerships, insurance companies, bank subsidiaries and tax-exempt institutions. (p. 28)

The largest part of the loan, roughly 55 percent of the LBO financing, would ordinarily be debt secured by the assets and receivables of the target corporation. Thus using the target company's assets as collateral, the acquiring organization would secure the loan with senior debt typically from a syndicate of banks and insurance companies.

Perhaps the best example is the method that James Ling perfected in the late 1950s. Because he did not have the equity to expand, he would use the assets of the company about to be purchased. Backed by those assets, he would borrow money on a short-term note—generally at a very high rate. He would then sell longer-term bonds with lower interest rates and use the proceeds to pay off the short-term loans. Of course, the lower-interest, long-term debt was preferred to high-interest, short-term debt, but the negative effects of long-term debt were that, if the economy turned downward or the firm's productivity declined, the debt was more difficult to pay off from the proceeds of the purchased firm. In order to pay off the long-term debt, Ling would then sell off the assets (portions) of the purchased firm. The positive effect was that Ling did not have to dilute the stock (by issuing more) in order to increase the value of the firm. Another positive effect was that debt, unlike equity, is tax deductible.

Through LBOs, Ling was able to purchase companies much larger than his own, because the purchase was not dependent upon the assets of his firm, but rather on how much money he could borrow—his access to bonds. Ling began in 1955 by raising eight hundred thousand dollars to take Ling Electric Company public. Five years later in 1960, he had purchased Temco Electric. The resulting combination was renamed Ling-Temco-Vought (LTV), a Fortune 500 company (Sobel 1984b).

Throughout the decade of the 1960s, Ling borrowed against the value of LTV and the assets of the larger target firms he was taking over. The debt was then lowered by selling the target firms' assets. This would leave the newly acquired firm vulnerable and LTV's assets would look weak. Therefore, Ling would buy back large portions of the acquired firms' assets, which would increase the price of their stock. By 1965, Ling had reorganized LTV as a holding company, each holding having its own stock (p. 207).

Between 1965 and 1970, Ling purchased many firms and created the prototype unrelated conglomerate or holding company. In their order of acquisition, they were Okonite, a wire manufacturer; Wilson and Company, a meat processing and production plant that also held four other unrelated companies—a sporting goods manufacturer, a pet food company, a soap company, and a growing pharmaceutical company; Great America Corporation, which was another holding company for several insurance firms, banks, Braniff Airways, and National Car Rental; and finally Jones and Laughlin Steel (pp. 207–8).

Ling's philosophy depicts the financial concept of the firm. In 1969, at the height of his acquisitions, he was quoted by *Fortune:*

> In the most general sense, my function is to be sure we come up with the most creative use of assets of the corporation that will build values and increase earnings per share. Redeploying assets in this way is building values and these values are measured by the stock market. And in turn they are useful financially as a means of building new values. (McDonald 1969, p. 162)

His definition of what a good executive was lays out the importance of the social embeddedness of corporate executives in the financial world:

> I personally believe the best background for corporate life is that of a financial analyst working in the Wall Street area—someone who has been exposed to all the technological markets and knows the basic ways of getting good information in and about companies. A man with this background would know the financial values of these operations. (p. 164)

By late 1969 Ling was fighting off a serious antitrust challenge, and was seeking purchasers for Braniff and Okonite. Jones and Laughlin was failing. Threatened with illiquidity, Ling was trying to locate buyers for parts of Jones and Laughlin and other parts of LTV (Sobel 1984a, p. 180). Sobel felt that Ling was the most innovative of the conglomerate kings; ironically, he was the only one who failed to survive into the 1980s.

The Role of Investment Bankers in the Leveraged Buyouts of the 1980s

The LBOs of the 1980s were different. They were not financed by entrepreneurs patching together a group of small firms; rather they were engineered by financial managers of multibillion-dollar holding companies or takeover boutiques. In the 1980s LBOs were much more common than they had been during the conglomerate period, and they were more often hostile takeovers, often resembling warfare. Such terms as *white knight* (a firm to which a targeted or besieged firm would look as a possible merger partner when about to be taken over by an unfriendly firm) and *black knight* (an unfriendly potential acquirer) were invented. The *scorched-earth policy* referred to the threat to dismiss entire management teams if they opposed the takeover. On Wall Street, the gigantic struggles among the multibillion-dollar corporations for control of one another were called *nuclear war*.

Eccles and Crane (1988, pp. 96–97) examined the number of mergers and acquisitions performed by the nineteen leading investment bankers between 1984 and 1986. They found a total of 1,338 mergers and acquisitions with another investment banker on the other side. Drexel ranked fifth in the number of mergers and acquisitions, with 113, behind Goldman, Sachs; Stanley; First Boston; and Shearson, Lehman. Investment bankers generally chose consistently to represent either acquirers or targets, and thus planned offensive or defensive strategy. Goldman, Sachs, because it has always represented the blue-chip stock companies that were being attacked, had an announced policy of not representing acquirers in a hostile takeover. It represented the target in 66.0 percent of its M&A activities. Kidder, Peabody was also a major player in representing the target with 63 percent of its activity on the side of targets. Drexel stood out for doing the largest proportion of its M&A deals for acquirers, 63.7 percent. However, other firms including Merrill Lynch, First Boston, Stanley, Lazard Freres, and Donaldson, Lufkin & Jenrette represented acquirers in more than half of their deals. Thus Drexel was the major underwriter for raiders during the height of the 1980s mergers and acquisitions period, but not the only one.

This is important for yet another reason: M&A bankers moved between firms and thus could appear on the team opposing the firm they had represented at a previous time. Second, a firm that was willing to trade inside information would attempt to make contact with a firm that was working for the opposite side of a transaction. Thus, those who were representing acquirers might wish to establish relationships with those who were defenders of targets. For example, Drexel gained more from its relationships with Kidder, Peabody and Goldman, Sachs, which represented targets, than it did from other representatives of acquirers. It was secretly and covertly informed when the target was willing to make a deal.

Secretary of the Treasury Brady (1989, p. 28) saw LBOs of the 1980s as a major trend in the restructuring and capitalization of American corporations—the replacement of corporate equity with debt and the consequent leveraging of corporate balance sheets. From 1978 to 1983, the total value of LBOs was around $11 billion. In the following five years, LBOs totaled $160 billion, with 1988 accounting for $60 billion. Ironically, his data revealed a lesser trend of LBO activity concentrated in industries better able to support substantial leverage.

Brady's analysis of the individual LBOs revealed that these transactions introduced "unprecedented levels of debt," which in some cases left the corporations unable to service their debt with existing cash flow. Brady writes that it is

> apparent that many such transactions require immediate asset sales at higher prices in order to reduce the debt to manageable levels. In other cases, the corporation will be required to cut back on non-interest expenditures; for example, expenditures for research and development. (p. 29)

Brady and his staff see the recent level of LBO activity as a result of six conditions: the relationships between debt and equity tax structures, the emergence of the junk bond market, arbitragers' activity, low stock prices, speculative returns, and fees paid to investment bankers and other advisors. The last seems to be the major driving force for the large number and size of LBOs . All are discussed below.

The Role of Tax Codes

The growth in LBOs caused both the Senate and the House to hold hearings on the financial restructuring of debt based partially on the assumption that the tax deductibility of corporate debt encourages corporations to take on more debt. One such meeting of the Senate Finance Committee was held on Tuesday, January 24–26, 1989, at which time Senator Lloyd Bentsen announced that the committee would hold hearings on "The recent trends in corporate restructuring, mounting debt in the corporate sector, and the relationship of these trends to the tax law" (1989, p. 1). Specifically he said:

> [T]he massive corporate conversion of equity to debt causes me concern about the ability of our country's corporations to weather an economic downturn. I am also concerned about the possible adverse effects of this mounting debt on Federal tax revenues, at a time when reducing the budget deficit is a critical priority . . . One cause for this trend may be our tax system's bias in favor of debt financing, as opposed to equity financing. I intend to examine this problem and explore the possibilities for reform. (p. 1)

Bentsen goes on to note the increasing level of corporate debt in American, and that the debt was being tied to a reduction in corporate equity. He noted that between 1984 and 1987 the nonfinancial corporations of the United States received a net $313 billion in equity and, at the same time, borrowed a net $613 billion.

From the perspective of the acquiring firm, LBOs are rational because the tax system treats equity and corporate debt differently. Since interest payments are deductible, but corporate dividends are not, a substantial tax advantage accrues to LBOs and other transactions that effectively replace corporate equity with debt. But the tax efficiency conditions do not fully explain the extent and timing of the LBO activity, because the tax advantages of debt capitalization have existed for most of the history of the corporate income tax. It is a necessary, but not a sufficient condition for the development of the junk bond market.

It could be argued that the Tax Reform Act of 1986, including the reduction in the corporate tax rate and the elimination of the so-called general utilities doctrine, may actually have diminished the tax benefits available from LBOs, yet the number and value of aggregate LBOs has increased every year since 1986, until the end of the decade.

The target of proposed legislation is the interest deductibility of corporate debt used to finance takeovers or issued by companies already highly leveraged. To prevent overleveraging of corporations, some would like to tie the tax deductibility enjoyed by a company as a result of its interest payment to its debt-to-equity ratio. Theorists (namely, Williamson and Jensen) who advocate the new economic organization perspectives argue that American corporations are already overtaxed and are at a disadvantage against foreign competition in Japan and Germany (Auerbach and Andow 1977; Ellsworth 1985). On the other hand, one might argue that corporations that are highly leveraged cannot use their profits to expand, to build new plants, and to increase productivity through research and development to meet international competition. They must use their profits to service and reduce their debt.

The Role of the Bond (Debt) Market

As control of the large multidivisional firms was taken over by financiers, the perception of how to expand in order to survive shifted from expansion through internal research and development to expansion through mergers and acquisitions. Expansion through research and development required large sums of money over relatively long periods; however, expansion through mergers required even larger sums of capital but over very short periods.

During the 1980s the economy grew, stock prices increased, and borrowing power expanded. Borrowing money for expansion was more efficient than using the firm's capital (largely because debt was tax deductible) and therefore firms chose LBOs over investment of their reserve capital. Many large firms were created solely though large-scale mergers. Entrepreneurs who were not industrial barons began by buying two or three unrelated firms and through a process of divestiture acquired some capital through which they were able to borrow even more capital to purchase their fourth and fifth firms. The Large organizations were created solely though large-scale mergers with the financial entrepreneurs having little or no understanding of the operation of the firms they purchased. Other firms soon discovered that mergers and buyouts were successful methods of capital expansion.

The CEO's role was to invest and divest so that assets and profits would increase. Indeed, the strategy of diversification through mergers and acquisitions of unrelated multidivisional firms provided a spectacular growth rate, which set a new pace for American industry. Many firms began to follow suit by decentralizing and diversifying in order not only to compete, but to avoid being taken over in a hostile attack by more powerful firms.

The Role of Junk Bonds. Unlike equities, debt issues are evaluated by major bond-rating agencies. These ratings provide guidelines for the risk of the bonds offered by the issuer. Thus the U.S. bond market is dominated by two giant bond-rating agencies, Moody's and Standard & Poor's, who for generations have guided investors seeking to gauge the risk in fixed-income investments. The value of the bond depends on an issuer's ability to make interest payments until the bond matures, and then repay the principal. Companies with weaker balance sheets have correspondingly lower ratings. Some companies are so risky that they receive no rating whatsoever. Interest rates on corporate debt fluctuate with the U.S. Treasury market rates and with the level of risk of the firm issuing the debt. The lower the debt rating, the higher is the interest the issuing firm must pay in order to attract investors.

Technically, *high-yield bonds (junk bonds)* are those rated below Ba by Moody's and BBB– and below by Standard and Poors. That is, they are bonds having a below–investment grade rating. Unrated corporate bonds are usually included in the junk bond category as well. Under this definition, junk bonds have existed since the first bond rating was published by John Moody in 1909. In fact, junk bonds were a significant source of corporate funds throughout the pre–World War II period, accounting for 17 percent of total rated, publicly issued straight corporate debt from 1909 to 1943 (Atkinson 1967). Between 1944 and 1965 they accounted for only 6.5 percent of total corporate bond issues (Atkinson 1967); from 1965 to 1975 they were used even less frequently. By 1977, junk bonds accounted for only 3.7 percent of total corporate bonds outstanding (Altman and Nammacher 1985b).

On the one hand, corporate investment grade bonds are purchased almost exclusively by institutional investors and are traded less frequently in secondary markets than equities. Because of the ratings and pricing guidelines there is little need to make a market in investment grade bonds. There is a low level of uncertainty in distinguishing between issuers of these bonds. Thus, there is little room for investment banker innovation in making a market.

On the other hand, corporate junk bonds are low-grade, high-risk, unrated or low-rated bonds traditionally used by small firms desperately in need of capital funds for expansion, but lacking equity and a reliable financial track record. The market for these non–investment grade bonds is much less certain than investment grade debt. There is less certainty about the issuer. They too are purchased by institutional investors. However, the investors who purchase these bonds are generally higher-risk investors. Because these bonds are more speculative, the placement of this debt by investment bankers is more difficult. It is complicated by the market's knowledge of the potentially high default rate. The bond sellers and traders have to know more about the companies issuing the bonds and their related financial statistics. Such bonds pay high interest rates and are quite lucrative, if divested while the firm is still solvent. Coffee (1986, p. 4) and Jensen (1988, p. 37) note that junk bonds pay 3–5 percent higher interest than that paid to holders of government bonds of comparable maturity, but during the mid-to-late 1980s the differential in interest rates was much larger than this.

By the end of the 1970s and early 1980s, the equity of many firms had eroded to such an extent that they became easy targets for takeovers. Often financiers bought the firm by paying what in the existing market was a premium, and selling the pieces at a profit. Frequently the acquiring firm had to take on additional debt in order to successfully execute the takeover. Thus the acquiring firm engaged in issuing bonds. Often this left the acquiring firm in an unstable situation and the bonds that were issued were not highly rated. In other words, they were low-quality, high-risk (junk) bonds.

A broad and active market for lower-grade corporate bonds has emerged only since 1977. Prior to the late 1970s, the market for lower-grade corporate bonds was dominated by what was known as *fallen angels*— issues of formerly financially sound corporations that had been downgraded by Standard & Poor's and Moody's rating services. The active and broader market began to develop in the late 1970s and expanded greatly in the 1980s. According to Drexel Burnham Lambert, new issues of lower-grade straight debt was $0.56 billion in 1977; just ten years later, in 1986 and 1987 combined, such new issues totaled nearly $63 billion. The majority of these bonds were issued or traded through Drexel. For the first time, less-than-investment grade bonds were given access to the capital markets.

But there were no widely accepted indexes for lower-grade bonds as there were for equities markets and investment grade bonds. The houses that traded in these bonds (Drexel Burnham Lambert, and Salomon Brothers) began to create indexes, but both indexes had problems. For example, Salomon used dealer quotes for a minimum trade of five hundred bonds. Blume and Keim criticized this practice:

> [U]ntil recently, the return on their index was derived from the average yield, average coupon and average maturity of the bonds in the index, not from the realized returns of the individual bonds; it thus represented the return on a hypothetical bond and only approximated the returns of a portfolio of lower grade bonds. (1990, p. 5)

In 1986, Salomon introduced a new index based on the realized return of individual bonds, which more closely approximates the returns of an actual portfolio.

An even more serious problem of both Salomon's and Drexel's indexes is that they "drop a bond from their indexes if the bond defaults, if the quality of the bond increases to investment grade, or if there is no demand for the bond" (p. 5). As none of these events is known in advance, excluding the bond return for the month in which the event occurs may bias the index. Blume and Keim (p. 5) fault the index because if bond prices fall upon default, the return implied by these indexes may overstate the returns that an actual investor might obtain.

In 1990, while the junk bond market crashed, Edward Altman (1990a) edited a book of papers from the foremost financial authorities on the market. In the preface to the book, he notes that the high-risk, non–investment grade market is now a relatively large and important segment of the corporate bond market, comprising over 20 percent of total corporate, publicly held indebtedness. He states that this market is of interest to issuing firms, investors, underwriters, traders, regulators, and the media. Several of the articles by well-known finance scholars extolled the virtues of junk bonds. In his contribution, Altman writes: "Despite some relatively high cumulative mortality rates over long holding periods, return spreads on all corporate bonds are positive, *with impressive results for the high-risk, low grade categories*" (1990b, pp. 53–54, emphasis added). Ma, Rao, and Peterson in this same volume write, "In contrast to popular conjectures, the high-risk bond market demonstrates surprisingly strong resiliency. This study compares implied default probabilities around four major adverse events between May 1986 and November 1988" (1990, p. 73). Neither of these studies analyzed the performance of the junk bond market in a depression. And neither took into account the tremendous costs of the fraud associated with the junk bond–financed takeovers. Evidently these authors did not realize that even before their book was published this market would be of interest to the public in general, especially those who had their pension and retirement funds invested by insurance companies and other institutional investors who had bought into the junk bond market.

In 1987, the junk bond market was a $30 billion business and according to Barrie Wigmore (19809), partner in Goldman, Sachs investment bank, the fraction of the junk bonds issued for purposes of mergers and acquisitions shot up from 6 percent in 1987 to nearly 80 percent in 1989. Corporate debt was rising and this debt was largely junk bonds.

The Use of High-Yield Bonds in Leveraged Buyouts

Having dispensed, I think inappropriately, with the argument that LBOs expanded due to the more favorable tax structure for debt financing than equity financing, the staff of the Secretary of Treasury, Brady (1989) came to the conclusion that the key impetus for the recent resurgence in LBOs was the emergence of the junk bond market, which supplied much of the net capital on which LBOs were based. The most rapid growth was between 1984 and 1987; in each of these four years Drexel controlled between 40 and 65 percent of this market. Thus the staff of the secretary of the treasury reasoned that since neither banks nor the traditional bond markets could provide for the substantially increased rate of transactions, an alternative source of financing was sought. They concluded that the junk bond market has vastly facilitated LBO and LTO (leveraged takeovers) activity.

Led by Drexel and fueled by the LBO wave of the 1980s, the junk bond market became a significant arena of financial activity. By 1983 junk was 17.9 percent of the bond market and by 1984, at its highest point to that time, it reached 21.5 percent. Cumulating new issues and fallen angels, the total value of outstanding junk bonds was estimated in Drexel's 1988 annual report to be $159 billion by the end of 1987, and by the middle of 1988 $170 billion or 20 percent of the entire bond market. Joseph (1990) estimated that by the end of 1988 it would be $185 billion in principal and 25 percent of all publicly owned debt.

Finance economists saw this process of takeovers, mergers, and junk bond trading as a process of displacing inefficient managements and replacing them with managements that operated with higher levels of debt (often junk bonds) promising higher rates of return. They offered the rationale that American corporations were underleveraged. Managers were blamed for the vulnerability of the firms because they had let their stock prices fall (Jensen and Ruback 1983). Efficient managers understood the markets and took actions to raise the price of their stocks while inefficient managers were acquired through takeovers or mergers. The effect of these actions was to replace equity with debt for both the acquiring and the acquired firm.

Jensen (1988, p. 25) reasoned that these bonds played a direct role in less than 10 percent of the financing of all tender offers from January 1981 through 1986. Yago (1991, p. 36) points out that from 1980 through 1986, 74 percent of the proceeds from all junk bonds was used to finance corporations' internal growth, and 22 percent to finance their unopposed acquisitions; only 3.25 percent was used for unsolicited takeovers. Using a different method of calculation the *Wall Street Journal* (1991, p. C2), citing Drexel, comes to a different conclusion—that by 1988, only 2 percent of all junk bonds was being used to finance corporations' internal growth, and 98 percent was being used to finance LBOs.

Between 1988 and 1990 the General Accounting Office conducted a review of the high-risk bond market. Burnett and Philippi (1990) reported that they approached the question of the use of high-risk bonds to finance hostile corporate takeovers in two ways. First, they examined fifty-four takeovers in 1985 and 1986 that the SEC had identified as hostile. The takeover was completed either by the unwelcome bidder, a white knight, or the target firm's management. They reviewed tender offers, filings, bond prospectuses, and annual reports and found that the high-risk bonds accounted for about 12 percent of the value of the initial financing for these takeovers (pp. 148–49). Another 42 percent, the large majority, came from bank loans. But after the initial financing, they found that bank and bridge loans were refinanced (and in the final analysis, 22 percent of the financing of the deals) through high-risk bonds. Thus, contrary to Jensen's reasoning, considerably more than 12 percent of the financing of these deals came from the junk bond market.

The second approach they used was to review the "use of funds" section of bond prospectuses filed with the SEC. This showed that 13 percent of high-risk bonds was issued for the purpose of carrying out acquisitions. Another 15 percent was for future acquisitions, and 23 percent was to retire debt of previous merger and acquisitions. Thus 61 percent of the high-risk bonds was involved in the takeover process at some point (p. 149).

THE ROLE OF DREXEL IN THE CREATION OF THE JUNK BOND MARKET—A NEAR MONOPOLY

Joseph is correct when he writes that "opening the public debt markets to less-than-investment grade companies—roughly 95 percent of U.S. companies with sales in excess of $35 million—is helping to change established norms in capital structure" (1990, p. 120). He perceives that the high-risk market itself has "grown, matured, and evolved into a far more sophisticated entity which now accommodates a wide range of investor needs, facilitating transactions that might have been impossible 15 years ago" (p. 120). Drexel gained a near monopoly on this market largely because major investment banks did not wish to deal in low-grade bonds. Their clients did not wish to take on the risk. Drexel, however, was willing to move its initially small clientele into these higher-risk bonds. This must have appealed to the major investment banking firms because it initially kept them from having to compete with Drexel, and it must have appealed to Drexel because the special- and major-bracket firms had no interest in such low-class issuers and buyers. As soon as Drexel had been successful in this new market, the special- and major-bracket firms began to try to move into the market, but Drexel had such control that clients of the major houses came to Drexel to trade in its market.

Market makers are very important in low-rated and unrated bonds because, prior to 1975, most investment banking firms would not make a market in these risky bonds. Most of these bonds were secondary issues, which did not have to be registered with the SEC, and there was no public listing of their rate of return. As early as 1977, Drexel had established itself as the number one player in the junk bond market. Milken's operation controlled 75 percent of the then small, high-yield securities market. Drexel was the first and major player attempting to establish the liquidity of this market, and it was creating the price and the market as it traded these bonds. Drexel was the key to liquidity of these bonds, assuring the holders of the bonds that it would buy them when they needed cash. The market was no more than a network of issuers and Drexel buyers with Drexel at the center (see Chapter 2).

Purchase of the bonds was dependent on the firm's knowledge that Drexel could resell the bonds at a profit. The network of buyers was the key to Drexel's sales success. Milken's knowledge of these trades and Drexel's records of ad hoc exchanges were the creation of the high-yield bond market. There was no separate objective market such as the NYSE or the NASDAC. Drexel created a large number of high-risk securities to appeal to both issuers and investors: collateralized bond obligations, split coupon securities, pay-in-kind bonds, and increasing rate notes.

It was not until 1977 that Drexel underwrote its first original public bond issue: Texas International (TI), for $30 million. It offered seven original issues, including TI, that year (Yago 1991, p. 23). As the market expanded and other firms began to trade high-yield bonds, Drexel's portion of the market decreased, but until the late 1980s Drexel always controlled the largest portion of the high-yield market. Drexel's portion of the market never shrank to less than 40 percent until after it was indicted on securities fraud.

By 1983, high-yield bonds comprised nearly 40 percent of all outstanding corporate debt (p. 24). Drexel's junk bonds resembled standard corporate bonds. They paid interest twice a year; matured in three, five, or some designated number of years; and were generally sold in lots of $1 million or larger to institutional investors. However, other investment banks made loans to raiders, stipulating that their more traditional, lower-interest-rate loans would be paid off before any repayment of third-level debt, which Drexel was underwriting with higher-interest-rate junk bonds. Thus, should a takeover attempt fail, or the takeover firm later file for bankruptcy, the senior debt and second-level debt of the banks' and major investment banks' loans were repaid entirely before the holders of junk bonds could receive any interest payments or any repayment on their principal (Yago 1991, pp. 19–20; Jensen 1988, p. 37; Lipton et al. 1987, pp. 15–17). Therefore, although they paid the higher yield of 11 to 22 percent, they were highly speculative. The real assets of junk to the raiders were, first, that it secured this difficult to sell third-level debt. Second, the raiders used the capital that they secured from their junk bond issues as collateral in borrowing additional underwritten capital from major investment banking houses. Third, Drexel's junk did not carry the stigma that there might not be a market for it if the deal was not made or failed, because Drexel assured the potential seller that if it could not find a market, Drexel would purchase the bonds, albeit not at full price. Thus there was always a market.

KKR was Drexel's largest issuer of high-yield bonds and exemplified the environment that Drexel created and operated within. KKR raised billions of dollars to take over firms between 1977 and 1991 and is still doing so, though at a greatly reduced rate. Peter Ackerman, Michael Milken's head trader, managed the KKR account and helped to finance over a dozen of KKR's largest buyouts:

(1) In 1984, Cole National Corporation of Cleveland, $318 million (KKR supplied only 26.1 percent of the investment in equity). Drexel later purchased this corporation with management.

(2) In 1985, Motel 6 Inc., a Dallas-based chain, $881 million (KKR supplied only 14.2 percent of the investment in equity).

(3) In 1985, Storer Communications Inc., a Miami-based television and cable TV company, $2.5 billion (KKR supplied only 8.8 percent of the investment in equity).

(4) In 1986, Beatrice Companies, a Chicago-based food and unrelated product conglomerate, $6.2 billion (KKR supplied only 6.6 percent of the investment in equity).

(5) Also in 1986, Safeway Stores, an Oakland, California–based grocery

chain, $4.2 billion (KKR supplied only 3.0 percent of the investment in equity).

(6) In 1987, Owens-Illinois, Inc., a Toledo-based maker of glass and plastic bottles, $3.7 billion (KKR supplied only 4.7 percent of the investment in equity).

(7) Also in 1987, Jim Walter Corporation, a Tampa, Florida, homebuilding, coal mining, and pipe-making conglomerate, $2.4 billion (KKR supplied only 6.0 percent of the investment in equity).

(8) In 1989, RJR Nabisco, Inc., a New York–based tobacco and food conglomerate, $26.4 billion (KKR originally supplied only 5.6 percent of the investment in equity, but later raised it to 12.1 in the July 1990 refinancing).[12]

Two of these were the largest LBOs of the past decade. In 1986, KKR's purchase of Beatrice for $6.2 billion was the largest LBO in the history of capitalism. Before the buyout, Beatrice was a consumer products company formed through mergers and LBOs. To purchase the company KKR contributed only $407 million in equity and borrowed $3.3 billion from banks. Drexel raised another $2.5 billion of funded debt in the high-risk market, a record amount of debt for a single buyout. The notes ran between 11 and 15–1/4 percent.

Three years later, Drexel helped underwrite KKR's buyout of RJR Nabisco for a record $25.07 billion. Joseph reported that this "is something we are not likely to see often, due to limits on the availability of debt, high-risk and otherwise" (p. 122). Here he blames the politicians for not raising the level of high-risk debt that banks can hold. KKR required $11.9 billion in bank financing, and a recent study by Moody's Investors Service noted that eleven of American's largest banks held a total of $21 billion in LBO loans.

In 1990, Joseph reported that Drexel was among the largest employee-owned companies in the country. In 1988, the firm had close to $4 billion in revenues, over $2 billion in capital, and was 75 percent owned by officer-employees. He reported that "Our employees' personal fortunes are tied to the firm's performance, and our people have a vested interest in the firm's continued growth" (p. 125). In fact, nearly every trader in the high-risk bond department was a millionaire and some were multimillionaires. Michael Milken, vice president and head of the High-Yield Bond Department, was a billionaire.

The Role of Investment Bankers in Setting Strategy

One of the strongest reasons for the increase in LBOs in the mid- and late 1980s was the ability of investment advisers, bankers, underwriters, and LBO fund managers to earn substantial up-front fees in the transactions. Fees routinely totaled at least 6 percent of the corporation's purchase price and lent considerable momentum to the process itself. Investment bankers, underwriters, and traders earn substantial income if the LBO is completed, and thus have strong incentives to identify the targets, arrange financing, and conclude the transaction. At the same time, investment bankers have little or no interest in the long-range success of the new corporations formed. Investment bankers stake the players by raising the billions necessary to finance mergers, raids, and LBOs. But they are not impartial lenders: They also supply expertise and coach their clients in how to raid. They market the stocks and bonds of the company needing financing. They make loans based on the assets of the target firm.

Increasingly, these financial intermediaries have become major players, not only in their role as advisers to the firms in the exchange, but also in their own interest. They are paid handsomely for their efforts. They design and promote deals that they know will pay both initially and also over several related transactions. Often an initial takeover will lead to the raiding firm being taken over a few months or a year later. The bankers who make the initial deal are in the best position to know the innate weaknesses of the former raider and are therefore in the best position to inform the new raider of the best takeover strategies. They assist in putting a firm into play as part of the take-over process. This generally causes the stock to skyrocket in value. Some bankers have been known to buy this stock before it gets put into play and, when they themselves have limited funds for such purchases, to sell information about impending takeovers to others who trade on it (e.g., Levine's sell to Boesky). Arbitragers like Boesky can affect the outcome of deals by acquiring and selling large blocks of stock to the raider, management, or the market. The corporations become like pieces on a chess board where the investment banker is the master of the game.

Offensive Strategies. Investment bankers play a triple game of making the deals (facilitating the mergers), running the business of stock trading, and stock arbitrage operations. They play a game within a game—vying against one another to underwrite the debt. They compete against other investment bankers to substitute their deal, their strategy for the takeover, their underwriting for that of the corporation's chosen firm.

To defeat management, investment bankers with their legal counsel design two-tiered raids for the takeover corporation. They entice stockholders into selling out quickly by offering more for shares sold early than for those sold later in the deal. Management, with its own legal and financial advisers, retaliates through such tactics as "poison pills" and "shark repellent" strategies designed to deter raiders. The firm and its management also incur huge debts in order to pay high dividends to stockholders and make shares available to them at ruinously low prices to keep them from selling out to the raider. Management may flood the market by issuing stock to prevent raiders from raising their percentage control of the firm's equity. Management may attempt to "lock up options" to defeat raids by contracting in advance to sell especially valuable corporate assets to third parties in the event of an outside takeover.

Investment bankers are ever conscious of their percentage of the market because this is not only an indication of their status in the industry, but it is advertising to their potential customers. Merger kings, like T. Boone Pickens, Ronald Perelman, and Carl Icahn, know the rankings of investment banking firms. They know who can do the deal and who cannot. They know which firms can compete and which cannot. In a game in which even one-hundredth of a percentage point is a large commission, they know that they will get the best rate from the larger firms. The competition among investment bankers is thus fierce and corrupt.

Investment bankers compete with insurance companies, which manage the retirement funds of state and corporate workers. Such banking firms provide billions to fund LBOs for firms like KKR. Henry Kravis made his substantial fortune through buying, selling, and restructuring firms built by others. KKR's subordinate debt was often financed by Drexel's High-Yield Bond Department. For example, in 1986 Donald P. Kelly joined with KKR and, with funding from Drexel's junk bonds, bought control of Beatrice Foods for a record $6.25 billion plus commissions and fees ($5.8 billion was debt). To pay for Beatrice, KKR raised a buyout fund (equity capital) of $1.35 billion, approximately half of which was supplied by pension funds and other institutional investors. The rest of the purchase price consisted of debt: $4 billion in bank loans and $2.5 billion in high-risk junk bonds from Drexel.

Who benefited from the takeover? KKR; Drexel; Kidder, Peabody; Lazard Freres; and Salomon Brothers received $162 million in fees, and the new president of Beatrice who had helped to take it over received $19.75 million for the takeover in addition to his $1.3 million annual salary. Another $22 million in golden parachutes was paid to Beatrice's top six executives to obtain their agreement to the takeover.

But the largest LBO of the 1980s was KKR's takeover of RJR Nabisco for $25.07 billion in December 1988. Ross Johnson, the CEO of RJR Nabisco, put the company into play just two months earlier by attempting to buy the firm and take it private for $17 billion. Johnson wanted to split up the conglomerate to profit from the sale of its parts (Helyar, Morris, and Stewart 1989). As depicted by the *Wall Street Journal* (Ander 1989), this was one of the most colorful of LBOs. Less than a week after Johnson put the company into play, KKR offered $21 billion for RJR Nabisco, and for the next two months the two companies battled over who would control the nation's nineteenth-largest firm. Another smaller buyout firm, Forstmann Little, became involved by consolidating the backing of three corporate sponsors. The cost of the deal rose, with an ever-increasing benefit to go to Johnson. On November 30, the board chose KKR as the winner with a record offer of over $25.07 billion.

The deal was so large that the electronic transfer of funds necessary to complete the deal exceeded the physical capacity of the Federal Reserve Bank's wire transfer. Drexel was at that very time under indictment and pleaded guilty to six counts of securities fraud, which carried a record fine of $650 million, but Drexel's fee for underwriting KKR's takeover of RJR Nabisco was $600 million, which would nearly cover the fines.

Thus the fees to Drexel had the side effect of covering its payoff to the government. This could hardly have been a productive use of capital for the U.S. economy. Wells may have put it best when he wrote,

> Seldom had greed and ego, common features of Wall Street life, been so nakedly on display. [It was an] unseemly spectacle of deal aspirants fighting like kids in a sand box for the right to reap millions in profits, not by creating anything but by tearing apart one of the nation's best known companies. . . . A healthy appetite for profits is what makes capitalism work. But at these levels, it is just a power game in which money is a means of keeping score and the deals themselves are sometimes pointless and destructive. (1988, p. 2, quoted from *Time* business editor, Stephen Koepp, 1988b, p. 22; see also 1988a)

Defensive Strategies. The view of the organization from the perspective of the financier is in terms of its financial structure (Jensen 1983). The financial structure is the debt (value owed creditors, largely bondholders and banks) to equity (value of shareholder's stake) ratio. Equity and debt are alternative ways for managers to fund firms' capital structures. Jensen would want to know the optimum debt-to-equity ratio in order to maximize short-term returns to shareholders. Managers take a different view. During the peak years of LBO activity, seated managers often had to take a defensive strategy against financiers. This was more often than not a restructuring of their firm. A corporate restructuring is any transaction that could have an effect on equity ownership, including a merger, a management buyout or a recapitalization. Coffee, writing in the mid-1980s, defines three types of restructuring: (1) stock repurchase or leveraged buyout at a higher price by management and its shareholder allies; (2) the paying of higher dividends to shareholders outright in order to reduce a firm's liquidity; and (3) "operational restructuring," which involves the sale of corporate divisions or other assets, usually occurring after a takeover (1986: 54). During the mid-1980s restructuring was a euphemism for a management buyout or divestiture after a takeover.

Toward the end of the 1980s it was used to mean a recapitalization after a bankruptcy, usually of a firm that had been taken over and had its corporate assets and divisions sold off (between 1985 and mid-1986, 23 percent of the top 850 corporations engaged in operational restructuring (p. 54). As a defensive mechanism, management eliminated as much equity as possible to remove the incentives for a raid. They could do this by bringing the value of the firm's stock—and the dividends paid to shareholders—in line with the value of the firm's assets, or they could themselves take on more debt, through a takeover, or expansion. The *Wall Street Journal* (Hertzberg and Monroe 1985) points out that at its peak between January 1984 and July 1985, 398 of the 850 largest corporations in North America restructured. Only 52 of these restructurings were in response to an actual takeover bid or threat. The others were self-initiated, in many cases defensive strategies.

An essential question during the 1980s was, When does a firm in need of capital increase its debt as opposed to issuing stock, thereby increasing equity and lowering the value of each share? This is not a simple financial decision because it has political ramifications. Stockholders tend to prefer that the corporation borrow money (increase their debt holdings) rather than dilute the value of their stock by issuing more stock and thereby lowering the value of shareholders' stock and reducing their earnings. On the other hand, managers may prefer to dilute the control of stockholders by issuing more stock. At the same time, if they dilute the value of the stock too much, stock prices will fall and they run the risk of a takeover. If a firm does not have substantial retained earnings, which is the most desirable option, how does a firm acquire funds for growth, expansion, etc.? Generally the firm will *acquire debt*. It will only resort to the issuance of equity if all other sources of funds are exhausted. *Thus the expansion of the 1980s was obtained largely through the dependence of corporate America on the bond market, which linked them to investment bankers.*

Because corporations preferred bonds over stocks, the stock market declined significantly in the 1970s. High inflation drove investors out of the stock market and into the bond market, where they could protect their investments through higher yields. Firms had to enter the bond market because they were afraid to issue stock, which would drive their stock prices down even further. Large firms were operating under conditions of high inflation, which meant higher interest rates on their bonds and increasing indebtedness; their equity was declining and thus their profits were eroding (Fama and Schwert 1977; Fama 1981; Taggart 1985).

The bond market was in turn fueled by the merger movement. Firms that were targets of takeovers had to increase the price of their stock to avoid acquisition. The corporation could purchase shares of their own stock, but in order to do this they had to spend their retained earnings or borrow funds. Borrowing to purchase stock usually meant incurring further debt through issuing bonds. This additional debt simultaneously made the firm less attractive as a takeover target, thus repelling the acquirer.

A second, more aggressive strategy to avoid takeover is known as *PacMan*, named for the video game that was popular in the 1980s. It is an apt name, because in this kind of strategy, the potential target is protected because the potential acquirer is itself acquired. A *PacMan* strategy was used in 1982 by Martin Siegel when he was employed by Kidder, Peabody. William Agee had launched a $1.5 billion hostile takeover of Martin Marietta, a major defense contractor. Marietta retained Kidder, Peabody, and Siegel retaliated by asking Boesky to buy shares of Bendix, an Agee-held firm. Siegel knew that if the price of Bendix shares began to rise, it would be a signal to Agee that Siegel's verbal threat to take over Bendix was credible. Siegel testified (*SEC v. Martin A. Siegel* 1987, pp. 10–14) that Bendix stock rose instantly after he spoke to Boesky. (When one company tries to take over another, the price of the target's stock generally rises, while the price of the acquirer's falls. In this case, the acquirer's stock, Bendix, was rising.)

Agee continued his pursuit of Marietta, the expense of which seriously weakened Bendix, and triggered a bidding war for Bendix between Allied Corporation and United Technologies. Ultimately Allied took over Bendix. Thus a white knight came in to rescue not the originally targeted firm Marietta, but the firm that was the original acquirer, Bendix. Martin Marietta was greatly weakened, but Martin Siegel had protected it from the Agee/Bendix takeover. Siegel and Kidder, Peabody earned substantial fees, but the real profits were made by Boesky, who made $120 million on the Bendix stock he purchased on the inside tip from Siegel. This was the beginning of the Siegel/Boesky link.

Firms that are not themselves involved in takeovers are likely to be targets of takeovers. Therefore, a third strategy employed by target firms to prevent being taken over is to become involved in taking over a third firm. In order to do so, it has to borrow the capital, thereby incurring debt and making itself less attractive to a merger or takeover attempt. Of course, increasing indebtedness also weakens the stability of the firm, and often the target firm's long-term survival depends on its ability to divest itself of underperforming divisions of the newly acquired firm. Ultimately, being able to apply the strategies of raiders may be the best defense and the best way to maintain autonomy and independence.

A fourth defensive strategy is to keep the stock for each of the divisions of the corporation above book value. The best method of achieving this end is to make certain that the profits for each division are high. If the stock price falls significantly below the book value, it is perceived by raiders as obviously undervalued and the division becomes attractive as a target.

THE TRANSFORMATION OF THE CAPITAL STRUCTURE
AND THE PRODUCTION OF CORPORATE DEBT

Repurchases of existing stock exceeded the new equity issued in the 1980s. American corporations shifted from equity producers to debt holders. In other words, a *de*capitalization process was taking place. In 1984, equity across corporate America shrank by $85 billion (Coffee 1986, p. 42). The debt-to-equity ratio in American corporations increased from 73 percent in 1983 to 81.4 percent in 1984 (pp. 41–42).

American corporate wealth was transferred from corporations to shareholders. Jensen points out (1988, p. 21) that the value of transfers of corporate control peaked at $180 billion in each of 1985 and 1986 (47 percent above the previous record of $122 billion in 1984). Shareholders in target firms received $346 billion (in 1986 dollars) from 1977 to 1986, and shareholders of acquiring firms received another $50 billion. This combined total of nearly $400 billion represented 51 percent of the total cash dividends paid to all investors from 1977 to 1986. In 1985 alone, such transactions totaled $37.4 billion or 32 percent of all public acquisitions, and in 1986 they totaled $44.3 billion or 39 percent. Average premiums paid to shareholders in these transactions exceeded 50 percent (p. 32). Shareholders' wealth increased as corporate assets decreased.

As corporations were taken over, the top-level managers of targets were often seen as fungible commodities. Nearly half of all top managers of target firms are typically displaced within three years of any takeover, hostile or voluntary (p. 35). These managers generally protect themselves with large shares of equity. Thus although after 1984 total wages paid to nonproductive workers (managers) grew more slowly, these nonproductive workers reaped benefits as a result of the breakups of these firms.

The Transformation of Corporations and the Junk Bond Market

The junk bond market peaked in 1986 with nearly $32 billion in high-interest bonds being issued in that year alone (Ramiriz 1991, p. C1). All of the publicly held junk bonds outstanding in 1986 totaled $125 billion, or 23 percent of the total corporate bond market (Jensen 1988, p. 37). By this time it was no longer the other issuers of Drexel paper that were buying these bonds but institutional investors: 30 percent by mutual funds and another 30 percent by insurance companies, 15 percent each by pension funds and savings and loans and 10 percent by foreign investors (Yago 1991, p. 199). By the end of 1989, the junk bond market exceeded $200 billion in total value and comprised 25 percent of the entire corporate bond market (p. 199).

Toward the end of the 1980s the financial nature of American corporations had changed. Unlike the early days when takeovers, underwritten with junk bonds, were relatively secure because of the surplus equity of firms (nearly twice the capital needed to service their debt or interest payments), a typical junk bond issue in 1988 was no longer based on sufficient capital to meet its debt service *on the day it was issued* (Ramiriz 1991, p. C1, quoting Barrie Wigmore of Goldman, Sachs). Rather, in order to meet the debt payments and avoid bankruptcy, raiders had to arrange the resale of the target simultaneously with the takeover; the raider no longer had the luxury of selling off the parts to provide sheer profits. The debt-to-equity ratio of most firms was far less favorable.

By the end of the decade, the size and composition of the corporations entering the junk bond market had changed. In 1979, junk bonds were issued on small, innovative, high-growth firms, seeking debt as a substitute for venture capital; 50 percent of the entire junk bond market was composed of firms with revenue of less than $100 million. By 1988, 60 percent of the junk bond market was made up of firms with revenues exceeding $500 million. These were low-growth, low-innovation firms, seeking short-term debt.

Drexel was contributing to the instability of corporations by providing corporate raiders not with capital, but rather with "highly confident" letters indicating that Drexel could raise the capital. This expedited the deal, whether it was sound or not. Until Drexel was indicted in 1988 it never faulted on a commitment to raise capital. However, after its indictment in the wake of the failure of the high-yield bond market in 1989, it could not meet these commitments.

COMPETITION-FUELED TAKEOVER MOVEMENT

One phenomenon that undoubtedly fueled the takeover boom was the sight of other people making money by buying companies and selling them. Suddenly "cash flow," needed to support interest payments, and "asset value" in the event of a takeover became the major indicators of the value of a company. The notion of earnings became obsolete. Concern over industry and market sector competitors lessened, while concern over stock prices and rates of return of firms in other industries increased in importance. Internal competition became more important than external competition. Each division was evaluated solely on its rate of return to the company; thus each unit was concerned with its profit relative to the other units held by the firm. What the market sector as a whole was doing was not relevant. Each division sought its highest rate of return and its profits

were often used by the company to invest in other industries against which
the profitable units would have to compete. Each division became a potential target. At the same time, the company could either become involved
in the merger and acquisition mania or risk being the target of mergers and
possible reorganization by other companies. Thus the relevant firms for
any large corporation were other large corporations that were expanding
through mergers.

Corporations realized that just about any firm, no matter how small,
could buy another company using the assets of the target, if the assets of
the target were sufficiently liquid and its existing debt was not excessive.
The raiders realized that large profits could be made by buying companies,
taking them private, slashing expenses, and breaking out divisions and
selling them off at a profit.

CAPITAL SUPPLY AND THE CONTROL OF CAPITAL MARKETS

Stearns provides an insightful explanation of the relationship between
corporations and financial institutions by analyzing the impact of the
capital market on the control relationships between corporations and
financial institutions: "The capital market is viewed as a resource environment in which corporations meet their capital needs: (1990, p. 175). She
also acknowledges that the capital market is the social context in which the
power relations between financial institutions and corporate managers
evolve within a capitalist economy, but she does not analyze these processes. Rather, she views organizations from a structural-contingency
perspective, which assumes that variation in the capital market (the supply
of capital) will change the relationships between the corporation and the
bankers. Stearns offers empirical evidence of specific changes in corporate
capital needs and capital market conditions that were related to different
levels of corporate financial dependency in two different time periods:
between 1945 and 1960, and between 1965 and 1980. She concludes that,
because of differences in money supply levels, managerialists may have
correctly depicted managers as the major source of control of organizations
during the earlier period, while financial control arguments are correct in
depicting financial institutions as controlling organizations during the
latter period.

Stearns rightly points out that because capital is an uncertain but crucial resource, control over capital flows provides financial institutions
with a means of control over corporations. She then posits that the availability of investment capital is essential: "Major decisions in which corporate control is exercised typically require, and are therefore conditional

upon, the availability of investment capital" (1990, p. 176). This is an important point but does not go far enough. Investment capital may exist in the external environment and therefore be presumed to be available, but it is obviously available only to organizations that have access to equity or debt instruments (stocks or bonds) and have investment bankers who are willing to make deals and sell these securities. Financial institutions have discretion over the corporation in terms of making capital available.

Stearns (pp. 177–78) assumes that availability of resources in the environment in which the corporation obtains its resources is crucial to the power/dependency relationship. Certainly she is correct—the corporation cannot obtain resources that are not available, but because resources are available does not necessarily mean that the corporation has access to them.

Stearns (p. 177) examines two questions: Was capital in scarce or plentiful supply? Was there a high or low degree of concentration and coordination among financial institutions? She correctly argues that these factors limit the options available to corporations and affect the power of financial institutions to exercise control. But this does not tell us if financial institutions are exercising control over corporations. Corporations become dependent on financial institutions when they must rely on a financial institution for a strategic or critical resource that is not obtainable from another financial institution in their environment or that they cannot generate themselves.

Organizations may attempt to generate financial capital themselves through research and development or by obtaining it in the environment. Thus at any given time a single corporation may be less vulnerable through meeting its own strategic contingencies. However, if the amount of capital needed is too great for it to generate, it must obtain a loan. At this point the surplus of capital in the environment becomes a factor in access to capital. When capital supply is munificent (availability of financial capital is great), financial institutions cannot control the corporation because the strategic contingency can be acquired from other capital suppliers. However, the environment may be munificent, but the corporation may have little power or ability to obtain funding. Conversely, financial capital may be scarce, but the corporation may have access to, and control over, networks that give it access to capital.

The Role of Investment Bankers in Capital Markets

The capital market (securities market) is the financial environment in which the corporation exists. If the corporation requires capital for expansion or survival and cannot generate the capital through production or the sale of its stock on the market, it must do so by going into the bond market (acquiring a loan), through the sale of bonds. Thus the capital market consists of three types of organizations: those which use and need capital, those which supply the capital needed, and intermediaries. Not only do suppliers of capital as corporations and governments control the outcomes for corporations that need capital, but financial intermediaries such as commercial banks, savings and loans, and investment bankers also control outcomes.

A corporation that seeks funds by selling its equity (stock) will be influenced not only by the amount of capital in the market but also access to that capital. If the equities are traded publicly and capital is munificent, access may be relatively uncontrolled. Likewise, if the corporation is selling its debt (bonds) it will be influenced not only by the amount of capital in the market but also by access to that capital. If the bonds are traded publicly and capital is munificent, access may be relatively un-controlled. However if the amount of capital is scarce, and the equities or the bonds are not traded publicly or are not graded high enough to compete, intermediaries may have a great deal of control over whether or not the corporation is able to sell its stocks and bonds. Under the condition of trading nonpublic or high-risk securities, intermediaries often control the strategic contingencies, in this case money supply. They may have knowledge, skill, or simply access to networks that do not exist in the market.

If a financial institution controls a strategic contingency and is the sole or limited source to fill that contingency, it may be able to demand that a corporation do business with no other financial institution or do business with a closely held partner, or that the corporation buy bonds or equities of other corporations that the financial institution is selling. The financial institution may funnel business away from the corporation if it considers the business too high risk. It may attempt to place its own officers on the board of directors of the corporation, or to influence the retention, ad-vancement, and replacement of personnel. If the loan itself is considered high risk, the financial institution may restrict the firm from acquiring additional debt, limit the type and length of loans that may be incurred, or require that the firm sell warrants along with the bonds as sweeteners. Other types of intervention into the discretionary policy of the corporation may have to do with hierarchical arrangements for the use of profits, such that paying off debt to the financial institution may take precedence over employee bonuses or over paying dividends to stockholders.

Several other conditions increased the capital market that fueled the junk bond market in the 1980s. First, the deregulation and competition forced on American banks induced them to offer their depositors high rates of interest. But banks had to get higher rates of interest for their money in order to offer their depositors higher rates. In order to raise rates of interest on their money, they charged corporate borrowers. This created a disadvantage for the U.S. borrower of capital. The cost of capital in the United States was 10.7 percent, compared to 4.1 percent in Japan. U.S. corporations were far less leveraged than Japanese, German, and Canadian firms. When Drexel began to underwrite original junk bond issues in 1983, the corporate debt as a percentage of GNP was 34 percent, but by 1987 it was 42 percent (Yago 1991, pp. 30–31).

Deregulation governing pension funds allowed money managers to seek higher-yield investments and to take greater risks, even as they were prohibited by law from buying non–investment grade bonds. These deregulations of the banks and pension funds attracted international investors. The depth of competition for American corporations was greater than at any time in the past. The reasons for this rested largely in the multiple and diverse foreign market with which they now competed. This was evidenced by the balance of trade in which the U.S. ratio of imports to exports was greater than at any time in history.

The theory developed to explain the functioning of firms in the late 1970s and 1980s (Fama 1980; Fama and Jensen 1983a, 1983b) viewed the corporate form as embodied in the separation of ownership from management and as capable, if not actually efficient. In its circularity, it reasoned that if it were not an efficient form, it could not exist. (If it exists it is because it is efficient.) Thus the form was accepted as optimal and the analysts proceeded to explore ways to understand why that form dominated, and hence was efficient.

This theory further reasoned that not only is the present form of corporate governance the most efficient, but so is the stock market. Through the functioning of the stock market, the price of a firm's stocks and bonds changes instantaneously with changes in information concerning the firm's prospects. This includes an assessment of the effectiveness of management. If management is thought to be inefficient, then that information is reflected in the price of the stocks and bonds. Thus the market operates as one important mechanism of control and feedback (Fama 1965). Although this argument has not been made about the bond market, in order for this thesis to be supported, the bond market must be assumed to operate in a similar fashion.

CONCLUSIONS: TOWARD NEW THEORIES OF ECONOMIC ORGANIZATIONS

According to economic organizational theory, the formal role of directors (Fama and Jensen 1983a, 1983b) is to control managers to ensure that their use of stockholders' equity is in keeping with the goal of increasing at least their long-range wealth, if not immediate gains. This goal is ensured in financial corporations as well as industrial corporations by tying managers' compensation directly to the corporation's profits through such mechanisms as bonuses, stock options, and commissions (see Chapter 4 for a discussion of how this was done in Drexel). Thus as the manager maximizes profits for the stockholder, his or her own interests are maximized. Because these managers are self-interested, they will return profits to shareholders in order to maximize their own profits.

The corporation is viewed as a market, a nexus of contracted transactions between buyers and sellers. Transactions are performed efficiently according to agreed-upon exchange. The corporation ideally functions in market-mimicking fashion. Transaction cost theorists and agency theorists quite consciously attempt to transfer concepts drawn from rational choice and neoclassical economic theory into corporate functioning. There is no accounting for the fact that the organization is more than the sum of its divisible parts. That is, it can, by its functioning as a whole, increase the value produced. There is no difference between functioning efficiently and increasing societal value. There is no accounting for power within firms or the power of firms.

Power of the Firm

In economic organizational theory the firm is conceptualized as a power-neutral and literally boundaryless aggregate nexus of exchange much like an ideal market. Jensen and Meckling (1976) do not view corporations as wielders of collective wealth and arbitrary power. They are like shareholders in the market, which has a life and existence of its own. Power has no place in economic organization theory. Thus any phenomenon based on power wielding cannot be explained. The origin, development, and history of market forms is outside the purview of economic theory (Friedland and Robertson 1990, p. 7). The existing concentration of wealth and power in corporations, the distribution of wealth and power among firms, and the transformation of wealth and power are outside economic models of organizations. Economic organizational theory treats the wielding of power, should it occur, as an inefficiency that can be overcome by market forces alone. The market will weed out actors who are inefficient, just as it will weed out those who are corrupt. These inefficient managers and the corrupt are revealed as such when the corporation's competitors countervail, as they respond to market forces. By the same logic, efficient, positive, innovative actions are revealed as such because they enhance shareholders' private wealth and by some leap of faith contribute to the social wealth and well-being. Competitive markets always win out over power wielders and the corrupt in the marketplace.

Economic organization theories of the firm cannot take into account the power exercised by firms in the economic arena. According to these views, the only social collective that can act arbitrarily, and is therefore a threat to the individual and market processes, is the state. These theories fail to explain what happens when a corporate entity, such as Drexel and its constituent parts, such as the junk bond division, are freed from their existing normative duties. They are capable of exercising their collective wealth and power as arbitrarily as the state. In fact, they may be more powerful in economic markets than the state. Put another way, economic theories of organization cannot explain the power that corporations generate to control their own organization and others in their environment, because theories of the market cannot explain power.

Takeovers and Fraud

Economic organizational theorists view management as being sanctioned by hostile takeovers underwritten by the junk bond market. Somehow the shareholders strike a deal with a raider, independent of management, and wrestle control of the corporation from management. Such a process is not seen as a power play, but a market mechanism, which makes the firm more efficient. The deviant behavior of managers, behavior not in the interest of shareholders, is sanctioned by the market in organizations (takeovers). What is essentially a power play is redefined as a market mechanism. The taking on of debt is defined as a control mechanism to make managers more efficient. What these models do not say is that this is efficiency in the interest of shareholders, the uppermost class in United States society. These models advocate the redistribution of wealth away from the middle class to the upper class—a decidedly political action and a decidedly political view.

Likewise, illegal behavior in the market is disciplined by takeovers. Presumably the market eliminates fraud. Yet our analysis demonstrates that in some cases fraud is facilitated by such takeovers and in other cases fraud makes these takeovers more efficient. The market model is placed in the precarious position of having to define insider trading, securities fraud, etc., as positive innovation because they made the market transactions of the 1980s more efficient through hostile takeovers and the divestiture of corporations.

Where is the analysis of power in these models? Proponents of these models should be asking the question, Who controls these takeovers and who benefits? Although arguments originate from many different sources, there is considerable agreement that investment banks and institutional investors, through the direct ownership of equity or large holdings of corporate bonds, have come to control large corporations in the 1980s.

Who Controls: Corporations or Bankers?

Throughout history, there have been competing propositions about who controls large corporations. One such proposition that originated in the classic work of Adolf Berle and Gardiner Means's (1932) *The Modern Corporation and Private Property* is that managers have increasingly come to control corporations through the ever-increasing dispersion of stock among investors in private corporations. With stock ownership spread thinly among many stockholders, there is no way for owners to collectively exercise control. This, Berle and Means posit, has resulted in a separation of ownership and control. Similarly, Burt (1983) argues that the capture of financial investors or suppliers on boards allows firms to coopt these financial institutions. As early as 1959, Dahrendorf believed that this resulted in owners no longer controlling and managers no longer owning, a situation that would contribute to the disintegration of the capitalist class. In Dahrendorf's words the capitalist class had become a "plurality" (1959, p. 47). Pluralists use this argument to suggest that ownership of capital is increasingly irrelevant in understanding class. Rather, those who operate individual firms are viewed as managers whose interests are those of their firm rather than those of the capitalist class (Mizruchi 1982).

A view accepting the separation of ownership and management, but repositioning the source of control, sees banks and insurance companies as controlling corporations either directly or through control of their boards of directors (Mintz and Schwartz 1985). Mintz and Schwartz use two types of data to show the centrality of banks, insurance companies, and other institutional investors: corporate interlock data and selected cases of organizational intervention by banks. Network analysis reveals that banks and insurance companies are the central links between firms (Mintz and Schwartz 1985; Mizruchi 1982; Pennings 1980). This research demonstrates that when corporations are in crisis, large debt holders often supervise reorganization. Mintz and Schwartz argue that this produces financial hegemony. They lodge this research squarely in the resource dependency theory of Pfeffer and Salancik (1978) because, they argue, the dependency of firms on financing leaves them vulnerable to being controlled by these financial agencies. Kotz (1978) makes a slightly different argument that financial institutions use their control over firms to increase their business. Hence such firms would be more likely to go into debt and to engage in mergers.

Maurice Zeitlin (1974) launched a decidedly different attack on Berle and Means's thesis by challenging the empirical basis of the separation of ownership and control. Still others such as Baran and Sweezy (1966) and Miliband (1969) accepted the separation of ownership and control but argued that this separation had little effect on the nature of corporations or class in the United States.

Financial Conceptions and Financial Control Theories

Fligstein (1990a) makes still another argument—that the actions of corporations are a result of the manager's attempts to promote the survival of the firm as the forces of competitors and the government converge upon it. Antitrust legislation is seen as an impediment to the ability of the firm to control competition. Fligstein's thesis is that organizations search for stable patterns of interaction with their largest competitors, to eliminate uncertainty by eliminating competition. Once the pattern of interaction proves to be legal and profitable, other organizations establish the same pattern, which he calls "the conception of control." Conceptions of control are worldviews held by managers about what are appropriate and inappropriate responses to competition and regulation. According to Fligstein, over the past one hundred years, four conceptions of control have organized corporations: direct, manufacturing, sales and marketing, and financial. The sales and marketing conception of control dominated the largest U.S. firms after World War II until 1970. The primary method of survival during this period was research and development.

As early as the 1950s, the financial conception of the firm began to appear. According to Fligstein this conception of control stresses the use of financial tools to evaluate product lines and divisions on the basis of profitability because profitability, specifically short-run profitability, is all that matters. Financial and accounting tools are the only methods of assessment that count. The tools of the past generations of strategic decision-makers from production and sales are obsolete. Fligstein found that by 1970, the largest firms had become multiproduct, multi-industry firms generally formed through the process of mergers. Firms divest themselves of any product line or division that underperforms financially. The structure of the firm is multidivisional and decision-making is decentralized.

Fligstein's book on the transformation of corporate control did not analyze the 1980s, however, when financial firms controlled organizations. This view is held across large firms in established organizational fields and operates to support reactions to actions of competitive firms that might be defined as putting the firm into play. In addition, this control across firms operates to select managers who share the same worldview, in this case that of the firm as financial actor (Fligstein 1987). However, this does not mean that the values, conceptions, and socialization of these managers determined their ability to control in the 1980s.

The finance conception of control can be defined as the point of view that conceives of the firm as purely a financial unit. A firm is a number of divisions, each earning varying rates of return on its assets. Short-run return is all that matters. Mergers, divestitures, stock repurchases, and judicious use of debt and equity are strategies to be managed to bring about short-run profits. Firms are restructured from multidivisional units of the same or related products to totally unrelated units of conglomerates, characterized by their product mixes. These unrelated units are treated as stock, to be bought and sold; the corporation is a portfolio of stocks.

Managers of large conglomerates need an easy way to evaluate each of their units. Reducing each component to rate of return earned becomes the only common denominator (Fligstein 1990a). But is this not a conception of firms that gives some corporate and financial actors more power than others? Fligstein also points out that managers have to be able to evaluate a wide variety of product lines if they wish to expand—during the early postwar era, the federal government strictly enforced the antitrust laws prohibiting the formation of vertically differentiated firms through the acquisition of competitors or suppliers by mergers.

By the 1970s, a whole new breed of American corporate entrepreneur had emerged: for example, James Ling, Harold Green, and Ted Turner. A counterpart financial entrepreneur emerged in the 1980s for the express purpose of buying and selling corporations, exemplified by KKR. Both types successfully used junk bonds in leveraged acquisitions. Mergers, LBOs, and other forms of acquisition became the new method of expansion. If major corporations wanted to continue to survive, they had to protect themselves by buying back their stock, taking on large amounts of debt, or manipulating their stock prices. In order to become a CEO of a major corporation, it became increasingly important that one know and be ahead of the merger movement in terms of these strategies and tactics. Therefore, finance executives have increasingly moved to head the largest corporations, as opposed to the marketers and manufacturers of previous eras.

These heads of major corporations have the same worldview as the banking financiers. At the same time, the Reagan and Bush administrations all but abolished the enforcement of antitrust laws, opening the door to all types of diversification, vertical and horizontal, and mergers, related and unrelated. The firms that are leaders in the takeover and buyout mergers are those with finance CEOs; those which are prone to reorganize are headed by finance CEOs. Both of these activities require that organizations take on greater amounts of debt. Organizations that are more likely to be the object of takeovers do not have finance CEOs, do not take on a great deal of debt, and are not skilled in the arts of taking on debt to fend off takeovers. But some firms have a head start: They are the firms that define the strategies, method of diversification, and divestitures; supply the capital for the takeovers and buyouts; reap the commissions, fees, and warrants; and even profit beyond the norm. Being both a financial firm and an investment banking firm, Drexel was in a position to be a powerful player in the transformation of corporate control. Few investment banking firms had any real power prior to the 1980s. The transformation of corporate control provided the investment banking firms with power because they are located at the nexus of the transactions. Even so, many investment banking firms did not have the knowledge and skill to take advantage of their strategic positions—but Drexel did. The real power center of Drexel was in the High-Yield Bond Department, not only because it gained control of the internal structure of the organization, as described in a previous chapter, also because it was strategically placed in the economic context in which it functioned.

The High-Yield Bond Department used its control of corporations to transform them through mergers and acquisitions, many of them becoming unrelated conglomerates. It used its power to change their capital structure from equity to debt. It used its control of profits, the strategic contingency of Drexel, to gain control over the corporation. And it used its power over the market and Drexel to wield power over Congress. (These relationships are discussed in the next chapter.)

At the same time, the High-Yield Bond Department took on the structure and strategy of the financially driven firms with which it did business. The employees were rewarded based on the business they brought into the firm, the fees they generated from putting the mergers and acquisitions together, and more importantly the financial fees they generated from these mergers and acquisitions together. The salaries of employees were a small part of their compensation. The West Coast office was not only financing the mergers and acquisitions with high-yield bonds, but from the mid-eighties on they were also bringing in most of the M&A clients. This meant that its share of the bonus pool was correspondingly larger than any other department. This ultimately meant it had more power at Drexel than any other department. But this did not lead to greater value for Drexel; it led to the failure of Drexel.

CONCLUSIONS: A STRUCTURAL MODEL

Both agency theory (i.e., Jensen's work), an economic model of organizations, and the financial conception of organizations (i.e., Fligstein's work), an institutional model, define the bases for organizational action in the same way (isomorphically). Both differ greatly on the causal factors of the transformation. Both agency theory and the financial conception of firms are normative models of the firm. The former rests on the normative economic model of neoclassical economic theory, in which the individual is viewed as a utility maximizer who rationally calculates and assesses alternatives to maximize benefits and minimize costs. Agency theory, like neoclassical economic theory, defines preferences as the basis for both individual and organizational actions. The financial conception of the firm rests on consensus, which is the result of common socialization of financial managers. This socialization teaches them to define the organization in terms of the bottom line. The concept is that firms are portfolios of other firms, which are to be bought and sold. The concept is not something that needs to be agreed upon, because the manager has internalized it. The idea or "conception" is, in Durkheim's terms, a "non-contractual element of contract," which is by its very nature assumed ([1893] 1933, p. xviii, and Book I, Chapter 7, Part 2, for discussion).

In my analysis, I use a structural model based not on the "distributional" structural approach of Blau (1982; Blau and Schwartz 1984), but on the "relational" form of structural analysis. In this model, structure is developed through people interacting with each other in direct social relationships. This structural perspective is different from both of the normative perspectives described above. It is rooted in the networks of interactions that lie outside the normative constructs and attributes of everyday categories (White, Boorman, and Breiger 1976, p. 733).

The structural perspective makes no assumptions about what the basis of action should be, and it makes no assumptions about microlevel motives and preferences. Like Cyert and March's (1963) and Granovetter's actors (1985, p. 506), the actor is intended rational. But rationality is problematic. Decisions made by actors are limited by social-structural constraints, such as other actors (for example, the actions of competitors, sellers, and buyers). The interests of the corporation can also be affected by social structural constraints (for example, economic and legal) that the firm faces.

Jensen's agency theory and Fligstein's financial conception of control lack theories of organizational power. In both theories those who control the firm have authority, but this is problematic for these models. There are actors who control corporations (Kotz 1978) from outside these corporations, who are neither managers nor shareholders. Organizations pursue their interests both individually and collectively, by attempting to control the behavior of other organizations. Regardless of the assumptions of various economic models of organizations and the fact that often what appears to be collective action is actually the consequences of similar behavior by like actors, there is also a great deal of common collective action taken on the part of corporations. But it is not necessary for firms to act collectively in order to promote their interests and achieve their goals. They may act unilaterally as aggregates that have like interests and have the same impact as LSL and Drexel did in attempting to affect the bank regulatory boards (see Chapter 7 for an analysis).

Corporations are under constant pressure to control the constraints placed on them by other powerful actors in their environment—to reduce environmental uncertainty (Pfeffer and Salancik 1978). Drexel was constantly attempting to control buyers and sellers through forming networks in which sellers became buyers of other issues that Drexel was selling. But still more powerful actors in Drexel's environment—Congress—threatened to limit Drexel's interests by enacting laws that constrained its ability to sell high-risk bonds to savings and loans and pension funds. The attempt to influence political officials and regulatory boards was an important way to restrict constraints on the firm's behavior and thus reduce environmental uncertainty.

Often these buyers and sellers became economically dependent upon Drexel. Because of this dependency they supported what was in Drexel's interest, just as Drexel supported legislation and regulation that was in the interest of its buyers and sellers. The basis for their collective action was not social ties or kinship; it was not that they had attended the same Ivy League schools, because they had not; it was not that they had the same financial conception of the firm, or other values. It was rather that they were structurally, economically interdependent upon each other as financial institutions as their clients and customers often were. Drexel was the hub of a giant mergers and acquisitions machine of buyers and sellers of junk bonds. The role of this interdependency was underestimated by all until Drexel went bankrupt and the junk bond market failed.

Drexel failed for at least three reasons. First, as Richard Breeden points out (1990, p. 20) at the time of the government settlement on the six counts of securities fraud, Drexel had a substantial inventory of junk bonds. Why did Drexel carry such a large inventory of junk bonds? Second, Drexel after its indictment continued to rely heavily on mergers and acquisitions and activities related to the junk bond securities. Why did it not change? Third, Drexel was unable to borrow by issuing commercial paper. To effect such a program, it would have had to possess liquid, pledgeable assets as a backup. This would have permitted Drexel to satisfy its liquidity needs through secured bank loans if for any reason it lost access to commercial paper. Drexel had only illiquid, privately placed investments in unregulated subsidiaries and in uncollateralized securities (predominantly junk bond securities).

All three of these economic reasons led directly to Drexel's past and persisting dependency on the junk bonds that were controlled by the

High-Yield Bond Department. When the junk bond market failed in 1989, Drexel could not change its corporate strategy, its power structure, its decentralization of discretionary decision-making, its major market, or its capital base.

Few sociologist have empirically analyzed the effects of economic interdependency on the political action of firms. Although Mintz and Schwartz (1985) analyze the power of financial institutions, it is their ability to resolve interindustry conflict, not their control of environmental certainty or their ability to control legislation, that affects their ability to do business.

Thus in developing the model of this analysis two criteria were generated from the limits of the literature and the nature of the financial institutions being analyzed: (1) a focus on the corporation rather then the individual, and (2) the relationships among financial firms and corporations, and, in the next chapter, government agencies. Keeping these criteria in mind, the guiding questions were: What are the financial interdependencies which exist between these entities? Which entities have power?

NOTES

12.   The underwriting was originally for $25.07 billion but the actual price was $26.4 billion. That is the reason for the two different figures for the deal here and earlier.

Chapter 7

Political-Legal Context

Drexel not only worked to control its economic environment of competitors, sellers, and buyers; it also attempted to control uncertainty in its political environment (1) by reforming laws that restricted junk bond–LBOs and punished securities fraud (such as antitrust laws, securities laws, and RICO laws), (2) by supporting laws that facilitated LBOs (such as tax laws that allow companies to write off interest on debt), and (3) by blocking potential laws from being enacted if they inhibited takeovers (such as antigreenmail laws). Corporations are far from passive actors—rather they are active participants in the making and reform of laws that affect their business. Furthermore, businesses that are economically interdependent work together to bring about political actions that facilitate their business interests. This chapter speaks to the question of the relationship between corporations, banks, and the state. In the last half of this chapter I map out the joint action relationships among a number of the most powerful financial firms in the 1980s to demonstrate how Drexel worked with LSL, to control the regulatory structures and to reform RICO in the interests of Drexel, Michael Milken, Charles Keating, and LSL.

My position is that corporate and financial elites, unlike less powerful actors, have direct access to politicians, especially congresspersons, through constituent relations, campaign contributions, PAC contributions, lobbies, and speaking engagements. Through these relationships, they directly influence the political-legal environment in which they operate. These direct relationships are exposed through a structural network analysis of the reform of RICO, presented in the last half of this chapter. The reform of RICO is only one example of Drexel's influence on the legal context in which it conducted business. [Other examples are fully explicated in a forthcoming book on the relationships between investment bankers, corporations and the state in the 1980s. (Zey, forthcoming).]

The Congress, which made and reformed securities, tax, antitrust, bankruptcy, and RICO laws, became essential to Drexel's daily existence. Fred Joseph, Drexel's CEO, participated in congressional hearings on the long-run consequences of the proliferation of mergers and acquisitions funded through LBOs. The High-Yield Bond Department organized and controlled the Alliance for Capital Access to lobby for the deregulation of banking both directly and through its relationship with Charles Keating. All of this was being done as it worked for the reform of the RICO Act under which Michael Milken and Charles Keating were indicted and under the threat of which Drexel had pleaded guilty to six counts of securities fraud.

This structural analysis of interorganizational relations is based on the resource dependency model. This model is part of a rich tradition that includes Selznick's (1949) analysis of the Tennessee Valley Authority, Zald's (1970) analysis of the Young Men's Christian Association, and the more contemporary works of Pfeffer and his associates (Aldrich and Pfeffer 1976; Pfeffer and Salancik 1978).

The guiding premise drawn from this perspective is that organizations exist in environments that are potentially turbulent and therefore threatening. The threat and uncertainty in the environment are overcome by gaining access to resources. The effectiveness of the organization in dealing with the environment has a major impact on its internal working and success. Drexel's power in relation to other organizations, both economic and political, was a function of its ability to gain access to resources and use these resources to control political organizations in its environment. During the 1980s, Drexel was constantly working at managing and limiting uncertainty, including developing a stable and predictable relationship with its political environment.

Drexel established various ways of doing this: One was to create interlocking networks of buyers and sellers to control its economic and, indirectly, its political environment. Thus the organizations with which it did business were dependent on it both to underwrite and sell their bonds and to buy other corporation's bonds. In fact, Drexel required that issuers buy high-yield bonds. Indirectly these organizations and Drexel were interdependent because any changes in the legal structures that affected these corporations affected Drexel's ability to do business. Thus if laws were made that limited the amount of junk a buyer could purchase, it affected the ability of Drexel to sell junk. Thus the sellers, buyers, and Drexel were jointly affected.

Drexel also established interlocking boards of directors. Bond salesmen and traders as well as investment bankers served on the boards of many of the targets that Drexel defined as takeovers for their clients. For example, Leon Black, the head of the M&A Department in New York, was appointed to the board of directors of Harris Graphics because Drexel held 1.2 million shares of Harris Corporation when it was formed. There is a considerable body of literature on such interlocking boards. Most of this research assumes that financial institutions are being co-opted by corporations in order to control the latter's potentially disruptive environment. Thus banks' and corporations' needs for financial support are simultaneously brought under control of the corporation. Significant among those who view the bank representatives as recruited to corporations' boards are Thompson and McEwen (1958), Burt (1983), and Mizruchi and Stearns (1988). They all found that high levels of debt were associated with interlocks between corporations and financial institutions.

A weakness of most of the research on the relationships between financial institutions and both economic and political organizations is that it assumes that the corporation or the state initiates relationships with banks in order to control access to ready capital. The origin of the interlock is not investigated, only its existing structure. It is often difficult to determine if the bank is co-opted by the corporation or if the bank infiltrates the corporation. Some theorists have attempted to make the case for both directions in the formation of the link (Koenig, Gogel, and Sonquist 1979; Palmer 1983; Mizruchi and Stearns 1986).

In my analysis, I found that investment banks often placed their representatives on a target's board after a takeover in order for the bank to more closely monitor the solvency of the corporation, a condition that was generally highly marginal for a number of years after a takeover. In these cases, the bank infiltrated the corporation in order to protect its short-term investments. But other types of direct relationships were established between banks, corporations, and political legal agencies. Some of these are discussed later in this chapter.

Regardless of whether banks or corporations initiate relationships between them, there is a second and equally important question of how these relationships are sustained and which party actually controls the other. From the examination of the relationships between corporations and banks in Chapter 6, it is obvious that the question of ownership was not important [this is the reason that many Marxists reject the empirical basis of Berle and Means's thesis (see Zeitlin 1974; Zeitlin, Ewen, and Ratcliff 1974)]. As early as the turn of the century, Corey (1930) found that, even though stock was widely dispersed among many owners, this did not place corporations in the hands of managers. In fact, financiers controlled corporations. The control of U.S. corporations by financiers in the 1980s similarly defies the Berle and Means thesis, as well as Jensen's thesis that managers control American corporations. Stock ownership is as irrevelant today when KKR and Drexel control Beatrice and RJR Nabisco as it was when J.P. Morgan controlled U.S. Steel. Corey writes:

> The House of Morgan and other financial masters did not own the corporations under their control. Nor was ownership necessary. Stockholders

being scattered and numerous, control was easily usurped by minority
interests, particularly when interests were institutionalized in the formidable combination of the House of Morgan. (1930, p. 284)

Substitution of Drexel and KKR for the House of Morgan easily describes
the 1980s and leads us to question Jensen's arguments. Owners are not in
control of corporations, but neither are managers. Stock ownership is
unimportant, because the companies that are taken over and the relationships that facilitate their takeover are a result of financial pressures, relations with financial institutions, and sometimes interlocks and other
relationships, which are dependent on stockholders' lack of participation
in the management of the firm. The roles of stockholders and managers
are limited by relations with other corporations, financial firms, and
government agencies. For example, Mintz and Schwartz (1985) found that
loan consortia consisting of several dozen financial institutions placed
constraints on corporations. In fact, corporations may influence each other,
whether management or owner controlled, because they are controlled by
the same financial institution (see Chapter 2). This occurred in the 1980s.

Many corporations, savings and loans, insurance agencies, and investment fund firms were dependent on Drexel because it held a near monopoly
on the high-yield bond market. Because these financial firms were paying
high rates for their money, they needed to invest in high-yield bonds, which
paid even higher rates. Thus the interdependence of these organizations
was due to "market constraints" (Burt 1978). Burt uses the term *market
constraints* to mean the extent to which dependence is affected by the
absence of alternatives. Market constraint is the extent to which organizations in one industry sector impose limits on the ability of members of
another industry sector to realize profits. This definition can be generalized
to financial institutions such as investment banks, which impose constraints on banks and industries that affect their profits. The dependence
of various corporations on Drexel was a result not only of the portion of
the market held by Drexel, but also of the portion of their business that these
firms had in high-yield debt. Even though the high-yield portion of the total
debt package was usually small, less than 30 percent in takeovers, Drexel
controlled 40–60 percent of the high-yield bond market from 1984 to 1987.
Dependencies of corporations and investment firms on Drexel were great
because of their holdings in high yield bonds.

Firms that were issuers of junk bonds and institutional investors that
were buyers of junk bonds were linked to each other through their relationship with Drexel. Not only did they have a vested interest in the
legislation that affected mergers and acquisitions, they also had an indirect
structural relationship through Drexel that caused them to take the same
position toward government policies, laws, and regulations. Koenig and

Mizruchi (1988) found a strong positive association between indirect interlocks (a form of relationship) through major banks on the one hand and a similarity in corporate political behavior on the other. These direct relationships have been unexplored.

Institutional investors have a special reason to support the political actions of Drexel. Institutional investors are now the largest stock- and bondholders of U.S. corporations. Shortly before the 1980s, Kotz (1978) found that a small portion of the *Fortune* 500 firms had more than 5 percent of their stock held by a single bank. This was also true in the 1980s, but institutional investors often held large amounts of stocks and bonds and often simultaneously bought and dumped their holdings. Such actions were a significant threat to managers and small shareholders of such corporations. As the hub of a sizable group of institutional investors, Drexel often dictated these buys and sells. Thus corporate issuers of bonds had a common interest as well as a structural reason (linked in the same network) to support government policies and legislation that were supported by institutional investors as well as those supported by Drexel.

LAWS

Five types of laws are especially important to our analysis of securities fraud: securities, tax, bankruptcy, antitrust, and RICO laws.

1.   Securities laws are designed to guard against fraud in the financial marketplace. They apply to corporate deals by specifying the kinds of information that must be publicly disclosed, who must disclose it, when it must be disclosed, and who may and may not trade on it.

2.   Tax laws specify the sorts of business expenses that can be deducted from corporate income and are therefore exempt from taxation. For example, interest expenses to service debt can be deducted, whereas dividend payments to stockholders are effectively taxed twice—first as income received by the firm, and then as income received by stockholders. Tax laws also allow losses from prior years to be carried forward on a company's profit and loss statement, and thus they can be used to shelter corporate income and protect it from taxation.

3.   Bankruptcy laws specify under what conditions a corporation can declare bankruptcy, how the courts are to allocate assets among creditors, and after Chapter 11 was reformed, how corporations would be restructured.

4.   Antitrust laws, when government chooses to enforce them, prohibit mergers and acquisitions whose effect may be to substantially lessen competition or tend to create a monopoly in any line of commerce in any section of the country.

5. RICO is the Racketeering Influenced Corrupt Organization Act, which forbids an organization from racketeering activities in the performance of securities trading.

The extent to which any law is enforced depends on many political considerations, such as the extent to which the executive branch pushes for regulation; the vigor with which the attorney general pushes for prosecution; the composition of commissions, regulatory boards, and indirectly the SEC and the Federal Trade Commission (FTC), especially the head of the Antitrust Division; the majority control of the houses of Congress and their position on antitrust legislation; and how liberal the Supreme Court is in interpreting the antitrust laws. The role of firms, bankers, and institutional investors is seldom analyzed. But as will be demonstrated in the analysis below, firms that issue bonds, investment bankers who sell them, and institutional investors who buy them have a major impact on laws through their influence on Congress, regulatory boards, the SEC, and the FTC.

Securities Laws

The federal securities laws were enacted in 1933 and 1934. They consist mainly of three acts: the Securities Act of May 1933, the Glass Steagall Act of June 1933, and the Securities Exchange Act of June 1934. Each of these acts was developed as a component of Roosevelt's New Deal for a specific purpose in bringing about economic recovery during a time of depression.

Securities Act of 1933. The Securities Act of 1933 placed the responsibility for disclosure and truth in disclosure on those who offer securities for sale. For its time, it was thought to provide for both public disclosure of new issues and severe penalties for failure to comply to the law. By today's standards it was weak in both areas. New issues were registered with the FTC and, when sold, were to be accompanied by full written information, which would permit investors to judge the security's worth. To assure adequate time to evaluate each offering, the law specified that registry of the issue with all relevant disclosures was to be completed at least twenty days before the security could be sold. It was then left to the FTC to decide if the information was inaccurate, incomplete, and ultimately if the offering was fraudulent in some way. Those who were not in compliance were guilty of civil, not criminal acts.

The Securities Act of 1933 is important to our analysis because it prohibits misrepresentation of securities being issued to the public. In other words, if stocks or bonds are represented by a firm to be as safe as government bonds, it is the issuer who must prove this to be true. It is not the FTC's responsibility to prove that it is false.

Glass-Steagall Act of 1933. The Glass-Steagall Act is generally thought to be a banking act because it was written to ensure that the structure and functioning of banks would promote solvency. Under this act the Federal Reserve Board was empowered to limit the amount of credit bankers made available for speculative purposes.

This act is important to our analysis in two ways: (1) It limits the amount of high-yield bonds a bank can purchase (the portion of its assets it can invest in high-risk securities). It therefore reduces the amount of risk a non–investment bank can bear. (2) The Glass-Steagall Act also created the FDIC to protect small deposits of less than $15,000. More important to our analysis of fraud, however, is that under Glass-Steagall, banks were barred from taking deposits and offering new securities for sale or distributing securities to the public. Thus, a bank could not be both a commercial deposit bank *and* an investment bank. This is an important regulation because it restricted Drexel and other investment banks to functions separate from those of commercial banks. This separation of functions endured until the great push for deregulation of banks in 1986.

Securities Exchange Act. The Securities Exchange Act (SEA) was written largely to regulate the conduct of the markets. The SEA outlawed some practices such as dissemination of false or misleading information, which could be used to control the market in certain stocks. In other cases it simply extended the securities regulations that already existed. It extended the registry and disclosure requirements applied to new securities to all securities traded on the exchanges. Finally the SEC was established to take over registration functions from the FTC.

The SEC was established in 1934 to register stock exchanges, monitor the rules of the exchanges, and guarantee that stock exchanges operated in compliance with the spirit of the securities acts. Implied within its stated function may have been that the SEC was to serve the function of monitoring exchanges for irregularities and breaches of the SEA. However, if this was the intention, monitoring was irregular to nonexistent throughout the 1980s.

Prior to the 1980s there existed scarcely any U.S. legislation concerning the regulation of insider trading. The securities acts of 1933 and 1934, which are the foundation of the securities regulatory system, made only passing reference to the practice of insider trading. There were a very few court decisions rendered in the 1940s.

Insider Trading and the Securities Exchange Act. The largest legislative case history was developed by the SEC between the early 1960s and the mid-1970s. Most important among its various achievements was the SEC's ability to persuade the courts to define certain kinds of insider trading as fraud, thus making it a legitimate subject for regulation under the anti-fraud provision of the securities laws (Karsch 1984). The SEC used the full and fair disclosure clause, which is at the heart of securities legislation, to impose obligations on securities traders to disclose characteristics of purchases and the true identity of purchasers. Under this law, parking is illegal. The SEC further imposed regulations requiring disclosure of percentage of stock acquired in a company, beginning at a total of 5 percent and above. Thus if a company accumulated over 5 percent or more of the stock in any other firm, it was obligated to report its holdings to the SEC. Finally the SEC refashioned the doctrine of fiduciary obligation to impose obligations not to trade for profit on those who were involved in trading securities, in other words, it broadened the range of insiders. Securities officers became trustees of the securities they were investing for others. Over time, some trustees were more worthy of their clients' trust than others. As a result of the enactment of the 1984 congressional legislation imposing heavy sanctions on those convicted of insider trading, the SEC began to take aggressive action to enforce the legislation against insider trading.

Secondary Bond Issues. The SEC also regulates the trading of bonds. When a new issue is sold by a company the transaction is subject to securities regulation. After the primary offering, however, the sale of the bonds does not have to be registered with the SEC. Secondary offerings are unregulated, and a large portion of the transactions that were executed by the High-Yield Bond Department of Drexel were secondary offerings. For example, if a large insurance company or pension holder decided to sell a large bond position that it had acquired from the original issuer, it might have Drexel buy the bonds and sell them to its network of bond buyers. More important for the transaction process, there is no published listing of the price at which such offerings are sold. This is like buying stocks on a market for which one does not have published market information.

Only the traders with superior knowledge of what junk bonds were worth could deal in this market and make money. Those who traded in the rated bond market often did not know what junk bonds were worth. Even Milken's colleagues at Drexel did not know, and they reported that the High-Yield Bond Department often took advantage of them. Stewart reports that in 1976 Gary Winnick, a salesman in Drexel's New York office, bought for one of his customers a bond from Milken: "Winnick earned one-eighth of a point on the spread, or the difference between the price the customer paid and what Milken charged him" (1991, p. 47). (A point means a *basis point*, or one-hundredth of a cent per dollar on a bond. One-eighth of a point on the spread in a $1 million purchase represents about $125.). The spread had actually been 30 points and Milken had kept 29–7/8 points for himself. The lack of regulation not only worked to the disadvantage of the customer in relation to the bankers, but it also worked to the disadvantage of the purchasing salesman. Knowledge and a willingness to trade tough, if not unethically, were the determining factors.

Tax Laws

Some researchers have found that leveraged takeovers are motivated by tax subsidies that acquirers exploit without creating any real economic value (see Chapter 3). They further hold that acquirers will pay more than ordinary shareholders in the market, because the former can liquidate or merge the target to realize the tax benefits. Others (for example, Gilson, Scholes, and Wolfson 1988) argue that the gains to the acquiring company are often offset by tax losses to the target company and its shareholders. The answer lies in the extent to which these losses are implicit costs for the acquirer.

Auerbach and Reishus (1988) examined a sample of hostile takeovers from 1968 to 1983 for the purpose of quantifying the tax incentives for mergers and found there was little if any tax gain from the stepped-up basis or from the increase in interest deductions from long-term debt. They found instead that transfers of net operating losses and tax credits, of the type described in Chapter 3 for Triton when it took over the more profitable Simplicity Patterns, did appear to generate merger tax benefits. They conceded that there is a risk that an aggregated database such as theirs may conceal significant benefits from some sources such as a basis step-up.

The attractiveness of these bonds benefited greatly from the very generous tax treatment of interest payments on debt, which are fully deductible for the corporation. Thus buying assets on borrowed funds means shifting much of the cost (at least the interest) to the federal government and the U.S. taxpayer. This practice was discussed in Chapter 6.

The deduction of interest on corporate debt has long been part of the U.S. tax code, but it was nowhere as beneficial as it was during the LBOs of the 1980s. Restructuring corporations to take on large amounts of debt so that their equity could be used to finance additional takeovers made maximum use of the law. Other taxes have also been shifted from the corporation to the U.S. taxpayer. Net operating loss deduction (NOL) is a tax break that allows corporations to reduce this year's taxes—and next year's—because of money lost last year. [For an example of this type of tax advantage, see Barlett and Steele's (1992, pp. 40–64) discussion of Guaranty Federal Savings and Loan of Galveston.]

Bankruptcy Laws

Congress revised the United States bankruptcy laws in 1978 for the first time in approximately forty years. This set the stage for the heavy leveraging that took place in the 1980s. The new Chapter 11 law created a limbo state in which corporations were neither solvent nor insolvent, but could stay in business as they tried to resolve their financial problems. The rate of bankruptcies increased astronomically. Corporations could take on debt, and if they failed they could declare bankruptcy. This declaration gave them government protection while they restructured. Under the old statute, Chapter 7, when a corporation declared bankruptcy, the courts provided for the liquidation of its assets to pay its debts and the subsequent liquidation of the corporation. Chapter 11 had existed for a number of years; however in 1978, it was reformed to allow corporations to continue to operate and reorganize (restructure) under existing management while being protected from their creditors.

The reforms that "liberalized" Chapter 11 came at the beginning of the transition to bank control of corporations—at the beginning of the mergers and acquisitions and the junk bond explosion. Bankruptcy was no longer a stigma; it became just another way of restructuring the enormous debt, which companies could not bear at such high rates of interest. Easing of the bankruptcy laws effectively sanctioned unrestrained leveraging, a practice defined as positive by the financial and corporate communities. Financial executives who did the takeovers, managers of acquiring firms, and financiers who underwrote the failing companies retained their jobs, because bankruptcy was no longer defined as failure (and carried no stigma) but rather an interim stage of growth (growth was defined as taking on more debt).

Compared to 24,900 in the 1970s, during the 1980s, 63,500 bankruptcy petitions a year were filed in the United States (Barlett and Steele, p. 68), an increase of 155 percent—the largest increase since the Great Depression. Barlett and Steele point out that both the number and the size of bankruptcies increased. As various takeovers and junk bond–funded entities failed between 1989 and 1992, "the combined assets of large companies seeking bankruptcy court protection swelled to more than $70 billion in 1990" (1992, p. 68). Among the largest of these were several Drexel clients: In first place was Financial Corporation of America at $33.9 billion in 1988. In third place was First Executive Corp. at $15.2 billion in 1991. In fifth place was Imperial Corp. of America, parent company of Imperial Savings and Loan, at $12.3 billion in 1990. At twenty-first place was Drexel at $3.7 billion.

In keeping with agency theory, the taking on of debt is defined not as a necessary tool for corporate growth, to be used cautiously, but as a method of government financing (a tax-free loan), to impose discipline on the corporation's management. In essence, it is a power tool through which shareholders and investment bankers trump management. These take-overs and restructurings are not in the long-run interest of corporate America, but are in the short-run interest of attorneys, consultants, accountants, and shareholders of large firms.

As a consequence of the 1978 Bankruptcy Reform Act, legal counsel for those participating in takeovers and restructuring became the most lucrative type of law practice. These debt-financed bankruptcies created victims of the targets that were taken over. These professionals with specialties in finance, law, and accounting who had created strategies to take over targets subsequently created strategies to turn the failing targets around. The costs for creating both types of strategies are passed on to the target, creating more debt. These professionals bill by the hour. They are paid to track the time they spend consulting, packing to fly, flying, going to airports, attending conferences, scheduling, phoning, packing files, filing, word processing, transcribing, and so on. The courts recognize and allow these charges. (A firm which specializes in such restructuring is Sigoloff and Associates, a "crisis manager," in Santa Monica, California, headed by Stanford C. Sigoloff. He bills himself as a specialist in corporate turnarounds and restructuring.)

The largest price for the takeovers, protection, and restructuring is paid by the work force. For example, in 1987 Doskocil, a relatively small, solvent, growing meat packing plant in Hutchinson, Kansas, initiated a takeover of the larger Wilson Foods as a result of Drexel's targeting Wilson for takeover. Wilson outclassed Doskocil in every way. It had sales of $1.3 billion to Doskocil's $215 million, five thousand employees to Doskocil's nine hundred; twelve plants to Doskocil's five plants. Doskocil sold $750 million in high-risk junk bonds to finance the acquisition. Wilson resisted the takeover and fought for nearly half a year. The resulting expenses were $11.8 million in financial, legal, and banking fees, commissions, and other charges. All of these transaction costs were borne by Wilson. Over one hundred employees of Wilson's headquarters in Oklahoma City were fired immediately and other firings followed. Profitably for Drexel, just one and one-half years later, the deal, which costs millions of dollars, came apart. Unable to sell the Wilson components, Doskocil, unable to pay the interest on the debt and under "liquidity crisis," filed for bankruptcy protection under Chapter 11 on March 5, 1990, and then immediately began to restructure with Drexel's assistance. Workers, paid five to six dollars an hour, lost their jobs, and plants closed, while lawyers, accountants, and bankers received extraordinary fees (for additional information on the fee structures of attorneys for the creditors of Doskocil and its management consultants, see Barlett and Steele 1992, pp. 78–79).

Barlett and Steele, quoting Steven N. Kaplan at the University of Chicago, sum up the problem: "The large debt service payments force managers to find ways to generate cash and prevent managers from spending money unproductively" (1992, p. 85). The intended result was to impose discipline on management through the high debt service payments; instead the liability drove many companies out of business. The transaction costs imposed by attorneys, accountants, bankers, and consultants increased the insolvency of these highly vulnerable corporate entities.

Antitrust Laws

Generally antitrust laws are enacted to maintain and increase competitiveness in the U.S. economy. They are intended to allow small firms to compete with large firms. Conglomerates, mergers, and the like are generally considered to be anticompetitive strategies of corporate expansion. The two major pieces of legislation that have regulated the formation of such acquisitions are the Clayton Antitrust Act of 1914 and the Celler-Kefauver Act of 1950, with the FTC having oversight responsibility. In this section I discuss the passage of the Celler-Kefauver Act to demonstrate the transition from lack of enforcement of antitrust laws to the passage of new laws with far more stringent enforcement. In the 1980s, this transformation provided an incentive for corporate expansion through diversification and conglomerates (for a more complete discussion see Fligstein 1990a).

Before discussing the Celler-Kefauver Act, we will look at the Clayton Act. The Clayton Act was an attempt to outlaw specific types of anticompetitive behavior that were thought to lead to monopolies. Examples include purchasing a firm's stock to control its actions. The Clayton Act did not pertain to existing firms but prevented what it considered unfair concentrations from being newly formed. Large firms that had been created prior to its enactment benefited by its restrictions on growth of their competitors, and thus many large firms supported the passage of the Clayton Act.

The merger movement of the 1920s occurred largely because the federal government was generally not enforcing the existing antitrust laws. The Supreme Court had narrowly reinterpreted the Clayton Act in order to nullify any effect it might have on limiting the merger movement. The Supreme Court heard only four antitrust cases in that decade. Since the Court decides which cases to hear, its reluctance to hear cases demonstrated its lack of enthusiasm in enforcing this law. Section 7 of the Clayton Act impedes the development of monopolies through the purchase of the stock of a competing firm. Three of the four firms in the cases heard in the 1920s purchased the competing firm's assets and then stock. One of the cases was against a firm that had purchased the stock first and then the assets. In all four cases the Supreme Court decided for the purchasing firm even though the mergers were anticompetitive. Of course, the corporate world defined these rulings as nullifying the Antitrust Act in practice and conducted business in keeping with their newfound freedom.

Not until the late 1930s did a reversal of this policy take place. Beginning in 1937, Roosevelt encouraged Thurman Arnold, head of the Antitrust Division, to make use of the antitrust laws. At the same time, Senator Joseph O'Mahoney and Representatives Estes Kefauver and Emmanuel Celler became interested in antitrust legislation. The FTC also became more active in prosecuting violations of antitrust laws. In 1937, these congressmen and the FTC were brought together to form the Temporary National Economic Commission to deal with the problem of monopolies and oligopolies in key markets.

The Temporary National Economic Commission recommended the amendment of Section 7 of the Clayton Act to make anticompetitive mergers through the purchase of *assets* unlawful, thereby closing a loophole in the original law, which prohibited only the purchase of *stock*. Kefauver and Celler introduced legislation in every Congress from 1945 to 1950 to amend the Clayton Act, but the Celler-Kefauver Act could not pass until the democrats gained control of the Senate in 1950. The Celler-Kefauver Act made horizontal and vertical mergers illegal and was intended to slow the growth of monopolies to prevent product concentration as well as to prevent mergers among firms that produced related products.

Four conditions were relevant for deciding whether a violation had occurred:

> 1) the character of the acquiring and the acquired company, 2) the characteristics of the markets affected, 3) immediate changes in the size and competitive range of acquiring company and in the adjustments of other companies operating in the market directly affected, and 4) probable long range differences that the acquisition may make for companies actually or potentially operating in those markets. (U.S. Attorney General 1955, p. 125)

However, the Celler-Kefauver Act was ineffective, not because it did not limit vertical and horizontal concentration, but because corporations found other ways to expand. Conglomerates and diversified multidivisional firms were *not* unlawful. Fligstein points out that between 1945 and 1969 the largest firms rapidly diversified mostly through mergers:

> The business community had one important example of the pure financial strategy: the acquisitive conglomerate. The acquisitive conglomerates were

built by people on the edges of the American corporate sector, often outside
New York, where most of the large firms were located. (1990a, p. 30)

The Eisenhower, Kennedy, and Johnson administrations continued antitrust prosecution and Earl Warren, Chief Justice of the Supreme Court,
supported the government's position. The Warren Court relied on the argument that markets were the only relevant facts in considering the legality
of a merger, and did not consider the issue of firm performance. At the
same time, product-related and -unrelated mergers were lawful and were
pursued with a vengeance. In order to facilitate this method of expansion,
firms developed a purely financial conception of control, selecting as their
CEOs and executives those who saw firms as financial entities (Fligstein,
1990a). Financial control became the reigning type of corporate control.
Financial control emphasized performance: not industry performance, but
a very specific type of firm performance—return to shareholders.

Fligstein views the antitrust enforcement in the postwar era as directly
linked to the emergence of the financial concept of control (his theory of
financial control). According to Fligstein, the Antitrust Division of the FTC
used the Cellar-Kefauver Act to discourage vertical and horizontal mergers, which encouraged mergers through diversification.

The merger movement of the 1960s ended at least in part because of the
antitrust policy of the Nixon era. Richard McLaren, assistant attorney
general in charge of the Justice Department's Antitrust Division, prepared
cases against ITT and LTV (see Chapter 6). Nixon had to make a decision
between enforcing the law and his support for big business. He wanted
to stop the antitrust suits, but was advised not to do so. In 1971, Nixon
established a policy group to assist him in finding a way out of his
dilemma. John Ehrlichman, one of Nixon's chief advisors, headed the
committee.

The committee focused on the concentration in the given industrial
sector of the market that resulted from the mergers, not its concentration
before the merger. By 1972, the Supreme Court, headed by Warren Burger,
a Nixon appointee, rejected the idea that ownership of stocks and assets
was enough to demonstrate potential monopoly. Now the arguments
against such mergers had to demonstrate *how* they were potentially anticompetitive in their consequences. Those who made the laws began to
question whether or not mergers in fact were anticompetitive. Arguments
were developed to defend the position that mergers were efficient for the
merged firms. In the 1970s and 1980s, scholars argued that mergers could
result in efficiencies and that concentration of production could lower costs
for larger firms. The important issue of the time was the competitiveness
of American firms. The structure of industry was secondary. The logic was
tautological: The most successful organizations survived through mergers,

and mergers reflected the working of the market to produce efficient industrial organizations. Any merger that did not produce a more efficient organization would fail; therefore there was no reason to regulate mergers because the market would select only those which were efficient. By definition, any merger that survived was efficient. The resulting view was that mergers enhance shareholders' value. This argument has produced quite a shift in antitrust policy.

The Carter and Reagan administrations continued the Nixon trend and declined to enforce the antitrust laws, allowing the proliferation of mergers and acquisitions to continue. In fact, the Reagan administration almost ended antitrust enforcement entirely. Under Reagan, the Justice Department challenged only 26 of the nearly 11,000 corporate deals that included notification of impending mergers and acquisitions. During his administration, one of the first official acts of the Justice Department was to drop the government's massive ten-year antitrust case against IBM. In each of 1982, 1984, and 1986 the administration asked Congress to relax the merger laws further. In 1986, Secretary of Commerce Malcolm Baldridge went even further and urged that merger laws be abolished outright. While antitrust laws still stand, the Justice Department's Antitrust Division staff of attorneys had been reduced by 44 percent. Its full-time staff (including economists, paralegals, and clerical support) has been cut by 37 percent. Donald Baker, Secretary of the Treasury under Reagan, is reported to have said in 1987, "The Antitrust Division today is less than two-thirds its size when President Reagan took office. It is smaller than when I came to it first in October 1966" (Elias 1987, p.8). Bush encouraged the same lax antitrust policy that perpetuated the merger wave from 1976 to the time he took office.

During the period of nonenforcement of the Celler-Kefauver Act, large unrelated mergers became lawful in practice, if not in statute. Even the largest vertical and horizontal mergers were positively sanctioned by the noninvestigative policy of the Antitrust Division in the 1980s.

The lack of enforcement of the Celler-Kefauver Act was supported by the rhetoric of globalization of markets and the exigencies of international competition. In the 1980s large corporations were deemed necessary to compete with the even larger corporations developing in Japan and Germany. Both product-related and -unrelated firms were expanding through mergers and acquisitions. Such expansion was justified as U.S. markets dwindled and the national debt increased.

POLITICAL ACTION COMMITTEES AND LOBBIES

Drexel had a political action committee (PAC) throughout the 1980s, but it was considerably more active in the mid-1980s than at earlier times.

According to the Federal Election Committee database, the Drexel Burnham Lambert Political Action Committee (DBL-PAC) received contributions from the employees of Drexel (for example, $771,000 in 1985–1986) and in turn made contributions to legislators, including nearly all members of the Keating Five and Representative Timothy Wirth of Colorado. However, Drexel had no formal lobbying mechanism until 1985, when Congress began to hold hearings on hostile takeovers and the junk bond market. On August 8, the Alliance for Capital Access was incorporated for just this purpose. The directors of the alliance were Carl Linder, president of American Financial Corporation in Cincinnati, and Richard Grassgree, president of Kinder-Care Learning Centers in Montgomery, Alabama—both Milken's clients. The incorporation papers were filed by Craig Cogut, a lawyer with Cambrent Financial Group, one of the companies supported by Milken's junk bond sales. Cogut was part of the external legal counsel of the High-Yield Bond Department and was a partner in the MacPherson partnership.

Barlett and Steele write, "over the next five years more than half of the 120 companies which contributed to the Alliance had ties to Michael Milken" (1992, pp. 207–10). In fact, of the largest contributors, over 80 percent had direct or indirect ties to Milken. More important to the thesis of this book, many financiers belonged to the alliance: Some dealt in tax shelters, such as LSL; annuity companies, such as First Executive Life Insurance; investment management firms, such as Shamrock Holding Corporation; and retail insurers, such as Zenith National Insurance.

The Alliance worked effectively to educate the media and the government about the "virtues" of takeovers, leveraging, and junk bonds. All of the companies that were involved in junk bond issuing and buying were portrayed to Congress as successful, dynamic business ventures that were building jobs and industrializing the American economy. However, as was revealed in Chapter 3, many of these corporations are now bankrupt, banks are insolvent, and financial firms have disappeared.

Representative Timothy Wirth, a democrat from Colorado, chaired the Subcommittee of the House Energy and Commerce Committee, the goal of which was to "assess the fairness" of takeovers and the role of junk bonds. He introduced a bill in the House outlawing greenmail. Wirth appointed David K. Aylward as the subcommittee's staff director and chief counsel. As the hearings were beginning, Aylward resigned from Wirth's staff and went over to the opposition: He took a position with a lobbying company working for the newly formed Alliance for Capital Access, whose goal it was to block legislation that would restrict the use of junk bonds in funding takeovers. Shortly after Aylward's defection, Wirth himself would make a conversion to support junk bond–funded LBOs.

The next year, Drexel opened a lobbying office and hired Robert Strauss, a former Democratic National Committee Chairman, and John Evans, a former SEC commissioner. Drexel made $177,800 in PAC contributions in 1986. Senator Alan Cranston (the only member of the Keating Five to be censured by the Senate), a Democrat from California, received $41,750 in campaign contributions from Drexel in 1986 alone. Also in 1986, Drexel executives were asked to contribute over $56,750 to Senator Alfonse D'Amato, chairman of the securities subcommittee. At the 1986 Predators' Ball (see Chapter 1) Timothy Wirth was a key speaker in favor of high-yield bonds. Subsequently, Drexel contributed $23,900 to Wirth's successful Senate campaign, and his attempt to outlaw greenmail and limit the tax deductibility of corporate bonds disappeared. Although other congressmen received contributions, there were none so directly linked to the outcomes of Drexel or its executives as these three (Jackson and Ricks 1988): PAC contributions coupled with contributions to some of these same actors and DeConcini by Keating reinforced Milken's message to the nation. The forces in this country buying high-yield securities had overpowered all regulation because the forces behind the corporate elite were financial elite who controlled the lawmakers.

In the Tax Reform Act of 1986, the Congress repealed numerous tax breaks for individuals, including IRAs and consumer interest; but Congress neither enacted laws against takeovers funded by bonds or against greenmail, nor did it restrict the deduction of interest on corporate debt. Though it operated for only six years, the Alliance for Capital Access was successful in blocking legislation that could restrict Drexel's direct and indirect business. Among the corporate members of the Alliance for Capital Access were four banks—Centrust Savings Bank, Columbia Savings and Loan, Imperial Savings and Loan, and LSL—all of which failed at least in part or largely due to holdings in the junk bond market. The parent companies of two of these banks, Imperial Corporation and American Continental Corporation, were forced into bankruptcy after their banks were seized by regulators. Failure of these banks is costing the U.S. taxpayer billions of dollars in the form of the savings and loan bailouts.

As a result of being overextended with debt, another group of Alliance for Capital Access members has sought protection under bankruptcy laws: First Executive Life Insurance Corporation (the largest insurance company to declare bankruptcy), Doskocil Companies, the Forum Group, Inc., Integrated Resources, Living Well, Inc., Southmark Corporation, and U.S. Home Corporation. Other members of the alliance, whose successes were financed with junk bonds, have ultimately had to be restructured, including Western Union, Ingersoll Publications Company, and Kinder Care, Inc., the nation's largest day-care center operator. This may seem like poetic justice because these companies fell prey to the financial mechanism from which they benefited so greatly. However, their failure has meant that unsuspecting investors and the overall American economy suffer as well, and continue to do so.

RICO ACT

In 1989, the 101st Congress attempted to reform the Racketeer Influenced and Corrupt Organizations Act (RICO).[13] Passed in 1970 as Title IX of the Organized Criminal Control Act of 1970,[14] RICO is perhaps the strongest and most controversial criminal code for the prosecution of corporate crime.[15] The law attempts both to limit the infiltration of legitimate organizations by those who commit illegal acts, and to restrict the conduct of otherwise legal business through racketeering procedures.

RICO is one of the least understood statutes in the federal criminal code. The core of the RICO statute is 18 U.S.C. 1962 (1970), which created four new crimes:

1.   Under 1962(a), it is a crime for any person to "use or invest any income he has derived" from a "pattern of racketeering activity or through collection of an unlawful debt" to establish, operate, or acquire an interest in "any enterprise" engaged in or affecting interstate commerce.

2.   Under 1962(b), acquiring or maintaining an interest in or control of any such enterprise "through a pattern of racketeering activity or through the collection of an unlawful debt" is prohibited.

3.   Under 1962(c), it is a crime for any person "employed by or associated with any enterprise" in or affecting commerce "to conduct or participate, directly, in the conduct of such enterprise's affairs through a pattern of racketeering activity or collection of unlawful debt."

4.   Under 1962(d), "conspiracy" to violate the other three prohibitions is a crime.

Subsections 1962(a) and 1962(b) make it a crime for someone outside a business to infiltrate a legal business through the investment of ill-gotten gains or criminal profits. Section 1962(c) provides the means to prosecute not only the infiltration of legitimate businesses, but also those who conduct some affairs of an otherwise legitimate business through "racketeering types" of actions. The criminal acts of so-called legitimate businessmen who take advantage of their organizational prerogatives to commit crimes already defined by the penal codes can be prosecuted under 1962(c).

But why not prosecute mail fraud, wire fraud, and securities fraud under the earlier penal codes? Because section 1962 substantially increases the criminal penalties for these kinds of violations.[16] Present RICO indict-

ments carry the possibility of freezing assets, requiring that they be surrendered if the defendant is found guilty, fines of $25,000 per count, up
to twenty years in jail per count, and forfeiture of "all interests in the
enterprise," whether or not the interest was illegally acquired. In addition,
under civil RICO only,[17] the defendant who is found or pleads guilty can
be assessed triple damages.

The bill prohibits acts that are typical of organized crime, among them
drug dealing, gambling, and criminal violence. Bankruptcy fraud and
bribery of federal officials were added in 1982,[18] as well as embezzlement
from unions, welfare and pension fraud, and interstate transportation of
property stolen or taken by fraud.[19] In 1982 and 1984, Senate committees
amended the final version of RICO, and added violations of federal laws
involving mail, wire, and securities fraud.[20] The consequences of the last
changes were that any corporate executives, savings and loan officers, or
investment bankers who conduct the affairs of their firm "through a
pattern of" fraud would violate RICO. Thus between 1970 and 1984, RICO
was expanded to cover most types of corporate crime. These expansions
had the concomitant effect of drastically increasing the potential penalties
facing many corporate criminals (see case analysis on severity of penalties
below).

Who Has the Power to Change the Law?

One might assume that laws controlling acts of the financial elite are
reformed in the same ways as those bearing upon the criminal syndicate.
(The use of the term *financial elite* is purely a matter of linguistic conve-
nience, and does not connote that the analysis is rooted in elite theory. The
word *syndicate* instead of *organized crime* is used to denote the mob because
securities fraud is also organized crime.) This question can only be examined when laws apply equally to the crimes of the "syndicate"[21] and
the financial elite because they are involved in the same criminal acts. Thus
the reform of RICO is a natural context in which to examine this important
question because RICO addresses itself to racketeering on the part of
corporate elites.

Judging from the reform, it appears that the Congress must have asked
a different question: How can the law control the syndicate while at the
same time creating exceptions for financial elites when both syndicate and
financial elites are engaged in the same types of behavior? The congressional reform committee's stated legal reasons for the reform of RICO can
be debunked and an argument can be made that this law is being reformed
because of the social and political embeddedness of financial elites.

A congressional committee of the 101st Congress drafted a bill, the

Senate RICO Reform Act,[22] exempting certain types of corporate crime, particularly those committed by persons in the securities industry and savings and loan banks, from prosecution under the RICO act. The rationale was that investment bankers and savings and loan officers were already regulated by the SEC and bank boards. The same frauds would be prosecuted under RICO if committed by nearly anyone else—including, of course, the syndicate. In doing so, the committee argued that legally RICO was being reformed because it is "too vague," "too broad," and "too severe." The unstated reason was that potentially prosecutable financial elites had links to powerful congressional actors, including the chairman of the RICO reform committee.

How might the reform of RICO by congressional committees be explained? We know that corporate economic power carries with it the potential for political power, but according to some, this potential cannot be realized because corporations cannot mobilize themselves as a politically cohesive force. Others contend that the corporate elite does not have to be a unified coalition to bring about change in its interest because the ruling elite acts in the interest of capitalism and therefore in the corporate elite's interest. Thus, increasing economic concentration in advanced capitalist societies has led to an increase in the political power of corporations (Useem 1982, 1984; Domhoff 1983; Jacobs 1988). But how does the financial elite go about reforming those laws to better serve their interests?

Legal Explanations

The RICO reformers argue that only recently—since the Princeton/ Newport indictment, the first investment banking firm indicted under RICO—has RICO been used to prosecute white-collar crime. They maintain that it was written solely to control the syndicate and therefore should be applied only to the syndicate. I demonstrate that RICO has, since its inception, been used to prosecute white-collar crime, but only recently has it been used against financial elites (i.e., investment bankers and savings and loan officers). Interestingly enough, only recently has it been labeled by the congressional reform committees as "vague," "too broad," and "too punitive." Furthermore, only recently have congressional reformers claimed it is intended solely for the prosecution of syndicated crime. Congress has only become interested in reforming RICO since 1987, not because of the types of crimes that are being prosecuted, but because of the individuals being prosecuted and their elite position in "legitimate businesses."

I find, contrary to claims of the Committee to Reform RICO, that RICO has not been used disproportionately to prosecute the syndicate and is not now being used to inappropriately prosecute corporate crimes. From its enactment in 1970 through 1985, RICO was used 2.5 times more frequently to prosecute business firms (excluding other types of white-collar employees, labor managers, and government workers), than to prosecute the syndicate. Only recently has it been used to prosecute a special category of white-collar criminals—savings and loan officers and investment bankers—and it is the prosecution of this socially embedded, well-networked, financial elite that has led Congress to attempt to weaken RICO. The legal rationale for the reform of RICO—that it is vague, too broad in scope, too severe, and constructed for the prosecution of the syndicate—has little validity when judicial precedent is taken into consideration. These were considered to be appropriate, even desirable, characteristics of a law for the prosecution of the "heinous crimes of the mob." In fact, the U.S. attorneys general find these characteristics quite helpful, not only for the prosecution of the mob, but also for the prosecution of the financial elite, because it allows them to cast a wide net.

Structural/Network Explanation

Congress's ability to make laws and the courts' ability to punish corporations operating outside these laws is constrained by the power of corporations to resist the influence of external agencies, as well as their ability to amend and reform such laws (Hawkins 1984; Clune 1983). Corporations have multifaceted capacities to control. Among the mechanisms that intensify their control are the implicit assumptions at the basis of neoclassical economics, which underlies the economic theory of the capitalist system in which they operate (Coleman 1984; Etzioni 1988). The culture of business and the marketplace (Burk 1988) and the bureaucratic structures of corporations (Stone 1975; Vaughan 1989) buttress this resistance. Others see corporate influences upon legal structures and regulatory agencies as inhibitors of enforcement (Carosso 1970), while still others cite the ineffectiveness of legal sanctions by regulatory agencies as the key to corporate resistance (Burk 1988, pp. 102–5; Hawkins 1984).

The social organization of corporate elites consists of the formal and informal networks of economic and social relations among corporate owners and managers (Useem 1979). Corporations are intricately linked formally and informally with financial firms and government agencies. Financial firms have an even greater ability to control and resist their environment than other types of corporations. This has been demonstrated by three groups of researchers who see the relationship between financial organizations and their environments in at least three different ways.

The first group represents the managerialist view and argues that corporations (specifically managers) control boards and their environments, including financial firms (Berle and Means 1932). The second group argues that financial organizations, specifically banks, have come increasingly to dominate nonfinancial corporations because their directors sit on the boards of these corporations (Useem 1979; Mintz and Schwartz 1985; Mizruchi and Stearns 1986; Kotz 1978). Here the bankers are proactive infiltrators of corporate boards who wish to gain control of the policy decisions of the corporations (Zeitlin 1974; Aldrich 1979: 296; Mizruchi 1982; Mintz and Schwartz 1985). Financiers intervene in corporate strategies and tactics during periods of crisis and help management to collude or cooperate in taking actions to constrain or respond to their environment (Mintz and Schwartz 1985). However, when the effects of financial corporations on nonfinancial corporations are studied, investment banks are omitted from the sample (for examples, see Useem 1979, p. 559; Mariolis 1975). Stearns (1983) suggests a third view, in which large firms have become more dependent on external financing over the past thirty years. Management has taken on debt to raise capital for the expansion of operations either internally or through mergers and acquisitions. This capital has come largely from the bond market and from commercial banks. Corporations ask financiers to sit on boards in order to co-opt them in times of economic decline and uncertainty (Mizruchi and Stearns 1988). During the most recent merger and acquisition period, as the bond market grew and junk bonds became the leverage of choice for many large mergers and acquisitions, these bondholders increasingly served on each other's boards (Bruck 1988). They were encouraged to purchase each other's debt (junk). Buyers and sellers were networked in overlapping exchanges.

Stearns's position (1983) is that corporations act independently to gain resources from financiers. Management invites financiers to serve on these boards in order to co-opt them to make loans to the firms when they are in financial trouble. This is demonstrated by the appointment of representatives of financial institutions to corporate boards during periods of declining solvency, declining profit rates, the correspondence of increased demand for capital with declining interest rates, and the correspondence of increased demand for capital with contracting stages of the business cycle (Mizruchi and Stearns 1988).

Because investment bankers have been omitted from the samples of these structural analyses, we do not understand the role of investment bankers in relation to banks, corporations, and government agencies. We do know that investment bankers play an important role in corporate formations and mergers because of their central position in the issuing and sales of securities (Navin and Sears 1955; Carosso 1970; Mizruchi 1982; Roy 1983). As the major provider of capital in periods of intense competition and increasing concentration, investment bankers appropriate a major share of the profits for themselves, appoint their own representatives to sit on corporations' boards, and exert influence over corporate policy (Sweezy 1942; Zey 1990). Investment bankers have played a substantial role in the 1980s mergers and acquisitions movement.

It is often impossible to distinguish co-optive from infiltrative interlocks in the structural analysis of the above researchers. Structural analysis tells us the relationship between economic conditions of organizations and the composition of the board at the time the analysis is conducted, but we do not know why these links were initially established or what sustains them. The network, or interlock, may not be a result of anything that is occurring at the time the research is conducted, but may exist as a result of the relationship, which was meaningful and logical at a previous time.

We do not know the nature of the relationship that links financial to nonfinancial organizations, nor what links investment banking firms to other financial and nonfinancial organizations. What we need is an understanding of how elites are linked in networks, and under what conditions these elites form direct links to change the environment, as opposed to using some other mechanism such as political contingencies or PAC formation. More is known about indirect links through PACs than about direct networks (Mizruchi 1989a; Koenig and Gogel 1981; Etzioni 1984; Clawson, Neustadtl, and Bearden 1986; Burris 1987).

Most of the studies of financial control do not assess power. Rather they use network participation as a proxy for power. This leads to another related limitation. As Alford and Friedland (1975) have argued, participation cannot necessarily be equated with power or control. Many of these studies that analyze the structure of participation do not reveal if overrepresentation of financial organizations on boards and in governance structures means that they are decisively shaping the policies of the subject organizations. These studies do not reveal what is being exchanged. To understand the exchanges that take place, it is necessary to collect data about the content of interactions—this is difficult to do when the actions are illegal. Only after this information is made public can such analysis be done.

Organizational analyses have not revealed the relationships between investment banking, savings and loan officers, and various political entities that make the laws that regulate and control their behavior. However, social embeddedness (Granovetter 1985; Fligstein 1985, 1989, 1990a) and the external control perspective (Pfeffer and Salancik 1978; Burt 1983) help explicate these relationships. The reform of the laws is embedded in the interaction of congressional committee members and financial elites. Networks of corporate elites, investment bankers, savings and loan officers, and their congresspersons not only come from a common social class that shares values and interests and that sees the economic well-being of the nation similarly, but these elites also interact with each other in social exchange networks in which each provides for the continued survival of the other and thus ensures its own.

External control theory and resource dependency theory (Pfeffer and Salancik 1978; Burt 1983) posit that actors in organizations with strong ties to resources outside the organization are more powerful within their own organization. They influence the course of their organization more readily than those without such ties. Actors who can deliver inputs (i.e., clients) and control outputs (i.e., trades and deals) and profits are likely to influence the internal allocation of resources disproportionately (Pfeffer and Salancik 1978) as well as make decisions to act for or against certain aspects of the organization's environment.

External control theory focuses on organizations that interact in order to do business. Strategies for co-pting and exploiting the environment are necessary in order to promote organizational goals of profit and survival. Organizations can be controlled by other organizations on which they are most dependent (Pfeffer and Salancik 1978). Linking network analysis with resource dependency theory suggests that firms tend to interact with other firms with whom they share some link in order to reduce uncertainty about their dependencies (Burt 1983). Thus, financial corporations may form relationships with lawmakers to control regulatory boards and legal structure, thereby reducing uncertainty and the risk of doing business.

I argue against Fligstein's concept of organizational environments as organizational fields and against his definition of organizations as predominantly constrained corporations. Rather, I argue that networks are much less structured and more overlapping, often blurring the boundaries of organizations. In this context corporations attempt to construct and reform laws that control them. This section explains how financial corporations go about shielding themselves and their acts from the purview of the law through reforming laws and changing regulatory policy.

Institutional theory tells us that corporate entities interact with and depend upon the normative environment (Meyer and Rowan 1977; Meyer and Scott 1983; DiMaggio and Powell 1983), specifically the legal environment, in the form of bank regulators and congressional members who are lawmakers (Edelman 1990, 1992). However, when threatened with prosecution, these same networks may act as channels through which corporate executives seek reform of the law—modifying the scope of actors to which the law applies, the types of crimes covered, or the penalties. Corporations act on their legal environment as powerful components of the constituency of their congresspersons.

The actions taken by organizations are suggested by the circumstances in which they are embedded and the nature of their ongoing relationships. This integrated perspective focuses on understanding organizational actions as based in the arenas in which they interact (DiMaggio and Powell 1983; Meyer and Rowan 1977; Fligstein 1987, 1989; DiMaggio 1985; White 1981). Burt (1983) makes a similar argument when he contends that boards of directors are used by firms to co-opt the segment of the firm's environment that is represented by a particular board member, whether it be customers, suppliers, or bankers. Similarly, the financial elite may be used to subsidize campaigns and make donations to the candidacies of members of Congress, while members represent the interests of business by amending and reforming laws and influencing regulation.

Money is not the decisive element in this equation: Certainly securities industry actors, investment bankers, and savings and loan officers have the wealth to purchase their well-being, but then so do criminal syndicate members. Class status, in addition to wealth, affords the corporate elite the legitimacy to redress the existing laws through direct and indirect social interaction with the members of Congress and regulatory agencies. Both the syndicate and financial elites have access to redress though the courts by appealing lower-level decisions, but because syndicate members lack legitimacy, they cannot appeal directly to their congresspersons for reform of the laws under which their crimes are prosecuted. In addition to wealth and class status, a third factor is necessary for the exercise of control over the legal environment—networks. The financial elites have money, status, and therefore legitimacy, but most importantly they are also members of networks that give them direct and indirect access to members of Congress. They can use legitimate means such as PACs to influence political decisions, but they can also use illegitimate and difficult-to-trace means (Alexander 1976).[23] When threatened with indictment, they use a variety of methods to seek deregulation and reform (Sabato 1984). We know little about the nature and content of networks that deal in illegal exchanges.

Methods and Data

Congressional reformers and the courts have leveled three charges against RICO: It is too vague, its scope is too broad, and its penalties are too severe. I argue that the challenges to RICO are pretexts for wanting to alter it to better accommodate the needs of the financial elite, not to refine the law to conform to legal guidelines of clarity, limited scope, and appropriate penalty as the congressional committee has claimed. Below, I will present the challenges to RICO as hypotheses. I then present the case data and analysis. To refute the legal arguments made by Congress, I trace RICO cases from 1970 to 1987, analyzing the charges of vagueness, scope, and severity of penalty, and pointing out where the courts have upheld these challenges and how the Supreme Court's position has changed in the last few years. The scope challenge refers to the reformers' claims that RICO was originally intended for and has been primarily applied to the syndicate, not to white-collar crime. I examine the validity of this claim by analysis of the percentages of syndicate and white-collar cases tried in the appellate courts between 1970 and 1985.

After disposing of each of the challenges to RICO, I turn to the alternative thesis that RICO is not being reformed because it is a poor law, but because it threatens business elites. Key financial elites are politically and socially embedded in networks of potential influence and therefore in a position to "reform" it to their benefit. This is studied by analyzing depositions, court testimony, and congressional hearing testimony to construct networks of reciprocity between the key financial elites and congressional committee members. This network analysis links the financial elites (investment bankers, savings and loan officers) and key congressional elites to the reform of RICO.

Legal Challenges to RICO

The first challenge came in 1985, when the Supreme Court declared that it was up to Congress, not the courts, to revise RICO (*Congressional Quarterly Almanac* 1985, p. 8-A).[24] The National Association of Manufacturers, accountants' organizations, and the AFL-CIO immediately asked Congress to rewrite RICO. The 100th Congress in both 1987 and 1988 attempted to do so. In 1989, the Senate Committee of the 101st Congress for the Reform of RICO was led by Dennis DeConcini, Democrat from Arizona, and consisted of Patrick J. Leahy, Democrat from Vermont, and Orrin G. Hatch, Republican from Utah. Under the RICO Reform Act of 1990 (Senate Bill 438), a congressional committee challenged RICO on the following three grounds and made a recommendation for retroactive action:[25]

> **Hypothesis 1:** *RICO is being reformed because it is legally vague—the challenge of vagueness.* Authors of the reform legislation argued that the language of the law, which defined the concepts of organized crime, enterprise, and racketeering activities, is too vague.

> **Hypothesis 2:** *RICO is being reformed because it is legally broad—the challenge of breadth or scope.* In reaction to the 1982 and 1984 amendments to RICO, which provided for the prosecution of mail, wire, and securities fraud, reformers charged that these select "white-collar" crimes should *not* be prosecuted under criminal RICO.

> **Hypothesis 2a:** *RICO has been applied largely to the prosecution of organized crime (the syndicate).* They argued that the law had been applied specifi-

cally to the prosecution of syndicate crimes (e.g., of *cosa nostra*). The congressional reformers alleged that RICO has only recently been used for the prosecution of white-collar crime.

Hypothesis 2b: *RICO has not been applied to the prosecution of organizational crime or white-collar crime until the past five years.* They argued that those who work in the securities industry should not be subject to RICO prosecution because these are industries that are "regulated" by state and federal agencies and are subject to a corresponding set of statutes. Consistent with this argument, they proposed that RICO be reformed to provide that bankers be exempt from prosecution under RICO. Further, they argued that financiers and other such professionals should not be branded with the "harsh" label of racketeer.

Hypothesis 3: *RICO is being reformed because the punishment is too severe— challenge of severity.* Congressional reformers questioned the severity of the penalties attached to RICO, specifically, the treble damages under civil RICO and seizure under criminal RICO. Under the bill before the 101st Congress, alleged securities fraud or fraud of commodities transactions would be exempt from treble damages. Forfeiture statutes were challenged on grounds of due process and were subsequently modified by the Justice Department. The reformers maintained that prison sentences of up to twenty years under criminal RICO are too severe for "financiers."

Recommendation of Retroactivity. Finally, the bill would have retroactively applied to those presently under indictment and pending trial.[26] Financial elites would not be totally immune from prosecution because some parts of the proposed bill concentrated on civil RICO. Businesses that were defrauded could bring separate suit under civil RICO. Michael Milken and Charles Keating were indicted under criminal RICO and were pending trial at the time the law was being reformed. Drexel, Dennis Levine, and Ivan Boesky pleaded guilty under threat of indictment under criminal RICO. The magnitude of the threat was the freezing of assets with possible forfeiture, which would have prevented Drexel from underwriting KKR's $25.07 billion takeover of RJR Nabisco, a deal that netted Drexel $600 million, nearly the amount of their fines ($650 million). To Fred Joseph, CEO of Drexel, pleading guilty was "more rational" than having assets frozen pending trial. In fact, Princeton/Newport, the only other investment bank that had been indicted under RICO, had its assets frozen and subsequently filed bankruptcy just one month before Drexel settled, a fact that weighed heavily in Joseph's decision-making process.[27]

Case Analysis: Vagueness Hypothesis. The case analysis yields no support for the vagueness hypothesis. Vagueness challenges generally apply to the clarity of the definition of the crime or to the clarity of the penalty to be applied. The principle of legality requires that in order to be acceptable, penal legislation must describe with some precision the conduct it prohibits and the consequences that may follow from the conviction for such conduct (Packer 1968, pp. 79–100).[28] However, the behaviors considered illegal under RICO are well defined in the predicate acts of the law and its amendments in 1982 and 1984.[29] Likewise, the maximum penalties, up to twenty years in prison and up to twenty-five thousand dollars per count, as well as the forfeiture provisions, are very clear.

The vagueness challenge of the reformers seems to rest more on the ambiguities in the language of the original statute. A statute violates the Due Process Clause of the Fifth and Fourteenth Amendments if its language is so vague that it fails to convey sufficiently clear warning as to the proscribed conduct such that humans of common intelligence must necessarily guess as to its meaning.[30] However, a statute is not unconstitutionally vague where an appropriate judicial construct removes vagueness.[31]

The courts generally have *not* been receptive to challenges to RICO along lines that it is unconstitutionally vague either in terms of the acts covered or the penalties. I found more than thirty federal district court cases in which, with varying degrees of analysis, the void-for-vagueness challenge was rejected on various aspects of RICO. I found no case showing sympathy for the vagueness argument, save Scalia's concurrence in *H.J. Inc. v. Northwestern Bell*[32] (see Appendix for a listing of the cases analyzed), although in that case, the Justices unanimously declined to narrow the scope of RICO.

Scalia passed the gauntlet to Congress and, at the same time, implied that Congress may *not* be inclined to reform the law, thus upholding the position that the law is intentionally vague so as to cast as wide a net as possible for the prosecution of the syndicate at least. Three terms that are intentionally vague and that the courts have allowed are *pattern of racketeering, enterprise,* and *organized crime.* Although these terms have been challenged repeatedly by defense attorneys, the courts have upheld them as originally constructed. Senate Bill 438 alters this language.

Pattern of racketeering.   A pattern of racketeering activity as defined in 18 U.S.C. 1961(5)(1976) is the commission of two or more predicate acts within a ten-year time frame. *Act* is defined as any of the activities that are predicate such as extortion, bribery, embezzlement, counterfeiting, gambling, and obstruction of justice.[33] With the 1982 and 1984 amendments, mail and wire fraud and securities fraud are included. The courts have held that the law applies to anyone who commits "a pattern of racketeering acts" while participating in any fashion in the operation of any enterprise.

The statute is extremely broad, but there is little definitional ambiguity over the activities and perpetrators to which the law was meant to apply. The Congress has amended it to include an increasingly broad set of crimes and the courts have upheld its application. Only since 1987 has it come under attack.

The proposed RICO reform act holds that the label of racketeer is a harsh penalty and, in paragraph (10) amending section 1964(c), that with regard to civil suits containing no violence the term *unlawful activity* be used in place of the term *racketeering activity.* Similarly, the reform act holds that the term *pattern of unlawful activity* be used instead of the term *pattern of racketeering.*[34] Thus, investment bankers and savings and loan officers are not, under this language, labeled as racketeers unless they are involved in violent acts.

Enterprise. An enterprise is defined in 18 U.S.C. 1961(4)(1976) as "any individual, partnership, or corporation, association, or other legal entity, and any union or group of individuals associated in fact although not a legal entity."[35] Enterprise has recently been interpreted by the Supreme Court as including both "legitimate and purely illegitimate" associations.[36] The decision of the court in *U.S. v. Frumento* held that the general definition of enterprise in 1961(4) was meant to extend beyond specific references. In other words, the term *enterprise* was meant to be defined broadly so as to encompass all parts of legal and illegal entities that might be involved in the crime. In fact, an enterprise has been defined by the courts to include as few as two persons.

To the original drafters of RICO, the vagueness of the term *enterprise* was an asset, for they were concerned about the expansion of the syndicate into legal business. Reformers of RICO, however, do not want so-called legal corporations (i.e., savings and loans and investment banking firms) to be defined as enterprises through which so-called racketeering activities can be carried on. Limiting the term *enterprise* solely to illegal organizations would negate twenty years of judicial extension of the concept.

Organized crime. The RICO bill did not originally, nor has it been amended to, define organized crime in terms of the syndicate, much less *solely* in terms of the syndicate. Its predecessor bills did so, but the language was omitted from RICO. Instead, the RICO bill implicitly defined organized crime by what it did, the criminal acts, rather than what it was. The bill lists a variety of crimes (predicate acts)[37] to which the prohibitions of the act apply. RICO thus makes no attempt to define its target and limit its applicability to the syndicate (Lynch 1987, p. 683).

Again, the judicial precedent has been quite clear about the interpretation of the term *organized crime.* The courts have upheld the definition that organized crime is any entity that carries on the criminal activities enumerated in the act (the predicate acts). Organized crime could have been defined in terms of an organization—"a society that seeks to operate outside the control of the American people and their government," as the precursors of title IX tried to do.[38] However, the judicial system might have difficulty applying a law that made certain actions illegal when performed by members of a specific, organization (e.g., the Mafia) but could be performed without penalty by other citizens and organizations (e.g., investment banking firms). Even if *organization* could be satisfactorily defined, there would be political and ethical ramifications and the constitutionality of a law based on such a definition would be dubious. The reformers' argument that the term *organized crime* is vague and should be rewritten to apply only to the syndicate and not to securities and regulated industries may be both discriminatory and unethical.

A critical case in the challenge of vagueness of the term *organized crime* is *U.S. v. Mandel*.[39] After analyzing RICO's legislative history, in that case the court concluded that limiting RICO's applicability to organized syndicate crimes would severely "cripple the statute, if not render it unconstitutional." This seems the most obvious response to the reformers of RICO who wish to limit organized crime to syndicate types.

Based on two arguments, the courts have separately, repeatedly, and emphatically rejected the argument that RICO applies only to defendants who are part of organized, syndicated crime.[40] First, the law was not written to apply solely to the syndicate. Second, judicial precedent has defined organized crime as the act of committing certain criminal behaviors (the predicate acts), not as syndicate activities. Congress itself has amended RICO to include predicate acts of mail, wire, and securities fraud in 1982 and 1984, activities that are, in fact, more likely to be committed by the class of actors the reformers wish to exclude, investment bankers and savings and loan officials, than by the syndicate. Thus Congress itself has contributed to the broad interpretation of the term *organized crime*. This does not mean that a highly conservative court will continue to uphold RICO as originally constructed. Both Justices Scalia and Rehnquist have qualified rulings in ways that encourage such revisions.

Case Analysis: Scope Hypothesis.   In *U.S. v. Stofsky*,[41] the Court reported, "This [Act] may be broad, but it is not vague." Subsequently in June 1989, in *H.J. Inc. v. Northwestern Bell Telephone Co.*, the Court declined to narrow the scope of RICO, as noted above. This was prompted by four justices who agreed that the statute's definition of a "pattern of racketeering" is so vague that it might be unconstitutional (*Congressional Quarterly Weekly Report* 1989). In the interest of avoiding vagueness and imprecision in the core concepts of the RICO statute and in the interest of prosecutorial use, the act has been extended to cover many types of activities such as rack-eteering. This gives the law breadth. Certainly this is what recently prompted Rehnquist (1989) to conclude that he thought that the time had arrived for Congress to enact amendments to civil RICO to limit its scope to the sort of wrongs that are connected to organized crime, or have some other reason for being in federal court.

However, Rehnquist (1989) said he wanted to eliminate "garden variety fraud" from prosecution under RICO and thereby lighten the case load in the court system. RICO reformers have used this statement to argue that Rehnquist feels that the law is too broad, and therefore that securities fraud should not be prosecuted under RICO because it is already regulated by the SEC.

There is no doubt that the application of RICO is broad in scope, but it was originally so constructed to provide latitude in prosecuting the syndicate. Only recently has this latitude been called into question and then only because the law is broad enough in scope to prosecute the financial elite, a less politically convenient application of the law for the elites. Undoubtedly, it would be more efficient to have a single type of crime prosecutable under a single law. However, this generally is not the case; RICO is the statute of choice for prosecutors because of its penalties. The labeling of RICO as too broad has occurred since the amendments that defined mail and wire fraud and securities fraud as prosecutable under the law in 1982 and 1984, respectively, and since the act has been used to prosecute the financial elite. If RICO is too broad, why not eliminate labor or government officials from prosecution under it? Why choose the securities industry and other regulated industries? The answer lies in the political and social embeddedness of Congress, not in the breadth of RICO.

Inappropriate application and scope. The RICO reform committee, headed by DeConcini, charges that RICO has been used primarily to prosecute the syndicate, and therefore, application of this law to white-collar crime (what we call corporate crime) is inappropriate. This is a charge that can be empirically investigated: (1) Do the number of cases prosecuting the syndicate far exceed those brought against other types of organizations? (2) Is corporate crime prosecuted far less than any other type?

Following the lead of Lynch (1987), I surveyed all published criminal RICO cases decided in the courts of appeals from 1970 to 1985, from the first reported appellate decision involving the RICO statute in 1974 to the end of 1985.[42] Why 1985? I am hypothesizing that RICO *has* been applied to corporate crime since its enactment and that the syndicate has been prosecuted in relatively few cases, so I did not want to bias my data in the direction of supporting my hypothesis by including the last few years during which RICO has been applied heavily to corporate crimes. Many more cases of corporate crime, including securities fraud, have been prosecuted under RICO since the 1984 amendment. Assuming that both the syndicate and white-collar criminals would have the economic means to appeal lower-level decisions, I analyzed only appellate court cases. I also analyzed only criminal cases because syndicate crimes are criminal more often than civil, again biasing the data against my hypothesis and in favor of the reformers.

My research disclosed 250 indictments containing RICO counts, of which 236 could be studied. Fourteen cases did not include sufficient information to determine whether or not the syndicate was involved and the nature of the occupations and organizational affiliations of the actors. Subsections 1962(a) and (b) prohibit the investment of racketeering proceeds to acquire an interest in an enterprise. Syndicate cases would have to be filed under these subsections narrowing the search of cases for syndicate involvement to subsections (a), (b), and (c). Subsection 1962(d) prohibits conspiring to violate (a) and (b).

Only seventeen (8 percent) of the 236 cases involved the syndicate. Six of the seventeen cases were dismissed or convictions were later reversed on appeal.[43] Thus, only eleven cases (4.6 percent) were convicted, syndicate-type infiltrations of legitimate businesses. Thus I rejected the hypothesis that the preponderance of RICO cases had dealt with syndicate crimes.

Then the types of organizations and occupational affiliations of the defendants in each of the cases were coded to determine if those prosecuted under the act had been in sectors other than corporate organizations and white-collar occupations. The largest proportion of cases, ninety-four (40 percent), were concerted criminal activities, seventy-one (30 percent) cases were government corruption, forty-two (18 percent) cases were corporate crimes, and twenty-nine (12 percent) cases were labor corruption.[44]

By far the largest number of cases were criminal activities, followed by government corruption. Corporate crime composed only 18 percent of the cases that were tried in the appellate courts. Thus, nearly one-fifth of these cases were what the reformers classify as corporate crimes, if they mean business alone (a conservative definition of white-collar crime because labor and government officials who were white-collar criminals were excluded).

Whereas only 8 percent of the cases were syndicate related, 18 percent were corporate crimes. The percentage of white-collar cases was well over 2.5 times that of syndicate crimes. To say that RICO has been used primarily to prosecute the syndicate is inaccurate. Likewise to hold that it has not been used to prosecute white-collar crime is equally false. Thus both of the reformers' assumptions are false. Its use to prosecute corporate crime has, of course, increased since 1985.

The case analysis yields some support for the general scope of RICO being broad, but its breadth was intentionally expanded by Congress during the 1980s. There is no support for either scope subhypothesis. Between 1970 and 1985, RICO was not applied largely to syndicate cases. However, RICO was 2.5 times more often applied to corporate crimes than to syndicate crimes.

Case Analysis: Severity of Penalties. Careful and deliberate attachment of penalties to particular offense categories is effectively undermined if a prosecutor is empowered to increase those penalties dramatically by indictment under RICO. That is, securities fraud, which is a felony punishable by five years' imprisonment and, until recently, a relatively low fine, can now be indicted under RICO with much stiffer penalties. A person who is indicted on, say, two counts of securities fraud can be sentenced to a maximum of forty years in prison (twenty years for each count) and a fifty-thousand-dollar fine and can further be required to forfeit interest in the business enterprise used to defraud. The mandatory character of the forfeiture aspect of RICO places even greater sentencing power in the hands of the prosecutor. The government prosecutor's ability to freeze assets prior to trial, and seek seizure and forfeiture if the defendant is found guilty, is a heavy penalty on a firm's ability to conduct business in the interim and is unfair if the firm or party is not found guilty. The government can freeze at least the amount it claims that a corporation profited from the alleged wrongdoing. In fact, it could freeze all assets tainted by the alleged wrongdoing for forfeiture upon a finding of guilty.

Reformers, including the DeConcini-headed congressional committee, consider the freeze and forfeiture clauses of the RICO statute to be unduly severe. The Constitution protects citizens' justified expectations that conduct is only punishable to a particular extent in the same way that it protects the expectation that particular conduct will be defined as lawful. Securities firms deal primarily in capital. If they have their assets frozen at the time of indictment (any assets involved in, deriving from, or commingled with illegal funds), the resulting forfeiture may greatly inhibit the firms' ability to conduct normal business. If the verdict is guilty, the inhibition of normal business may be merited; however, if the verdict is not guilty, business has been unjustly impeded.

In October 1989, the Justice Department distributed new, more lenient guidelines to U.S. attorneys for the prosecution of RICO crimes. Now the government may seek a temporary restraining order upon the filing of RICO indictments in order to preserve all forfeitable assets until the trial is completed and judgment entered. Seizure is no longer possible because pretrial freezing of assets is equivalent to seizure without due process.

Treble damages under civil RICO are also being attacked. Section 5 of reform bill 438, which limits the damages recoverable by plaintiffs under civil RICO, is the most elaborate part of the statute. This section specifies that treble and double damages can be sought in "extraordinary cases." These are largely limited to government entities. The proposed reform bill reads:

> It is anticipated that detrebling the potential damages in these cases will reduce the misuse of civil RICO. Civil RICO should, however, remain available to victims of a pattern of criminal fraud or a pattern of other criminal conduct who only fit in this category. (p. 20)

Thus, if the fraud is regulated by the securities industry, it can be prosecuted by the SEC under other statutes. Therefore, according to the reform bill, it is no longer prosecutable under RICO. The bill exempts those accused of securities and commodities fraud from prosecution and therefore from both the forfeiture clause and increased damages.

In light of the recent Justice Department rulings, the case analysis yields no support for the severity of penalties hypothesis.

Recommended to Be Retroactive.   The RICO reform bill 438 was originally written to apply to all pending cases, all cases under indictment, and cases that had not had verdicts rendered at the time the bill was enacted. Two relevant cases were the savings and loan securities fraud case of Charles Keating and the investment banking securities fraud case of Michael Milken. If the bill's retroactive clause had remained intact and the bill had been enacted, both Michael Milken's and Charles Keating's indictments under RICO would have been abandoned. In September 1989, DeConcini was brought under fire for his involvement with Charles Keating; in 1990, the retroactive feature of the bill was eliminated and the bill was made applicable to civil cases only (p. 10).

Conclusions Concerning Legal Explanations

The vagueness and severity arguments set forth by the reformers of RICO do not hold up under examination—both hypotheses 1 and 3 were rejected based on the case data. There is evidence that RICO has been broadly applied to many types of crimes; however, the reformers' contention that RICO is a law both constructed for and applied to syndicate and not to white-collar crime is not supported. In fact, the law has been at least 2.5 times more frequently applied to white-collar crimes than to the syndicate. Thus, hypotheses 2a and 2b are not supported by the data. The language of the original statute does not mention the syndicate and the drafters were careful not to imply such limited application. The intentional breadth of the law can be supported by the fact that since 1984 Congress itself has expanded RICO to include the predicate acts of mail, wire, and securities fraud.

STRUCTURAL/NETWORK ANALYSIS

The sociopolitical embeddedness explanation of the reform of RICO results from an analysis of the social interactions among members of Congress, corporate elites, and financial elites of savings and loans and investment banks. It is not just that these leaders share a common socialization and therefore a common view of the world based on their values, norms, and beliefs. This may be true, but it is a very limited understanding of what occurs between various political, legal, and economic organizations. Congresspersons, judges, and investment bankers may well share common interpretations of the business world and how business operates, but they also participate directly in the well-being of each other's institutions through extensively linked social networks.

Hypothesis 4: *RICO is being reformed because of the social and political embeddedness of financial elites in congressional networks.*

In this section I demonstrate the social embeddedness of key congressional committee members who favored the reform of RICO and the regulation of banking. The exchanges among financial elites of investment banking firms (particularly Drexel and Michael Milken through the Alliance for Capital Access), savings and loans (particularly LSL and Charles Keating), and the congressional committee (headed by Dennis DeConcini) are laid out.

The data presented below explain the network shown in Figure 7.1.

1. *Drexel*: Investment banking firm with largest junk bond department in the nation. It controlled 40 percent or more of the junk bond market for each of four years (1984–1987).
   a. *Crime*: December 1988, DBL pleaded guilty to six felony counts of mail and wire fraud and securities fraud in order to avoid the much harsher penalties under RICO indictment. Under RICO, the government could have, immediately upon indictment, seized the company's assets to protect them for later forfeiture if Drexel were found guilty.
   b. *Network*: Milken and his traders were employees of DBL.
   c. *Punishment*: CEO Fred Joseph cooperated to prevent indictment under RICO and Drexel was fined $650 million. Fred Joseph was not indicted. Drexel filed bankruptcy in 1990.

1a. *Michael Milken*: Vice president of Drexel, head of the High-Yield
    Bond Department. Milken held interest in additional partnerships,
    number yet undetermined. From 1984 to 1987, he received a total
    of more than $3.5 billion from Drexel in salary, commissions, and
    bonuses. This amount was augmented substantially by his part-
    nership holdings.
    a. *Crime*: Pleaded guilty in April 1990 to six felony counts of se-
       curities fraud in connection with Drexel.

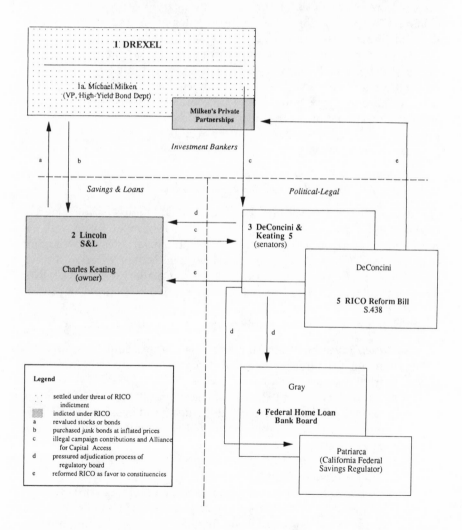

Figure 7.1 Political-Legal Networks.

b. *Network*: Milken parked stock for Boesky;[45] provided insider information to Boesky; revalued stock for Keating;[46] indirectly influenced DeConcini to reform RICO, through the Alliance for Capital Access and the Drexel PAC; indirectly influenced the Keating Five to intervene with the bank regulatory board, through the Alliance for Capital Access.

c. *Punishment*: Milken was assessed $600 million in fines and restitution (a $400 million restitution fund has been established), and was sentenced to ten years in prison with possible reduction for cooperation, and three years of full-time community service. Between the time of his sentencing in late 1990 and March 2, 1991, when he began serving his term, he was escorted around the country to provide information on possible and pending criminal and civil cases of alleged frauds related to his crimes. (He was released from prison after serving just twenty-two months.)

2. *Charles Keating*: Owner of the failed LSL (seized April 11, 1989), an Irvine, California–based part of American Continental Corporation (presently under seizure). LSL is the largest savings and loan to have failed to date, at a cost of $2 billion.

a. *Crime*: Keating has been found guilty on sixteen out of seventeen counts of securities fraud under California criminal code. And on July 10, 1992, a jury awarded $3.3 billion in damages to plaintiffs who had been defrauded though LSL. Keating is also under indictment for two felony counts of RICO in connection with LSL. Keating illegally contributed to campaigns of five U.S. senators.

b. *Network*: Michael Milken revalued Playtex stock for Keating. Keating purchased large quantities of overpriced high-risk bonds from Milken. Keating contributed $1.3 million to five senators, political contributions in exchange for the modification of regulatory statutes: Alan Cranston received $39,000 from Keating in 1986; $85,000 went to the California Democratic Party, and $850,000 went to several voter registration organizations; $48,000 went to Dennis DeConcini's 1988 campaign, and $33,000 went to his 1982 campaign (subsequently returned); two of DeConcini's aides received $50,000 in real estate loans from LSL; Donald Riegle received $78,250 for his 1988 campaign (subsequently returned); John McCain reimbursed Keating $13,000 for the use of his plane and vacation home in the Bahamas and has promised to return the $112,000 which he received from Keating if they are found by the Senate Ethics

Committee to be improper; John Glenn received $34,000 in campaign contributions, and Keating gave a political action committee associated with Glenn another $200,000. DeConcini is alleged to have intervened with bank regulator Edwin J. Gray, Chairman of the Federal Home Loan Bank Board, on behalf of Keating's failing LSL. In this deal, DeConcini is alleged to have requested compliance from Gray that, if LSL increased its relative holdings of home mortgage loans, the board would drop a regulation limiting the ability of state-chartered S&Ls to make riskier investments, specifically investments in junk bonds.

c. *Punishment*: A jury in the California trial of Charles Keating fined him $3 billion, an award that the judge later reduced to about $1 billion. Keating has declared bankruptcy and the cost to the taxpayer is estimated at $26 billion. The federal court found Keating guilty of seventy-three counts of securities fraud, bank fraud, and racketeering charges in indictments in 1991. Keating is presently serving his sentence, which has not been defined (Stevens 1993).

3. *Dennis DeConcini*: Democratic senator from Arizona, leading sponsor of the Senate RICO Reform Bill 438 and leader of Keating Five.

a. *Possible crimes*: DeConcini is testifying before the Senate Ethics Committee regarding his alleged intervention in the regulation of LSL by the Federal Home Loan Bank Board. Keating was interested in increasing LSL's holdings in junk bonds and, allegedly through DeConcini, offered the board a deal: LSL would increase its share of low-risk home mortgage loans in exchange for the regulatory board decreasing its efforts to regulate his purchasing of high-yield junk bonds. At the time of the intervention, the regulatory board was charging that LSL had exceeded a limit on the portion of its investment that can be held in high-risk instruments. Michael Patriarca, a federal savings regulator, testified that DeConcini applied the most pressure of any of the Keating Five on the regulating body to change its position that LSL's holdings of high-risk securities were in violation of the law. The senators are also charged with having unlawfully attempted to persuade the regulatory board to allow the purchase of LSL. All of this was occurring at a time when the regulatory board was adjudicating the LSL case. Dennis DeConcini, with four other senators, allegedly accepted more than $1.3 million in political contributions from Keating and his associates. In exchange for such contributions, DeConcini and

his colleagues Cranston and McCain, in April of 1987, allegedly asked Edwin Gray, chairman of the Federal Home Loan Bank Board, to revoke a regulation that LSL was challenging in the courts. LSL would then alter its operating procedures to minimize its junk bond holdings. The Federal Home Loan Bank Board was conducting an investigation of LSL.[47] The retroactive provision of the original reform act, S. 438, would have applied to the RICO lawsuit filed against Charles Keating and Michael Milken, thus shielding them from prosecution under some penalties.
   b. *Network*: DeConcini took campaign contributions from Keating. DeConcini intervened in the regulatory board's action to enforce the law limiting the holdings of a bank in high-risk investments. He also intervened to attempt to persuade the board that LSL was solvent. DeConcini was the head of the Senate committee working to reform RICO in ways that would limit its applicability to banks and securities firms.
   c. *Punishment*: The object of Senate Ethics Committee hearings for which he received a reprimand.

CONCLUSIONS OF NETWORK ANALYSIS

Vagueness and severity challenges to RICO were found to be flawed. The law is found to be intentionally broad both as constructed and as amended. Furthermore, empirical analysis of the cases demonstrates that the contention of the reformers—that RICO was written for and has been applied solely to syndicate crimes—is fallacious. The supporting contention of reformers that RICO has not been applied to white-collar crime is also fallacious since an analysis of appellate cases from 1970 to 1985 demonstrates that corporate crime cases were 2.5 times more prevalent than syndicate cases. The three legal arguments for the reform of RICO, contained in Senate Bill 438, are either quite limited or totally contradict the data.

The social and political embeddedness thesis provides a greater understanding of both why and how the reform has come about and what form it has taken. The economic and political reciprocities of the congresspersons, financial elites, and corporations are laid bare to explain not only the proposed changes in the laws, which would reduce the scope and penalties of elite crimes as explained, but also the changes in judicial interpretation. These changes were the direct consequences of interorganizational and interinstitutional networks.

Actors such as Milken, Keating, and DeConcini are located at network hubs not only in their focal organizations, but also importantly among various social institutions. There are strong ties demanding reciprocity among these influential actors. Milken and Keating, both powerful organizational players in their financial arenas, have influence over DeConcini in Congress, who in turn influences lawmakers and regulatory agencies. Milken and Keating would not enjoy such access to influential political figures if they had less status in the economic arena. Their status in these interorganizational networks provides information and leverage that, in turn, enhances their status in their focal organizations (Pfeffer and Salancik 1978) and provides them with the power to make internal policy and affect strategy. Thus these actors become even more powerful. Through this power, financial elites construct the moral norms and institutional frameworks in which they conduct business.

The underlying source of cohesion between these networks is not their similar family backgrounds (DiTomaso 1980) or their similar political behavior (Mizruchi 1989b), but rather their economic and political interdependence. The interdependence among financial corporations and between financial corporations and political and regulatory bodies leads to cohesion even when these firms might have conflicting or competing interests for profits. Like Mizruchi and Koenig (1984), I found that the ability of one organization to constrain another was positively associated with the interdependence of the organizations in these networks. It is not the density of interaction and number of interactions, but the nature of the interaction in terms of the ability of one organization to constrain and influence the survival of the other which creates powerful relationships.

The moral order embodied in laws and enforced through regulatory agencies should act as a control mechanism on the behavior of even these elite financiers (Meyer and Rowan 1977). However, when laws not previously applied to the financial elite, begin to be applied to them with the same punishments as imposed on the nonelite, the law is suddenly defined by these elites, Congress, and the judicial system as severe, vague, and inappropriately applied. Illegal conduct among elites does not necessarily lead to conviction, nor do elites change their behavior to conform to the law. Instead of changing their behavior, they use wealth, status, and their resulting legitimacy to gain access to networks of influential players to change the very laws intended to regulate behavior such as theirs. Thus, Milken and Keating, through DeConcini and his associates and the Senate committee that drafted the reform, attempted to alter the legal constraints of the Federal Home Loan Bank Board to raise the risk level and thus ensure that LSL's risk fell within acceptable limits. They also tried to have RICO reformed to reduce the penalties and liabilities for securities fraud.

The responsibility for reforming RICO has been debated by both Congress and the Supreme Court (see Rehnquist 1989), with Congress taking the lead. Both of these bodies are themselves part of the network and use their authority to bring about change through such mechanisms as judicial prerogative and congressional reform of legislation in ways that preserve the privileges of the dominant class and retain the present class structure.

Although we have some data on how social reforms (reforms directed against elite interests) come about, we have little evidence on how the elite uses legitimate relationships to conduct the illegal business of reforming the law. I have presented evidence of how the elite changes the laws that control its members' behavior through the networks in which they are embedded. The major drafter of the RICO bill is not only linked to the Keating Five and the reformers of RICO in a political network, but to economic networks made up of bankers (Keating) and investment bankers (Milken), and also to a regulatory network (Gray and Patriarca). A major contribution of this research is the finding that the same networks that were designed to control the corporate elite are used by the corporate elite to influence members of Congress to weaken the very laws and regulations that were written to control the behavior of corporate elites.

After 1985, the conservative courts began to reinterpret RICO and, at the same time, to speak out in ways that demonstrated to the financial elite that they were reinterpreting the law (see Rehnquist 1989 and Scalia in *H.J. Inc. v. Northwestern Bell Telephone Co.*). Because these reforms were initiated by elite interests having direct access to the legal system, they did not require popular pressure from organized constituencies (although such constituencies were in existence), which would have asked Congress to consider them. Pluralistic interest group formation was unnecessary. Had Keating not been indicted under RICO and DeConcini's relationship to Keating not been exposed, the reform bill would have easily been enacted with a minimum of public involvement and little media attention, save for the endorsement of the *Wall Street Journal*. Surely this would not have been the end of interest in RICO, but the beginning. There would then have been a struggle over reforming the regulatory system. Here the elite interests are in even stronger positions than they are in the legislative arena. Poorly funded regulatory agencies have boards that are, in some cases, directly controlled by the financial elite, and in other cases, indirectly controlled through Congress as was demonstrated above. This control is of a different nature than that of the formally mandated oversight of agencies by Congress.

The difference between the elites and the syndicate when it comes to seeking the attention of policymakers is that the elites have both legitimacy and wealth, whereas the syndicate has only wealth. The difference between elites and nonelites in the legitimate sector is that the elites do not have to build pluralistic interests through the formation of constituency groups as would other legitimate reformers of less elite status, because they have more direct access to those who make the laws and regulate the boards. Not only does a double standard exist in the application of the law to the financial elites and other organizational criminals, including the syndicate, but a double standard also exists in the access to legislative arenas and judicial treatment. These advantages are due not just to the structural advantages of the elite class (Merton 1968), but to the social interaction patterns and processes (networks) that they develop as they gain status.

At the macro level, this research has implications for the subfields of corporate crime, economic sociology, legal politics, organizational environments, and interorganizational networks. It also has implications for network analysis. But more importantly, it has implications for our understanding of the sociopolitical embeddedness of political-legal actions and economic actions. An understanding of the construction and the reform of laws is found not so much in legal arguments about the nature of the laws, but in the embeddedness of the actions of those who construct and reconstruct our laws. At the micro level, this analysis has implications for understanding the nature of exchange, power relationships within exchange, and reciprocity. Even more importantly, it has implications for our understanding of the nature of trust. The nature and level of trust is quite different for those involved in illegal activities than for those involved in legal exchanges. We know little about the consequences of the breach of trust between these powerful actors such as Boesky and Milken.

The links among cases of investment banking fraud, junk bond market fraud, and savings and loan fraud are undoubtedly related to market failures and impending recession. At present, there have been few attempts to measure the social cost or damage to the moral order.

APPENDIX: CASES

American National Bank and Trust Company of Chicago v. Haroco, Inc
H.J. Inc. v. Northwestern Bell Telephone Co.
Sedima S.P.R.L. v. Imrex Co., Inc.
United States v. Brown 583 F. 2nd at 669–70
United States v. Campanale 518 F. 2nd at 352, 363 (9th Cir. 1975)
United States v. Cohen Grocery 335 U.S. 81, 41 S. Ct. 298, 65 L. Ed. 519 (1921)
United States v. Computer Science Corp. 689 F. 2nd at 1189–91
United States v. Jacobson 691 F. 2nd at 110
United States v. Mandel F. Supp. 997 (D. Md. 1976)
United States v. Ramano 736 F. 2nd at 1432, 1441 (11th Cir. 1984)
United States v. Ranney 719 F. 2nd at 1186

United States v. Romano 736 F. 2nd at 1434–35
United States v. Rubin 559 F. 2nd at 975, 991 N. 15 (5th Cir. 1975)
United States v. Rubio 727 F. 2nd at 790–91
United States v. Stofsky 409 F. 609 (S.D.N.V. 1973)
United States v. Turkett 101 S. Ct. 2524 (1981)

NOTES

13. 18 U.S.C. 1961–1968 (1982 & Supp. III 1985).

14. P. L. No. 91–452, 84 Stat. 941 (1970).

15. Corporate crime is distinguished from the broader category of white-collar crime. which includes government and labor management crimes. Corporate crime includes some but not all crimes committed by employees of firms. Corporate crime differs from employee crime in that employee crime is committed against the organization, such as padding expense accounts, whereas corporate crime is committed for the benefit of both the employee and the corporation and could not be committed without a position in the corporation.

16. Whereas penalties for investment of unreported income had a maximum sentence and a $50,000 fine [S. 2048, 90th Congress, 1st Sess. (1967)]. In the 91st Congress, the penalty was set at ten years and not more than $10,000 [S. 1623, 91st Cong. 1st Sess. 2(a), 2(c) (1969)]. No forfeiture provision was made. As enacted in 1970, RICO permitted a twenty-year jail term and a fine up to $25,000 and contained elaborately defined forfeiture provisions. See 18 U.S.C. 1963(a), (1982) amended 1984.

17. Civil RICO is generally used when one business files suit against another. RICO is a criminal enforcement mechanism. "The provision for a private civil remedy in the statute was designed to provide a supplementary way to enforce its basic purposes and to add substantial private resources to the enforcement of the criminal law. Thus the commonly accepted rationale for the private civil RICO action is that it serves to convert each individual plaintiff, into [one] who can enforce the RICO statute's prohibitions against criminal conduct in a civil lawsuit" (Abrams and Harlan 1989).

18. See 18 U.S.C. 1961(1)(D) (1982).

19. See S. 1961, 91st Cong. 1st Sess. 2(a) (1969) provision to have been codified as 1961(1)(B).

20. See 18 U.S.C. 1961(1)(B) (1982) (amended 1984).

21. The author is aware of the popular debate over the existence of the syndicate, mob, and related terms as families and as organizations. The terms are used in this paper in quotes as they are terms used by Congress in the debate concerning the reform of RICO.

22. Senate Bill 438, 1990.

23. The Federal Election Campaign Act of 1971 grants corporations explicit permission to establish PACs, which, although legally distinct organizations, are funded by firms. All corporate contributions to political campaigns must be filed

with the FEC and knowledge must be made available to the public. The law limits PAC contributions to $5,000 per each election.

24. Amending the Racketeering Influenced and Corrupt Organizations Act, 101st Congress, 2nd Sess., 101–269, April 24, 1990. Only the portions of the act relevant to our analysis of financial corporations are listed here.

25. When DeConcini's connection to Keating was discovered and publicized, the bill was amended by omission of its fourth point.

26. See *Sedima S.P.R.L. v. Imrex Co., Inc.* and *American National Bank and Trust Company of Chicago v. Haroco Inc.*

27. Testimony of Frederick Joseph (*U.S. v. Michael Milken* 1990a).

28. This principle finds expression in the federal constitutional doctrine of vagueness, which holds that a penal statute that does not give fair warning of the nature of its prohibitions violates the constitutional command that deprivation of life, liberty, or property must be based on due process of law. 29. 18 U.S.C. 1962, and (1982) and (1984).

30. *United States v. Cohen Grocery*, 335 U.S. 81, 41 S. Ct. 298, 65 L. Ed. 519 (1921).

31. 6A Am. Jour. 2nd Constitutional Law 818 (1988).

32. The Supreme Court in a June 1989 ruling in *H.J. Inc. v. Northwestern Bell Telephone Co.* said, "RICO may be a poorly drafted statute, but rewriting it is a job for Congress, if it is so inclined, and not for this court." A minority of the judges (four) concurred that the statute's definition of a "pattern of racketeering" may be vague.

33. 18 U.S.C. 1961(1) (1976).

34. Amending the Racketeer Influenced and Corrupt Organizations Act, 101st Congress, 2nd Sess. (1990): 9.

35. 18 U.S.C. 1961(4) (1976).

36. *United States v. Turkett*, 101 S. Ct. 2524 (1981).

37. The predicate acts include bail bond violations, bribery, burglary, conspiracy, drug and narcotics violations, extortion, falsification of records, fraud, gambling, labor and union violations, mail and wire fraud, obstruction of law enforcement, robbery, securities violations, travel acts violations, and miscellaneous racketeering activities.

38. President's Commission on Law Enforcement and Administration of Justice (Katzenbach Commission), "The Challenge of Crime in a Free Society" (1967). The commission was created by President Lyndon Johnson in 1965. See Exec. Order No. 11,236 (July 23, 1965), Task Force Report at 6–10. Two bills introduced by Senator Roman Hruska: S. 2048, 90th Cong., 1st Sess. (1967); see also H.R. 11,266, 90th Cong., 1st Sess. (1967) (same bill introduced in House) and S. 2049, 90th Cong., 1st Sess. (1967); see also H.R. 11,268, 90th Cong., 1st Sess. (1967) (virtually identical bill introduced in House). See also S. 1861, 91st Cong., 1st Sess. (1969) (Senators Hruska and McClellan). Although this bill itself was entitled "Corrupt Organizations Act of 1969," the proposed new chapter to title 18 of the United States Code was called "Racketeer Influenced Organizations." The two titles were later combined to yield the present acronymic title.

39. F. Supp. 997 (D Md. 1976).

40. See also *United States v. Rubin*, 559 F. 2nd at 975, 991 N. 15 (5th Cir. 1977), vacated and remanded, 439 U.S. 810 (1978), rev'd in part on other grounds, 591 F. 2nd at 278 (5th Cir ?), cert. denied U.S. 864 (1979); United States v. Campanale, 518

F. 2nd at 352, 363 (9th Cir. 1975) art. denied, 423 U.S. 1050 (1976); United States v. Ramano, 736 F. 2nd at 1432, 1441 (11th Cir. 1984), vacated in part on other grounds, 755 F. 2nd at 1401 (11th Cir. 1985).

41.   409 F. 609 (S.D.N.V. 1973).

42.   These same 236 cases were also examined by Lynch for other purposes. His figures are somewhat similar: 94 were concerted criminal activities, 71 cases were government corruption, 42 cases were business crimes, and 29 were instances of labor corruption.

43.   *Ranney*, 719 F. 2nd at 1186; Jacobson, 691 F. 2nd at 110; Romano, 736 F. 2nd at 1434–35; Brown, 583 F. 2nd at 669–70; Rubio, 727 F. 2nd at 790–91; Computer Science Corp. 689 F. 2nd at 1189–91.

44.   Concerted criminal activity consists of narcotics, gambling, sports bribery, arson, violent extortion, political violence, loan sharking, prostitution, theft and fencing, and diversified syndication. Government corruption consists of police corruption, contracts and purchasing, courts, tax and regulatory bodies, legislators, governors, and miscellaneous. Corporate crime consists of business fraud, violence and theft, and copyright violations. Labor corruption consists of all crime in which labor was involved.

45.   Boesky and Milken each held stock for the other to conceal ownership of more than 5 percent from the SEC. Ownership of 5 percent or more must be reported under the assumption that it should be public information because it signals potential acquisition.

46.   One of Keating's alleged fraudulent activities that has been linked to Michael Milken and Drexel is the revaluing of Playtex. In December 1984, LSL bought 2.1 million shares of Playtex (a restricted stock not trading publicly) from Drexel. Drexel was the underwriter of the Playtex junk bond issue and sold the stocks as a "sweetener." Drexel's junk bond unit, headed by Milken, set the stock's price at 20 cents per share. Four months later (April 1987) Lincoln's parent corporation, American Continental Corporation (ACC), controlled by Keating bought the Playtex stock for $1.00 a share, a price set by Drexel. Lincoln recorded a $1.68 million profit, or 400 percent, in four months. In December 1987 ACC sold 1.5 million of the original 2.1 million shares to CenTrust, run by David Paul, at $6.95 a share, or $10.4 million. Again Drexel set the price. The 600 percent increase in the value of the stock in eight months had netted ACC $8.9 million. As would be expected, in June 1988 CenTrust sold 1.5 million shares back to ACC for $10.6 a share, a price determined by Drexel and a 53 percent increase in the price of the stock in six months. CenTrust recorded a $5.5 million profit (*Business Week* 1990, p. 26).

47.   Lincoln Case, p. 3134; ethics probe, p. 3132.

Part IV

Toward Theory

Chapter 8

Toward Theories of Economic Organizations and Organizational Crime

Closed doors, close relationships, and mystery govern business here.
—Chandler and Kanabayashi, *Wall Street Journal*,
Tuesday, June 25, 1991

The above quote concerning the operations of the market, ironically, was written about the Japanese market and was preceded by the sentence, "In fact the widespread scandal underscores how far Japan still lags [behind] the standards of many of the world's markets." Obviously the author was attempting to demonstrate how insular the Japanese market is compared to Western markets. However, closed doors, close relationships, and mystery do exist in securities markets in the United States. The same quotes might well have been used to describe U.S. markets in the 1980s, especially the high-yield bond market. Codes of silence and unlawful disclosure of inside information among traders, the myth of the self-regulating markets, and the links between markets, regulators, and Congress allowed securities fraud to flourish.

The securities fraud of the 1980s was the largest in the history of Wall Street, even larger than that underlying the market crash of 1929, which is purported to have been the impetus for our contemporary securities laws (Fligstein 1990a). It did irreparable damage to markets and had pervasive consequences for the transformation of corporate America from multidivisional related-product producing structures to unrelated-product holding companies. Many large companies vanished in takeovers (Carnation, Beatrice, General Foods, Diamond Shamrock). Others became part of huge conglomerates of unrelated products (Nabisco and R.J. Reynolds). Many of these takeovers were characterized and assisted by market manipulation, insider trading, parking, and other forms of securities fraud.

The magnitude of the fraud associated with takeovers in the 1980s may have been augmented by a change in motivation for the transactions. Unlike mergers in earlier periods, which were conducted for the purpose of expanding production or expanding into new markets, the mergers in the 1980s were undertaken for immediate profits generated by reselling some or all of the acquired firm. Thus, each buyout led to a large number of related financial transactions. Unlike "industrial capital," which generates profits through increased production and the buying and selling of goods, "financial capital" generates profits though monetary transactions. These transactions have the characteristics discussed in Chapter 5. Fraud is cleaner and more efficient in a solely monetary arena than in an arena in which goods must be produced and then exchanged for money. This is true because it takes a shorter period of time to exchange money than it does to produce a product and then exchange that product for money. The amount of time necessary for industrial capital to make a profit is greatly increased when an entire product line must be created or a market established. Industrial capital transactions are based on tangible and visible products, which are being exchanged for money. Thus the deficiencies in the product and its exchange are more readily detectable than are problems in purely financial transactions.

The transformation of American corporations from multidivisional production firms to holding companies or financial entities resulted in unemployment for millions of Americans. Many companies were overleveraged and today are using precious profits to pay interest rates sometimes three times higher than the current rates. Still others are bankrupt. Many of our corporate giants have been restructured (often a euphemism for Chapter 11 bankruptcy), most more than once. The current value of their securities is far less than was represented to bondholders. Some of these bonds are worthless junk. There is no absolute measure of the contribution of this fraud to the current United States recession. Richard C. Breeden, chairman of the SEC, estimated the cost of Drexel-related fraud to the U.S. taxpayer at $40–$50 billion (Breeden 1991). The figure seems low to this author.

As important as the consequences of fraud of the 1980s are for corporate America, they are having a long-lasting effect on institutional investors: savings and loans, pension funds, insurance trusts, and the investment funds that hold the retirement and annuities of most state and federal employees. A substantial portion of stocks and bonds are held by institutional investors. As James Burk points out, institutional investments tie "the stock market, the state, and the society together into a single community of fate" (1988, p. 139). Private and public well-being are one.

The pillars of capitalism are private ownership of property (especially in the form of corporations) and the free transfer of ownership. For decades, investment bankers were essentially the gatekeepers of capitalism. But, in the decade of the 1980s, investment banking firms not only executed the transactions but defined and initiated the deals, and in some cases chose which actors could participate. Investment bankers themselves invested in the targets, becoming "merchant bankers," similar to J. P. Morgan's merchant banking at the turn of the century.

Although the decade of the 1980s glorified free-market capitalism, this analysis shows that, in fact, during this period, markets were corrupted and subverted for the organizational and individual interests of powerful players. The players constructed a myth of free competition, enterprise, intelligence, innovation, and hard work—the bases on which the market is supposed to reward participants. While they talked of the virtues of the level playing field, they participated in the greatest thefts in the history of American markets, the kind of theft that destroys our confidence in overall fairness. The actions of these investment bankers resulted not only in a loss of confidence in the market, but also in investment bankers and in securities firms in general. Everyone who owns a pension fund or an annuity or pays taxes is a victim of these crimes.

These crimes were committed just prior to the U.S. economy plunging into the deep and protracted recession of the early 1990s. During periods of recession we examine ourselves in attempts to answer questions about our individual well-being, the well-being of the corporations in which we work, and the well-being of our society. A fair question to ask is, How much of this recession was due to securities fraud of various kinds? In a capitalist democracy we are generally positive about capitalism and its underlying markets. When the markets are going well we feel that the economy of the country is doing well, and therefore that we are doing well. But crime and immorality in the marketplace destroy our confidence in the market, which often results in demands for tighter regulation.

In exchange for fair and ethical treatment, we reward those who know and understand the market with reverence and elevated titles such as the one mythicized in *Bonfire of the Vanities*: "master of the universe." Michael Milken was deified on Wall Street with the titles "wizard of Wall Street" and the "junk bond king." The capitalist system rewards these elite securities traders with salaries and compensation packages in the millions of dollars.

The assumption underlying capitalism is that the material prosperity of the country depends on private ownership and market trades. Yet most of us do not understand how markets function. We trust that those who study and deal in markets know how they work. We further trust that these same individuals will deal fairly and ethically with those who enter markets. Market exchanges rest on trust; fraud succeeds by abusing this trust. As a result of the success of fraud, trust is destroyed. When we find those who are the masters of the game, such as Dennis Levine, Martin Siegel, and Michael Milken, are participating on an uneven playing field, it shakes our confidence in these actors and the corporations they represent, if not in the entire capitalist system. We begin to realize that those who participate in the market as investors can defraud the even savvy managers, who do not understand how the market functions. Because of special characteristics of market transactions, the superior knowledge of traders, and the apathy of government officials, repeated acts of fraud can go undetected for long periods of time. We come to understand that the corporations in which these actors operate do not have effective systems of policing themselves or protecting the public. More shocking is that corporations themselves are either actively or by inertia sanctioning participation in fraud. Many of our regulatory statutes and securities laws have not kept up with the innovations in the securities fraud industry. Others are not enforced. The laws that are effectively enforced or used for indictments are being altered by Congress with the support of the Supreme Court, to support the financial elite whom they were designed to control.

There was a market failure in October 1987 and another minifailure two years later. By market failure, I do not mean that the normal market mechanisms were not functioning, but rather that the prices of stocks were declining. Market failure could be the consequence of many actions: It could occur because of monopolistic control, the high cost of securities fees (transaction costs), or market manipulation and fraudulent practices (Williamson 1975, pp. 211–18). When one or more of these phenomena takes place, the market is more likely to fail. If one of the major ways in which businesses are being financed (through junk bonds) is conducted as a near monopoly, the company that controls this market monopoly can charge exceptionally high prices for both interest and financial consulting services. If many of the monopolistic transactions were executed by manipulating the market or by securities fraud, such situations could cause market failure or, at the very least, compound the failure.

Some have argued that, when these phenomena occur, perfect competition is inhibited and goods and resources are not allocated efficiently. Thus, monopoly and fraud cause the price of stock to be inflated. A crash is the normal readjustment of the market to the true value of corporate stock. These types of phenomena interfere with the market and are therefore harmful to public interests (or at least to those with interest in the market). Others argue that the market failure of the Great Depression resulted in the public demanding and the government providing increased monitoring and regulation. In other words, these theorists hold that the securities regulations of 1933 and 1934 were a result of market failure stemming from fraud, as well as other causes (Pecora 1939; Cowing 1965; Sligman 1982; Carosso 1970).

MARKETS, ORGANIZATIONS, AND FRAUD

Securities markets have a long and well-documented history of fraud. Before the 1930s, the New York Stock Exchange, the largest securities market in the world, was legendarily unscrupulous. Perhaps the best source on the fraudulent practices of the great bull market of the 1920s is Sobel who wrote, if a "rascality index" could be devised, the 1920s would mark a peak (1965, p. 236). The aftermath of this period of fraud was the great crash, Congressional hearings, indictments and prosecution of the fraudulent, the 1933 and 1934 Securities Acts, and the establishment of the Securities and Exchange Act.

In the United States of the late 1970s, it was estimated that 30 percent of all corporate liquidations were the result of fraud (Comer 1977, p. 3). The proportion increased in the 1980s to approximately 46 percent. This, of course, was fraud that was detected. We do not know to what extent undetected fraud contributed to the success of some organizations and the demise of others. These statistics do not speak specifically to securities fraud or to investment banking fraud. We have few analyses of the pervasiveness of securities fraud. However, as I explored the networks between various securities organizations, I came to realize that the extent of securities fraud in the 1980s was greater than I had ever imagined, certainly much greater than what was being reported in the press or prosecuted in the courts.

Such fraud was prevalent not only in commercial banking and savings and loans but also in investment banking. Investment banking fraud was not limited to small- and medium-sized firms such as Princeton/Newport, but included larger firms such as Drexel and Kidder Peabody. To forestall the idea that fraud was a movement limited to the 1980s, note that in the summer of 1991, the largest and most prestigious investment banking firm in the United States, Salomon Brothers, manipulated the Treasury bond market by buying 46 percent of the securities sold in a December 1990 auction, 57 percent of those sold in the February 1991 auction, and 94 percent of those sold in the May 1991 auction (Cohen and Siconolfi 1991). Treasury Department rules require a bid limit of 35 percent at any single sale of government securities. As in the junk bond market, there was collusion among the investment banking firms to organize these bids. Cohen and Siconolfi reported:

> Collusion and price fixing in the $2.3 trillion Treasury securities market have been routine for more than a decade, according to traders and top Wall Street executives. The most prevalent and potentially damaging practice has been the sharing of confidential information among an elite group of bond traders about their bids at auction of Treasury securities. (1991, p. C1)

Securities fraud is interpreted by newspapers and the popular press as the product of individual greed and uncontrolled ambition. This is a curious interpretation for several reasons, which will be developed below. However, for immediate purposes, it is curious because these crimes are committed through the transactions and networks of complex and sophisticated organizations. It is truly corporate crime that is intentionally or unintentionally facilitated by the organizational structure and processes of the employing organizations. The magnitude of corporate crime rests on the power and influence that the employing organization has at its disposal.

FINDINGS

This section summarizes and synthesizes the most important findings related to ownership and control and suggests future directions for organizational analysis:

1. A single department, the High-Yield Bond Department in the case of Drexel, can gain control of an organization and enhance or destroy it by controlling the strategic contingency, in this case organizational profits.
    a. Structuring rewards in keeping with the premises of agency theory creates internal contradictions that replace authority with functional control, in this case financial control.

2. Control of external resources increases the internal power of a single department. In this case the control of networks of buyers and sellers increased the High-Yield Bond Department's control of Drexel.
    a. Sellers were controlled because of the High-Yield Bond Department's knowledge and control of the bond market and expertise in doing deals. The department controlled 40–65 percent of the high-yield bond market between 1984 and 1987. Drexel was the most effective investment banker, selling high-risk, third-level subordinate debt.
    b. Buyers were controlled because junk bonds returned a higher rate of interest than any other security. Thus they provided a profit margin that was necessary for the buyer, usually an institutional investor, to return a high rate of interest to its investors.
        1. Institutional investors were controlled by making them partners in illegal activities and profits related to the bonds they were buying for their funds. (For example, Patricia Ostrander

of Fidelity and J. Mulheren of Jamie Securities were principals in the MacPherson Partnership.)

3. Deals (mergers and acquisitions) were often facilitated by fraud such as market manipulation, insider trading, parking, and tax evasion. Fraud increases the efficiency of some transactions.

4. Financial firms initiate and control corporations. Drexel defined which corporations were the most vulnerable and therefore the most acceptable targets as well as designated the acquirer.

5. Financial firms controlled political/legal actions such as regulatory boards, the reform of RICO, tax laws, and bankruptcy laws.
   a. To change laws on which they were economically dependent, financial firms interacted directly with powerful/legal actors.
   b. Financial firms indirectly controlled political/legal entities through PACs. Drexel organized its own PAC and lobby, the Alliance for Capital Access, which was written into existence by Craig Cogut, a high-ranking member of the High-Yield Bond Department's external legal counsel and a partner in Milken's privately held partnerships.
   c. Financial firms indirectly controlled political/legal entities by influencing those who were economically dependent upon them (buyers and sellers) to act in concert with them to change laws (e.g., LSL worked with Drexel to reform the regulatory structures for banks and RICO).

The High-Yield Bond Department controlled the strategic contingencies of corporate profits and thus the internal operations of Drexel. The department controlled networks of buyers and sellers because it had the expertise, knowledge, and access to the high-yield bond market. In fact, the high-yield bond market had its origins in the later 1970s. However, Drexel did not control it until the mid-1980s, when it invented a number of financial instruments, such as the "highly confident" letter and zero coupon bonds. The High-Yield Bond Department's control of buyers and sellers increased its control of the internal operations of Drexel. In order to do larger and more profitable deals, the High-Yield Bond Department used two types of external organizations—the Boesky organizations and the employee private partnerships—for illegal actions in the market and with buyers and sellers. This network of buyers allowed Drexel to gain control of 40–65 percent of the junk bond market. This control augmented Drexel's advantage over its competitors and gave it access to networks of congressmen who oversaw regulators and wrote legislation, including the reform of RICO, under which the firm's and Milken's fraud were being indicted.

INFORMING PERSPECTIVES

Although there are a number of perspectives that attempt to inform us about organizational crime in economic organizations and markets, I have chosen to discuss three of these: popular press psychological explanations; economic organizational theory explanations, specifically Jensen's agency theory; and the structural/embeddedness theory developed in this book. Here I will critique each of the two more popular alternatives to the structural model and then continue to build the structural model developed in earlier chapters.

Psychological Explanations in the Popular Press

This analysis examines only the popular press's use of psychological explanation. I am not criticizing social-psychological explanations of crime in general. In fact, there are excellent works on crime from social-psychological perspectives, some with social constructionist roots. One such work is Katz's (1988) *Seduction of Crime: Moral and Sensual Attraction in Doing Evil*, an outstanding treatment of noncorporate crime. In the final chapter, Katz suggests ways in which his approach can enlighten studies of organizational crime. Yet organizational scholars have not generally followed his lead.

On the other hand, countless popular press books have described various aspects of Drexel's junk bond market fraud as the result of the personal characteristics of a single person or a small number of people. These works assumed that such fraud was occurring only in Drexel and only because key individuals were obsessively greedy or driven by power. These portrayals of the character of Drexel employees are obviously limited and one-sided. They suggest that other firms, with employees of different character, were not involved in such illegal activities. In some cases these theories go deeper, attributing the development of these characteristics to their fathers' and mothers' treatment of the individuals, but this type of superficial psychoanalytical analysis can be very weak [for example, see Kornbluth's (1992) analysis of Michael Milken's actions].

In these psychological explanations, the individual is the unit of analysis and the moral character of the individual is the cause of the fraud. These psychologically based accounts are most often rendered by journalists and journalists turned book authors [for example, Connie Bruck (1988) and Sarah Bartlett (1991)]. Those who have worked in securities firms and are now exploiting their past by publishing accounts of their experiences have also adopted psychological interpretations, with an additional agenda of rationalizing their actions. Some who worked in firms that have been involved in recent scandals wrote about their experiences before the public exposure of scandal (e.g., Michael Lewis 1989). More recently, securities firm employees (e.g., Dennis Levin 1991) who participated in the crimes have written exposés of their personal illegal acts. Some accounts have found their way into movies and television scripts such as *Wall Street*. These accounts are all focused on key individuals, using what is basically the great man (in this case infamous man) theme. They analyze personality characteristics rather than the systemic character of the fraud.

My analysis acknowledges the importance of self-interest and greed as motivations of many of the actors involved: Boesky, Levine, Siegel, and Milken. However, the real driving force of the 1980s was a far more sophisticated and complex set of financial innovations and economic environments, of transformations of legal structures, of contradictory organizational structures and strategies, and of interorganizational powers that enabled market manipulation, if not market control, through a network of issuers, investment bankers, and buyers. An understanding of the rise and fall of the merger and acquisition boom of the 1980s requires an understanding of the centrality of the capital supply and the tax deductibility of debt that are systemic to the economic and legal processes of the times. Other laws were changed to facilitate the junk bond–leveraged merger and acquisition movement. The centrality of self-interest and maximization of profits are innate to the financial method of corporate control of the 1980s. Although they form the core of Drexel, they are no less salient for firms that are not at the center of such fraud networks. Thus self-interest and greed cannot explain why Drexel but not other firms was so pervasively involved in this fraud.

The power of this small group of market makers was greater than any other at that time. Their market power came not only from controlling the strategic contingency of profits for the organizations in which they operated, but also from controlling the legal and economic structures that supported these organizations. Thus insider trading and securities fraud were carried on through Drexel and its networks of clients, buyers, other investment banking firms, private partnerships, and arbitragers. Drexel controlled the corporations with which it did business, and influenced relevant congressional committees and regulatory bodies. As we saw in Chapter 7, investment banking firms can manipulate not only the economic environment in which they operate, but also their legal environment.

As our systems of regulation, control, and transactions falter, the press and, in turn, the American public view these cases as isolated, unrelated instances of fraud that occur because those involved are greedy, evil, immoral, or at best amoral. When the level of acquisition is beyond all imagination and the defrauder is worth billions, the motivation must be "bigger and bigger deals." Certainly, I am not denying that these actors are willing to go to any lengths to increase their wealth and status among deal makers. They are willing to defraud not only buyers of securities, but also those for whom they are selling the securities. Greed could motivate a person to become involved in such activities. However, when those involved are billionaires, their continued illegal actions are less plausibly motivated by greed.

A more plausible psychological explanation was revealed in the interviews with traders for continued involvement in fraud: the exhilaration of doing larger and larger illegal deals and getting away with it. Each successive deal is touted as the largest to date and each is assumed to be completely legal. The doing of deals, especially fraudulent deals, that are progressively riskier is seductive. The seduction of crime is not a novel idea (see Katz 1988). The doing of the deal acted much as a fix; which provided a needed rush of excitement. However, the rush was followed by inevitable let down and anxiety about one's status in the deal-making game. This anxiety provided the impetus for the next fix—another deal.

I am not attempting to absolve individuals of their actions, but to expose the dual process of individual actions and structural embeddedness that lead to the opportunity to commit fraud. We castigate those who sell worthless securities to the public and control the market in particular securities. However, we do little to alter the transaction systems that facilitate the fraud and the social networks in which these transactions are embedded.

Neoclassical Economic Explanation

The second argument, the one best known to academicians, is the neoclassical economic model. It served as the point of departure for the perspective developed in this book because the economic organization models that I argue against are derivatives of neoclassical economics. These models, which have their roots in the works of Adam Smith, claim that markets create their own moral norms from the transactions among market participants. These exchanges, which emerge naturally, unregulated by external structures, are the most efficient. Those who do not operate according to the norms of the market are inefficient. That is, those who act fraudulently are operating outside the accepted markets norms and will be sanctioned by the market. If their acts breach the norms of exchange too greatly, they will be expelled by the market because of exchange inefficiency.

Those who participate in the market to satisfy their desires will be attentive to the desires of others, not because they are altruistic, but because they cannot fulfill their own desires unless they meet the needs of others. If they attempt to fulfill their needs without meeting the needs of others, or if they attempt to maximize their needs at the expense of others, they will find themselves without transaction partners and will therefore fail to meet their own needs. Thus, in the short run, those who act solely self-interestedly, exploitatively, or fraudulently in the exchange process may benefit greatly. However, over the long run, transaction partners learn that they can benefit more from transactions with others. Thus narcissism, exploitation, and crime do not pay. The smooth functioning of the market depends on the good character of its participants, and the consequences of the naturally regulated market are the reinforcement of profit mechanisms. Those who do not play by the rules do not profit.

According to this model, markets function autonomously within society. Markets regulate themselves, establish the norms under which others participate in their exchanges, and expel and economically punish those who do not play by the rules of the game. Herein lies our concern with this model. What if the empirical evidence is that those who do not play according to the rules of the game are the winners? What if those who act fraudulently are able to manipulate the market over long periods of time? What if the cumulative consequences are not major losses or expulsion, but success? Still more detrimental to society, what if cheaters are discovered and the punishment dealt them is relatively light? Neoclassical economics has never provided a fully adequate understanding of the economies that it seeks to analyze.

It can be demonstrated empirically that not all market participants share the same norms of exchange. What is fair exchange is socially constructed, dependent on group beliefs, and the specifics of the trading situation. Not all exchange partners are equally desirable in a specific exchange. Some have greater potential for long-run payoffs than others. As Williamson (1975) points out, participants may not only seek to satisfy their self-interest, they may do so opportunistically and with guile. In other words, individuals attempt to realize an advantage by manipulating the playing field to their advantage, by constructing innovative rules, or by using nonmarket strategies such as fraud. In sum, there is considerable evidence that market actors create their own moral orders.

Neoclassical economic ideas enjoyed immense popularity during the 1980s, along with other conservative economic and political ideas, such as a return to the natural market system and a belief in inevitable progress through free-market enterprise, laissez-faire capitalism, and the imprudence of enforcement of antitrust regulations. This remarkable revival of classical free-market economics has served to fulfill the public's need for some kind of understanding of what guides the day-to-day actions and transactions on Wall Street.

Sociological, economic, and political explanations of American institutions seemed to revolve around rational choice and neoclassical economic theories. The market economy became predominant not only in the United States and the West, but in former East Germany and other Eastern European countries. At the end of the 1980s, the Berlin Wall fell and the Communist Party in Russia lost a great deal of its power. Beginning in the 1990s, the U.S.S.R. began to experience dissolution of its centrally controlled state and a transformation toward market systems. Capitalism, or some new form of social democracy, enjoyed a new world status in what had previously been communist countries. Gorbachev and later Yeltsin joined Western leaders in a move toward *glasnost*. England's Margaret Thatcher and Germany's Helmut Kohl led their countries toward a less-regulated form of capitalism of the U.S. type. There seemed to be a greater value consensus about capitalist values than had ever existed before. Political conservatism prevailed, signaled not only by the new appointees to the United States Supreme Court, but also by the United Nations response in the Gulf War and by the notion of the military supremacy of the Western world. Nowhere was the return to a conservative perspective stronger than in the United States. We returned to the belief that, if left alone, Western capitalism would bring about "near" utopia. The best (most efficient) economic order results from a free-market system.

Economic Organization Theories

In the United States during the 1980s, the question that dominated the study of society, institutions, and organizations was not the role of markets versus the state, but how to make markets, and therefore organizations and society, more efficient. A minimum of government interference was assumed to be best. Two outgrowths of rational choice and neoclassical economics—transaction cost analysis and agency theory—suggest that reducing transaction costs and agency costs increases efficiency. Both models suffer from the limitations of neoclassical economics (see Zey 1992 for an extensive discussion of these limitations). However, in this chapter, I am concerned with a very limited aspect of these models, the manner in which they treat organizational deviance—in their terms, "opportunism." Our analysis leads us to understand opportunism, including illegal acts, as central to the functioning of the political economy of the United States in the 1980s. Unlike economic-organization models, we do not view opportunism as an inefficient side game, a small part of the error term, or an unlikely occurrence.

The neoclassical explanation and its variants, transaction cost theory and agency theory, can be integrated with the greed explanations described above, because they are all based on the assumption that wealth is the goal of individual action. The neoclassical explanation is also appealing because the bond floor, unlike the department and the firm, most closely approximates the workings of an ideal market (See Chapter 4 for this discussion). The bond floor is the place where self-interest and opportunism dominate trust and cooperation. The trading floor is the context or structure that shapes the behavior that organizational economics defines as universal (e.g., Williamson 1975, 1985; Jensen and Meckling 1976; Jensen 1983; Barney and Ouchi 1986).

Williamson (1975) posits that those entrusted with the control of others' assets have an inherent propensity to be opportunistic, to shirk, and to create moral hazards for those who trust them. The major limitation of organizational economics is the assumption that human nature shapes the behavior of organizational actors and that behavior, or its anticipation, shapes organizational design. Both neoclassical and organizational economics hold that the attributes of economic man are intrinsic to human nature (Barney 1990). Accordingly, transaction partners or contract partners are expected to behave opportunistically, resulting in transaction costs and agency costs.

The second explanation begins with the assumption that attributes of economic man are stylized interpretations (constructs) of human nature. I argue that when economic action in markets and organizations approaches the ideal type portrayed in the economic model of humans and the economic models of organizations, it is because the setting is constructed to support it. It is not because such behavior is natural, or functionally necessary. In other words, the action is embedded in the social context. However, as Eisenhardt (1989, p. 71) points out, this has only partial validity. Even in organizations which should most closely approximate markets, such as investment banking firms, other types of behavior are present.

Structural Embeddedness Explanation

The third perspective, the one set forth here and demonstrated throughout the analysis, is that of structural embeddedness. The structural character, as explained in Chapters 4, is based on the social interaction between the organizations analyzed. The embeddedness character, as explained in Chapters 6 and 7, is based on the relationships formed with economic and government actors.

The concept of embeddedness originates in the writings of Granovetter. Essential to the embeddedness perspective is the assumption that markets do not and cannot create the moral norms on which they function. These moral norms emerge from the society in which the market functions.

Granovetter writes that institutions, even market institutions, "are so constrained by ongoing social relations that to construe them as independent is a grievous misunderstanding" (1985, p. 482). However, because societies are not unified consensual entities, these norms enjoy greater and lesser agreement depending on the nature of the norm, the interests of the groups involved, and other characteristics of the relationship. This position does not challenge the existence of rational and opportunistic behavior, both of which exist in supportive contexts that are constructed by humans to promote specific modes of action.

Organizational deviance, as well as organizational conformity, is socially embedded. That is, securities fraud is socially embedded (p. 483) in larger structural relationships. I agree with Granovetter that rational-choice models hold an undersocialized view of humans, while the institutional perspective holds an oversocialized view of humans. Social actors are not clones of their social environments. Views in which actors are abstracted out of the complex societal and institutional arenas in which they participate and to which they are connected are inaccurate. Nor can they be separated from their history and the structural context in which interaction is constructed:

> Standard economic analysis neglects the identity and past relations of individual transactors, but rational individuals know better, relying on their knowledge of these relations. They are less interested in general reputations than in whether a particular other may be expected to deal honestly with them mainly a function of whether they or their own contacts have had satisfactory past dealing with the other. (p. 491)

Indeed standard economic analysis cannot explain the origin and development of trust. If both social relationships and economic relationships are based in trust, how can the maintenance of markets and their accompanying hierarchies be explained without the trust that is built up in social relationships?

The question for this analysis was, What are the organizational, legal, and economic contexts that supported the development of opportunism in the high-yield bond market? It was found that opportunism is a learned strategy for action. It is learned during the socialization process and the normal work of the firm. It is developed when normal market mechanisms do not work. The learned opportunism is then modified to fit each interaction episode as is any other social action. Most important, a particular form of opportunism can be used or not used depending upon the nature of the transaction and the extent to which it facilitates the deal. In some cases opportunism is rational. It is one of the most efficient and logical ways to reach the desired organizational goal. Thus markets and their organization are socially and culturally constructed through both legal and illegal actions. U.S. capitalism rests on a mix of markets and limitations of markets, including economic and legal constraints such as those that make for the definition and enforcement of fraud.

Second, from my research, I have found that government and society in general not only shape the moral norms for economic organization from without, but economic organizations are deeply embedded in the social networks that define what the market is, how it functions, and how it is constrained. This is achieved through networks which are largely made up of other economic and government organizations. This is so much the case that it is often difficult to distinguish whether these organizations function in the interest of the government or the economy. Further I hold that the abandonment of government and societal controls and the related countermovement toward the neoclassical economic model reduce the long-range vitality of the capitalist economy, at least partially, through affording greater opportunism.

In the case of Drexel there were potentially four types of regulation: the self-regulating organization, industry regulation, market regulation, and government regulation. Theoretically, regulation is pervasive. However, at the organizational level, Drexel provided maximum individual performance incentive systems of bonuses and commissions based on profits from trades. These incentives far exceeded the control the firm had through the salary structure. At the same time the firm's control through authority structures, professional review systems, compliance officers, and feedback from clients was eroded. In fact, the High-Yield Bond Department's compliance officers worked to justify the department's actions to the firm and to make certain the department's trades were presented to the government regulatory boards so as to appear to be in compliance. The authority of a peer review process in the form of the underwriter review committee was ignored by the decision-makers in the High-Yield Bond Department. Because the High-Yield Bond Department controlled the strategic contingencies of profits through networks of buyers and sellers, it operated relatively autonomously from Drexel.

At the industry level, the National Association of Securities Dealers (NASD) is responsible for regulation. But it has been more active in regulating the interface between retail brokers and the general public. It did not oversee the operations of the bond department. I dare say that the bankers and traders on the high-yield bond floor did not consider the NASD in making illegal transaction decisions. The industry simply did not regulate the High-Yield Bond Department's opportunism whether it was directed at savings and loans, insurance firms, or mutual funds.

Finally, at the market level, theory tells us that the opportunity for fraud is highest when market growth is rapid, volatility is high, and traders are uncertain about market prices. Under these conditions, traders with better information can take advantage of transaction partners. Withholding information, deception, insider trading, skimming, etc., are all information dependent. Since Drexel controlled between 40 and 65 percent of this market in the mid-1980s, it had more information than any other banker on current prices. It often helped to determine the price. Thus it could create volatility and therefore the opportunity to defraud its transaction partners.

The deregulation of the Reagan era and the passivity of the SEC (Fligstein 1990a) provided an almost free reign of opportunism, limited only by what the consumer could bear. In 1981, Reagan appointed a wealthy, thirty-one-year veteran of Wall Street, John Shad, to the chair of the SEC. Shad was a vice-chairman of E.F. Hutton, a major investment banker and brokerage house, which later in the 1980s failed due to fraud. Vise and Coll (1989) report that when Reagan was seeking election in 1980, his campaign organizers approached Shad and asked him to handle the New York fund-raising. In exchange Shad negotiated "a job in Washington if Reagan were elected." Shad was chairman from 1981 to 1987.

At the very time that the fraud was escalating, Shad was trying to cut back the budget and breadth of monitoring, especially the regulation of Wall Street. Shad pulled the commission back from close scrutiny of Wall Street brokerage houses' operations, particularly sales practices. He believed that investment firms—and the stock exchange to which they belonged—were well equipped to police themselves. Shad appointed a corporate lawyer, not a commission insider, as enforcement officer and further restricted the filing of charges against large brokerage houses, which according to Vise and Coll led to a breakdown in discipline at the largest investment firms. In this atmosphere, SEC staffers no longer bothered to propose charges except in the most insignificant cases.

Most important to our analysis, Vise and Coll note that though the commission had extensive power, Shad did little to restrain "junk bond financed corporate raiders as they rattled the executive suites and shop floors of the country's largest companies with hostile bids." Obviously these takeovers were lining the pockets of investment bankers.

After discussing Shad's admiration for Michael Milken, Vise and Coll point out that "at a key moment when some in the Reagan administration feared Shad was about to push for takeover restriction, officials and economists privately told him that he was deviating from the free-market philosophy of the administration." Although the SEC is not part of the executive branch, and not part of the president's economic policymaking apparatus, several conservative economists in the administration lobbied Shad to make sure he did not intervene with regulations.

In fairness to Shad, in 1984, while chairman of the SEC, he gave a speech titled "The Leveraging of America," in which he warned about the dangers of financing takeovers through LBOs. He pointed out that many of the companies that were targets had strong, not weak management as Jensen had claimed. He warned about the long-range economic and social consequences with the words, "The more leveraged takeovers and buyouts today, the more bankruptcies tomorrow." Then Shad appointed a committee of mostly Wall Street takeover professionals to study the consequences of LBOs. Reportedly, Shad's speech was not well received by the administration. According to Greg Jerrell, SEC chief economist, the administration wanted to "influence Shad's approach to takeover." Specifically, Jerrell worked to change Shad's position by appointing conservative economists to the study committees. Jerrell defined it as his role to develop studies "that would support the administration's position that takeovers—even the Drexel-sponsored hostile takeovers mounted by corporate raiders who had little cash to finance their bids—were good for shareholders, the economy and the country" (Vise and Coll 1989). The floating interest rates and the rampant speculation in mergers and acquisitions of the mid-1980s provided an even wider arena in which traders and bankers could take advantage of trading partners.

Boundaries between corporations (especially financial firms) and markets have collapsed. The market is no longer a market based on commodities, but is a market in the buying and selling of firms. Securities firms are making markets in corporations and corporate subsidiaries. The collapse of differences between firm and market has major consequences for society as a whole. Now, when the Federal Reserve Board lowers the interest rate to pump money into the economy, it has little or no effect. Its actions are based on the assumption that corporations are producing commodities, a process for which they need to borrow capital at a lower rate. But many corporations are no longer production entities—they are financial entities. Thus the government pumps up capital markets, which facilitates further *financial* activity, because lowering the interest rate encourages corporations to borrow more money. Corporations use this money to fuel takeovers or financial functions, which do not contribute to the growth of the economy, instead of production functions, which do. Major corporations intervene to prevent the Federal Reserve Board's intended outcome by establishing their own monetary strategies and reallocating and redistributing capital to the firms that they own or are purchasing. These corporations are assisted by investment banking firms and lawyers who, as a side game to what the Federal Reserve Board intended, drive up the price of these monetary transactions. Sometimes prices are driven up by competition, but often they are driven up through fraud disguised as competition. Sometimes the competing organization is operating out of self-interest. At other times it is operating in the interests of those who are doing the deals.

THE ARGUMENT IN SUPPORT OF STRUCTURAL
EMBEDDEDNESS AS AN ALTERNATIVE TO NEOCLASSICAL
ECONOMIC MODELS OF ORGANIZATIONS

The neoclassical economic model assumes instrumental behavior. However, *it also assumes that economic actors obey the rules of the economic game. The two assumptions are contradictory.* Williamson quoting Diamond (1971, p. 31) writes: "Economic models [treat] individuals as playing a game with fixed rules which they obey. They do not buy more than they know they can pay for, they do not embezzle funds, they do not rob banks" (1975, p. 7). I hold that this kind of idealistic argument is not only logically inconsistent but also empirically inaccurate.

First, it is logically inconsistent because the pursuit of self-interest is not—as Weber said of historical materialism—a streetcar that one can get on and off as one pleases; once one boards, one must proceed to the final destination. If the analyst assumes individuals are only instrumental, he or she must also assume individuals always act opportunistically and, in so doing, violate the rules of the game to take advantage of others and benefit themselves.

To be sure, a calculus of self-interest can explain why people follow the rules of the game when there is a reasonable chance they will be caught and penalties are stringent. However, if people do not behave opportunistically when the chances of detection are slight and/or the penalties are not stringent, their behavior is not purely instrumental. In short, there is something else going on. I hold that the existence of nonopportunistic behavior is evidence of embeddedness and of the power of noneconomic variables, such as the ongoing relationships of a network, and the strength of personal ties of buyers and sellers. People refrain from committing fraud out of commitment to these relationships.

On the other hand, if people do behave opportunistically when the chances of detection are great and/or the penalties are stringent, their behavior is, once again, not purely instrumental. There is something else going on. These cases are much more interesting than the cases in which the actor is socially rewarded for being normative. Opportunism in the face of social control is a force to be understood. When actors are so deeply embedded in legal and economic networks that they feel they can control outcomes, even when they are acting opportunistically, the fraud is organized and systemic.

From Adam Smith ([1790] 1971) to Habermas (1976), social theorists have argued that the effective functioning of competitive markets depends on the creation of a moral order capable of disciplining and restraining the capitalist's appetite. In his essay on the culture of the market, Max Weber stresses the methodical and calculating nature of capitalism—the constant calculation of means-ends relationships. To Weber this means that capitalist rationality also restrains the acquisitiveness of humans:

> The impulse of acquisition has in itself nothing to do with capitalism.... Capitalism may even be identical with the restraint, or at least a rational tempering, of this irrational impulse.... The universal reign of absolute unscrupulousness in the pursuit of selfish interests has been a specific characteristic of precisely those countries whose bourgeois-capitalistic development... has remained backward. ([1903–1906] 1985, pp. 17, 57)[48]

This moral order must deal with Adam Smith's ([1790] 1971) problem, regarding the consequences of individuals maximizing their self-interests. The consequences become the natural by-product of competition. Economic and psychological theories that make the assumption of maximized self-interest sever actions from consequences for society. These theories rest on the assumption that what is good is in the individual's self-interest, ignoring consequences for society. Yet there are greater goods for the group and society, which are often negated by maximization of self-interests. Self-interest and societal interests do not necessarily occur together. Thus organizational theorists substitute one determinism for another by linking the outcomes for the individual to those for the group or organization. But issues of consequences are more complex than group outcomes. Norms about what is fair, ethical, and moral in any given situation may be correctly satisfied in any of a dozen ways, each of which represents a different consequence.

Second, the assumption of neoclassical economic theory that instrumental actors operate within the rules of the game is empirically invalid. If humans are purely instrumental, the rules of the game are of little concern to them. In reality, the rules of the game are selectively adhered to. I maintain that structural embeddedness explanations reveal the nature of relationships in which the rules govern behavior and those in which they do not. Specifically, when the actor is inextricably embedded in social networks, has no other methods of competing, no legal method of doing the deal or upholding the contract, he or she will break the rules of the game and become involved in illegal behavior.

Illegal as well as legal deviant behaviors are often instrumental—efficiently instrumental. In fact, opportunistic behavior is often more efficient than legal behavior. The argument that instrumental behavior includes opportunism follows logically from the assumption that rational pursuits are pursuits of self-interest. The failure to build the likelihood of opportunism into economic models has been a logical inconsistency of economic organizational models. These analyses have no viable explanation for why actors do not pursue their self-interest through rule violation, opportunism, and illegal acts, such as insider trading and securities fraud.

Third, the failure to build crime into our organizational models derives from the lack of a dualistic perspective that sees individuals and organizational units as twin-born (Mead 1934). It is important that we do not view the individual or organization as determined by the immediate conditions of the transaction process or by a willingness to conform to the regulatory processes of the society, its government, or peer groups. Economic actors use the social order created by their interactions in relationships with others to access resources, create legitimacy, and gain power in pursuit of their goals. How effective they are varies.

To reiterate, structural embeddedness does not negate the potency of the individual or of groups of individuals. Economic institutions, including the market, are affected by larger societal forces. However, equally important in their formation are actors in economic organizations. These actors have the ability to determine the shape of their organizations and institutions. In many cases they influence the control structures that govern them. Despite external social constraints, legal and economic structures, including markets and their organizations, are largely created by the actors who inhabit them.

Thus markets and other economic institutions are both socially emergent and socially embedded. These institutions are not independent creations of some larger natural economic law, but emerge as a microcosm of the larger society and are structured as a result of interactive relationships with other social actors. The structural embeddedness perspective provides theoretically and methodologically richer and more complex understandings of the relationships and processes underlying networks within and between organizations than does the neoclassical economic paradigm. The structural embeddedness perspective is not overly deterministic as are both neoclassical economics and the psychological approach. The structural embeddedness approach avoids substituting one deterministic perspective for another.

Fourth, neoclassical economists do not analyze markets and how they are made (function). When one examines how markets are made, as we do in this book, it becomes readily apparent that markets do not function on the ideal assumptions and principles set forth in the neoclassical model. For example, there is the assumption that markets tend toward an equilibrium state, the result of which is efficiency of the economy. Thus all the markets—stock, bond, commodity—are systematically linked in a way that contributes to this greater efficiency of the economy. This is not the case with respect to the high-yield bond market. I doubt it is true with regard to other securities markets.

Fifth, the neoclassical economist assumes that, where there are multiple buyers and sellers, there is no particular buyer or seller with enough power to unilaterally influence price. Yet, in the junk bond market, the prices of bonds, as well as of stocks, were repeatedly set, manipulated, and controlled. If market participants can influence and control prices, then there is no natural equilibrium. Thus, both the assumptions of equilibrium and of the inability of participants to control the market are in question.

Sixth, the neoclassical economist assumes that there is equal information and, because of this, no one has an unfair advantage. It is assumed that all information is public, and thus buyers have equal access to information. This is a major characteristic of the level playing field. If some buyers are trading on insider information, the model does not function efficiently. If insider trading is a routine method of doing business, buyers with information get an unfair price advantage and sellers do not get the price they deserve. The balance between supply and demand is impaired. Regulation is imposed to prevent unequal information. However, regulation rests on the willingness of actors to voluntarily curb their opportunistic behavior and of the employing and legal organizations to impose restraints when actors do not.

Seventh, the neoclassical economist assumes that market exchanges are more or less one-time transactions between strangers who are unencumbered by normative expectations that build up in repeated transactions. Thus transactions are driven by price, not relationships. If transactions are driven by favors, the investment banker with the most effective strategy and access to the largest pool of capital, or who is part of an inside network, has an advantage. However, these transactions are not one-time occurrences among strangers. They are ongoing established relationships, which carry commitments, loyalties, and normative structures.

Eighth, the neoclassical tradition insists that the economy is analytically distinct from the rest of society and culture. All other components are external to the economy. This assumption is practically as well as theoretically important to neoclassical theory because it preserves the status of the economic order to separate it from the so-called lesser social institutions. Thus the family, state, etc., can be defined as secondary to, and in service of, the capitalist economic order and markets. While neoclassical economists may disagree about the effects of other social institutions on markets, they agree that all other social institutions are external to the economy.

The structural embeddedness argument views markets as emerging and changing with other social institutions. It views government regulation of business as a necessary set of checks and balances rather than external interference with the market economy. It does not see business as external to social movements such as business regulation. Often businesses actively participate in constructing the laws under which they operate. Unlike Fligstein (1990a), the structural embeddedness perspective does not perceive corporations as responding automatically to legal structures such as antitrust legislation. Rather, the structural embeddedness perspective views markets as embedded in various social relationships some of which are networks, each of which is essential for the vitality of the other. Although neoclassical and organizational economists are well aware that society attempts to control business firms, their theories often overlook the attempts of business to control society, particularly government agencies. Capitalist democracies are composed of these two countervailing forces (Polanyi 1944). In our analysis, investment banking firms often proved to be more powerful than corporations buying and selling bonds and more powerful than the government organizations with which they interacted.

Ninth, neoclassical and organizational economists ignore the vast domain of organizational and interorganizational networks that is the focus of this book. When organizational characteristics are the focus, organizations are viewed as hierarchical (see Williamson 1975), which is not the structure of most financial organizations, including investment banks (Eccles and Crane 1988). A broader emphasis on power—so crucial to decision-making within economic organization—would be more fruitful. The roles of intra- and interorganizational competition, bargaining, co-operation, co-optation, adjudication, extortion, buyoffs, and buyouts are important. These relationships are not based on authority. They are based on influence. Organizations create their own rules (their own social and moral orders) through which they attempt to constrain not only their employees, but also other organizations and institutions, both the state and markets. Individual and work group actions are embedded in the rules and social relationships of these organizations.

Thus the extent to which a firm and its members can act opportunistically depends on the fit between the market, the regulatory structures of the state, and the self-regulation of the organizational context. *When change is rapid, the context is volatile, and control is missing at the state and organizational levels, opportunism is to be expected.*

The extent to which securities transactions parallel the ideal market model is more or less limited. This limited marketness is due in part to invalid assumptions about the nature of exchanges that were never reflected in an empirical marketplace. An analysis of the junk bond market makes these limitations apparent. High-yield bond transactions bore little resemblance to a neoclassical market model.

Securities fraud is initially embedded in the specific economic and legal contexts of the 1980s, which facilitated the types of transactions that are involved in fraud. As such they are important to this analysis, but they do not explain why some organizations and not others are involved in securities fraud. This lies in the nature of securities transactions, the power of the High-Yield Bond Department developed within Drexel, and the economic relationships developed outside Drexel.

During the 1980s, in the name of increasing U.S. competitiveness against Japanese market expansion, the Reagan and subsequently the Bush administration all but dismantled the regulation of trusts. Even the most conservative businesspeople, who may have little sympathy for antitrust legislation, hold fast to the regulation of insider trading and securities fraud because they see unfair market manipulation as limiting their competitiveness. However, they failed to see trusts as limiting the competitiveness of U.S. firms, viewing them instead as necessary to compete against the Japanese, the Germans, etc. Thus, on the one hand, the mergers and acquisitions wave of the 1980s with its associated junk bond financing has been seen as positive by the economic organizational theorists and the conservative administrations. On the other hand, the insider trading, parking of stocks, and securities fraud associated with this era are generally viewed as interfering with market mechanisms and inhibiting free competition—and thus as bad for the U.S. economy.

My central thesis is that the increase in securities fraud in the 1980s in the United States is related to the long-term shift in the conception of how large firms grow and operate. This shift includes the financial definition of the firm and the strategy of growth through junk bond–funded leveraged mergers and acquisitions, which caused the proliferation of multidivisional, unrelated-industry holding companies. These changes occurred at a time when the corporate tax structure supported the acquisition of debt. Investment bankers, especially Drexel, controlled the high-yield bond market, wielding a great deal of power over issuers, buyers, comanagers of underwriting, regulatory boards, and congressional committees. The coalescing of the growth in markets, a tax structure that greatly favored debt over equity financing, the development of the junk bond market, and the increase in LBOs brought about the rise to power of investment banking firms in a context of lax enforcement of antitrust laws, corporate manipulation of regulatory agencies, and reform of RICO.

The financial definition of corporations and the resulting power of financial and accounting subunits; the expansion of mergers and acquisitions and the resulting structure of unrelated, multifirm conglomerates; the lack of federal control of mergers and takeovers; the deregulation of trading commissions; and the favorable corporate debt tax structure combined to create an environment ripe for investment banking fraud.

WHO CONTROLS?

Ownership and Control

This volume is a debate with economic theories of organizations. In the section above, discussion concentrated on the limitations of economic models of organizations. This section focuses on what I consider to be the major limitation of economic theories of organizations: They do not recognize the central role that power plays in the operation of the organization and the control of markets. This failure was demonstrated by the discussion of the structural contradictions between power and formal authority within Drexel (Chapter 4).

The starting point for an alternative definition of power must be the inadequacies of agency theory and its inability to explain the transformation of American corporations in the 1980s. This inability is due to agency theory's view of control as ownership alone. That is, agency theory assumes those who own should also control. Rarely is this assumption more explicitly made than in agency theory. However, if we conceptualize power as multidimensional with at least two of the dimensions being ownership and control, we begin to see some other problems with agency theory. For example, if we conceptualize ownership as control over investments—the flow of financial resources into and out of production (Wright 1985, p. 46)—then we can begin to define other dimensions of control such as control over the physical means of production and workers. Organizational theorists break these dimensions down into strategic and operational control. The assumption here is that one can own the actual shares (real ownership) while others control them. For example, Drexel controlled the takeover of public firms and delivered controlling interest to the acquirer. Thus control is separate, but may overlap ownership.

Figure 8.1 demonstrates how agency theory's distribution of ownership and control differs from the actual distribution of ownership and control before and during the 1980s merger and acquisition movement. Agency theory says nothing about workers. It deals with the relationship between managers and owners. I have placed workers in cell 4 to acknowledge that workers generally do not own the company, nor do they control it. Jensen, the major exponent of agency theory, does not consider employee stock ownership participation (ESOP) organizations. When workers do own shares they are usually widely dispersed among many shareholders (Patman 1964).[49] Before the 1980s, Jensen holds, managers, who generally were not owners, controlled large American corporations' financial decisions as well as other strategic and operational decisions. His solution is that managers' interests can be brought in line with owners/shareholders' interests by making managers shareholders: That is, if managers become owners, they can and will therefore act in the shareholders' interest because they act in their own interest. Notice that cell 2 specifies that agency theory does not permit control without ownership.

What really existed before the 1980s mergers and acquisitions period was a cadre of upper-level managers who were also owners (capitalists in the true sense of the word), as well as a larger group of managers and some

	OWNERS	
	YES	*NO*
	Cell 1	Cell 2
YES	A: Shareholders/ managers	A: Does not permit control without ownership
	B M&A: Capitalists (manager/owners)	B M&A: Managers and investment bankers
	M&A: Merchant bankers, capitalists, & managers	M&A: Some investment bankers
CONTROLLERS		
	Cell 3	Cell 4
NO	A: Does not permit ownership without control	A: Not discussed
	B M&A: Dispersed Shareholders	B M&A: Workers
	M&A: Dispersed Shareholders	M&A: Workers

A, agency theory; B M&A, before M&As of 1980; M&A, M&As of 1980s.

Figure 8.1. The theoretical distribution of ownership vs. control in agency theory compared with the actual distribution of ownership vs. control in the periods before and during the M&As of the 1980s.

bankers who were not owners, but who controlled corporations. The shareholders were the largest group of owners. However, individually they each owned such small portions of publicly held corporations that they had no control over them. Thus, they are labeled dispersed shareholders and are placed in cell 3 as owners, but not controllers.

Agency theory predicts that the results of mergers and acquisitions through LBOs will be that managers become owners when the firm is taken private. However, contrary to Jensen's thesis, most companies do not stay private. After the company is again taken public by selling shares to raise capital (see discussion of KKR and RJR Nabisco in Chapter 3), managers, along with many other dispersed shareholders, become owners. Rather than conforming to the specifications of agency theory, mergers did not cause managers to manage in the interest of shareholders or to relinquish control to shareholders. Investment bankers became merchant bankers, holding large shares of the companies taken private. Thus, the mergers and acquisitions period had unexpected consequences for agency theorists. Merchant bankers gained some ownership, but great control. In Figure 8.1, they moved from cell 2 before the mergers and acquisitions period to cell 1 during the mergers and acquisitions period. He did not expect investment bankers to become so powerful. Jensen also prophesied the end of the public corporation, which did not occur. Even KKR took many of its most profitable firms public in 1991. However, it retained large blocks of shares, as did many other merchant banks.

If we drop the assumption that the relationship between ownership and control is isomorphic and instead assume that they are two different dimensions of power, we get an entirely new solution to the mapping of the relationship between managers and owners. We see that managers and investment bankers can be both owners and controllers, occupying more than one position at a time.

The earlier label that was often given these actors had to do more with their original positions (titles) in relations to the corporation and not with their involvement with the various dimensions of power. It undoubtedly seems contradictory to an agency theorist to think that managers or investment bankers could, for a short period of time, have more control over a corporation than its owners or managers. However, this was sometimes the case. It was true when Milken controlled Drexel and when Drexel was targeting corporations for KKR and other raiders.

From a Marxist perspective it does not matter if managers are owners, because the interests of management and shareholders are basically the same. The most obvious aspect of this model is that the position of the worker does not change. Furthermore, the worker does not generally gain ownership or control either before or during the mergers and acquisitions of the 1980s. Neo-Marxists would also see managers as salaried workers, and therefore proletariat. Marxists would view agency theory as promoting an opportunity for managers to move into the propertied class. But, as Wright (1985) points out, the concepts of management and control are far too complex for this simple categorization process. Managers include not only executives, but professionals and upper-, middle-, and lower-level managers, as well as supervisors. Agency theory does not specify how each will or will not share in ownership.

Another complexity is added because control includes not only financial control, but also strategic control of other major decisions in addition to financial decisions. Upper-level managers, with control over strategic decisions, who receive shares as part of their compensation and reward for returns to shareholders, will obviously, as neo-Marxists might say, reflect "the inherently contradictory interests of the owner capitalists and the wage-paid proletariat." Agency as well as Marxist theory must find more complex conceptualizations [e.g., Wright (1985) presents solutions to some of these problems in relation to class].

Bank Control: Historical Antecedents

The reader should not assume that the 1980s were the only time in U.S. history in which investment bankers dominated corporations and markets. In 1907, Wall Street experienced a dramatic stock market decline. Fears of the existence of a "money trust" in the United States reemerged and galvanized the call for government reform of the financial system. These reforms were, in large measure, reactions to J. P. Morgan's ability to act as a one-person Federal Reserve Bank when he prevented the Wall Street panic from escalating into a national disaster. As a consequence of Morgan's power, Robert M. LaFollette of Wisconsin accused the leaders of the financial community—"those who withheld and dispersed prosperity"—of being "deliberately responsible for having brought on the late panic, to serve their own ends" (*Bankers' Magazine* 1908, p. 480; *Commercial and Financial Chronicle* 1913, pp. 680–81).

The idea of J. P. Morgan, or a group of cooperating individuals such as bankers, controlling the fate of the American economy suggested that our manufacturing capacity was being misused, even destroyed, to enrich the controlling group. Domination by these financiers implied a systematic manipulation of stock issues and corporate investment, resulting in regressive profits for insiders, while producing as "side effects" stock market crashes, economic stagnation, and a decline in public welfare. Industrial firms were the pawns of financial firms, and financial firms were the instruments of a small number of individual bankers.

Concern about the abuse of financial trust led to the formation of the Pujo Committee, a subcommittee of the House Banking and Currency Committee, in 1912 (U.S. House of Representatives 1913a). It began with the explicitly antitrust assumption that "competition is the most effective 'regulator of economic activity'" (Carosso 1970, p. 137); that such competition had broken down due to the "concentration that existed among a very few Atlantic Coast Banks"; and that it was necessary to understand how these banks had developed and preserved "their dominant position" (p. 140–41). The report identified an infrastructural network of a small group of banks including J. P. Morgan & Co., the First National Bank of New York, and the National City Bank of New York, together with their affiliated trust companies, Guaranty Trust and Bankers Trust; a set of close allies of this inner group (including Higginson & Co.; Kidder, Peabody &

Co., and the three largest commercial banks in Chicago); and Kuhn, Loeb
& Co., which was labeled by the committee as "qualifiedly allied with the
inner group" (p. 141; *Money Trust Investigation: Report 90*). "The Pujo
committee argued that these financial institutions dominated corporate
capital and credit in the United States, and that the cooperation between
these firms was so consolidated that 'virtually no competition existed
among them'" (*Money Trust Investigation: Report 90*; DiDonato, Glasberg,
Mintz, and Schwartz 1988).

The committee insightfully linked this small infrastructure of investment banks to larger groups of several hundred small banks and investment firms that were dependent on the inner group for development and
sale of securities. At the same time that this inner circle was linked to a
larger network of banks, it also dominated, through the control of investment and expansion capital, some of the largest industries. The Pujo
Committee concluded that American business and smaller banks were
controlled by a small infrastructure of investment and commercial banks.

Based on the Pujo Report, Louis Brandeis ([1914] 1967), former Supreme
Court Justice, stressed the fact that this financial power was achieved with
other people's money, including the deposits of the very corporations
these banks financed and controlled. The largest investment banking firm,
J. P. Morgan, acquired half of its deposits from just seventy-eight interstate
corporations, thirty-two of which had a Morgan partner on their boards
(*Money Trust Investigation: Report 90*, pp. 56–57). The implication was that
these banks exploited their relationships by making a profit from production firms without producing anything themselves. Brandeis argued
that control was enacted and maintained through the interlocking corporate boards of directors defined by the Pujo Committee (Carosso 1970,
Chapter 6, p. 137). The Pujo Committee demonstrated that the inner group
of six banks held "341 directorships in 112 corporations having aggregate
resources or capitalization of over twenty-two billion dollars" (Allen 1935,
p. 178), a tremendous sum for that time.

Brandeis further argued that these banks not only controlled the growth
and expansion of firms through the control of capital, but they also determined corporate strategy. Presumably this meant that these financial
firms could control competition, preventing banks and corporations that
did not cooperate from becoming players.

The Pujo Report, as well as Brandeis's remarks seemed to develop the
logic that financial domination implied a process of accumulation that
placed increasing amounts of investment capital, as well as political and
economic power, in the hands of commercial banks that derived profits
from nonproductive investments. This is the theme underlying the concept
of *social capital* that is currently gaining popularity in the analysis of

business structure (Bearden 1982, 1987) as is the related concept of corporate control by a "concentration in interests" (Scott 1978).

In the anticapitalist tradition, Rochester (1936) and Stanley (1932) developed the idea that corporations, rather than people, were the active agents in the business world. They suggested that firms actively wrested control from each other, with banks winning the battle, presumably because banks controlled a strategic contingency, capital (Pfeffer and Salancik 1978; Hickson et al. 1971). Both authors came to the conclusion that socialism was the answer because industry would be recaptured by the people and would be run to serve their interests rather than for the profit of capitalists (Stanley 1932, p. 282). Rochester came to this conclusion through the sophisticated argument of financial capital theory.

In Rochester's view, entrepreneurs had little need for the corporate form because they controlled their firms through daily direction. She saw the corporate form as a device that facilitated the investment and safe accumulation of capital by outside investors who were not involved in management. The development of stock and bond markets were part of the evolution of a set of institutional mechanisms that imposed profit maximization on even the most autonomous managers. Therefore, when expanding production and rapid growth in the late nineteenth century led to oligopolies, it did not reduce the profit motive or the need for outside capital. The new corporate giants sold their stock in the public market and borrowed huge sums of money because large amounts of capital were necessary to maximize growth and profits and to cushion the effects of business cycles. The increasing importance of stock sales and borrowing led to the dramatic growth and centralization of the financial sector and, ultimately, to the domination of the banking industry by a handful of Wall Street firms (DiDonato et al. 1988, pp. 144–45).

According to Rochester (1936, p. 26) markets in capital and credit (stocks and bonds) took precedence over production and distribution of products as the more profitable and therefore "honorable" activity. An ever-increasing share of the total surplus value produced by the workers was drawn off as profits for bankers. The market was no longer an exchange of goods or an exchange of goods for money, but was simply the trend of prices and sales from stocks and bonds. Interlock networks were the methods of cementing relationships. The interlock signified the fusion of industrial and financial capital. This was not only a power dependency relationship for Rochester, but also one in which banks took on decision-making for industrial firms.

The separation of management and control did not come about because managers became more powerful (Berle and Means 1932), but because as companies bought out other companies the acquirers obtained substantial fortunes, which they deposited in banks to draw interest. These were owners of "loan capital," seeking investment without participation in management. "The economic power of the financial rulers is supported by the structural mechanisms through which they control other men's capital" (Rochester 1936, p. 104). The same group of capitalists invested directly in the stock market. The largest companies, in order to expand, sold stock publicly. Ultimately stockholders became passive investors, exercising little voice in corporate strategy and policy (p. 104).

Rochester (p. 103) pointed out that, although this trend was hailed as the "new democracy," because it scattered ownership of leading corporations among many stockholders, the actual consequence was that it concentrated control in the hands of the financial elite who controlled the distribution of capital. Obviously, hundreds of thousands of stockholders were helpless to organize to control the corporations in which they owned stock, not to mention the fact that they were uninterested in controlling the corporations. Stockholders were interested only in making profits from trading stocks and bonds.

Rochester laid out the difference between her analysis and that of the managerial perspective of Berle and Means. Berle and Means saw the separation of ownership and control as giving owners less power and managers more power, whereas Rochester saw the separation of ownership from control as a contributing factor in the development of the rise of financial hegemony and the fusion of financial and industrial capital. She argued that Berle and Means had stopped short of relating the corporation to the financial group that is behind management (Rochester 1936, p. 120). Whereas Berle and Means argued that the decline of stockholders' power produced a less single-minded concern with profits, Rochester argued that financial institutions sought control and used it for the purpose of extracting profits:

> Banks and bankers have the richest pickings from the advancing of credit, the trading of capital, the promotion of mergers, and the manipulation of protective committees and reorganizations than they could gather in merely from the ownership of stocks and bonds. (p. 120)

She argues that this led to bank domination instead of managerial autonomy as Berle and Means suggested. Her picture is of corporate and financial unity instead of corporate autonomy.

Thus, although Berle and Means's and Rochester's arguments rest on the same assumption, that intercorporate coordination (or lack thereof) derived from the capacity of firms with different needs to overcome these differences through accommodation or exercise of power, they disagree about whether the firm was controlled or an autonomous actor. They do agree, however, that the central process was an industrial/capital relationship that was not based in neoclassical economic competition but in cooperation.

Who Controls Corporations

The recent trends in acquisitions and mergers reaffirm the idea of control, not of owners over managers, but of investment banks over owners, managers, and corporations. Owners have taken the control of corporations out of the hands of managers through the mechanism of takeovers, mergers, and LBOs. The managers who have risen to the tops of major corporations in the past decade are the ones who were able to negotiate these methods of control. Leveraged buyouts are more likely to be used by financiers and accountants. Thus CFOs are more likely to become CEOs. Those who have adopted a definition of the corporation as a profit center, and are themselves single-mindedly concerned with profits, are more likely to rise to the top of organizations.

Who controls corporations? Organizational analysts have argued for decades about whether organizations are controlled internally by their managers (the managerialist argument), externally by financial institutions (financial control theory argument; Mintz and Schwartz 1985; Mizruchi and Stearns 1988), or by the government (Skocpol 1985). We have only recently come to consider that financial control, management control, or state control may change over time. During some periods managers within organizations may be more in control than external financial firms and the state. At other times, managers may be more dependent on financial firms for resources.

Although resource dependency theory does not acknowledge a hierarchy of resources, strategic contingency theory attempts to define the resources that are most critical to the survival of the organization at a given time. Certainly the importance of a resource may change with the development of the corporation, the nature of the environment, and other factors. Financial control theory views capital as the most important resource. It is the generator of inputs, sustainer of production, and distributor of products to the external environment. Likewise, capital provides the organization the ability to adapt to its environment (research and development, diversity) or to change the environment to ensure continued support and survival (constituencies development, campaign contributions to those who make and reform laws and the control boards, and buyouts of competitors). When corporations require external funds, not only the capital supply but financial institutions that control access to the supply become important to the corporation.

Corporations are largely controlled by the strategic contingencies on which they are dependent. During the past decade, financial institutions, specifically investment banking firms, have demonstrated significant control over corporations. Investment banking firms, in particular, have gained prominence among banking firms due to the growth in mergers and acquisitions financed by debt in the form of junk bonds.

Managerialism became the dominant theory of corporate control from the 1930s through the mid-1970s. Organizational theories did not, in most cases, deal with acquisition of economic resources. These theories, from the scientific and classical management models to structural contingency theory, emphasized the power and control of corporate managers over the functioning of organizations. Managers were expected to define and control the uncertain external environment of the corporation. One method of doing so was for the firm to generate its own capital, by the sale of existing products or by the discovery of new products and new markets by research and development through sales and marketing. Sales and marketing became powerful departments and many of those managers rose to the top of the organization.

During this period, organizational theorists did not believe that financial control existed in the United States. They certainly agreed that corporations were vulnerable to firms outside the organization that controlled finance capital. However, because these corporations were in the business of generating their own capital, this was not a strategic contingency. As late as 1966, Baran and Sweezy wrote: "Each corporation aims at and normally achieves *financial independence* through the internal generation of funds which remain at the disposal of management" (1966, p. 16). Although a corporation may choose to borrow through financial institutions, "it is not normally forced to do so and hence is able to avoid *the kind of subjection to financial control* which was so common in the world of Big Business fifty years ago" (p. 16, emphasis added).

Perhaps Zeitlin's (1974) critique of managerialism, although not the first departure from this position, was a critical turning point in our recognition that corporations do not control their financial capital. Zeitlin noted that the increase in corporations' reliance on external finance capital, the presence of larger stockholdings by financial institutions, and the high incidence of interlocking directorates gave financial institutions control over corporations. Although we were not told the direction of the power/dependence relationship between these corporations and financial agencies, these relationships were assumed to demonstrate corporations' dependence on financial institutions. Subsequent studies have demonstrated the centrality of financial institutions in stockholding and in interlocking directorate networks. Often the measure of the financial organization's exertion of control was assumed to be greater if the amount of capital obtained by the corporation was greater. However, although the amount of external funding that a corporation obtained from financial institutions was used as an indication of financial control, it could mean that the corporation was very powerful because it could garner substantial amounts of resources to support its expansion. Again, there is little research on the content or the nature of the relationships between banks and corporations, although more recently the direction of the power dependence relationships have begun to be analyzed.

Drexel had power over its competitors because it was able to constrain them by limiting their market through controlling a large share of the bond market itself. Drexel had control over organizations *for* whom it sold bonds and those *to* whom it sold bonds. Drexel insisted that bond issuers buy other high-yield bonds that it was offering or else their own would not be sold. Thus issuers were also buyers. Issuers had to buy in order to have Drexel do their next offering. My findings are consistent with those of Mintz and Schwartz (1985), who argue that financial institutions influence the behavior of nonfinancial firms with which they have transaction relationships, and also with Zeitlin (1974), Domhoff (1983), and Useem (1984). Finally, my arguments are consistent with those of White et al. (1976) and Burt (1987), who discuss the importance of indirect relationships. Drexel had power because other organizations who were economically dependent on the firm would act in its interest. In some cases, investment bankers and corporate interests were the same and influenced political/legal actors in the same way. In other cases corporations took economic or political/legal action that was beneficial to Drexel because their competitor was taking such action and they were mimicking successful behavior (Burt 1987).

However, my research extends the argument in two directions. First, it demonstrates that relationships with corporations are initiated and controlled by financial firms; corporations were more dependent on financial institutions in the 1980s than the reverse. Second, it shows that these financial firms did not have to rely only on the indirect relationships defined in previous research. Merchant bankers had indirect access, but also direct access to Congress.

Financial Control

In the 1980s, the development of financial control of the corporation and the development of organizational theory converged to support an economic/financial theory of control among managers (Fligstein 1990a) and an economic paradigm about how hierarchies originate (Williamson 1975). However, those who studied how organizations, including economic organizations, originate, how they are perpetuated, how they change, and how organizational deviance takes place were using alternative explanations focused around networks and structural embeddedness theories (Granovetter 1985).

The development of firms and new markets cannot be explained as a consequence of market efficiency as the neoclassical economists and the economic organizational theorists would have us believe (for example, see Williamson 1975). Because power, culture, and other social factors have no place in neoclassical theory (Swedberg 1987), the changes in strategies and structures of corporations and in market forms remain outside the purview of economics. In the 1980s, the development of new forms of organizations (holding companies) created through mergers and acquisitions was the result of a specific set of economic and legal factors, defined in Chapters 6 and 7, respectively.

The development of the junk bond market was an integral part of this period. Its development was not unlike the development of other markets. As Lie (1988) demonstrates, the emergence of the market in the seventeenth and eighteenth centuries was not an organic coalescence of existing local markets, but a new aggregation of transactions among numerous individual buyers and sellers. It was a social construction, brought about through the political acts of a group of London-based wholesale entrepreneurial merchants. They profited from their exclusive access to information and new national distribution networks. They acted politically to extract from government agencies the repeal of existing legislation against middlemen-merchants who, it was rightly feared, would disrupt face-to-face, normatively regulated local markets. In reality, the "invisible hand of the market" was a small group of middlemen-merchants who exploited the price differentials across regions (p. 109). By bypassing traditional local markets, in which producers and consumers traded directly, by constructing new distribution networks that had different principles of operation and different structures of market power between producers, buyers, and distributors, they created a market.

Through the entrepreneurial efforts of these investors, the capacity of the consumer to control prices was radically reduced. It is impossible to explain the origins of the market as a consequence of market efficiency when the market does not yet exist. This is also true for the junk bond market. The junk bond market did not exist and thus could not have originated as a result of efficiency.

It is more accurate to describe the development of firms and markets as the result of inefficient, politically negotiated deals among powerful opportunistic actors. These markets and firms depended on the collusive exercise of power derived from advantageous positions in economic and political-legal networks. Owners and traders brought their power to bear on the state and potential competitors to redefine the conditions and parameters of doing business. It should be no surprise to find that the development of the junk bond market and the mergers and acquisition movement of the 1980s emerged and developed through a similar collusion.

Structural embeddedness explanations remain outside neoclassical economic theory. They are viewed as exogenous parameters that affect the distribution of resources in inefficient ways (Williamson 1975; Williamson and Ouchi 1981). Here markets and firms themselves are political. Until we understand the politics of efficient and inefficient markets and firms, we cannot understand efficient markets. When political and legal processes are conceived to be external to the market and the firm, we cannot understand markets and the firm, because markets and the firm do not operate separately from these processes.

Pursuit of power and control pervades the behavior of firms that trade in the market as well as the market itself. It pervades the regulatory and legislative organizations that control and are influenced by the market and its firms. However, the analysis of power lies outside neoclassical models. Neoclassical economic theory takes property rights as given. But property rights are not determined by the interests of shareholders, banks, boards of directors, managers, or those who control corporations. The conflicts over property rights are not played out in the market, but in the courts, the legislature, and regulatory agencies. To understand how firms and markets operate, we must bring political-legal issues—takeovers, buyouts, buybacks, divestitures, stock parking, increased debt, high-yield bonds, insider trading—from the periphery to the center of our analysis.

Some of the most interesting organizational and economic questions involve how bond markets were redefined in the 1980s, how junk bonds became redefined as high-yield, acceptable instruments of debt (see Chapter 6), how and why RICO was redefined and reformed (see Chapter 7). Through the redefinition of the categories of actors to which RICO applied, investment bankers and savings and loan officers attempted to influence congressional committees to reform RICO to exclude industries (such as banks and savings and loans), which were so-called "board-regulated" industries, thus protecting them from the more severe penalties of RICO. The political resolution of these conflicts and questions did not simply redirect the flow of capital into and out of firms and markets but redefined the means by which material gains were pursued.

Williamson's (1975) economic organizational theory prescribes where the state has some chance of succeeding when markets fail. Firms as hierarchies (and presumably the state) are relegated to these areas. But Williamson does not tell us where the boundaries are or what the nature of the relationships among markets, firms, corporations, and the state are.

Generally the state's or firms' extraction and redistribution of market resources are seen as a coercive and inefficient preempting of what would be efficient market mechanisms. The relationships between markets, financial firms, and the political-legal structure of the state cannot be explained with modified neoclassical economic theory.

A qualifying statement must be made: I am not here advocating the primacy of the state over the market. In fact, I have found that the direction of the relationship generally is from financial firms to political/legal organizations. I am analyzing market firms and financial firms to understand how the government influences them and how they use the government to maintain control over their operations. What is known is that, depending upon the strategy of fiscal extraction, states have sometimes facilitated and sometimes obstructed the extension of markets (Tilly 1985; Skocpol 1985).

During the 1980s, the key imagery of the firm became that of a financial structure, consisting of *equity* (the value of shareholders' stake in the firm, i.e., the stock price times the number of shares), and *debt* (the value of that which the firm owes its creditors, in particular, banks and bondholders). Debt and equity are alternative ways for managers to fund or support the firm's capital structure, its survival, growth, and development. The desirable debt-to-equity ratio was never more important or more debated by financial experts than during the 1980s. The debate was over how much debt a firm should hold in order to optimize returns.

The decade of the 1980s ended with the failure of banks, insurance companies, and pension funds that had invested in Drexel-issued junk bonds (see Chapter 3). Defaults became so widespread that 38 percent of all junk bonds issued in 1988 failed to pay interest at the appropriate times. The 1990s' recession exposed the vulnerability of leveraged companies and institutional investors who held large issues of junk bonds. The largest takeover in which Drexel participated was KKR's takeover of RJR Nabisco. On January 27, 1990, RJR Nabisco's bonds were downgraded by Moody: Its biggest junk bonds sank to 66 cents on the dollar, then to 56 cents on the dollar, followed by a restructuring to refinance the debt of the company.

Ironically KKR made the transition from debt to equity in the 1990s by transforming Safeway, RJR Nabisco, and Owens-Illinois from private ownership financed by debt to public ownership financed by equity. Stock was offered at a premium and KKR used the revenue to reduce the debt on each company. RJR Nabisco's 1990 refinancing was the first of several major changes that took place over the next year and one-half. Equity offerings were increased. Debt was paid off. Cash flow, which had been used to finance debt, was now used to promote research and development of new products.

However, despite the fact that the corporation is healthy, as of October 1992, stock in RJR Nabisco was selling for the same $8 to $10 at which it reentered the market in 1990. It may take some time for the firm to recreate the internal stability needed to increase its stock prices.

Some companies were not able to make the transition. The two biggest buyers of KKR junk bonds were insurance executive Fred Carr of First Executive and bank president Tom Spiegel of Columbia Savings and Loan. In late 1990 and early 1991, both companies failed due to the losses incurred as a result of the drop in the market. Their portfolios were overwhelmingly invested in Drexel junk bonds. High-yield mutual funds went under.

Jensen's prophecy of "the eclipse of the public corporation" (1989b) just one year earlier seemed grossly inaccurate. He too must have noticed the reversal of the trend that he had exaggerated to its inaccurate limit.

NOTES

48. I have run together quotations from separate chapters of Weber's *The Protestant Ethic and the Spirit of Capitalism.*

49. Berle and Means considered the ownership of a 20 percent block of a corporation's shares as the minimum necessary for its control. Recent investigators have used a block of 10 percent on the assumption that stock is now more widely dispersed than it was in the 1930s. However, the Patman Committee concluded that effective control may be assured with even less than a 5 percent holding, "especially in very large corporations whose stock is widely held" (Patman 1964, p. 832).

Central Actors

Actors are arranged in hierarchical order within their respective organizations. An asterisk (*) indicates that the person was an employee of more than one organization in this network during the time period analyzed.

Drexel, Beverly Hills

Michael Milken, vice-president and head of High-Yield Bond Department

Lowell Milken, attorney for the High-Yield Bond Department, head of compliance, supervised the employee-related private partnerships

Warren Trepp, head high-yield bond trading

Cary Maultasch, convertible-bond trader; in 1985 went to New York office to manage the Boesky account

Peter Ackerman, trader and banker, High-Yield Bond Department

James Dahl, bond trader

Terren Peizer, bond trader

Bruce Newberg, convertible-bond trader

Peter Gardiner, convertible-bond trader, took over Bruce Newberg's accounts

Gary Winnick, trader of High Grade Bonds, Drexel New York; moved to Beverly Hills with Milken to trade high-yield bonds; later head of convertible bond area

Alan Rosenthal, trader; head of convertible-bond area after Winnick; moved to Drexel New York office to handle the Boesky account

Lisa Jones, trading assistant

Charles Thurnher, accountant and bookkeeper

Donald Balser, bookkeeper

Kevin Madigan, legal counsel for the High-Yield Bond Department

*Craig Cogut,** attorney from Cogut, Taylor, Siegel, and Engelman (external legal counsel for the High-Yield Bond Department); creator of the Alliance for Capital Access

Richard Sandler, attorney from Victor, Sandler and Cogut, external legal counsel for the High-Yield Bond Department (principal duties were to work with employee-related partnerships)

Alliance for Capital Access

*Craig Cogut,** attorney from Cogut, Taylor, Siegel, and Engelman (external legal counsel for the High-Yield Bond Department); filed the charter for the Alliance for Capital Access

Larry Mizel, head of the Alliance for Capital Access
David Aylward, assistant to Senator Timothy Wirth; organizer of the Alliance for
   Capital Access

Drexel, New York

Frederick Joseph, CFO, then CEO
Dennis Levine, investment banker in M&A, Smith Barney; then Lehman; and
   finally Drexel
Martin Siegel,* investment banker, Kidder, Peabody; beginning 1986, head of
   M&A, Drexel
Leon Black, cohead of M&A
David Kay, cohead of M&A
Joseph Harch, first vice-president of corporate finance, senior corporate finance
   officer in charge of relationship between Drexel and Wickes

Kidder, Peabody & Company, New York

Ralph DeNunzi, CEO
Al Gordon, chairman
John T. Roche, president
Martin Siegel,* investment banker
Richard Wigton, head of arbitrage
Timothy Tabor, arbitrage employee
Peter Goodson, head of M&A

Goldman, Sachs & Co., New York

Robert Freeman, head of arbitrage

Princeton/Newport

James Regan, CEO, found guilty of insider trading under RICO along with Drexel's
   Bruce Newberg and Lisa Jones (perjury)

Merrill Lynch

John Mulheren,* arbitrager and trader of stock options

Lazard Freres, New York

Robert Wilkis, investment banker

Ivan F. Boesky Corporation, New York

*Ivan F. Boesky,** CEO and Head; later Head of Boesky Ltd. Partnership
Reid Nagel, CFO
Stephen Conway, investment banker
Lance Lessman, head of research
Michael Davidoff, head trader
Setrag Mooradian, chief accountant and bookkeeper
Maria Termine, assistant to Mooradian

OAD, Inc.

Peter Testaverde, partner and auditor; performed audit on Boesky Corporation
   when Boesky Limited Partnership was being established
Steven Oppenheim, partner

Kohlberg Kravis Roberts, Inc. (KKR)

Jerome Kohlberg, partner
Henry Kravis, partner
George Roberts, partner
R. Theodore Ammon, legal counsel

Major Raiders (Issuers), Clients of Drexel

Carl Icahn, corporate raider and future chairman of TWA
Ronald Perelman, CEO, MacAndrews and Forbes Holding Company
Victor Posner, CEO, Sharon
Nelson Peltz, owner of Triangle Industries, a holding company, later called Triangle
   International
*Carl Linder,** CEO, American Savings and Loan; CEO, American Financial
T. Boone Pickens, CEO, Mesa/Gulf
*Saul Steinberg,** CEO, the Reliance Group
Ted Turner, CEO, Turner Broadcasting

Investors in Drexel's High-Yield Bonds—Savings and Loans

American Continental Corporation and LSL, Charles Keating, owner and CEO LSL,
   parent company American Continental Corp.
*Columbia Savings and Loan, Thomas Spiegel,** CEO, American Continental Corp.
*Financial Corporation of American /American Savings and Loan, Carl Linder,** CEO
*Bank of Santa Barbara/Financial Corporation of Santa Barbara, Ivan Boesky,** owned
   controlling interest

Investors in Drexel's High-Yield Bonds—Insurance Companies

First Executive Corporation, Executive Life, Fred Carr, CEO
Reliance Insurance Company, Saul Steinberg,* CEO, the Reliance Group, Inc., a hold-
    ing company for Reliance Insurance

Investors in Drexel's High-Yield Bonds—Investment Funds

Fidelity High-Yield Investment Fund, Patricia Ostrander, head of fund; member of
    MacPherson Investments; found guilty of securities fraud in 1992
General Electric Bond Fund, Aubrey Hayes, manager of fund
Jamie Securities, John Mulheren,* owner and head
Solomon Assets Management, David Solomon, head
First Investment Management, Benalder Bayse, fund manager
First Investors, David Crayson, head
Atlantic Capital, Guy Dove, fund manager

Government

Milton Pollock, judge, U.S. District Court, Southern District of New York, to whom
    Drexel pleaded guilty
Kimba Wood, judge, U.S. District Court, Southern District of New York, to whom
    Milken pleaded guilty

United States Attorney's Office, New York

Rudolph Giuliani, U.S. district attorney
Benito Romano, deputy to Giuliani
Charles Carberry, assistant U.S. attorney
Bruce Baird, assistant U.S. attorney, later head of fraud unit
John Carroll, assistant U.S. attorney
Jess Fardella, assistant U.S. attorney

Securities and Exchange Commission, Washington D.C.

John Shad, chairman
Richard Breeden, chairman after Shad
Gary Lynch, chief of enforcement
John Sturc, assistant chief of enforcement

U.S. Congress, Washington, D.C.

William Bradley, Democratic senator from New Jersey
Alan Cranston, Democratic senator from California, Member of the Keating Five
Dennis DeConcini, Democratic senator from Arizona, Member of the Keating Five
Alfonse D'Amato, Republican senator from New York
John Glenn, Democratic senator from Ohio, Member of the Keating Five
Edward Kennedy, Democratic senator from Massachusetts
John McCain, Republican senator from Arizona, Member of the Keating Five
Howard Metzenbaum, Democratic senator from Ohio
Donald Riegle, Democratic senator from Michigan, Member of the Keating Five
Timothy Wirth, Democratic representative from Colorado

Glossary

Accumulating a position. Buying up stock in a company, as acquirers do when they take over a firm or as greenmailers do in order to later sell their shares to the acquirer at a higher than market price.

Acquisitions. When one company takes over a controlling interest in another.

Arbitrage. Generally a risk-free profit that occurs when two securities are mispriced relative to each other, so that it is possible to buy one and sell the other and make a risk-free profit. In the investment banking industry, the term *arbitrage* often refers to the activity that takes place when an acquisition is announced at a higher price than the current stock price of the target firm.

Arbitrage department. The department of an investment banking firm that makes decisions to buy stocks to take advantage of anticipated higher price offers.

Asset valuation. The valuation of assets in a merger and acquisition transaction. The investment banking firm estimates the value of the various parts of the corporation that is targeted.

Black knight. Unfriendly acquirer drawn to a target by news that the company has already been put into play by others.

Block trading. Trading a large quantity of securities. The NYSE considers a block trade to be equal to ten thousand or more shares.

Bonds. Debt; a security that obligates the borrower to repay principal and interest on specified dates.

Boutique takeover firm. A securities firm that specializes in takeovers and ownership of target firms.

Bridge loan. A short-term loan made by an investment bank to facilitate a transaction. It is made during the takeover until the bonds are sold and the loan can be repaid by the issuer.

Callable bond. Bond that the issuer has the right to redeem or pay off before the scheduled maturity date.

Cash flow. Net income plus depreciation, depletion and amortization.

Chapter 9 bankruptcy. Bankruptcy in which a corporation is taken over by the SEC and the courts distribute its assets among its creditors.

Chapter 11 bankruptcy. Bankruptcy in which a corporation is taken over by the SEC and remains in business. Its debt is restructured so that it may pay off its debtors and survive.

Chinese wall. The separation or barrier between bankers or mergers and acquisitions and the traders in an investment banking firm. It is a corporate constructed, imposed, and enforced regulation intended to prevent traders and arbitragers from acting on confidential information about clients. Chinese walls are especially important in times of takeovers, when client losses can be astronomical if information is leaked to traders.

Comanager.   Investment banking firm that works with lead manager investment banking firm to underwrite a security offering such as a bond offering.

Comfort letter.   Certification issued by auditors of a firm's books specifying that the firm's assets are as represented by the firm.

Commercial paper.   Commercial debt or a debt on the corporation.

Common stock.   Known simply as stock. Shares in a company, which represent ownership in a public corporation. Owners are entitled to vote on the selection of directors and other corporate policies. They typically receive dividends on their stock, but corporations are not required to pay dividends on common stock. *See also* Preferred stock.

Convertible bond.   A bond that can be exchanged for a specific number of shares of common stock.

Creditors.   Those to whom money is owed; those who hold debt instruments.

Debenture or debenture bond.   A certificate or voucher acknowledging a debt, typically for an unsecured bond.

Debt.   A security that obligates a borrower to repay principal and interest on a specified date. Debt includes bonds, notes, mortgages, and other forms of credit obligations.

Divestiture.   The sale of corporate assets, such as a division of the firm.

Dividends.   Generally a cash payment per share paid on ex-dividend dates over a twelve-month period. May also be reported on a declared basis where it has been established to be a company's payout policy.

Dividend recapture trade.   Process of the corporation that issued the stock, usually a preferred stock, to buy the stock back or convert the preferred to common stock in order to recapture dividends.

Due diligence.   Process an investment bank undertakes to assure that information provided in a security offering is accurate.

Earnings.   The amount a company reports as having been earned for the year on its common stock based on generally accepted accounting procedures and standards.

Equity.   (1) Ownership in a public corporation, generally in the form of common or preferred stock; (2) technically, common stock plus surplus and retained earnings, less any difference between the carrying value and liquidation value of preferred stock.

Ex-dividend.   The occurrence of dividend payment on a date specified by the corporation.

Fallen angel.   Bond issue formerly higher-rated, which has been lowered to depict higher risk and is now unrated.

Fatico hearings.   Hearings held to determine crimes in addition to those pleaded to by the defendant. In Michael Milken's case the Fatico was held October 11, 1990, for two weeks. Judge Kimba Wood allowed the government to explore six additional charges beyond those pleaded to by Milken.

Flip-over.   Part of a poison pill–share purchase rights plan in which if the acquirer purchases in excess of a specified percentage of the target's stock (e.g., 20 percent) and then acquires the remaining target common stock in a business combination transaction, the flip-over provision entitles the holder of a share purchase right to purchase the acquirer's common stock at half price.

Friendly offer. A merger proposal cleared in advance with the target company's board and top management, with the firm recommending it favorably to shareholders for approval.

Golden parachute. Provision in the employment contract of top executives that assures them a lucrative financial severance from the firm in the event of a takeover.

Greenmail. The practice of becoming a hostile acquirer, a raider, in order to accumulate a large stake in a company for the purpose of scaring management into buying out the raider at a premium price.

Hedge. An investment strategy used to reduce risk. It typically involves the purchase or sale of a contract designed to offset the change in value of another security.

High-yield bond. Unrated or low-rated bond, junk bond, which is high risk and therefore returns a high rate of interest.

Hired guns. Merger and acquisition specialists, other investment bankers, and lawyers employed by either side in any takeover.

Hostile takeover. An acquisition that takes place against the wishes of the management and the board of directors of the acquired (target) company.

"Highly confident" letter. A formal pledge, or contractual agreement that Drexel would raise the money it specified in a takeover bid. This mechanism saved time in closing the deal, thus preempting bids from others and assuring the takeover firm of capital needed to close the deal.

High-Yield Bond Department. At Drexel, the Junk Bond Department, headed by Michael Milken.

Illiquidity. Securities that cannot be traded; securities for which there is no market.

Insider trading. Trading on nonpublic information, an illegal activity.

Institutional investor. An organization, such as pension funds, life insurance companies, and mutual funds, that holds and trades large volumes of securities.

Investment grade bonds. Bonds graded at or above A by Standard and Poors.

Junk bonds. High-risk, high-yield bonds, publicly traded low-grade or ungraded corporate bonds, before the 1980s sold by new and restructuring corporations—defined as high-yield bonds by the industry as a promotional technique.

Leveraged buyout (LBO). The purchase of a company, or part of a company, with borrowed funds. In the 1980s the target company's assets frequently served as security for the loan taken out by the acquiring firm. In some cases there was little collateral and the bonds were considered junk. The loan is typically repaid from the acquired firm's cash flow.

Liquidity. A security for which there is a market or a buyer.

Long-term debt. Debts/obligations due after one year. Includes bonds, payable notes, mortgages, lease obligations, and industrial revenue bonds.

Making a market. Trading (buying and selling) a security in order to raise the price, thereby providing liquidity to holders of the security when they wish to sell it.

Merchant bank. An investment bank that commits its own capital to a transaction, as when it makes a bridge loan or when it makes equity investments in a company or acquires a stake in a company. Generally this is done for a company for which it is doing a takeover. A common British term, first used in U.S. to describe J. P. Morgan.

Merger. When two or more companies are combined.

Mergers and acquisitions (M&A) department or group. In an investment banking firm, the group that helps a firm take over a target or defends a target against takeover. Also works on such processes as divestitures and repurchasing of blocks of stock.

Majors. The second rank of securities firms, a category that ranks under the top-ranked investment banking firms, called "special bracket" firms.

Net asset value. The market value of stocks, bonds, and net cash divided by the outstanding shares.

Non–investment grade bonds. Bonds with credit ratings of less than A. They are typically issued by untested companies without a track record or sales and earnings, or by companies that have had financial difficulty and may have had to restructure their debt. Otherwise known as junk bonds and high-yield bonds; in the 1980s issued as a means to finance takeovers.

Nuclear war. Struggles among giant corporations to control one another.

Off-line trading. When an investment banking firm trades in the name of and through another firm so as not to be identified with the trade. Another name for the illegal practice of parking.

PacMan. A defensive strategy in which targets of takeovers turn on the acquirer and the acquirer is taken over.

Parking. Having another party buy and pretend to own stock or bonds to conceal ownership from the government, while agreeing to protect the holder from losses; parking is an illegal activity.

Point. Means a base point, which is one-hundredth of a cent per dollar on a bond.

Poison pill. Antitakeover strategy in which the target develops a package of incentives for its shareholders, thereby making the takeover prohibitively expensive for the acquirer.

Poison pill and scorched earth. The device most frequently associated with the term *poison pill* is the Share Purchase Right Plan (by 1989 adopted by 46 percent of the Fortune 500 companies and 54 percent of the Fortune 700 companies). Key provisions are the flip-over position coupled with the ability of the board of directors to redeem the rights issued pursuant to the rights plan for a nominal amount prior to a twenty percent acquisition. These provisions are designed to encourage an acquirer to negotiate with the board of directors of the target company rather than proceeding unilaterally with the takeover, and to dissuade the acquirer from employing abusive takeover tactics.

Predators' Ball. The nickname of the annual conference of the High-Yield Bond Department of Drexel.

Preferred stock. A class of securities that ranks somewhere between common stocks and bonds. Preferred stock takes precedence over common stock in the paying of dividends. In the event that a corporation is liquidated, the claims of creditors and preferred-stock-holders take precedence over the claims of those who own common stock. However, creditors take precedence over both common- and preferred-stock-holders in the case of liquidation and the company does not have a legal obligation to pay preferred-stock dividends.

Private placement.   Securities that are directly placed with an institutional investor, such as an insurance company, rather than sold through a public issue. Private placements do not have to be registered with the SEC, so placements can occur more rapidly, with less information in the public domain.

Price/earnings ratio.   The ratio of market price to earnings—essentially indicating the valuation investors place on a company's earnings; obtained by dividing the annual earnings into the average price for the year.

Private partnership vs. public corporation.   Private partnerships are owned by a small group of investors, whereas public corporations are owned by investors who purchase publicly traded shares on the market—shareholders.

Recapitalization.   A change in a corporation's capital structure, such as when it exchanges debt for equity. In other words, a financial restructuring. This has been done to avoid takeovers.

Restricted list.   A confidential list of clients involved in pending investment banking activities.

Restructuring.   *See* Recapitalization. Financial restructuring can also take place in order to avoid bankruptcy. In this case the debt is restructured to provide the company a longer period of time to pay off.

RICO (Racketeer Influenced Corrupt Organizations Act).   Enacted in 1970 primarily for the prosecution of organized crime including the syndicate. Beginning with the case of Princeton/Newport, it was used to indict the organized crime of securities firms.

Schedule 13-D.   A schedule that must be filed with the SEC if an investor accumulates 5 percent or more of a target company so a public disclosure of such action can be made.

Scorched-earth policy.   The threat to dismiss the management of a firm opposed to being taken over.

SEC (Securities and Exchange Commission).   The federal agency created by the Securities Exchange Act of 1934 to administer that act. Five commissioners are appointed by the president for the purpose of enforcing the laws related to disclosure and to protect the investing public against securities fraud. All issues (but not all sales) of securities in the U.S. must be registered with the SEC.

Self-dealing.   Dealing in a client's stock in ways that will benefit the interest of the investment banking firm.

Selling short.   Selling a security or commodity contract that is not owned by the seller to take advantage of an anticipated decline or to protect the profits of a long position.

Skimming warrants.   Retaining, deceptively and without the knowledge of the issuer, warrants that were intended to be attached to the sale of bonds.

Special-bracket firms.   The top-ranked investment banking firms, which lead the majority of securities underwriting in the United States. Ranking is based on subjective prestige among investment banking firms.

Stock.   *See* Common stock and Preferred stock.

Short sale. *See* Selling short.

Takeover. The purchase of majority ownership in a corporation; usually resisted by the target company but can be accomplished nonetheless by the acquirer paying a premium above the current market price for the firm's shares.

Target. The corporation that is the object of a takeover.

Target letter. A letter to a firm from the government notifying it that it is under investigation for indictment.

Target in play. When two or more investors acquire a large portion of shares (generally more than 5 percent) of a target firm in competitive buying.

Tender offer. An offer to buy shares of a corporation for cash or securities, or both, with the objective of taking control of a target company. Generally this is significant when the corporation has purchased more than 5 percent of the target and is required by law to register this accumulation with the SEC. The proposal is generally for an amount higher than its current market price.

Tombstone. An advertisement placed in financial presses by investment bankers to announce offerings of securities (underwriting, tender offers, divestments).

Two-tier tender offer. A tender offer for some but not all of a target's shares, to be followed by a squeeze-out merger with securities of less value, sometimes used to "stampede" shareholders into tendering their stock.

Underwrite. When a securities firm assumes the risk of buying an issue and then selling the securities to the public either directly or indirectly.

Warrants. A type of equity. *See* Equity.

White knight. Acceptable acquirer sought by a potential target to forestall an unfriendly takeover; the preferred suitor.

Zero-coupon bond. A bond that provides debt financing in transactions that cannot carry the current interest burden on the firm's full debt load. No payment is due on either principal or interest for three to five years.

References

Aaronovich, S. 1961. *The Ruling Class*. London: Lawrence and Wishart.

Abrams, Jill and Christie Harlan. 1989. "RICO-Reform Bill Won't Be Retroactive." *Wall Street Journal*, 28 September, B5.

Adams, Walter and James W. Brock. 1988. "Reaganomics and the Transmogrification of Merger Policy." *Antitrust Bulletin* (Summer):310.

———. 1989. *Dangerous Pursuits: Mergers and Acquisitions in the Age of Wall Street*. New York: Pantheon.

Aldrich, Howard E. 1979. *Organizations and Environments*. Englewood Cliffs, NJ: Prentice-Hall.

Aldrich, Howard E. and Jeffrey Pfeffer. 1976. "Environments of Organizations." Pp. 79–105 in *Annual Review of Sociology*, Vol. 2, edited by Alex Inkeles. Palo Alto: Annual Reviews, Inc.

Alexander, H. 1976. *Financing the 1972 Election*. Boston: Lexington Press.

Alford, Robert T. and Roger Friedland. 1975. "Political Participation and Public Policy." Pp. 429–79 in *Annual Review of Sociology*, Vol. 2, edited by Alex Inkeles. Palo Alto: Annual Reviews, Inc.

Allen, Frederick Lewis. 1935. *Lords of Creation*. New York: Harper & Bros.

Altman, Edward I. (ed.). 1990a. *The High-Yield Debt Market: Investment Performance and Economic Impact*. Homewood, IL: Dow Jones-Irwin.

———. 1990b. "Measuring Corporate Bond Mortality and Performance." Pp. 41–57 in *The High-Yield Debt Market: Investment Performance and Economic Impact*, edited by Edward I. Altman. Homewood, IL: Dow Jones-Irwin.

Altman, Edward I. and S. A. Nammacher. 1985a. *The Default Rate Experience on High-Yield Corporate Debt*. New York: Morgan Stanley.

———. 1985b. *The Anatomy of the High-Yield Debt Market*. New York: Morgan Stanley.

———. 1987. *Investing in Junk Bonds: Inside the High-Yield Debt Market*. New York: John Wiley & Sons.

Amihud, Yakov. 1988. "Management Buyouts and Shareholders Wealth." Paper presented at the Conference on Management Buyouts, New York University.

Amihud, Yakov, P. Dodd, and M. Weinstein. 1986. "Conglomerate Mergers, Managerial Motives and Stockholder Wealth." *Bell Journal of Economics* 12:605–16.

Anders, George. 1988. "Shades of U.S. Steel: J. P. Morgan Paved the Way for LBOs." *Wall Street Journal*, 15 November, A1, A9.

———. 1989. "RJR Finale Will Send Many Coursing." *Wall Street Journal*, 9 February, C1.

———. 1992. "KKR in Peril: The Flight to Save RJR." *Wall Street Journal*, 6 April, B1, B5.

Arrow, Kenneth J. 1992. "Rationality of Self and Others in an Economic System."
    Pp. 63–78 in *Decision Making: Alternatives to Rational Choice Models*, edited by
    Mary Zey. Beverly Hills, CA: Sage.
Atkinson, T. R. 1967. *Trends in Corporate Bond Quality*. Cambridge, MA: National
    Bureau of Economic Research.
Auerbach, A. J. (ed.). 1988. *Mergers and Acquisitions*. Chicago: University of Chicago
    Press.
Auerbach, A. J. and A. Andow. 1977. "The Cost of Capital in the United States and
    Japan: A Comparison." Working Paper 2285, National Bureau of Economic
    Research, Cambridge, MA.
Auerbach, A. J. and David Reishus. 1988. "Taxes and the Merger Decision."
    Chapter 19 in *Knights, Raiders, and Targets: The Impact of Hostile Takeovers*, edited
    by John C. Coffee, Louis Lowenstein, and Susan Rose-Ackerman. New York:
    Oxford University Press.
Baker, Wayne E. 1984. "The Social Structure of a National Securities Market."
    American Journal of Sociology 89(4):775–811.
Baldridge, Malcolm. 1986. "Hearing on Merger Law Reforms. Committee on the
    Judiciary, United States Senate. 99th Congress, Second Session. S.2022 Bill to
    Amend the Clayton Act Regarding Antitrust Enforcement and S.2160 Bill to
    Clarify and Improve the Analysis of Mergers Under the Anti-trust Law.
    Washington, DC: U.S. Government Printing Office. Serial J-99–93 (April 9):
    18–22.
Bankers' Magazine. 1908. 76(April): 480.
Baran, Paul A. and Paul M. Sweezy. 1966. *Monopoly Capital*. New York: Monthly
    Review Press.
Barlett, Donald L. and James B. Steele. 1992. *America: What Went Wrong*. Kansas
    City, MO: Andrews and McMeek.
Barney, Jay B. 1990. "The Debate Between Traditional Management Theory
    and Organizational Economics." *Academy of Management Review* 15(3):382–93.
Barney, Jay B. and William G. Ouchi. 1986. *Organizational Economics*. San Francisco,
    CA: Jossey Bass.
Barth, James R. 1990. "Thrift Institutions and High-Yield Bonds." Pp. 161–74 in *The
    High-Yield Debt Market: Investment Performance and Economic Impact*, edited by
    Edward I. Altman. Homewood, IL: Dow Jones-Irwin.
Bartlett, Sarah. 1991. *The Money Machine: How KKR Manufactured Power and Profits*.
    New York: Warner Books.
Baxter, William. 1983. "Reflections on Professor Williamson's Comments." *St.
    Louis University Law Review* 27:315–20.
Bayse, Benalder. Jr. 1986. "How to Tell High-Yield Bonds from Real Junk." *Bot-
    tomline* 3(8, August):29–33.
Bearden, James. 1982. "The Board of Directors in Large U.S. Corporations." Ph.D.
    dissertation, Department of Sociology, State University of New York at Stony
    Brook.
———. 1987. "Financial Hegemony, Social Capital and Bank Boards of Directors."
    Pp. 48–59 in *The Structure of Power in America: The Corporate Elite as a Ruling
    Class*, edited by Michael Schwartz. New York: Holmes & Meier.

Benson, Kenneth. 1975. "The Interorganizational Network as Political Economy." *Administrative Science Quarterly*, 20:229–49.

———. 1977a. "Innovation and Crisis in Organizational Analysis." *Sociological Quarterly* 18:5–18.

———. 1977b. "Organizations: A Dialectical View." *Administrative Science Quarterly*, 22:1–21.

Bentsen, Lloyd. 1989. *Leveraged Buyouts and Corporate Debt*. Hearing before the Committee on Finance, United States Senate, January 24, Washington, DC: U.S. Government Printing Office.

Berger, P. L. and T. Luckmann. 1966. *The Social Construction of Reality*. New York: Anchor.

Berle, Adolf A. and Gardiner C. Means. 1932. *The Modern Corporation and Private Property*. New York: Harcourt, Brace & World.

Blau, Peter M. 1970. "A Formal Theory of Differentiation in Organizations." *American Sociological Review* 35:201–18.

———. 1982. "Structural Sociology and Network Analysis: An Overview." Pp. 273–79 in *Social Structure and Network Analysis*, edited by Peter V. Marsden and Nan Lin. Beverly Hills, CA: Sage.

Blau, Peter M. and Joseph E. Schwartz. 1984. *Crosscutting Social Circles*. Orlando, FL: Academic Press.

Blinder, Alan S. 1989. "Want to Boost Productivity?" *Business Week*, 17 April, 10.

Block, Fred. 1990. *Postindustrial Possibilities*. Berkeley: University of California Press.

Blume, Marshall E. and Donald B. Keim. 1990. "Risk and Return Characteristics of Lower-Grade Bonds, 1977–1987." Pp. 3–17 in *The High-Yield Debt Market: Investment Performance and Economic Impact*, edited by Edward I. Altman, Homewood, IL: Dow Jones-Irwin.

Boies, John L. 1989. "Money Business and the State: Material Interests, Fortune 500 Corporations, and the Size of Political Action Committees." *American Sociological Review* 54:821–33.

Braithwaite, J. 1984. *Corporate Crime in the Pharmaceutical Industry*. London: Routledge & Kegan Paul.

Brancato, Caroly and Kay Gaughan. 1989. *Leveraged Buyouts and the Pot of Gold*. A Report of the U.S. House Committee on Energy and Commerce, Subcommittee on Oversight and Investigation. Washington, DC: U.S. Government Printing Office.

Brandeis, Louis. [1914] 1967. *Other People's Money and How Bankers Use It*. New York: Harper and Row.

Breeden, Richard C. 1989. Statement of Richard C. Breeden, Chairman of the Securities and Exchange Commission. Hearing Before the House Banking, Finance, and Urban Affairs Committee, November 14, United States Senate.

———. 1990. *Speech Concerning the Bankruptcy of Drexel Burnham Lambert Groups Inc.* Hearing Before the Committee on Banking, Housing and Urban Affairs, United States Senate, March. Washington DC: U.S. Government Printing Office.

———. 1991. *Address on the Economy and Mergers and Acquisitions.* Graduate School of Business, Stanford University, Stanford, CA. Washington, DC: U.S. Government Printing Office.

Bruck, Connie. 1988. *The Predators' Ball.* New York: Simon and Schuster.

Burawoy, Michael. 1979. *Manufacturing Consent: Changes in the Labor Process Under Monopoly Capitalism.* Chicago: University of Chicago Press.

Burk, James. 1988. *Values in the Marketplace: The American Stock Market Under Federal Securities Law.* New York: Walter de Gruyter.

Burnett, Michael A. and Frank Philippi. 1990. "New Developments in Regulation of the High-Yield Bond Market and Junk Bond Investments." Pp. 145–53 in *The High-Yield Debt Market: Investment Performance and Economic Impact,* edited by Edward I. Altman, Homewood, IL: Dow Jones-Irwin.

Burris, Val. 1987. "The Political Partisanship of American Business: A Study of Corporate Political Action Committees." *American Sociological Review* 52:732–44.

Burrough, Bryan and John Helyar. 1990. "The Jeremiah of Junk Bonds." *New York Times,* 23 January, 34–40.

Burt, Ronald S. 1975. "Corporate Society: A Time Series Analysis of Network Structure." *Social Science Research* 4:271–328.

———. 1977. "Positions in Multiple Networks. Part One: A General Conception of Stratification and Prestige in a System of Actors Cast as a Social Topology." *Social Forces* 57:106–31.

———. 1978. "Cohesion Versus Structural Equivalence as a Basis for Network Subgroups." *Sociological Methodology and Research* 7:189–212.

———. 1982. *Toward a Structural Theory of Action.* New York: Academic Press.

———. 1983. *Corporate Profits and Cooptation: Networks of Market Constraints and Directorate Ties in the American Economy.* New York: Academic Press.

———. 1987. "Social Contagion and Innovation: Cohesion Versus Structural Equivalence." *American Journal of Sociology* 92:1287–335.

Business Week. 1990. 15 January, 26.

Camic, Charles. 1986. "The Matter of Habit." *American Journal of Sociology* 91(5): 1039–87.

Carosso, Vincent P. 1970. *Investment Banking in America: A History.* Cambridge, MA: Harvard University Press.

Carruthers, Bruce, and Wendy Nelson Espeland. 1991. "Accounting for Rationality: Double-Entry Bookkeeping and the Rhetoric of Economic Rationality." *American Journal of Sociology* 97(1):31–69.

Carter, R. 1985. *Capitalism, Class Conflict, and the New Middle Class.* London: Routledge and Kegan Paul.

Castro, Janice. 1991. "A Sizzler Finally Fizzles." *Time* 22 April, 32.

Chandler, Alfred D. Jr. 1962. *Strategy and Structure: Chapters in the History of American Industrial Enterprise.* Cambridge, MA: MIT Press.

———. 1977. *The Visible Hand: The Managerial Revolution in American Business.* Cambridge, MA: Belknap Press of Harvard University Press.

———. 1990a. "The Enduring Logic of Industrial Success." *Harvard Business Review* (March/April):434–41.

———. 1990b. *Scale and Scope.* Cambridge, MA: Harvard University Press.

Chandler, Clay and Masayoshi Kanabayashi. 1991. "Japanese Stock Scandal Sends Strong Message: Small Investors Beware." *Wall Street Journal* 25 June, 1.

Clawson, Dan, James Bearden, and Alan Neustadtl. 1986. "The Logic of Business Unity: Corporate Contributions to the 1980 Congressional Election." *American Sociological Review* 51(December):797–811.

Clawson, Dan, Alan Neustadtl, and James Bearden. 1986. "Interlocks, PACs and Corporate Conservatism." *American Journal of Sociology* 94:749–73.

Clune, William H. 1983. "A Political Model of Implementation and the Implications of the Model for Public Policy, Research, and the Changing Role of Lawyers." *Iowa Law Review* 69:47–125.

Coase, R. H. [1937] 1952. "The Nature of the Firm." Pp. 386–405 in *Readings in Price Theory*, edited by G. J. Stigler and K. E. Boulding. Homewood, IL: Richard D. Irwin.

Coffee, John C. 1986. Business Organization and Finance: Legal and Economic. Minneola, NY: Foundation Press.

———. 1988. "Shareholders versus Managers: The Strain in the Corporate Web." Pp. 77–134 in *Knights, Raiders, and Targets: The Impact of the Hostile Takeover*, edited by John C. Coffee, Louis Lowenstein, and Susan Rose-Ackerman. New York: Oxford University Press.

Cohen, Laurie P. and Michael Siconolfi. 1991. "Solomon Reveals It Had Control of 94% of Notes at May Auction." *Wall Street Journal* 5 September, C1.

Coleman, James. 1984. "Introducing Social Structure into Economic Analysis." *American Economic Review* 74(2):84–88.

Comer, M. 1977. *Corporate Fraud*. London: McGraw Hill.

Commercial and Financial Chronicle. 1913. 96(8 March): 680–81.

Congressional Quarterly Almanac. 1985. Washington, DC: Congressional Quarterly, Inc.

Congressional Quarterly Weekly Report. 1989. June, p. 1624. Washington, DC: Congressional Quarterly, Inc.

Corey, Lewis. 1930. *The House of Morgan*. New York: G. Howard Watt.

Council of Economic Advisers. 1985. *Economic Report of the President*. Washington DC: U.S. Government Printing Office.

Cowan, J. 1992. "Flap over Value of Stock Options." *New York Times*, 26 October, D2.

Cowing, Cedric B. 1965. *Populists, Plungers, and Progressives*. Princeton, NJ: Princeton University Press.

Cyert, Richard M. and James G. March. 1963. *A Behavioral Theory of the Firm*. Englewood Cliffs, NJ: Prentice Hall.

Dahl, Robert A. 1957. "The Concept of Power." *Behavioral Science* 2:201–15.

Dahrendorf, Ralf. 1959. *Class and Class Conflict in Industrial Society*. Stanford: Stanford University Press.

Diamond, P. 1971. "Political and Economic Evaluation of Social Effects and Externalities: Comment." Pp. 30–32 in *Frontiers of Quantitative Economics*, Edited by M. Intrilligator. Amsterdam: North-Holland.

DiDonato, Donna, Davita Silfen Glasberg, Beth Mintz, and Michael Schwartz. 1988. "Theories of Corporate Interlocks: A Social History." *Research in the Sociology of Organizations* 6:135–57.

DiMaggio, Paul J. 1985. "Structural Analysis of Organizational Fields." *Research in Organizational Behavior* 7:335–70.

DiMaggio, Paul J. and Walter W. Powell. 1983. "The Iron Cage Revisited: Institutional Isomorphism and Collective Rationality in Organizational Fields." *American Sociological Review* 48:147–60.

DiTomaso, Nancy. 1980. "Organizational Analysis and Power Structure Research." Pp. 255–68 in *Power Structure Research*, edited by G. W. Domhoff. Beverly Hills, CA: Sage.

Domhoff, G. W. 1967. *Who Rules America?* Englewood Cliffs, NJ: Prentice-Hall.

———. 1983. *Who Rules America Now?* Englewood Cliffs, NJ: Prentice-Hall.

Drexel Burnham Lambert, Inc. 1985. *Financing America's Growth: High Yield Bonds.* New York: Author.

———. 1986a. *1986 Annual Report.* New York: Author.

———. 1986b. *The Case of High-Yield Securities.* New York: Author.

———. 1987. *1987 Annual Report.* New York: Author.

———. 1988. *Annual High-Yield Market Report.* Los Angeles: Author.

Drucker, Peter. 1950. *The New Society: The Anatomy of Industrial Order.* New York: Harper.

———. 1984. "Taming the Corporate Takeover." *Wall Street Journal*, 30 October, A2.

Durkheim, Emile. 1933 [1893]. *The Division of Labor in Society.* New York: Free Press.

Eccles Robert C. and Dwight B. Crane. 1988. *Doing Deals: Investment Banks at Work.* Cambridge, MA: Harvard Business School Press.

Eccles, Robert C. and Harrison C. White. 1988. "Price and Authority in Inter-Profit Center Transactions." *American Journal of Sociology* 94(Supplement):S17–S51.

Edelman, Lauren. 1990. "Legal Environments and Organizational Governance: The Expansion of Due Process in the American Workplace." *American Journal of Sociology* 95:1401–40.

———. 1992. "Legal Ambiguity and Symbolic Structures: Organizational Mediation of Civil Rights Law." *American Journal of Sociology* 97(6, May):1531–76.

Edwards, Richard. 1979. *Contested Terrain: The Transformation of the Workplace in America.* New York: Basic Books.

Ehrlich, I. 1973. "Participation in Illegitimate Activities: A Theoretical and Empirical Investigation." *Journal of Political Economy* 81:521–65.

Eisenhardt, K. 1989. "Agency Theory: An Assessment and Review." *Academy of Management Review* 14(1):57–74.

Elias, Christopher. 1987. "Scales Tip against Antitrust Statute." *Insight* 3(24):8–16.

Ellsworth, Richard R. 1985. "Capital Markets and Competitive Decline." *Harvard Business Review* 63(September/October):171–83.

Emerson, Richard M. 1962. "Power-Dependence Relations." *American Sociological Review.* 27:31–41.

Etzioni, Amitai. 1984. *Capital Corruption: The New Attack on American Democracy.* New York: Harcourt Brace Jovanovich.

———. 1988. *The Moral Dimension.* New York: Free Press.

Fama, Eugene. 1965. "The Behavior of Stock Market Prices." *Journal of Business of the University of Chicago* 38(1, January):34–105.

————. 1980. "Agency Problems and the Theory of the Firm." *Journal of Political Economy* 88(April):288–307.

————. 1981. "Stock Returns, Real Activity, Inflation, and Money." *American Economic Review* 71(September):545–65.

Fama, Eugene and Michael C. Jensen. 1983a. "Separation of Ownership and Control." *Journal of Law and Economics* 26(June):301–26.

————. 1983b. "Agency Problems and Residual Claims." *Journal of Law and Economics* 26:327–50.

Fama, E. and G. W. Schwert. 1977. Asset Return and Inflation. *Journal of Financial Economics* 5:114–46.

Fitch, R. and M. Oppenheimer. 1970. "Who Rules the Corporations," Parts I, II and III. *Socialist Review* 4:73–108, 5:61–114, 6:33–94.

Fligstein, Neil. 1985. "The Spread of Multidivisional Form." *American Sociological Review* 50:377–91.

————. 1987. "The Intraorganizational Power Struggle: The Rise of Finance Presidents in Large Corporations, 1919–1979." *American Sociological Review* 52:44–58.

————. 1989. "Bank Control, Owner Control, or Organizational Dynamics: Who Controls the Large Modern Corporation?" Paper presented at the American Sociological Association Meetings, San Francisco.

————. 1990a. *The Transformation of Corporate Control.* Cambridge, MA: Harvard University Press.

————. 1990b. "The Structural Transformation of American Industry." In *The New Institutionalism in Organizational Theory,* edited by W. Powell and D. DiMaggio. Chicago: University of Chicago Press.

Fligstein, Neil and Kenneth Dauber. 1989. "Changes in Corporate Organization." Pp. 73–96 in *Annual Review of Sociology,* no. 15, edited by Richard Scott. Palo Alto: Annual Reviews Inc.

Fowler, K. L. and D. R. Schmidt. 1988. "Tender Offers, Acquisitions, and Subsequent Performance in Manufacturing Firms." *Academy of Management Journal* 31:85–106.

Frank, Robert H. 1990. "Patching Up the Rational Choice Model." Pp. 53–88 in *Beyond the Marketplace: Rethinking Models of Economy and Society,* edited by Roger Friedland and A. F. Robertson. Chicago: Aldine.

Franko, L. G. 1989. "Global Corporate Competition: Who's Winning, Who's Losing, and the R&D Factor as One Reason Why." *Strategic Management Journal* 10:449–74.

Freudenheim, Milt. 1992. "U.S. Jury Awards $3.3 Billion to Investors from Keating." *New York Times* 11 July, 15, 19.

Friedland, Roger and A. F. Robertson (eds.). 1990. *Beyond the Marketplace: Rethinking Models of Economy and Society.* Chicago: Aldine.

Friedman, Benjamin. 1985. "The Substitutability of Debt and Equity Securities." Pp. 274–95 in *Corporate Capital Structures in the United States,* edited by B. Friedman. Chicago: University of Chicago Press.

————. 1988. *Day of Reckoning.* New York: Random House.

Gilbert, Nick. 1987. "A Closer Look at First Executive." *Financial World* 156(9, May 5):22–25.

Gilson, Ronald J., Myron G. Scholes, and Mark A. Wolfson. 1986. "Taxation and the Dynamics of Corporate Control: The Uncertain Case for Tax Motivated Acquisitions." Working Paper No. 24, Law and Economic Program, Stanford Law School.

Glasberg, Davita Silfen, and Michael Schwartz. 1983. "Ownership and Control of Corporations." *Annual Review of Sociology* 9:22–32.

Gordon, David, Richard Edwards, and Michael Reich. 1982. *Segmented Work, Divided Workers: The Historical Transformation of Labor in the United States.* Cambridge, MA: Cambridge University Press.

Granovetter, Mark. 1985. "Economic Action and Social Structure: The Problem of Embeddedness." *American Journal of Sociology* 91(93):481–510.

Habermas, J. 1976. *Legitimation Crisis.* London: Routledge & Kegan Paul.

Hage, Jerald. 1974. *Communication and Organizational Control: Cybernetics in Health and Welfare Settings.* New York: John Wiley & Sons.

Hage, Jerald and Michael Aiken. 1967. "Relationship of Centralization to Other Structural Properties." *Administrative Science Quarterly* 12:72–92.

———. 1978. "Program Change and Organizational Properties: A Comparative Analysis." *American Journal of Sociology* 72:503–19.

Hall, B. H. 1990. "The Impact of Corporate Restructuring on Industrial Research and Development." Pp. 85–135 in *Brookings Papers on Economic Activity*, edited by M. N. Baily and C. Winston. Washington, DC: Brookings Institution.

Hamilton, Joan and Judith H. Dobrzynski. 1987. *Business Week*, February, 110–11.

Hawkins, Keith. 1984. *Environment and Enforcement.* Oxford: Clarendon Press.

Heins, John. 1988. "Tom Spiegel's (Dubious) Claim to Fame," *Forbes* 142(11, November 14):153–56.

Helyar, John, Betsy Morris, and Steve Stewart. 1989. "RJR Nabisco Chief Considering Buy-Out of Concern for $17.6 Billion, or $75 a Share." *Wall Street Journal*, 13 January, 1.

Herman, Edward S. and Louis Lowenstein. 1988. "The Efficiency Effects of Hostile Takeovers." Pp. 211–40 in *Knights, Raiders, and Targets: The Impact of the Hostile Takeover*, edited by John C. Coffee, Louis Lowenstein, and Susan Rose-Ackerman. New York: Oxford University Press.

Herzel, L. and D. Colling. 1983. "The 'Chinese Wall' Revisited," *Company Lawyer* 15:14–19.

Hertzberg, Daniel and Aron Monroe. 1985. "Investment Banks See Gold Mine in Enthusiasm for Restructuring." *Wall Street Journal*, 12 August, 13.

Heydebrand, Wolf. 1977. "Organizational Contradictions in Public Bureaucracies." *Sociological Quarterly* 18:85–109.

Hickman, W. Braddock. 1958. *Corporate Bond Quality and Investor Experience.* Princeton, NJ: Princeton University Press.

Hickson, D. J., C. R. Hinings, G. L. Lee, R. E. Schneck, and J. M. Pennings. 1971. "A 'Strategic Contingencies' Theory of Intraorganizational Power." *Administrative Science Quarterly* 16(2):216–29.

Hilder, D. B. 1988. "Bank Board Staff Expects to Offer Rules Curbing Thrifts' 'Junk Bond' Investments." *Wall Street Journal*, 28 September, B4.

Hilferding, R. [1910] 1981. *Finance Capital.* London: Routledge and Kegan Paul (originally published in German).

Hirsch, Paul M. 1986. "From Ambushes to Golden Parachutes: Corporate Take-overs as an Instance of Cultural Framing and Institutional Integration." *American Journal of Sociology* 91(4):800–37.

———. 1987. *Pack Your Own Parachute: How to Survive Mergers, Takeovers, and other Corporate Disasters.* Reading, MA: Addison-Wesley.

Hirsch, Paul, Stuart Michaels, and Ray Friedman. 1987. "Dirty Hands" versus "Clean Models": Is Sociology in Danger of Being Seduced by Economics?" *Theory and Society* 16(3):317–36.

Hitt, Michael A., Robert E. Hoskisson, and R. Duane Ireland. 1990. "Mergers and Acquisitions and Managerial Commitment to Innovation in M-form Firms." *Strategic Management Journal* 11:29–47 (special issue).

Hitt, Michael A., Robert E. Hoskisson, R. Duane Ireland, and Jeffry S. Harrison. 1991. "Effects of Acquisitions on R&D Inputs and Outputs." *Academy of Management Journal* 34(3):693–706.

Hopkinson, Edward. 1952. *Drexel & Co.* New York: The Newcomen Society in North America.

Huber, George, and Reuben McDaniel. 1986. "Decision-Making Paradigm of Organizational Design." *Management Science* 32:572–89.

Jackson, Brooks and E. Ricks. 1988. "Lobbyists, Speaking Fees, Election Aid Didn't Keep Milken from Capital Hill." *Wall Street Journal,* 5 April, 16.

Jackson, Stanley. 1984. *J. P. Morgan.* New York: Stein and Day.

Jacobs, D. 1988. "Corporate Economic Power and the State: A Longitudinal Assessment of Two Explanations." *American Journal of Sociology* 93:852–81.

Jarrell, Gregg and Michael Bradley. 1980. "The Economic Effects of Federal and State Regulation of Cash Tender Offers." *Journal of Law and Economics* 23:371–407.

Jarrell, Gregg A. and Annette B. Poulson. 1986. "Shark Repellents and Stock Prices: The Effects of Antitakeover Amendments Since 1980." Mimeo, August.

Jeidels, O. 1905. *Das Verhaltnis der deutschen Grossbanker zur Industrie mit bersonderer Berucksichtigung der Eisenindustrie.* Leipzig: Verlag von Dunker & Humblot.

Jensen, Michael C. 1983. "Organization Theory and Methodology." *Accounting Review* 55(2):319–39.

———. 1986. "Agency Costs of Free Cash Flow, Corporate Finance and Take-overs." *American Economic Review* 76(May):323–29.

———. 1988. "Takeovers: Their Causes and Consequences." *Journal of Economic Perspectives* 2(Winter):21–48.

———. 1989a. "Is Leverage an Invitation to Bankruptcy? On the Contrary, It keeps Shaky Firms Out of Court." *Wall Street Journal,* 1 February, A14.

———. 1989b. "The Eclipse of the Public Corporation." *Harvard Business Review* 67(September/October):61–75.

Jensen, Michael C., and William H. Meckling. 1976. "Theory of the Firm: Managerial Behavior, Agency Costs and Ownership Structure." *Journal of Financial Economics* 3:305–60.

———. 1979. "Rights and Production Functions: An Application of Labor Managed Firms." *Journal of Business* 52(October):469–506.

Jensen Michael C. and Richard S. Ruback. 1983. "The Market for Corporate Control: The Scientific Evidence." *Journal of Financial Economics* 11:5–50.

John, T. A. 1991. "Corporate Restructuring and Incentive Effects of Leverage and Taxes." *Managerial and Decision Economics* 12:461–72.

Joseph, Frederick H. 1990. "A Wall Street View of the High-Yield Debt Market and Corporate Leverage." Pp. 115–30 in *The High-Yield Debt Market,* edited by Edward I. Altman. Homewood, IL: Dow Jones-Irwin.

Jung, Maureen. 1988. "Corporations and the Structure of Markets: The Comstocks and the Mining Economy in the Far West, 1848–1990." Unpublished Ph.D. dissertation, University of California, Santa Barbara.

Kanter, Rosabeth Moss. 1989a. "The New Managerial Work." *Harvard Business Review* 67(November-December):85–89.

———. 1989b. *When Giants Learn to Dance: Mastering the Challenge of Strategy, Management, and Careers in the 1990s.* New York: Simon and Schuster.

Kaplan, S. 1989. "Management Buyouts: Evidence on Taxes as a Source of Value." *Journal of Finance* 44:611–32.

Karr, Albert. 1991. "Labor Agency Backs Exception to Pension Law." *Wall Street Journal,* 9 July, A4.

Karsch, M. 1984. "The Insider Trading Sanctions Act: Incorporating a Market Information Definition." *Journal of Comparative Business and Capital Market Law* 6:283–305.

Katz, Jack. 1988. *Seductions of Crime: Moral and Sensual Attractions in Doing Evil.* New York: Harper Collins.

Kerwin, Kathleen. 1989. "Milken's Shadow Hovers over Fred Carr." *Business Week,* 17 April, 24.

———. 1990a. "Can Ed Harshfield 'Make the Taxpayer Whole'"? *Business Week* 10 September, 78.

———. 1990b. "I'm One of the Suckers." *Business Week* 24 September 24, 118–19.

———. 1990c. "The Avalanche of Junk Burying First Executive." *Business Week* 26 February, 41.

Koenig, Thomas and Robert Gogel. 1981. "Interlocking Corporate Directorates as a Social Network." *American Journal of Economics and Sociology* 40:37–50.

Koenig, Thomas, Robert Gogel, and John Sonquist. 1979. "Models of the Significance of Interlocking Directorates." *American Journal of Economics and Sociology* 38:173–86.

Koenig, Thomas and Robert Mizruchi. 1988. "Economic Concentration and Corporate Political Behavior: A Cross-industry Comparison." *Social Science Research* 17:287–305.

Koepp, Stephen. 1988a. "Fraud, Fraud, Fraud." *Time,* 15 August, 28–29.

———. 1988b. "Throwing the Book at Drexel." *Time,* 19 September, 38–40.

Kornbluth, Jesse. 1992. *Highly Confident.* New York: Basic Books.

Kotz, David M. 1978. *Bank Control of Large Corporations in the United States.* Berkeley: University of California Press.

Kuhn, Robert Lawrence (ed.). 1990. *Mergers and Acquisitions, and Leveraged Buyouts.* Homewood, IL: Richard D. Irwin.

Laffer, Arthur. 1985. "The Best Policy Is a Hands Off Policy." *Electronic Business* 11(June 15):104.

Laing, Jonathan. 1990. "Flawed Policies: Big Junk and Real-Estate Holdings Put Life Insurers at Risk." *Barron's* 70(October 1):10–11, 32–38.

Lambert, Wade and Richard B. Schmitt. 1991. "Fidelity Ex-manager faces Payoff Charge." *Wall Street Journal*, 11 October, B2.

Lane, Robert E. 1992. "Money Symbolism and Economic Rationality." Pp. 233–54 in *Decision Making: Alternatives to Rational Choice Models*, edited by Mary Zey. Beverly Hills, CA.: Sage.

Laumann, Edward O. and David Knoke. 1987. *The Organizational State: A Perspective on National Energy and Health Domains*. Madison: University of Wisconsin Press.

Lehn, Kenneth. 1990. "A View from Washington on Leveraged Buyouts." Pp. 154–60 in *The High-Yield Debt Market: Investment Performance and Economic Impact*, edited by Edward I. Altman. Homewood, IL: Dow Jones-Irwin.

Lehn, Kenneth and A. Poulsen. 1988. "Leveraged Buyouts: Wealth Created or Wealth Redistributed?" Pp. 48–62 in *Public Policy Toward Corporate Takeovers*, edited by Murray L. Weidenbau Publishers.

Levine, Dennis B. 1991. *Inside Out: An Insider's Account of Wall Street*. New York: G.P. Putnam's Sons.

Lewis, Michael. 1989. *Liar's Poker*. New York: W. W. Norton.

Lie, John. 1988. "Visualizing the Invisible Hand: From Market to Modes of Exchange." Department of Sociology: Unpublished Ph.D. dissertation, Harvard University, Cambridge, MA.

Lipton, Martin, James H. Fogelson, Andrew R. Brownstein, and Craig M. Wasserman. 1990. "Takeover and Defense Law I: The Takeover Environment." Pp. 441–85 in *Mergers, Acquisitions and Leveraged Buyouts*, edited by Robert Lawrence Kuhn. Homewood, IL: Richard D. Irwin.

Long, William F. and David T. Ravenscraft. 1984. "The Misuse of Accounting Rates of Return: Comment." *American Economic Review* 74:494–500.

Loomis, Carol J. 1991. "What Fred Carr's Fall Means to You." *Fortune* 123(9, May 6):60–62.

Lubatkin, M. 1987. "Merger Strategies and Stockholder Value." *Strategic Management Journal* 8:39–53.

Lubatkin, M. and H. M. O'Neil. 1987. "Merger Strategies and Capital Market Risk." *Academy of Management Journal* 30:665–84.

Lynch, Gerald E. 1987. "RICO: The Crime of Being a Criminal, Parts I & II." *Columbia Law Review* 84(4):661.

Lyng, Stephan and Lester Kurtz. 1985. "Bureaucratic Insurgency: The Vatican and the Crisis of Modernism." *Social Forces* 3:901–22.

Ma, Christopher, Ramesh P. Rao, and Richard L. Peterson. 1990 "Resiliency of the High-Yield Bond Market." Pp. 58–78 in *The High-Yield Debt Market: Investment Performance and Economic Impact*, edited by Edward I. Altman. Homewood, IL: Dow Jones-Irwin.

Magenheim, Ellen B. and Dennis C. Mueller. 1988. "Are Acquiring-Firm Shareholders Better Off after an Acquisition?" Pp. 171–93 in *Knights, Raiders, and Targets: The Impact of the Hostile Takeover*, edited by John C. Coffee, Louis Lowenstein, and Susan Rose-Ackerman. New York: Oxford University Press.

Mariolis, Peter. 1975. "Interlocking Directorates and Control of Corporations: The Theory of Bank Control." *Social Science Quarterly* 56:425–39.

————. 1977. "Type of Corporation, Size of Firm, and Interlocking Directorates: A Reply to Levin." *Social Science Quarterly* 58:511–13.

Markus, Lynne and Jeffrey Pfeffer. 1983. "Power and the Design and Implementation of Accounting and Control Systems." *Accounting Organizations and Society* 8:205–218.

Marx, Karl. [1867] 1977. *Capital,* Volume I. New York: Vintage Books.

McDonald, John. 1969. "Some Candid Answers from James J. Ling." *Fortune* 8(2, 19 August):92–95, 162–65.

Mead, George Herbert. 1934. *Mind, Self, and Society.* Chicago: University of Chicago Press.

Meese, Edwin, III, and Malcolm Baldridge. 1985. "The Reagan Administration's 1986 Anti-Trust Proposal in Congress." *Antitrust Law & Economic Review* 17(4):35–48.

Merton, Robert K. 1968. "Social Structure and Anomie." Pp. 188–214 in *Social Theory and Social Structure,* edited by Robert K. Merton. New York: Free Press.

Meyer, John, J. Boli and G. M. Thomas. 1987. "Ontological and Rationalization in Western Culture Account." Pp. 12–37 in *Institutional Structure,* edited by George Thomas et al. Beverly Hills, CA: Sage.

Meyer, John W. and Brian Rowan. 1977. "Institutionalized Organizations: Formal Structure as Myth and Ceremony." *American Journal of Sociology* 83:340–63.

Meyer, John W. and W. Richard Scott (eds.). 1983. Organizational Environments: Ritual and Rationality. Beverly Hills, CA: Sage.

Miliband, Ralph. 1969. *The State in Capitalist Society.* New York: Basic Books.

Miller, Merton H. 1991. "Financial Innovations and Market Volatility." Cambridge, MA: Basil Blackwell.

Mills, C. Wright. 1956. *The Power Elite.* New York: Oxford University Press.

Mintz, Beth and Michael Schwartz. 1984. *The Structure of Power in the American Corporate System.* Chicago: University of Chicago Press.

————. 1985. *The Power Structure of American Business.* Chicago: University of Chicago Press.

Mizruchi, Mark S. 1982. *The American Corporate Network, 1904–1974.* Beverly Hills, CA: Sage.

————. 1986. "Economic Sources of Corporate Political Consensus: An Examination of Interindustry Relations." *American Sociological Review* 51:482–91.

————. 1989a. "Market Relations, Interlocks, and Corporate Political Behavior." Reprint 118, Center for the Social Sciences, Columbia University, New York.

————. 1989b. "Similarity and Political Behavior Among Large American Corporations." *American Journal of Sociology* 2:401–24.

Mizruchi, Mark S. and Thomas Koenig. 1984. "Interdependency, Interlocking, and Corporate Political Behavior: A Test of the Interorganizational Theory of Class Cohesion." Paper presented at the Annual Meeting of the American Sociological Association, San Antonio, TX.

————. 1988. "Economic Concentration, and Corporate Political Behavior: A Cross-Industry Comparison." *Social Science Research* 17:287–305.

Mizruchi, Mark S. and Linda Stearns. 1986. "Organizational Responses to Capital Dependence: A Time Series Analysis." Paper presented at the Annual Meeting of the American Sociological Association, New York.

————. 1988. "A Longitudinal Study of Interlocking Directorates." *Administrative Science Quarterly* 33:194–210.

Modigliani, F. and Miller, M. H. 1958. "The Costs of Capital, Corporation Finance, and the Theory of Investment." *American Economic Review* 48:261–97.

Money Trust Investigation. 19??. Report 90:??–??

Morin, F. 1974. *La Structure Financiere de Capitalisme Francais.* Paris: Calmann-Levy.

Moses, Jonathan M. 1992. "Milken to Pay $500 Million More to Settle Civil Suits, Would Keep at Least as Much." *Wall Street Journal,* 18 February, A3.

Moses, Jonathan M. and Amy Stevens. 1993. "Milken Is Released to Halfway House in Los Angeles Area." *Wall Street Journal,* 5 January, B4.

Mueller, Dennis C. 1977. "The Effects of Conglomerate Mergers." *Journal of Banking & Finance* 1(December):344.

————. 1985. "Mergers and Market Share." *Review of Economics and Statistics* 67(May):266–67.

Navin, Thomas R. and Marian V. Sears. 1955. "The Rise of a Market for Industrial Securities, 1877–1902." *Business History Review* 29:105–38.

North, Douglass C. 1990. *Institutions, Institutional Change and Economic Performance.* Cambridge, MA: Cambridge University Press.

Packer, Herbert L. 1968. *The Limits of the Criminal Sanction.* Stanford, CA: Stanford University Press.

Palmer, Donald. 1983. "Broken Ties: Interlocking Directorates, and Intercorporate Coordination." *Administrative Science Quarterly* 28:40–55.

Parker, Marcia and Hillary Durgin. 1990. "Drexel Fall Shifts Focus to Insurers: Quality of Other Assets Under Scrutiny." *Pensions & Investments* 18(4, February 19):1, 45.

Patman Report. 1964. Report on the Robinson-Patman Act, U.S. House of Representatives Small Business Committee. U.S. Department of Justice. U.S. Government Printing Office. Washington, D.C. (Referred to as the Patman Report in the text).

Pecora, Ferdinand. 1939. *Wall Street Under Oath.* New York: Simon and Schuster.

Pennings, Johannes M. 1980. *Interlocking Directorates.* San Francisco: Jossey-Bass.

Perlo, Victor. 1957. *The Empire of High Finance.* New York: International Publishers.

Perrow, Charles. 1970. "Departmental Power and Perspective in Industrial Firms." Pp. 59–89 in *Power in Organizations,* edited by Mayer Zald. Nashville, TN: Vanderbilt University Press.

Pfeffer, Jeffrey and Gerald R. Salancik. 1978. *The External Control of Organizations: A Resource Dependence Perspective.* New York: Harper & Row.

Podolny, Joel Marc. 1991. "Status, Status Processes, and Market Competition." Ph.D. dissertation, Harvard University, Cambridge, MA.

Polanyi, Karl. [1944] 1957. *The Great Transformation.* Boston: Beacon Press.

Porter, M. E. 1987. "From Competitive Advantages to Corporate Strategy." *Harvard Business Review* 65(3):43–59.

Poulantzas, N. 1975. *Classes in Contemporary Capitalism.* London: New Left Books. (Originally published in French).

Powell, Walter W. 1990a. "Neither Market Nor Hierarchy: Network Forms of Organization." Pp. 295–336 in *Research in Organizational Behavior,* Vol. 12, edited by B. Straw and L. L. Cummings. Greenwich, CT: JAI Press.

————. 1990b. "The Transformation of Organizational Forms: How Useful Is Organizational Theory in Accounting for Social Change?" Pp. 301–30 in *Beyond the Marketplace: Rethinking Economy and Society,* edited by Roger Friedland and A. F. Robertson. Hawthorne, NY: Aldine de Gruyter.

Powell, Walter W. and Paul J. DiMaggio. 1990. *The New Institutionalism in Organizational Analysis.* Chicago: University of Chicago Press.

Prechel, Harland. 1991. "Irrationality and Contradiction in Organizational Change: Transformation in the Corporate Form of a U.S. Steel Corporation, 1930–1987." *Sociological Quarterly* 32(3):423–45.

President's Commission on Law Enforcement and Administration of Justice (Katzenbach Commission). 1967. "The Challenge of Crime in a Free Society." Report at 6–10.

Ramiriz, Richard. 1991. "Junk Bonds on the Rise." *Wall Street Journal,* C1, D1.

Ravenscraft, D. J. and R. W. Scherer. 1987. *Mergers, Sell-Offs and Economic Efficiency.* Washington, DC: Brookings Institution.

————. 1988. "Mergers and Managerial Performance." Pp. 194–210 in *Knights, Raiders, and Targets: The Impact of the Hostile Takeover,* edited by John C. Coffee, Louis Lowenstein, and Susan Rose-Ackerman. New York: Oxford University Press.

Rehnquist, C. J. 1989. Remarks at Brookings Eleventh Seminar on Administration of Justice, April 7. Brookings Institution, Washington, DC.

Reich. C. 1986. "Milken the Magnificent." *Institutional Investor* 20(August): 81–97.

Ricks, Thomas. 1988. "Milken Refuses to Testify in House Probe of Drexel Burnham's Junk-Bond Activity." *Wall Street Journal,* 28 April, 2.

Rochester, Anna. 1936. *Rulers of America.* New York: International Publishers.

Rose A. 1967. *The Power Structure.* New York: Oxford Press.

Rose, Frederick. 1991. "Executive Life Offer Rejected by California." *Wall Street Journal,* 7 November, A3, A5.

Roy, William G. 1983. "The Unfolding of the Interlocking Directorate Structure of the United States." *American Sociological Review* 48:248–57.

Sabato, L. J. 1984. *PAC Power: Inside the World of Political Action Committees.* New York: W.W. Norton.

Salancik, Gerald R. and Jeffrey Pfeffer. 1974. "The Bases and Use of Power in Organizational Decision Making: The Case of a University." *Administrative Science Quarterly* 19:453–73.

Salwen, Kevin G. 1991a. "SEC Reportedly Authorizes Charges Against American Continental, Keating." *Wall Street Journal,* 22 March, B3.

————. 1991b. "Three Ex-Officials of Lincoln Savings State Fraud Charges with the SEC." *Wall Street Journal,* 25 September, A5.

Schelling, Thomas C. 1978. *Micromotives and Macrobehavior.* New York: W.W. Norton.

Schipper, Katherine and A. Smith. 1983. "Effects of Recontracting on Shareholder Wealth: The Case of Voluntary Spin-Offs." *Journal of Financial Economics* 12(December):437–67.

Schipper, Katherine and Rex Thompson. 1983a. "Evidence on the Capitalized Value of Merger Activity for Acquiring Firms." *Journal of Financial Economics* 11:98–119.

―――. 1983b. "The Impact of Merger-Related Regulation on the Shareholders of Acquiring Firms." *Journal of Accounting Research* 21:184–221.

Scott, J. P. 1979. *Corporations, Class, and Capitalism.* London: Hutchinson.

―――. 1985. "Theoretical Framework and Research Design." Pp. 1–19 in *Networks of Corporate Power: A Comparative Analysis of Ten Countries,* edited by Frans Stokman, Rolf Ziegler, and John Scott. Cambridge: Polity Press in association with Basil Blackwell, Oxford.

SEC. 1986. "Triton Financial Report."

SEC v. Martin A. Siegel. 1987. Compliant for Injunction and Other Equitable Relief.

Selznick, P. 1949. *TVA and the Grass Roots.* Berkeley: University of California Press.

Sen, Amartya. 1987. *On Ethics and Economics.* Oxford: Basil Blackwell.

Shapiro, Susan. 1984. *Wayward Capitalism: Target of the Securities and Exchange Commission.* New Haven, CT: Yale University Press.

Simon, Herbert A. 1985. "Human Nature in Politics: The Dialogue of Psychology with Political Science." *American Political Science Review* 79(2):293–304.

Skocpol, Theda. 1980. "Political Response to Capitalistic Crisis: Neo-Marxist Theories of the State and the Case of the New Deal." *Politics and Society* 10:155–202.

―――. 1985. "Bringing the State Back In." Pp. 3–37 in *Bringing the State Back In,* edited by Peter B. Evans, Dietrich Rueschemeyer, and Theda Skocpol. Cambridge: Cambridge University Press.

Sligman, Joel. 1982. *The Transformation of Wall Street.* Boston: Houghton Mifflin.

Smith, A. 1989. "Corporate Ownership Structure and Performance: The Case of Management Buyouts." Working paper, University of Chicago.

Smith, Adam. 1790 [1971]. *The Theory of Moral Sentiment.* New York: Garland.

Smith, Randall. 1988. "Junk Market Can Weather Storm, Participants Predict." *Wall Street Journal,* 8 September, 7A.

Smith, Vicki. 1990. *Managing in the Corporate Interest: Control and Resistance in an American Bank.* Berkeley: University of California Press.

Smith, William French. 1991. *Law and Justice in the Reagan Administration: The Memoirs of an Attorney General.* Stanford, CA: Hoover Institute Press.

Sobel, Robert. 1965. *The Big Board: A History of the New York Stock Market.* London: Collier Macmillan.

―――. 1984a. *The Rise and Fall of the Conglomerate Kings.* New York: Stein and Day.

―――. 1984b. *The Age of Giant Corporations: A Microeconomic History of American Business, 1914–1984,* 2nd ed. Westport, CT: Greenwood Press.

―――. 1989. "Historical Perspectives on the Use of High-Yield Securities in Corporate Creations." Report prepared for Drexel Burnham Lambert, Institutional Research, New York.

South Bend Tribune and Nile Star. 1984. "Simplicity Pattern." P. 1.

Stanley, Louis. 1932. "The Spider of Wall Street." *World Tomorrow* 15(September 21):282.

Stearns, Linda. 1983. "Corporate Control and the Structure of the Capital Market: 1946–1980." Department of Sociology. Unpublished dissertation. SUNY, Stoney Brook, New York.

———. 1990. "Capital Markets Effects on External Control of Corporations." Pp. 175–202 in *Structures of Capital*, edited by Sharon Zukin and Paul DiMaggio. Cambridge: Cambridge University Press.

Stein, Benjamin J. 1989. November 13. "Watch Dog, Awake!—Fervent Plea to the New Chairman of the SEC." *Barron's* 69(46):6–7, 32–36.

Stevens, Amy. 1991. "Keating Is Found Guilty on 17 of 18 Counts." *Wall Street Journal*, 5 December, A3.

———. 1993. "Keating Convicted on Criminal Charges Stemming from Lincoln S&L Scandal." *Wall Street Journal*, 7 January, A3.

Stewart, James B. 1988. "Dubious Deals." *Wall Street Journal*, 15 July, A1.

———. 1991. *Den of Thieves*. New York: Simon and Schuster.

Stewart, James and Daniel Hertzberg. 1988a. "Five Princeton/Newport Partners Indicted in Racketeering, Fraud Case." *Wall Street Journal*, 5 August, 3.

———. 1988b. "SEC Accuses Drexel of Sweeping Array of Securities Violations." *Wall Street Journal*, 8 September, 1A, 7A.

Stigler, G. J. 1968. *The Organization of Industry*. Homewood, IL: Richard D. Irwin.

Stokman, Frans N. and Frans W. Wasseur. 1985. "National Networks in 1976: A Structural Comparison." Chapter 2 in *Networks of Corporate Power: A Comparative Analysis of Ten Countries*, edited by Frans Stokman, Rolf Ziegler, and John Scott. Cambridge: Polity Press in association with Basil Blackwell, Oxford.

Stokman, Frans N., Rolf Ziegler, and John Scott. 1985. *Networks of Corporate Power*. Cambridge, England: Polity Press in association with Basil Blackwell, Oxford.

Stone, Christopher D. 1975. *Where the Law Ends: The Social Control of Corporate Behavior*. New York: Harper and Row.

Stone, Katherine. 1981. "The Origins of Job Structures in the Steel Industry," Pp. 349–81 in *Complex Organizations: Critical Perspectives*, edited by Mary Zey-Ferrell and Michael Aiken. Glenview, IL: Scott Foresman.

Swedberg, R. 1987. "Economic Society: Past and Present." *Current Sociology* 35(Spring):1–221.

Sweezy, Paul M. [1942] 1956. *The Theory of Capitalist Development*. New York: Monthly Review Press.

Taggart, Robert A., Jr. 1985. "Secular Patterns in the Financing of U.S. Corporations." Pp. 13–75 in *Corporate Capital Structures in the U.S.*, edited by Benjamin Friedman. Chicago: University of Chicago Press.

———. 1988. "The Growth of the 'Junk' Bond Market and Its Role in Financing Takeovers." Pp. 5–24 in *Mergers and Acquisitions*, edited by Alan J. Auerbach. Chicago: University of Chicago Press.

Thomas, Paulette. 1991. "RTC Is Selling Part of Columbia S&L to Investors and Liquidating the Rest." *Wall Street Journal*, 16 September, A6.

Thompson, James D. and William J. McEwen. 1958. "Organizational Goals and Environment: Goal Setting as an Interacting Process." *American Sociological Review* 23:23–31.

Tilly, Charles. 1985. "War Making and State Making as Organized Crime." Pp. 169–91 in *Bringing the State Back In*, edited by Peter Evans, Dietrich Rueschemeyer, and Theda Skocpol. New York: Cambridge University Press.

U.S. Attorney General. 1955. *Report of the Attorney General's National Committee to Study Anti-Trust Laws*. Washington, DC: U.S. Government Printing Office.

U.S. House of Representatives. 1913a. "Investigation on Concentration of Control of Money and Credit." Committee on Banking and Currency. Washington, DC: U.S. Government Printing Office. (Referred to as Pujo Committee Report in text.)

———. 1913b. *Report of the Committee Appointed to Investigate the Concentration of Control of Money and Credit*. 62nd Congress, 3rd Session. Washington, DC: U.S. Government Printing Office.

———. 1968. "Commercial Banks and Their Trust Activities: Emerging Influences on the American Economy." Committee on Banking and Currency, Subcommittee on Domestic Finance. 90th Congress, 2nd Session. Washington, DC: U.S. Government Printing Office. (Referred to as Puttman Report in text.)

———. 1988a. "Confidential Report on National Can and Otter Creek to NYSE." Committee on Energy and Commerce, Subcommittee on Oversight and Investigation, pp. 3–9.

———. 1988b. *Report "Pensions and Leveraged Buyouts."* Subcommittee on Labor Management Relations, February 7. Washington, DC: U.S. Government Printing Office.

———. 1989. "Management and Leveraged Buyouts." *1988 Hearings before the Subcommittee on Telecommunications and Finance of the Committee on Energy and Commerce*, Serial No. 101–49, February 22 and May 25. Washington, DC: U.S. Government Printing Office.

U.S. v. Michael Milken. 1990a. Presentencing Hearing Documents. United States District Court, Southern District of New York, (S) 89 Cir. 41 (October 11–15). Testimony of Michael Davidoff, pp. 33–71; Gary Maultasch, pp. 72–212; Peter Richard Gardiner, pp. 223–362; Patsy Van Utt, pp. 374–93; Joseph Harch, pp. 394–485; Kevin Madigan, pp. 490–506; Thomas Connors, pp. 514–97; Benalder Bayse, pp. 599–664; Aubrey Hayes, pp. 654–86; Terren Peizer, pp. 697–773; R. Theodore Ammon, pp. 774–838; Craig Cogut, pp. 857–1023; Frederick Joseph, pp. 1028–1106; Richard Grassgreen, pp. 1107–51; James Dahl 1173–282 and 1308–15; Prescott Crocker, pp. 1283–307.

———. 1990b. Sentencing Document. United States District Court, Southern District of New York, (S) 89 Cir. 41 (October 21):1–57.

———. 1990c. Sentencing Memorandum. United States District Court, Southern District of New York, (S) 89 Cir. 41 (October).

———. 1990d. Reply to Sentencing Memorandum.

———. 1990e. SEC Disclosures, SS 89-CR-41.

United States Senate. 1989. *Leveraged Buyouts and Corporate Debt*. Hearing of Finance Committee. Testimony of Nicholas F. Brady, January 24. Washington, DC: U.S. Government Printing Office.

Useem, Michael. 1979. "The Social Organization of the American Business Elite and Participation of Corporation Directors in the Governance of American Institutions." *American Sociological Review* 44:553–72.

———. 1982. "Classwide Rationality in the Politics of Managers and Directors of Large Corporations in the United States and Great Britain." *Administrative Science Quarterly* 27:199–226.

———. 1984. *The Inner Circle: Large Corporations and the Rise of Business Political Activity in the U.S. and U.K.* New York: Oxford University Press.

Van Horne, James C. 1990. *Financial Market Rates and Flow.* Englewood Cliffs, NJ: Prentice-Hall.

Vaughan, Diane. 1983. *Controlling Unlawful Organizational Behavior.* Chicago: University of Chicago Press.

———. 1989. "Ethical Decision Making in Organizations: The Challenger Launch." Paper presented at Conference on Organizational Deviance, Harvard Graduate School of Business, Cambridge, MA.

Vise, David A. and Steve Coll. 1989. "The Man for Wall Street." *Washington Post,* 5 February, A1; 6 February, A1; 7 February, A1; 8 February, A1.

Wall Street Journal. 1985. "Surge in Restructuring Is Profoundly Altering Much of U.S. Industry." 12 August, 1, 12–13.

———. 1989. 3 February, 1.

Weber, Max. 1947. "Fundamental Concepts of Sociology." Pp. 3–62 in *Economy and Society,* edited by Guenther Roth and Claus Wittich. Berkeley, CA: University of California Press.

———. [1903–1906] 1985. *The Protestant Ethic and the Spirit of Capitalism.* Transl. by T. Parsons. London: Unwin.

Wells, Chris. 1988. "The RJR Greedfest Won't Stop LBO Mania For Long." *Business Week,* 5 December, 2.

White, Harrison C. 1981. "Where Do Markets Come From?" *American Journal of Sociology* 87(5):517–47.

White, Harrison C., Scott A. Boorman, and Ronald L. Breiger. 1976. "Social Structure from Multiple Networks. I.: Blockmodels of Roles and Positions." *American Journal of Sociology* 81:730–80.

Wigmore, Barrie A. 1989. "Speculation and the Crash of 1987." Paper presented at the Annual Meeting of the American Economics Association, New York City, December 28.

Williamson, Oliver E. 1975. *Markets and Hierarchies: Analysis and Antitrust Implications.* New York: Free Press.

———. 1981. "The Economics of Organization: The Transaction Cost Approach." *American Journal of Sociology* 87(November):548–77.

———. 1983. "Organizational Innovation: The Transaction-Costs Approach." Pp. 101–34 in *Entrepreneurship,* edited by J. Ronen. Lexington, MA: Heath.

———. 1985. *The Economic Institutions of Capitalism.* New York: Free Press.

Williamson, Oliver E. and William G. Ouchi. 1981. "The Markets and Hierarchies Program of Research: Origins, Implications, Prospects." PP. 131–60 in *Organizational Design,* edited by William Joyce and Andrew Van de Ven. New York: Wiley.

Wolfe, Tom. 1987. *Bonfire of the Vanities*. New York: Farrar, Strauss.

Wolfson, Mark. 1980. "Investment Banking." Pp. 423–32 in *Abuse on Wall Street*, edited by Twentieth Century Fund, Steering Committee on Conflicts of Interest in the Securities Markets. Westport, CT: Quorum Books.

Wright, Erik Olin. 1978. *Class, Crises and the State*. London: New Left Books.

———. 1985. *Classes*. London: Verso.

Yago, Glenn. 1990. "Economic Impact of High-Yield Securities and Public Policy Responses." Pp. 58–76 in *The High-Yield Debt Market*, edited by Edward I. Altman. Homewood, IL: Dow Jones Irwin.

———. 1991. *Junk Bonds: How High-Yield Securities Restructured Corporate America*. New York: Oxford University Press.

Yoshihashi, Pauline. 1991. "Junking of Pensions Angers Mill Workers: First Executive Woes Hit Maxxam Lumber Unit." *Wall Street Journal*, 18 April, A4.

Zald, Meyer N. 1970. *Organizational Change: The Political Economy of the YMCA*. Chicago: University of Chicago Press.

Zaltman, Gerald, Robert Duncan, and Jonny Holbeck. 1973. *Innovations and Organizations*. New York: John Wiley.

Zammuto, Raymond, and Kim Cameron. 1985. "Environmental Decline and Organizational Response." *Research in Organizational Behavior* 7:223–62.

Zeitlin, Maurice. 1974. "Corporate Ownership and Control: The Large Corporation and the Capitalist Class." *American Journal of Sociology* 79:1073–119.

Zeitlin, Maurice, Lynda Ann Ewen, and Richard E. Ratcliff. 1974. "New Princes for Old: The Large Corporation and the Capitalist Class in Chile." *American Journal of Sociology* 80:87–123.

Zeitlin, Maurice, and Richard E. Ratcliff. 1988. *Landlords and Capitalists: The Dominant Class of Chile*. Princeton, NJ: Princeton University Press.

Zeitz, Gerald. 1980. "Interorganizational Dialectics." *Administrative Science Quarterly* 25:72–88.

Zey, Mary. 1989. "Reform of RICO: Legal versus Social Embeddedness Explanations." Paper presented at the Annual Meeting of the Society for the Advancement of Socio-Economics, Harvard University, Cambridge, MA.

———. 1990. "Reform of RICO: Legal Explanations." Paper presented at the Annual Meeting of the Society for the Advancement of Socio-Economics, George Washington University, Washington, D.C.

———. 1992. *Decision Making: Alternatives to Rational Choice Models*. Beverly Hills, CA: Sage.

———. Forthcoming. *Investment Banks, Corporations, and the State in the 1980s*.

Zey-Ferrell, Mary. 1981. *Complex Organizations: Critical Perspectives*. Glenview, IL: Scott, Foresman.

Ziegler, Rolf. 1985. "Conclusion." Chapter 15 in *Networks of Corporate Power: A Comparative Analysis of Ten Countries*, edited by Frans Stokman, Rolf Ziegler, and John Scott. Cambridge: Polity Press in association with Basil Blackwell, Oxford.

Subject Index

ACC (American Continental
  Corporation), 6, 62–63
Accumulate a position, 19
Ackerman, Peter, 36, 64–65
Acquiring firm, 55–58, 130
Acquisitions (*See* Mergers and
  acquisitions)
Agee, William, 165
Agency theory, 79, 178, 190–191,
  253
Alliance for Capital Access, 197
Allied Corporation, 165
Altman, Edward, 6, 155
Altus, 70–71
American Continental Corporation
  (ACC), 6, 62–63
Ammon, R. Theodore, 12, 34, 36
Antimerger laws, 6
Antitrust laws, 130, 186, 192–195
Arbitrage, 3, 23
Asset value, 167
Autonomy, departmental, 87–91
Aylward, David K., 196

Baird, Bruce, 9
Balser, Donald, 10
Bankruptcy laws, 44, 62, 186, 190–192
Bankruptcy Reform Act of 1978, 190,
  191
Basis point, 188–189
Bayse, Benalder, 12, 39–41
Beatrice Foods takeover, 10, 32, 37–38
Below-investment grade bonds,
  88–89
Bendix, 165
Bentsen, Lloyd, 151
Bersoux, Henri, 69
Black knight, 149
Black, Leon, 71
Boards of directors, 182–183
Boesky, Ivan F.
  debt to Milken and, 3, 71

disclosure of Milken connection
  and, 41–42
extraordinary fraud networks and,
  19
Fischbach Corporation takeover
  and, 24–25
fraud process set up by, 19
Harris Graphics takeover and,
  26–27
Hudson Fund and, 3–4
MGM/UA takeover and, 28
Natomas Co. takeover and, 17–18
Pacific Lumber takeover and, 30
Storer Communications takeover
  and, 32, 33–34
surrender of, 6, 7
Wickes takeover and, 22–24
Boesky organizations (*See* specific
  names)
Bond floor control
  departmental, 94–95
  investment bankers and, 97–99
  Milken and, 94–95
  opportunism and, 91–94
  social context of, 91
  status of Drexel and, 95–97
  traders and, 97–99
Bond market, 152–156, 164, 188–189
Bonuses, 108–109
Boutique takeover firm, 31–32
Brackets, 95–96
Bradley, Bill, 5
Brady, Nicholas F., 147, 150–151
Bridge loans, 33, 132–133
Buyers of junk bonds, 15, 16–17,
  38–41

Cameron, Dort III, 25
Cannon Mills Corporation, 67
Capital
  accumulation, 86–87
  corporate, 166–167

298